51st Annual Meeting of the Association for Computational Linguistics (ACL 2013)

System Demonstrations

AA005894

Sofia, Bulgaria
4-9 August 2013

ISBN: 978-1-62748-977-5

Printed from e-media with permission by:

Curran Associates, Inc.
57 Morehouse Lane
Red Hook, NY 12571

Some format issues inherent in the e-media version may also appear in this print version.

Copyright© (2013) by the Association for Computational Linguistics
All rights reserved.

Printed by Curran Associates, Inc. (2013)

For permission requests, please contact the Association for Computational Linguistics
at the address below.

Association for Computational Linguistics
209 N. Eighth Street
Stroudsburg, Pennsylvania 18360

Phone: 1-570-476-8006
Fax: 1-570-476-0860

acl@aclweb.org

Additional copies of this publication are available from:

Curran Associates, Inc.
57 Morehouse Lane
Red Hook, NY 12571 USA
Phone: 845-758-0400
Fax: 845-758-2634
Email: curran@proceedings.com
Web: www.proceedings.com

Preface

Welcome to the proceedings of the system demonstration session. This volume contains the papers of the system demonstrations presented at the 51st Annual Meeting of the Association for Computational Linguistics, held in Sofia, Bulgaria, on August 5th, 2013.

The system demonstrations program offers the presentation of early research prototypes as well as interesting mature systems. The system demonstration chairs and the members of the program committee received 64 submissions, of which 34 were selected for inclusion in the program (acceptance rate of 53%) after review by two members of the program committee.

We would like to thank the members of the program committee for their timely help in reviewing the submissions.

Co-Chairs:

Miriam Butt, University of Konstanz
Sarmad Hussain, Al-Khawarizmi Institute of Computer Science, University of Engineering and Technology, Lahore

Program Committee:

Timothy Baldwin, University of Melbourne
Thierry Declerck, DFKI, Saarbrücken
Koenrad de Smedt, University of Bergen
Mark Dras, Macquarie University
Martin Forst, Netbase
Tracy King, eBay Inc.
Adam Przepiorkowski, Institute of Computer Science, Polish Academy of Sciences
Frédérique Segond, Viseo Reseach and Development
Heike Zinsmeister, IMS, University of Stuttgart
Ruvan Weerasinghe, University of Colombo
Mirna Adriani, University of Indonesia
Sivaji Bandyopadhyay, Jadavpur University
Ying Chen, China Agriculture University
Christopher Culy, University of Tübingen
Alexander Fraser, IMS, University of Stuttgart
Usman Ghani, Al-Khawarizmi Institute of Computer Science, University of Engineering and Technology, Lahore
Annette Hautli, University of Konstanz
Gurpreet Lehal, Punjabi University
Shoushan Li, Soochow University
Katja Markert, University of Leeds
Thomas Mayer, University of Marburg
Christian Rohrdantz, University of Konstanz
Virach Sornlertlamvanich, NECTEC
Alexandros Tantos, Aristotle University of Thessaloniki

Table of Contents

Conference Program

Monday August 5, 2013

(18:30 - 19:45) System Demonstrations A

WebAnno: A Flexible, Web-based and Visually Supported System for Distributed Annotations
Seid Muhie Yimam, Iryna Gurevych, Richard Eckart de Castilho and Chris Biemann

A Stacking-based Approach to Twitter User Geolocation Prediction
Bo Han, Paul Cook and Timothy Baldwin

An Open Source Toolkit for Quantitative Historical Linguistics
Johann-Mattis List and Steven Moran

AnnoMarket: An Open Cloud Platform for NLP
Valentin Tablan, Kalina Bontcheva, Ian Roberts, Hamish Cunningham and Marin Dimitrov

Detecting Event-Related Links and Sentiments from Social Media Texts
Alexandra Balahur and Hristo Tanev

DISSECT - DIStributional SEmantics Composition Toolkit
Georgiana Dinu, Nghia The Pham and Marco Baroni

DKPro WSD: A Generalized UIMA-based Framework for Word Sense Disambiguation
Tristan Miller, Nicolai Erbs, Hans-Peter Zorn, Torsten Zesch and Iryna Gurevych

Extending an interoperable platform to facilitate the creation of multilingual and multimodal NLP applications
Georgios Kontonatsios, Paul Thompson, Riza Theresa Batista-Navarro, Claudiu Mihăilă, Ioannis Korkontzelos and Sophia Ananiadou

FudanNLP: A Toolkit for Chinese Natural Language Processing
Xipeng Qiu, Qi Zhang and Xuanjing Huang

ICARUS – An Extensible Graphical Search Tool for Dependency Treebanks
Markus Gärtner, Gregor Thiele, Wolfgang Seeker, Anders Björkelund and Jonas Kuhn

Meet EDGAR, a tutoring agent at MONSERRATE
Pedro Fialho, Luísa Coheur, Sérgio Curto, Pedro Cláudio, Ângela Costa, Alberto Abad, Hugo Meinedo and Isabel Trancoso

Monday August 5, 2013 (continued)

PAL: A Chatterbot System for Answering Domain-specific Questions
Yuanchao Liu, Ming Liu, Xiaolong Wang, Limin Wang and Jingjing Li

PhonMatrix: Visualizing co-occurrence constraints of sounds
Thomas Mayer and Christian Rohrdantz

QuEst - A translation quality estimation framework
Lucia Specia, , , Kashif Shah, Jose G.C. de Souza and Trevor Cohn

SORT: An Interactive Source-Rewriting Tool for Improved Translation
Shachar Mirkin, Sriram Venkatapathy, Marc Dymetman and Ioan Calapodescu

Travatar: A Forest-to-String Machine Translation Engine based on Tree Transducers
Graham Neubig

PLIS: a Probabilistic Lexical Inference System
Eyal Shnarch, Erel Segal-haLevi, Jacob Goldberger and Ido Dagan

(19:45 - 21:00) System Demonstrations B

A Java Framework for Multilingual Definition and Hypernym Extraction
Stefano Faralli and Roberto Navigli

A Visual Analytics System for Cluster Exploration
Andreas Lamprecht, Annette Hautli, Christian Rohrdantz and Tina Bögel

Development and Analysis of NLP Pipelines in Argo
Rafal Rak, Andrew Rowley, Jacob Carter and Sophia Ananiadou

DKPro Similarity: An Open Source Framework for Text Similarity
Daniel Bär, Torsten Zesch and Iryna Gurevych

Fluid Construction Grammar for Historical and Evolutionary Linguistics
Pieter Wellens, Remi van Trijp, Katrien Beuls and Luc Steels

HYENA-live: Fine-Grained Online Entity Type Classification from Natural-language Text
Mohamed Amir Yosef, Sandro Bauer, Johannes Hoffart, Marc Spaniol and Gerhard Weikum

WebAnno: A Flexible, Web-based and Visually Supported System for Distributed Annotations

Seid Muhie Yimam[1,3] Iryna Gurevych[2,3] Richard Eckart de Castilho[2] Chris Biemann[1]
(1) FG Language Technology, Dept. of Computer Science, Technische Universität Darmstadt
(2) Ubiquitous Knowledge Processing Lab (UKP-TUDA)
Dept. of Computer Science, Technische Universität Darmstadt
(3) Ubiquitous Knowledge Processing Lab (UKP-DIPF)
German Institute for Educational Research and Educational Information
http://www.ukp.tu-darmstadt.de

Abstract

We present WebAnno, a general purpose web-based annotation tool for a wide range of linguistic annotations. WebAnno offers annotation project management, freely configurable tagsets and the management of users in different roles. WebAnno uses modern web technology for visualizing and editing annotations in a web browser. It supports arbitrarily large documents, pluggable import/export filters, the curation of annotations across various users, and an interface to farming out annotations to a crowdsourcing platform. Currently WebAnno allows part-of-speech, named entity, dependency parsing and co-reference chain annotations. The architecture design allows adding additional modes of visualization and editing, when new kinds of annotations are to be supported.

1 Introduction

The creation of training data precedes any statistical approach to natural language processing (NLP). Linguistic annotation is a process whereby linguistic information is added to a document, such as part-of-speech, lemmata, named entities, or dependency relations. In the past, platforms for linguistic annotations were mostly developed ad-hoc for the given annotation task at hand, used proprietary formats for data exchange, or required local installation effort. We present WebAnno, a browser-based tool that is immediately usable by any annotator with internet access. It supports annotation on a variety of linguistic levels (called annotation layers in the remainder), is interoperable with a variety of data formats, supports annotation project management such as user management, offers an adjudication interface, and provides quality management using inter-annotator agreement. Furthermore, an interface to crowdsourcing platforms enables scaling out simple annotation tasks to a large numbers of micro-workers. The added value of WebAnno, as compared to previous annotation tools, is on the one hand its web-based interface targeted at skilled as well as unskilled annotators, which unlocks a potentially very large workforce. On the other hand, it is the support for quality control, annotator management, and adjudication/curation, which lowers the entrance barrier for new annotation projects. We created WebAnno to fulfill the following requirements:

- *Web-based:* Distributed work, no installation effort, increased availability.
- *Interface to crowdsourcing:* unlocking a very large distributed workforce.
- *Quality and user management:* Integrated different user roles support (administrator, annotator, and curator), inter-annotator agreement measurement, data curation, and progress monitoring.
- *Flexibility:* Support of multiple annotation layers, pluggable import and export formats, and extensibility to other front ends.
- *Pre-annotated and un-annotated documents:* supporting new annotations, as well as manual corrections of existing, possibly automatic annotations.
- *Permissive open source:* Usability of our tool in future projects without restrictions, under the Apache 2.0 license.

In the following section, we revisit related work on annotation tools, which only partially fulfill the aforementioned requirements. In Section 3, the architecture as well as usage aspects of our tool are lined out. The scope and functionality summary of WebAnno is presented in Section 4. Section 5 elaborates on several use cases of WebAnno, and Section 6 concludes and gives an outlook to further directions.

2 Related Work

GATE Teamware (Bontcheva et al., 2010) is probably the tool that closely matches our requirements regarding quality management, annotator management, and support of a large set of annotation layers and formats. It is mostly web-based, but the annotation is carried out with locally downloaded software. An interface to crowdsourcing platforms is missing. The GATE Teamware system is heavily targeted towards template-based information extraction. It sets a focus on the integration of automatic annotation components rather than on the interface for manual annotation. Besides, the overall application is rather complex for average users, requires considerable training and does not offer an alternative simplified interface as it would be required for crowdsourcing.

General-purpose annotation tools like MMAX2 (Müller and Strube, 2006) or WordFreak (Morton and LaCivita, 2003) are not web-based and do not provide annotation project management. They are also not sufficiently flexible regarding different annotation layers. The same holds for specialized tools for single annotation layers, which we cannot list here for the sake of brevity.

With the *brat rapid annotation tool* (Stenetorp et al., 2012), for the first time a web-based open-source annotation tool was introduced, which supports collaborative annotation for multiple annotation layers simultaneously on a single copy of the document, and is based on a client-server architecture. However, the current version of brat has limitations such as: (i) slowness for documents of more than 100 sentences, (ii) limits regarding file formats, (iii) web-based configuration of tagsets/tags is not possible and (iv) configuring the display of multiple layers is not yet supported. While we use brat's excellent visualization front end in WebAnno, we decided to replace the server layer to support the user and quality management, and monitoring tools as well as to add the interface to crowdsourcing.

3 System Architecture of WebAnno

The overall architecture of WebAnno is depicted in Figure 1. The modularity of the architecture,

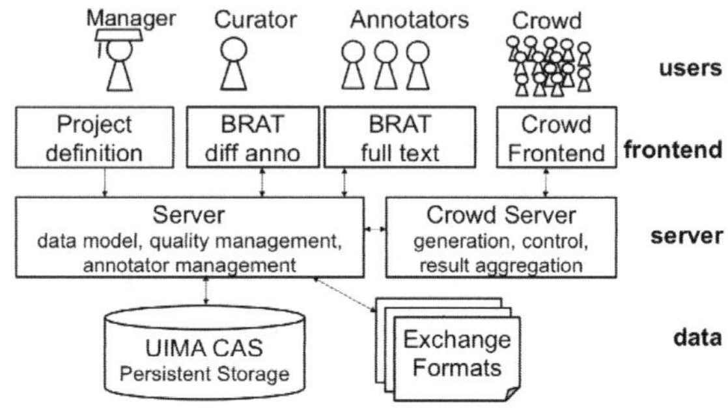

Figure 1: System architecture, organized in user, front end, back end and persistent data storage.

which is mirrored in its open-source implementation[1], makes it possible to easily extend the tool or add alternative user interfaces for annotation layers that brat is less suited for, e.g. for constituent structure. In Section 3.1, we illustrate how different user roles are provided with different graphical user interfaces, and show the expressiveness of the annotation model. Section 3.2 elaborates on the functionality of the back end, and describes how data is imported and exported, as well as our implementation of the persistent data storage.

3.1 Front End

All functionality of WebAnno is accessible via a web browser. For annotation and visualization of annotated documents, we adapted the brat rapid annotation tool. Changes had to be made to make brat interoperate with the Apache Wicket, on which WebAnno is built, and to better integrate into the WebAnno experience.

3.1.1 Project Definition

The definition and the monitoring of an annotation project is conducted by a project manager (cf. Figure 1) in a project definition form. It supports creating a project, loading un-annotated or pre-annotated documents in different formats[2], adding annotator and curator users, defining tagsets, and configuring the annotation layers. Only a project manager can administer a project. Figure 2 illustrates the project definition page with the tagset editor highlighted.

[1]Available for download at (this paper is based on v0.3.0): `webanno.googlecode.com/`

[2]Formats: plain text, CoNLL (Nivre et al., 2007), TCF (Heid et al., 2010), UIMA XMI (Ferrucci and Lally, 2004)

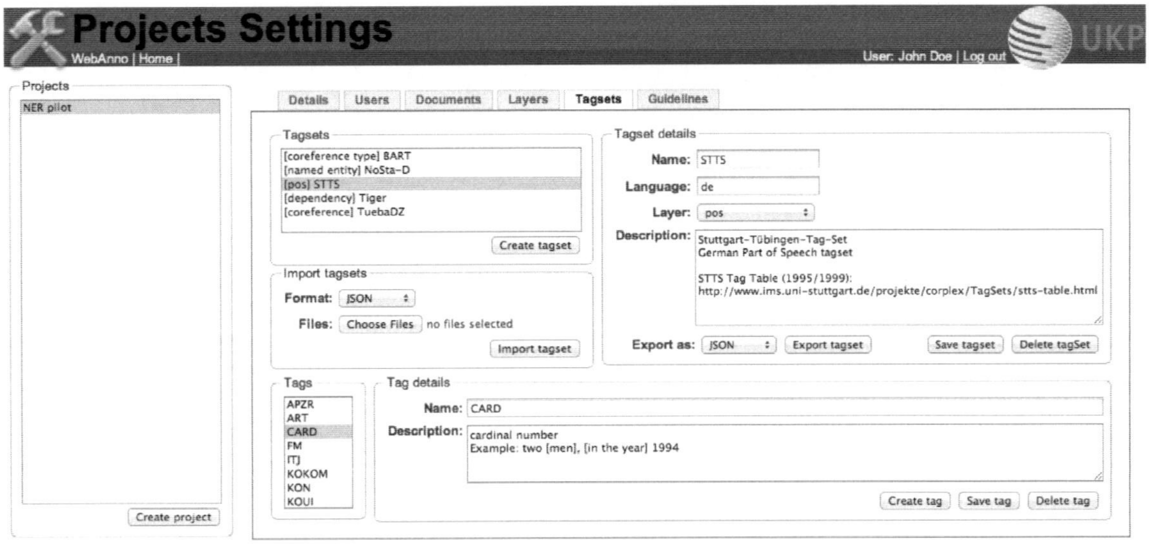

Figure 2: The tagset editor on the project definition page

3.1.2 Annotation

Annotation is carried out with an adapted version of the brat editor, which communicates with the server via Ajax (Wang et al., 2008) using the JSON (Lin et al., 2012) format. Annotators only see projects they are assigned to. The annotation page presents the annotator different options to set up the annotation environment, for customization:

- *Paging:* For heavily annotated documents or very large documents, the original brat visualization is very slow, both for displaying and annotating the document. We use a paging mechanism that limits the number of sentences displayed at a time to make the performance independent of the document size.

- *Annotation layers:* Annotators usually work on one or two annotations layers, such as part-of-speech and dependency or named entity annotation. Overloading the annotation page by displaying all annotation layers makes the annotation and visualization process slower. WebAnno provides an option to configure visible/editable annotation layers.

- *Immediate persistence:* Every annotation is sent to the back end immediately and persisted there. An explicit interaction by the user to save changes is not required.

3.1.3 Workflow

WebAnno implements a simple workflow to track the state of a project. Every annotator works on a separate version of the document, which is set to the state *in progress* the first time a document is opened by the annotator. The annotator can then mark it as *complete* at the end of annotation at which point it is locked for further annotation and can be used for curation. Such a document cannot be changed anymore by an annotator, but can be used by a curator. A curator can mark a document as *adjudicated.*

3.1.4 Curation

The curation interface allows the curator to open a document and compare annotations made by the annotators that already marked the document as *complete*. The curator reconciles the annotation with disagreements. The curator can either decide on one of the presented alternatives, or freely re-annotate. Figure 3 illustrates how the curation interface detects sentences with annotation disagreement (left side of Figure 3) which can be used to navigate to the sentences for curation.

3.1.5 Monitoring

WebAnno provides a monitoring component, to track the progress of a project. The project manager can check the progress and compute agreement with Kappa and Tau (Carletta, 1996) measures. The progress is visualized using a matrix of annotators and documents displaying which documents the annotators have marked as *complete* and which documents the curator *adjudicated.* Figure 4 shows the project progress, progress of individual annotator and completion statistics.

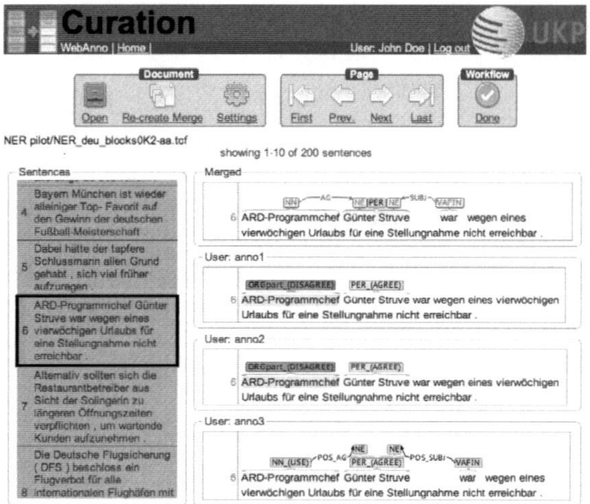

Figure 3: Curation user interface (left: sentences with disagreement; right: merging editor)

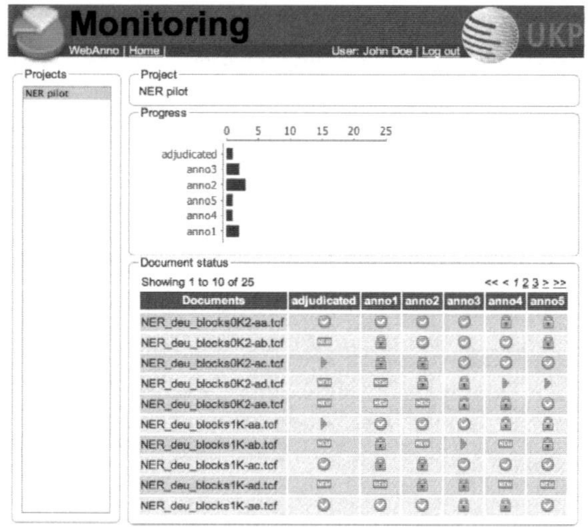

Figure 4: Project monitoring

3.1.6 Crowdsourcing

Crowdsourcing is a way to quickly scale annotation projects. Distributing a task that otherwise will be performed by a controlled user group has become much easier. Hence, if quality can be ensured, it is an alternative to high quality annotation using a large number of arbitrary redundant annotations (Wang et al., 2013). For WebAnno, we have designed an approach where a source document is split into small parts that get presented to micro-workers in the CrowdFlower platform[3]. The crowdsourcing component is a separate module that handles the communication via CrowdFlower's API, the definition of test items and job parameters, and the aggregation of results. The crowdsourced annotation appears as a virtual annotator in the tool.

Since it is not trivial to express complex annotation tasks in comparably simple templates suitable for crowdsourcing (Biemann, 2013), we proceed by working out crowdsourcing templates and strategies per annotation layer. We currently only support named entity annotation with predefined templates. However, the open and modular architecture allows to add more crowdsourced annotation layers.

3.2 Back End

WebAnno is a Java-based web application that may run on any modern servlet container. In memory and on the file system, annotations are stored as UIMA CAS objects (Ferrucci and Lally, 2004). All other data is persisted in an SQL database.

3.2.1 Data Conversion

WebAnno supports different data models that reflect the different communication of data between the front end, back end, and the persistent data storage. The brat data model serves exchanging data between the front end and the back end.

The documents are stored in their original formats. For annotations, we use the type system from the DKPro Core collection of UIMA components (Eckart de Castilho and Gurevych, 2009)[4]. This is converted to the brat model for visualization. Importing documents and exporting annotations is implemented using UIMA reader and writer components from DKPro Core as plug-ins. Thus, support for new formats can easily be added. To provide quick reaction times in the user interface, WebAnno internally stores annotations in a binary format, using the *SerializedCasReader* and *SerializedCasWriter* components.

3.2.2 Persistent Data Storage

Project definitions including project name and descriptions, tagsets and tags, and user details are kept in a database, whereas the documents and annotations are stored in the file system. WebAnno supports limited versioning of annotations, to protect against the unforeseen loss of data. Figure 5 shows the database entity relation diagram.

[3] www.crowdflower.com

[4] code.google.com/p/dkpro-core-asl/

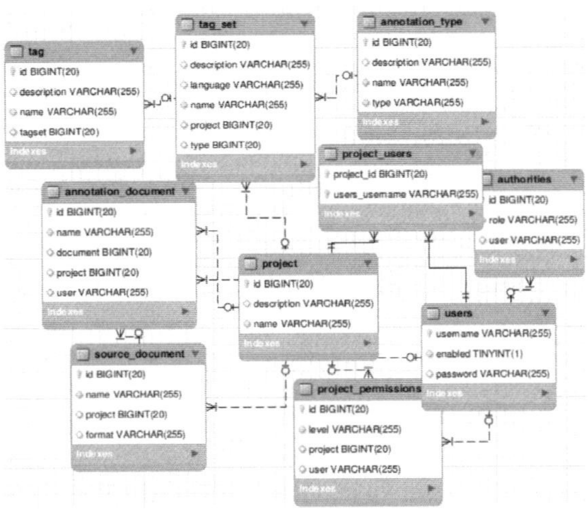

Figure 5: WebAnno database scheme

4 Scope and Functionality Summary

WebAnno supports the production of linguistically annotated corpora for different natural language processing applications. WebAnno implements ease of usage and simplicity for untrained users, and provides:

- Annotation via a fast, and easy-to-use web-based user interface.
- Project and user management.
- Progress and quality monitoring.
- Interactive curation by adjudicating disagreeing annotations from multiple users.
- Crowdsourcing of annotation tasks.
- Configurable annotation types and tag sets.

5 Use Cases

WebAnno currently allows to configure different span and arc annotations. It comes pre-configured with the following annotation layers from the DKPro Core type system:

Span annotations

- *Part-of-Speech (POS) tags*: an annotation task on tokens. Currently, POS can be added to a token, if not already present, and can be modified. POS annotation is a prerequisite of dependency annotation (Figure 6).

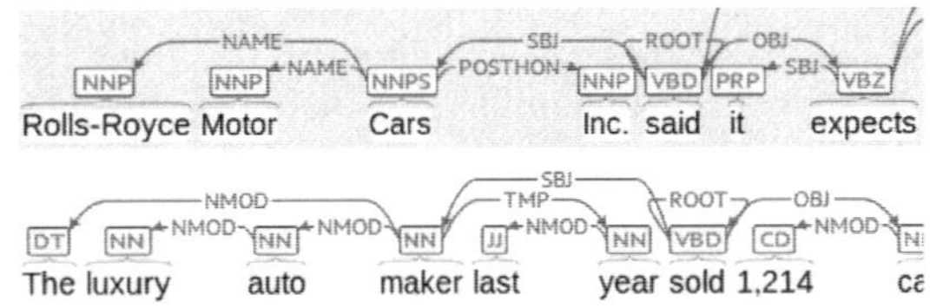

Figure 6: Parts-of-speech & dependency relations

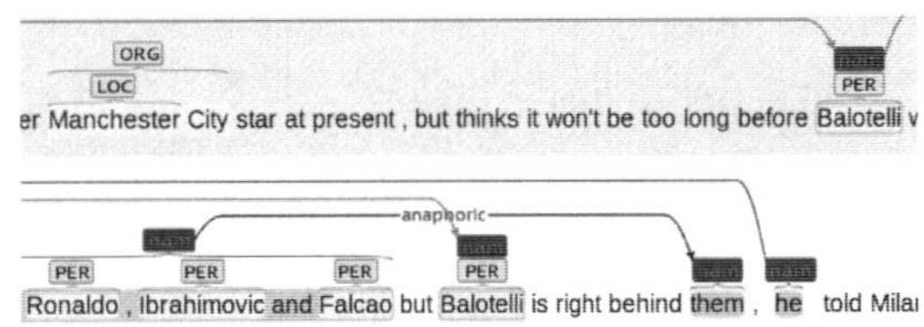

Figure 7: Co-reference & named entites

- *Named entities*: a multiple span annotation task. Spans can cover multiple adjacent tokens, nest and overlap (Figure 7), but cannot cross sentence boundaries.

Arc Annotations

- *Dependency relations*: This is an arc annotation which connects two POS tag annotations with a directed relation (Figure 6).
- *Co-reference chains*: The co-reference chain is realized as a set of typed mention spans linked by typed co-reference relation arcs. The co-reference relation annotation can cross multiple sentences and is represented in co-reference chains (Figure 7).

The brat front end supports tokens and sub-tokens as a span annotation. However, tokens are currently the minimal annotation units in WebAnno, due to a requirement of supporting the TCF file format (Heid et al., 2010). Part-of-speech annotation is limited to singles token, while named entity and co-reference chain annotations may span multiple tokens. Dependency relations are implemented in such a way that the arc is drawn from the governor to the dependent (or the other way around, configurable), while co-reference chains are unidirectional and a chain is formed by referents that are transitively connected by arcs.

Based on common practice in manual annotation, every user works on their own copy of the same document so that no concurrent editing occurs. We also found that displaying all annotation layers at the same time is inconvenient for annotators. This is why WebAnno supports showing and hiding of individual annotation layers. The WebAnno curation component displays all annotation documents from all users for a given source document, enabling the curator to visualize all of the annotations with differences at a time. Unlike most of the annotation tools which rely on configuration files, WebAnno enables to freely configure all parameters directly in the browser.

6 Conclusion and Outlook

WebAnno is a new web-based linguistic annotation tool. The brat annotation and GUI front end have been enhanced to support rapidly processing large annotation documents, configuring the annotation tag and tagsets in the browser, specifying visible annotation layers, separating annotation documents per user, just to name the most important distinctions. Besides, WebAnno supports project definition, import/export of tag and tagsets. Flexible support for importing and exporting different data formats is handled through UIMA components from the DKPro Core project. The monitoring component of WebAnno helps the administrator to control the progress of annotators. The crowdsourcing component of WebAnno provides a unique functionality to distribute the annotation to a large workforce and automatically integrate the results back into the tool via the crowdsourcing server. The WebAnno annotation tool supports curation of different annotation documents, displaying annotation documents created by users in a given project with annotation disagreements. In future work, WebAnno will be enhanced to support several other front ends to handle even more annotation layers, and to provide more crowdsourcing templates. Another planned extension is a more seamless integration of language processing tools for pre-annotation.

Acknowledgments

We would like to thank Benjamin Milde and Andreas Straninger, who assisted in implementing WebAnno, as well as Marc Reznicek, Nils Reiter and the whole CLARIN-D F-AG 7 for testing and providing valuable feedback. The work presented in this paper was funded by a German BMBF grant to the CLARIN-D project, the Hessian LOEWE research excellence program as part of the research center "Digital Humanities" and by the Volkswagen Foundation as part of the Lichtenberg-Professorship Program under grant No. I/82806.

References

Chris Biemann. 2013. Creating a system for lexical substitutions from scratch using crowdsourcing. *Lang. Resour. Eval.*, 47(1):97–122, March.

Kalina Bontcheva, Hamish Cunningham, Ian Roberts, and Valentin Tablan. 2010. Web-based collaborative corpus annotation: Requirements and a framework implementation. In *New Challenges for NLP Frameworks workshop at LREC-2010*, Malta.

Jean Carletta. 1996. Assessing agreement on classification tasks: the kappa statistic. In *Computational Linguistics, Volume 22 Issue 2*, pages 249–254.

Richard Eckart de Castilho and Iryna Gurevych. 2009. DKPro-UGD: A Flexible Data-Cleansing Approach to Processing User-Generated Discourse. In *Online-proceedings of the First French-speaking meeting around the framework Apache UIMA*, LINA CNRS UMR 6241 - University of Nantes, France.

David Ferrucci and Adam Lally. 2004. UIMA: An Architectural Approach to Unstructured Information Processing in the Corporate Research Environment. In *Journal of Natural Language Engineering 2004*, pages 327–348.

Ulrich Heid, Helmut Schmid, Kerstin Eckart, and Erhard Hinrichs. 2010. A Corpus Representation Format for Linguistic Web Services: the D-SPIN Text Corpus Format and its Relationship with ISO Standards. In *Proceedings of LREC 2010*, Malta.

Boci Lin, Yan Chen, Xu Chen, and Yingying Yu. 2012. Comparison between JSON and XML in Applications Based on AJAX. In *Computer Science & Service System (CSSS), 2012*, Nanjing, China.

Thomas Morton and Jeremy LaCivita. 2003. WordFreak: an open tool for linguistic annotation. In *Proceedings of NAACL-2003*, NAACL-Demonstrations '03, pages 17–18, Edmonton, Canada.

Christoph Müller and Michael Strube. 2006. Multi-level annotation of linguistic data with MMAX2. In S. Braun, K. Kohn, and J. Mukherjee, editors, *Corpus Technology and Language Pedagogy: New Resources, New Tools, New Methods*, pages 197–214. Peter Lang, Frankfurt a.M., Germany.

Joakim Nivre, Johan Hall, Sandra Kübler, Ryan McDonald, Jens Nilsson, Sebastian Riedel, and Deniz Yuret. 2007. The CoNLL 2007 Shared Task on Dependency Parsing. In *Proceedings of the CoNLL Shared Task Session of EMNLP-CoNLL 2007*, pages 915–932, Prague, Czech Republic.

Pontus Stenetorp, Sampo Pyysalo, Goran Topić, Tomoko Ohta, Sophia Ananiadou, and Jun'ichi Tsujii. 2012. brat: a Web-based Tool for NLP-Assisted Text Annotation. In *Proceedings of the Demonstrations at EACL-2012*, Avignon, France.

Qingling Wang, Qin Liu, Na Li, and Yan Liu. 2008. An Automatic Approach to Reengineering Common Website with AJAX. In *4th International Conference on Next Generation Web Services Practices*, pages 185–190, Seoul, South Korea.

Aobo Wang, Cong Duy Vu Hoang, and Min-Yen Kan. 2013. Perspectives on Crowdsourcing Annotations for Natural Language Processing. In *Language Resources And Evaluation*, pages 9–31. Springer Netherlands.

A Stacking-based Approach to Twitter User Geolocation Prediction

Bo Han,♠♡ **Paul Cook,**♡ and **Timothy Baldwin**♠♡
♠ NICTA Victoria Research Laboratory
♡ Department of Computing and Information Systems, The University of Melbourne
hanb@student.unimelb.edu.au, paulcook@unimelb.edu.au,
tb@ldwin.net

Abstract

We implement a city-level geolocation prediction system for Twitter users. The system infers a user's location based on both tweet text and user-declared metadata using a stacking approach. We demonstrate that the stacking method substantially outperforms benchmark methods, achieving 49% accuracy on a benchmark dataset. We further evaluate our method on a recent crawl of Twitter data to investigate the impact of temporal factors on model generalisation. Our results suggest that user-declared location metadata is more sensitive to temporal change than the text of Twitter messages. We also describe two ways of accessing/demoing our system.

1 Introduction

In this paper, we present and evaluate a geolocation prediction method for Twitter users.[1] Given a user's tweet data as input, the task of user level geolocation prediction is to infer a primary location (i.e., "home location": Mahmud et al. (2012)) for the user from a discrete set of pre-defined locations (Cheng et al., 2010). For instance, President Obama's location might be predicted to be Washington D.C., USA, based on his public tweets and profile metadata.

Geolocation information is essential to location-based applications, like targeted advertising and local event detection (Sakaki et al., 2010; MacEachren et al., 2011). However, the means to obtain such information are limited. Although Twitter allows users to specify a plain text description of their location in their profile, these descriptions tend to be ad hoc and unreliable (Cheng et al., 2010). Recently, user geolocation prediction based on a user's tweets has become popular (Wing and Baldridge, 2011; Roller et al., 2012), based on the assumption that tweets implicitly contain locating information, and with appropriate statistical modeling, the true location can be inferred. For instance, if a user frequently mentions *NYC*, *JFK* and *yankees*, it is likely that they are from New York City, USA.

In this paper, we discuss an implementation of a global city-level geolocation prediction system for English Twitter users. The system utilises both tweet text and public profile metadata for modeling and inference. Specifically, we train multinomial Bayes classifiers based on location indicative words (LIWs) in tweets (Han et al., 2012), and user-declared location and time zone metadata. These base classifiers are further stacked (Wolpert, 1992) using logistic regression as the meta-classifier. The proposed stacking model is compared with benchmarks on a public geolocation dataset. Experimental results demonstrate that our stacking model outperforms benchmark methods by a large margin, achieving 49% accuracy on the test data. We further evaluate the stacking model on a more recent crawl of public tweets. This experiment tests the effectiveness of a geolocation model trained on "old" data when applied to "new" data. The results reveal that user-declared locations are more variable over time than tweet text and time zone data.

2 Background and Related Work

Identifying the geolocation of objects has been widely studied in the research literature over target objects including webpages (Zong et al., 2005), search queries (Backstrom et al., 2008), Flickr images (Crandall et al., 2009) and Wikipedia editors (Lieberman and Lin, 2009). Recently, a considerable amount of work has been devoted to extending geolocation prediction for Twitter

[1] We only use public Twitter data for experiments and exemplification in this study.

users (Cheng et al., 2010; Eisenstein et al., 2010). The geolocations are usually represented by unambiguous city names or a partitioning of the earth's surface (e.g., grid cells specified by latitude/longitude). User geolocation is generally related to a "home" location where a user regularly resides, and user mobility is ignored. Twitter allows users to declare their home locations in plain text in their profile, however, this data has been found to be unstructured and ad hoc in preliminary research (Cheng et al., 2010; Hecht et al., 2011).

While popular for desktop machine geolocation, methods that map IP addresses to physical locations (Buyukokkten et al., 1999) cannot be applied to Twitter-based user geolocation, as IPs are only known to the service provider and are non-trivial to retrieve in a mobile Internet environment. Although social network information has been proven effective in inferring user locations (Backstrom et al., 2010; Sadilek et al., 2012; Rout et al., 2013), we focus exclusively on message and metadata information in this paper, as they are more readily accessible.

Text data tends to contain salient geospatial expressions that are particular to specific regions. Attempts to leverage this data directly have been based on analysis of gazetted expressions (Leidner and Lieberman, 2011) or the identification of geographical entities (Quercini et al., 2010; Qin et al., 2003). However these methods are limited in their ability to capture informal geospatial expressions (e.g. *Brissie* for *Brisbane*) and more non-geospatial terms which are associated with particular locations (e.g. *ferry* for Seattle or Sydney).

Beyond identifying geographical references using off-the-shelf tools, more sophisticated methods have been introduced in the social media realm. Cheng et al. (2010) built a simple generative model based on tweet words, and further added words which are local to particular regions and applied smoothing to under-represented locations. Kinsella et al. (2011) applied different similarity measures to the task, and investigated the relative difficulty of geolocation prediction at city, state, and country levels. Wing and Baldridge (2011) introduced a grid-based representation for geolocation modeling and inference based on fixed latitude and longitude values, and aggregated all tweets in a single cell. Their approach was then based on lexical similarity using KL-divergence. One drawback to the uniform-sized cell representation is that it introduces class imbalance: urban areas tend to contain far more tweets than rural areas. Based on this observation, Roller et al. (2012) introduced an adaptive grid representation in which cells contain approximately the same number of users, based on a KD-tree partition. Given that most tweets are from urban areas, Han et al. (2012) consider a city-based class division, and explore different feature selection methods to extract "location indicative words", which they show to improve prediction accuracy. Additionally, time zone information has been incorporated in a coarse-to-fine hierarchical model by first determining the time zone, and then disambiguating locations within it (Mahmud et al., 2012). Topic models have also been applied to the task, in capturing regional linguistic differences (Eisenstein et al., 2010; Yin et al., 2011; Hong et al., 2012).

When designing a practical geolocation system, simple models such as naive Bayes and nearest prototype methods (e.g., based on KL divergence) have clear advantages in terms of training and classification throughput, given the size of the class set (often numbering in the thousands of classes) and sheer volume of training data (potentially in the terabytes of data). This is particularly important for online systems and downstream applications that require timely predictions. As such, we build off the text-based naive Bayes-based geolocation system of Han et al. (2012), which our experiments have shown to have a good balance of tractability and accuracy. By selecting a reduced set of "location indicative words", prediction can be further accelerated.

3 Methodology

In this study, we adopt the same city-based representation and multinomial naive Bayes learner as Han et al. (2012). The city-based representation consists of 3,709 cities throughout the world, and is obtained by aggregating smaller cities with the largest nearby city. Han et al. (2012) found that using feature selection to identify "location indicative words" led to improvements in geolocation performance. We use the same feature selection technique that they did. Specifically, feature selection is based on information gain ratio (IGR) (Quinlan, 1993) over the city-based label set for each word.

In the original research of Han et al. (2012),

only the text of Twitter messages was used, and training was based exclusively on geotagged tweets, despite these accounting for only around 1% of the total public data on Twitter. In this research, we include additional non-geotagged tweets (e.g., posted from a non-GPS enabled device) for those users who have geotagged tweets (allowing us to determine a home location for the user).

In addition to including non-geotagged data in modeling and inference, we further take advantage of the text-based metadata embedded in a user's public profile (and included in the JSON object for each tweet). This metadata is potentially complementary to the tweet message and of benefit for geolocation prediction, especially the user-declared location and time zone, which we consider here. Note that these are in free text rather than a structured data format, and that while there are certainly instances of formal place name descriptions (e.g., *Edinburgh, UK*), they are often informal (e.g., *mel* for Melbourne). As such, we adopt a statistical approach to model each selected metadata field, by capturing the text in the form of character 4-grams, and training a multinomial naive Bayes classifier for each field.

To combine together the tweet text and metadata fields, we use stacking (Wolpert, 1992). The training of stacking consists of two steps. First, a multinomial naive Bayes base classifier (*L0*) is learned for each data type using 10-fold cross validation. This is carried out for the tweet text (TEXT), user-declared location (MB-LOC) and user-declared time zone (MB-TZ). Next, a meta-classifier (*L1* classifier) is trained over the base classifiers, using a logistic regression learner (Fan et al., 2008).

4 Evaluation and Discussion

In this section, we compare our proposed stacking approach with existing benchmarks on a public dataset, and investigate the impact of time using a recently collected dataset.

4.1 Evaluation Measures

In line with other work on user geolocation prediction, we use three evaluation measures:

- **Acc** : The percentage of correct city-level predictions.
- **Acc@161** : The percentage of predicted locations which are within a 161km (100 mile) radius of the home location (Cheng et al., 2010), to capture near-misses (e.g., Edinburgh UK being predicted as Glasgow, UK).
- **Median** : The median distance from the predicted city to the home location (Eisenstein et al., 2010).

Methods	Acc	Acc@161	Median
KL	.117	.277	793
MB	.126	.262	913
KL-NG	.260	.487	181
MB-NG	.280	.492	170
MB-LOC	.405	.525	92
MB-TZ	.064	.171	1330
STACKING	.490	.665	9

Table 1: Results over WORLD

4.2 Comparison with Benchmarks

We base our evaluation on the publicly-available WORLD dataset of Han et al. (2012). The dataset contains 1.4M users whose tweets are primarily identified as English based on the output of the `langid.py` language identification tool (Lui and Baldwin, 2012), and who have posted at least 10 geotagged tweets. The city-level home location for a geotagged user is determined as follows. First, each of a user's geotagged tweets is mapped to its nearest city (based on the same set of 3,709 cities used for the city-based location representation). Then, the most frequent city for a user is selected as the home location.

To benchmark our method, we reimplement two recently-published state-of-the-art methods: (1) the KL-divergence nearest prototype method of Roller et al. (2012) based on KD-tree partitioned grid cells, which we denote as KL; and (2) the multinomial naive Bayes city-level geolocation model of Han et al. (2012), which we denote as MB. Because of the different class representations, Acc numbers are not comparable between the benchmarks. To remedy this, we find the closest city to the centroid of each grid cell in the KD-tree representation, and map the classification onto this city. We present results including non-geotagged data for users with geotagged messages for the two methods, as KL-NG and MB-NG, respectively. We also present results based on the user-declared location (MB-LOC) and time zone (MB-TZ), and finally the stacking method (STACKING) which combines MB-NG, MB-LOC and MB-TZ. The results are shown in Table 1.

The approximate doubling of Acc for KL-NG and MB-NG over KL and MB, respectively, demonstrates the high utility of non-geotagged data in tweet text-based geolocation prediction. Of the two original models, we can see that MB is comparable to KL, in line with the findings of Han et al. (2012). The MB-LOC results are by far the highest of all the base classifiers. Contrary to the suggestion of Cheng et al. (2010) that user-declared locations are too unreliable to use for user geolocation, we find evidence indicating that they are indeed a valuable source of information for this task. The best overall results are achieved for the stacking approach (STACKING), assigning almost half of the test users to the correct city-level location, and improving more than four-fold on the previous-best accuracy (i.e., MB). These results also suggest that there is strong complementarity between user metadata and tweet text.

4.3 Evaluation on Time-Heterogeneous Data

In addition to the original held-out test data ($\texttt{WORLD}_{test}$) from WORLD, we also developed a new geotagged evaluation dataset using the Twitter Streaming API.[2] This new $\texttt{LIVE}_{test}$ dataset is intended to evaluate the impact of time on predictive accuracy. The training and test data in WORLD are time-homogeneous as they are randomly sampled from data collected in a relatively narrow time window. In contrast, $\texttt{LIVE}_{test}$ is much newer, collected more than 1 year later than WORLD. Given that Twitter users and topics change over time, an essential question is whether the statistical model learned from the "old" training data is still effective over the "new" test data?

The $\texttt{LIVE}_{test}$ data was collected over 48 hours from 2013/03/03 to 2013/03/05. By selecting users with at least 10 geotagged tweets and a declared language of English, 55k users were obtained. For each user, their recent status updates were aggregated, and non-English users were filtered out based on the language predictions of `langid.py`. For some users with geotagged tweets from many cities, the most frequent city might not be an appropriate representation of their home location for evaluation. To improve the evaluation data quality, we therefore exclude users who have less than 50% of their geotagged tweets originating from a single city. After filtering, 32k users were obtained, forming the final $\texttt{LIVE}_{test}$ dataset. In the final $\texttt{LIVE}_{test}$, the smallest class has only one test user, and the largest class has 569 users. The mean users per city is 27.76.

$\texttt{LIVE}_{test}$	Acc	Acc@161	Median
MB-NG	.268 (−.012)	.510 (−.018)	151 (−19)
MB-LOC	.326 (−.079)	.465 (−.060)	306 (+214)
MB-TZ	.065 (+.001)	.160 (−.011)	1529 (+199)
STACKING	.406 (−.084)	.614 (−.051)	40 (+31)

Table 2: Results over $\texttt{LIVE}_{test}$, and the absolute fluctuation over the results for $\texttt{WORLD}_{test}$

The results over $\texttt{LIVE}_{test}$, and the difference in absolute score over $\texttt{WORLD}_{test}$, are shown in Table 2. The stacked model accuracy numbers drop 5–8% on $\texttt{LIVE}_{test}$, and the median error distance increases moderately by 31km. Overall, the numbers suggest inference on $\texttt{WORLD}_{test}$, which is time-homogenous with the training data (taken from WORLD), is an easier classification than $\texttt{LIVE}_{test}$, which is time-heterogeneous with the training data. Training on "old" data and testing on "new" data is certainly possible, however. Looking over the results of the base classifiers, we can see that the biggest hit is for MB-LOC classifier. In contrast, the accuracy for MB-NG and MB-TZ is relatively stable (other than the sharp increase in the median error distance for MB-TZ).

5 Architecture and Access

In this section, we describe the architecture of the proposed geolocation system, as well as two ways of accessing the live system.[3] The core structure of the system consists of two parts: (1) the interface; (2) the back-end geolocation service.

We offer two interfaces to access the system: a Twitter bot and a web interface. The Twitter bot account is: @MELBLTFSD. A daemon process detects any user mentions of the bot in tweets via keyword matching through the Twitter search API. The screen name of the tweet author is extracted and sent to the back-end geolocation service, and the predicted user geolocation is sent to the Twitter user in a direct message, as shown in Figure 1.

Web access is via `http://hum.csse.unimelb.edu.au:9000/geo.html`. Users can input a Twitter user screen name through the web interface, whereby a call is made to the back-end geolocation service to geolocate that user. The geoloca-

[2] `https://dev.twitter.com/docs/api/1.1/get/statuses/sample`

[3] The source code is available from `https://github.com/tq010or/acl2013`

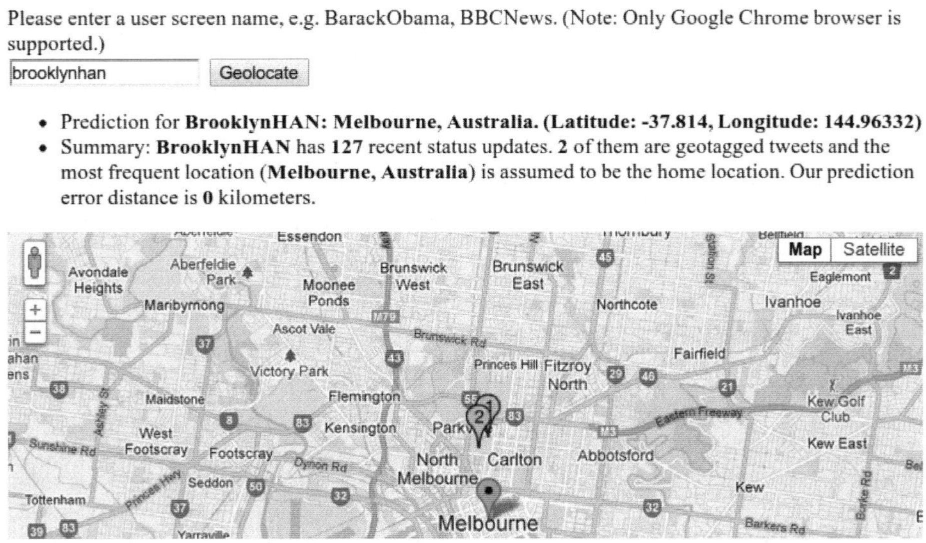

Figure 2: Web interface for user geolocation. The numbered green markers represent geotagged tweets. These coordinates are utilised to validate our predictions, and are not used in the geolocation process. The red marker is the predicted city-based user geolocation.

Figure 1: Twitter bot interface. When the Twitter bot is mentioned in a tweet, that user is sent a direct message with the predicted geolocation.

tion results are rendered on a map (along with any geotagged tweets for the user) as in Figure 2.[4]

The back-end geolocation service crawls recent tweets for a given user in real time,[5] and word and *n*-gram features are extracted from both the text and the user metadata. These features are sent to the *L0* classifiers (TEXT, MB-LOC and MB-TZ), and the *L0* results are further fed into the *L1* classifier for the final prediction.

6 Summary and Future Work

In this paper, we presented a city-level geolocation prediction system for Twitter users. Over a public dataset, our stacking method — exploiting both tweet text and user metadata — substantially outperformed benchmark methods. We further evaluated model generalisation on a newer, time-heterogeneous dataset. The overall results decreased by 5–8% in accuracy, compared with numbers on time-homogeneous data, primarily due to the poor generalisation of the MB-LOC classifier.

In future work, we plan to further investigate the cause of the MB-LOC classifier accuracy decrease on the new dataset. In addition, we'd like to study differences in prediction accuracy across cities. For cities with reliable predictions, the system can be adapted as a preprocessing module for downstream applications, e.g., local event detection based on users with reliable predictions.

Acknowledgements

NICTA is funded by the Australian government as represented by Department of Broadband, Communication and Digital Economy, and the Australian Research Council through the ICT centre of Excellence programme.

References

Lars Backstrom, Jon Kleinberg, Ravi Kumar, and Jasmine Novak. 2008. Spatial variation in search engine queries. In *Proc. of WWW*, pages 357–366, Beijing, China.

Lars Backstrom, Eric Sun, and Cameron Marlow. 2010. Find me if you can: improving geographical prediction with social and spatial proximity. In *Proc. of WWW*, pages 61–70, Raleigh, USA.

[4]Currently, only Google Chrome is supported. `https://www.google.com/intl/en/chrome/`

[5]Up to 200 tweets are crawled, the upper bound of messages returned per single request based on Twitter API v1.1.

Orkut Buyukokkten, Junghoo Cho, Hector Garcia-Molina, Luis Gravano, and Narayana Shivakumar. 1999. Exploiting geographical location information of web pages. In *ACM SIGMOD Workshop on The Web and Databases*, pages 91–96, Philadelphia, USA.

Zhiyuan Cheng, James Caverlee, and Kyumin Lee. 2010. You are where you tweet: a content-based approach to geo-locating twitter users. In *Proc. of CIKM*, pages 759–768, Toronto, Canada.

David J. Crandall, Lars Backstrom, Daniel Huttenlocher, and Jon Kleinberg. 2009. Mapping the world's photos. In *Proc. of WWW*, pages 761–770, Madrid, Spain.

Jacob Eisenstein, Brendan O'Connor, Noah A. Smith, and Eric P. Xing. 2010. A latent variable model for geographic lexical variation. In *Proc. of EMNLP*, pages 1277–1287, Cambridge, MA, USA.

Rong-En Fan, Kai-Wei Chang, Cho-Jui Hsieh, Xiang-Rui Wang, and Chih-Jen Lin. 2008. LIBLINEAR: A library for large linear classification. *Journal of Machine Learning Research*, 9:1871–1874.

Bo Han, Paul Cook, and Timothy Baldwin. 2012. Geolocation prediction in social media data by finding location indicative words. In *Proc. of COLING*, pages 1045–1062, Mumbai, India.

Brent Hecht, Lichan Hong, Bongwon Suh, and Ed H. Chi. 2011. Tweets from justin bieber's heart: the dynamics of the location field in user profiles. In *Proc. of SIGCHI*, pages 237–246, Vancouver, Canada.

Liangjie Hong, Amr Ahmed, Siva Gurumurthy, Alexander J. Smola, and Kostas Tsioutsiouliklis. 2012. Discovering geographical topics in the twitter stream. In *Proc. of WWW*, pages 769–778, Lyon, France.

Sheila Kinsella, Vanessa Murdock, and Neil O'Hare. 2011. "I'm eating a sandwich in glasgow": modeling locations with tweets. In *Proc. of the 3rd International Workshop on Search and Mining User-generated Contents*, pages 61–68, Glasgow, UK.

Jochen L. Leidner and Michael D. Lieberman. 2011. Detecting geographical references in the form of place names and associated spatial natural language. *SIGSPATIAL Special*, 3(2):5–11.

Michael D. Lieberman and Jimmy Lin. 2009. You are where you edit: Locating wikipedia contributors through edit histories. In *ICWSM*.

Marco Lui and Timothy Baldwin. 2012. langid.py: An off-the-shelf language identification tool. In *Proc. of the ACL*, pages 25–30, Jeju Island, Korea.

Alan M. MacEachren, Anuj Jaiswal, Anthony C. Robinson, Scott Pezanowski, Alexander Savelyev, Prasenjit Mitra, Xiao Zhang, and Justine Blanford. 2011. Senseplace2: Geotwitter analytics support for situational awareness. In *IEEE Conference on Visual Analytics Science and Technology*, pages 181–190, Rhode Island, USA.

Jalal Mahmud, Jeffrey Nichols, and Clemens Drews. 2012. Where is this tweet from? inferring home locations of twitter users. In *Proc. of ICWSM*, Dublin, Ireland.

Teng Qin, Rong Xiao, Lei Fang, Xing Xie, and Lei Zhang. 2003. An efficient location extraction algorithm by leveraging web contextual information. In *Proc. of SIGSPATIAL*, pages 55–62, San Jose, USA.

Gianluca Quercini, Hanan Samet, Jagan Sankaranarayanan, and Michael D. Lieberman. 2010. Determining the spatial reader scopes of news sources using local lexicons. In *Proc. of the 18th International Conference on Advances in Geographic Information Systems*, pages 43–52, San Jose, USA.

John Ross Quinlan. 1993. *C4.5: Programs for Machine Learning*. Morgan Kaufmann, San Mateo, USA.

Stephen Roller, Michael Speriosu, Sarat Rallapalli, Benjamin Wing, and Jason Baldridge. 2012. Supervised text-based geolocation using language models on an adaptive grid. In *Proc. of EMNLP*, pages 1500–1510, Jeju Island, Korea.

Dominic Rout, Kalina Bontcheva, Daniel Preoţiuc-Pietro, and Trevor Cohn. 2013. Where's @wally?: a classification approach to geolocating users based on their social ties. In *Proc. of the 24th ACM Conference on Hypertext and Social Media*, pages 11–20, Paris, France.

Adam Sadilek, Henry Kautz, and Jeffrey P. Bigham. 2012. Finding your friends and following them to where you are. In *Proc. of WSDM*, pages 723–732, Seattle, USA.

Takeshi Sakaki, Makoto Okazaki, and Yutaka Matsuo. 2010. Earthquake shakes twitter users: real-time event detection by social sensors. In *Proc. of WWW*, pages 851–860, Raleigh, USA.

Benjamin P. Wing and Jason Baldridge. 2011. Simple supervised document geolocation with geodesic grids. In *Proc. of ACL*, pages 955–964, Portland, USA.

David H. Wolpert. 1992. Stacked generalization. *Neural Networks*, 5(2):241–259.

Zhijun Yin, Liangliang Cao, Jiawei Han, Chengxiang Zhai, and Thomas Huang. 2011. Geographical topic discovery and comparison. In *Proc. of WWW*, pages 247–256, Hyderabad, India.

Wenbo Zong, Dan Wu, Aixin Sun, Ee-Peng Lim, and Dion Hoe-Lian Goh. 2005. On assigning place names to geography related web pages. In *ACM/IEEE Joint Conference on Digital Libraries*, pages 354–362.

An Open Source Toolkit for Quantitative Historical Linguistics

Johann-Mattis List
Research Center Deutscher Sprachatlas
Philipps-University Marburg
mattis.list@uni-marburg.de

Steven Moran
Department of General Linguistics
University of Zurich
steven.moran@uzh.ch

Abstract

Given the increasing interest and development of computational and quantitative methods in historical linguistics, it is important that scholars have a basis for documenting, testing, evaluating, and sharing complex workflows. We present a novel open-source toolkit for quantitative tasks in historical linguistics that offers these features. This toolkit also serves as an interface between existing software packages and frequently used data formats, and it provides implementations of new and existing algorithms within a homogeneous framework. We illustrate the toolkit's functionality with an exemplary workflow that starts with raw language data and ends with automatically calculated phonetic alignments, cognates and borrowings. We then illustrate evaluation metrics on gold standard datasets that are provided with the toolkit.

1 Introduction

Since the turn of the 21st century, there has been an increasing amount of research that applies computational and quantitative approaches to historical-comparative linguistic processes. Among these are: phonetic alignment algorithms (Kondrak, 2000; Prokić et al., 2009), statistical tests for genealogical relatedness (Kessler, 2001), methods for phylogenetic reconstruction (Holman et al., 2011; Bouckaert et al., 2012), and automatic detection of cognates (Turchin et al., 2010; Steiner et al., 2011), borrowings (Nelson-Sathi et al., 2011), and proto-forms (Bouchard-Côté et al., 2013).

In contrast to traditional approaches to language comparison, quantitative methods are often emphasized as advantageous with regard to objectivity, transparency and replicability of results. It is striking then that given the multitude of new approaches, very few are publicly available as executable code. Thus in order to replicate a study, researchers have to rebuild workflows from published descriptions and reimplement their approaches and algorithms. These challenges make the replication of results difficult, or even impossible, and they hinder not only the evaluation and comparison of existing algorithms, but also the development of new approaches that build on them.

Another problem is that quantitative approaches that have been released as software are largely incompatible with each other and they show great differences in regard to their input and out formats, application range and flexibility.[1] Given the breadth of research questions involved in determining language relatedness, this is not surprising. Furthermore, the linguistic datasets upon which many analyses and tools are based are only – if at all – available in disparate formats that need manual or semi-automatic re-editing before they can be used as input elsewhere. Scholars who want to analyze a dataset with different approaches often have to (time-consumingly) convert it into various input formats and they have to familiarize themselves with many different kinds of software. As a result, errors may occur during data conversion processes and the output from different tools must also be converted into a comparable format. For the comparison of different output formats or

[1] There is the STARLING database program for lexicostatistical and glottochronological analyses (Starostin, 2000). The Rug/L04 software aligns sound sequences and calculates phonetic distances using the Levensthein distance (Kleiweg, 2009; Levenshtein, 1966). The ASJP-Software also computes the Levenshtein distance (Holman et al., 2011), but its results are based on previously executed phonetic analyses. The ALINE software carries out pairwise alignment analyses (Kondrak, 2000). There are also software packages from evolutionary biology, which are adapted for linguistic purposes, such as MrBayes (Ronquist and Huelsenbeck, 2003), PHYLIP (Felsenstein, 2005), and SplitsTree (Huson, 1998).

for the evaluation of competing quantitative approaches, gold standard datasets are desirable.

Towards a solution to these problems, we have developed a toolkit that (a) serves as an interface between existing software packages and data formats frequently used in quantitative approaches, (b) provides high-quality implementations of new and existing approaches within a homogeneous framework, and (c) offers a solid basis for testing, documenting, evaluating, and sharing complex workflows in quantitative historical linguistics. We call this open source toolkit LingPy.

2 Lingpy

LingPy is written in Python3 and is freely available online.[2] The Lingpy website contains an API, documentation, tutorials, example scripts, workflows, and datasets that can be used for training, testing, and comparing results from different algorithms. We use Python because it is flexible and object-oriented, it is easy to write C extensions for scientific computing, and it is approachable to non-programmers (Knight et al., 2007). Apart from a large number of different functions for common automatic tasks, LingPy offers specific modules for implementing general workflows that are used in historical linguistics and which partially mimic the basic aspects of the traditional comparative method (Trask, 2000, 64-67). Figure 1 illustrates the interaction between different modules along with the data they produce. In the following subsections, these modules will be introduced in the order of a typical workflow to illustrate the basic capabilities of the LingPy toolkit in more detail.

2.1 Input Formats

The basic input format read by LingPy is a tab-delimited text file in which the first line (the header) indicates the values of the columns and all words are listed in the following rows. The format is very flexible. No specific order of columns or rows is required. Any additional data can be specified by the user, as long as it is in a separate column. Each row represents a word that has to be characterized by a minimum of four values that are given in separate columns: (1) ID, an integer that is used to uniquely identify the word during calculations, (2) CONCEPT, a gloss which indicates the meaning of the word and which is used to align the words semantically, (3) WORD, the orthographic

[2]http://lingpy.org

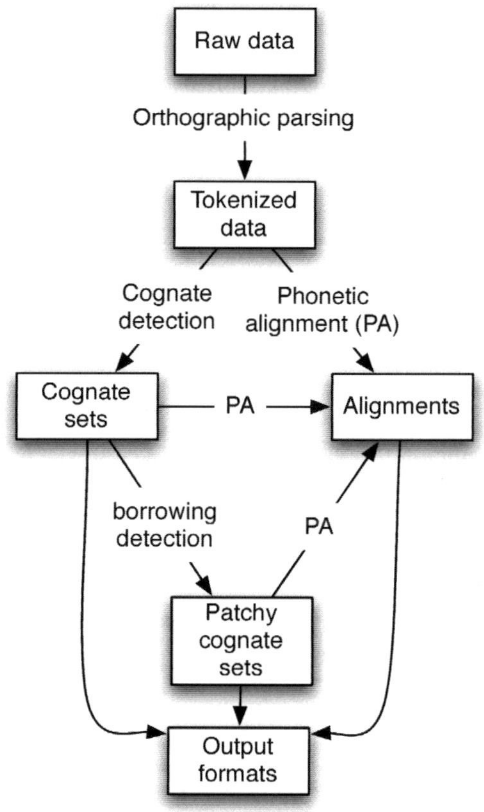

Figure 1: Basic Workflow in LingPy

representation of the word,[3] and (4) TAXON, the name of the language (or dialect) in which the word occurs. Basic output formats are essentially the same, the difference being that the results of calculations are added as separate columns. Table 1 illustrates the basic structure of the input format for a dataset covering 325 concepts translated into 18 Dogon language varieties taken from the Dogon comparative lexical spreadsheet (Heath et al., 2013).[4]

2.2 Parsing and Unicode Handling

Given a dataset in the basic LingPy input format, the first step towards sound-based normalization for automatically identifying cognates and sound changes with quantitative methods is to parse words into tokens. Orthographic tokenization is a non-trivial task, but it is needed to at-

[3]By this we mean a *textual* representation of the word, whether in a document or language-specific orthography or in some form of broad or narrow transcription, etc.

[4]This tokenized dataset and analyses that are discussed in this work are available for download from the LingPy website.

ID	CONCEPT	WORD	TAXON
...	...	...	...
1239	file (tool)	kí:rà	Toro_Tegu
1240	file (tool)	dì:sî:	Ben_Tey
1241	file (tool)	kírâl	Bankan_Tey
1242	file (tool)	dì:jú	Jamsay
...	...	...	...
1249	file (tool)	bìmbú	Tommo_So
1250	file (tool)	bìmbú	Dogul_Dom
1251	file (tool)	dì:zù	Yanda_Dom
1252	file (tool)	bí:mbyé	Mombo
...	...	...	...

Table 1: Basic Input Format of LingPy

tain interoperability across different orthographies or transcription systems and to enable the comparative analysis of languages. LingPy includes a parser that takes as input a dataset and an optional orthography profile, i.e. a description of the Unicode code points, characters, graphemes and orthographic rules that are needed to adequately model a writing system for a language variety as described in a particular document (Moran, 2012, 331). The LingPy parser first normalizes all strings into Unicode Normalization Form D, which decomposes all character sequences and reorders them into one canonical order. This step is necessary because sequences of Unicode characters may differ in their visual and logical orders. Next, if no orthography profile is specified, the parser will use a regular expression match `\X` for Unicode grapheme clusters, i.e. combining character sequences typified by a base character followed by one or more Combing Diacritical Marks. However, another layer of tokenization is usually required to match linguistic graphemes, or what Unicode calls 'tailored grapheme clusters'. Table 2 illustrates the different technological and linguistic levels involved in orthographic parsing.[5]

code points	t	s	ʰ	o	˜	̰	´	s	h	i
"characters"	t	s	ʰ	ṍ̰				s	h	i
graphemes	tsʰ			ṍ̰				sh		i

Table 2: Tokens for the string <tsʰṍshi>

So, given the dataset illustrated in Table 1 and an orthography profile that defines the phonemic units in the Dogon comparative lexicon, the LingPy parser produces the IPA tokenized output shown in Table 3.

ID	...	WORD	TOKENS	...
...	...	...	...	...
1239	...	kí:rà	# k í: r à #	...
1240	...	dì:sî:	# d ì: s î: #	...
1241	...	kírâl	# k í r â l #	...
1242	...	dì:jú	# d ì: ʤ ú #	...
...	...	...	...	...
1249	...	bìmbú	# b ì m b ú #	...
1250	...	bìmbú	# b ì m b ú #	...
1251	...	dì:zù	# d ì: z ù #	...
1252	...	bí:mbyé	# b í: m b j é #	...
...	...	...	...	...

Table 3: Orthographic Parsing in LingPy

2.3 Phonetic Alignments

Although less common in traditional historical linguistics, phonetic alignment plays a crucial role in automatic approaches, with alignment analyses being currently used in many different subfields, such as dialectology (Prokić et al., 2009), phylogenetic reconstruction (Holman et al., 2011) and cognate detection (List, 2012a). Furthermore, alignment analyses are very useful for data visualization, since they directly show which sound segments correspond in cognate words.

LingPy offers implementations for many different approaches to pairwise and multiple phonetic alignment. Among these, there are standard approaches that are directly taken from evolutionary biology and can be applied to linguistic data with only slight modifications, such as the Needleman-Wunsch algorithm (Needleman and Wunsch, 1970) and the Smith-Waterman algorithm (Smith and Waterman, 1981). Furthermore, there are novel approaches that use more complex sequence models in order to meet linguistic-specific requirements, such as the Sound-Class-based phonetic Alignment (SCA) method (List, 2012b). Figure 2 shows a plot of the multiple alignment of the counterparts of the concept "stool" in eight Dogon languages. The color scheme for the sound segments follows the sound class distinction of Dolgopolsky (1964).

2.4 Automatic Cognate Detection

The identification of cognates plays an important role in both traditional and quantitative approaches in historical linguistics. Most quantitative approaches dealing with phylogenetic reconstruction are based on previously identified cognate sets distributed over the languages being in-

[5] Note that even when a linguist transcribes a word with the International Phonetic Alphabet (IPA; a transcription system with one-to-one symbol-to-sound correspondences), explicit definitions for phonemes are needed because some IPA diacritics are encoded as Unicode Spacing Modifier Letters, i.e. characters that are not specified as how they combine with a base character, such as aspiration.

Taxon	Alignment								
Ben_Tey	t	ú	ŋ	g	ú	r	-	ú	m
Bankan_Tey	t	ú	ŋ	g	ú	r	-	ú	-
Jamsay	t	ú	ŋ	-	ú	r^{n}	-	ú	-
Perge_Tegu	t	ú	ŋ	-	ú	r^{n}	-	ú	m
Gourou	t	ú	m	-	ú	r	-	ú	-
Yorno_So	t	ɔ́	ŋ	-	ɔ́	-	-	-	-
Tommo_So	t	ú	ŋ	g	ú	r	-	ú	-
Tebul_Ure	t	ú	ŋ	g	ú	r	g	ɔ́	-

Figure 2: Multiple Phonetic Alignment in LingPy

vestigated (Bouckaert et al., 2012; Bouchard-Côté et al., 2013). Since the traditional approach to cognate detection within the framework of the comparative method is very time-consuming and difficult to evaluate for the non-expert, automatic approaches to cognate detection can play an important role in objectifying phylogenetic reconstructions.

Currently, LingPy offers four alternative approaches to cognate detection in multilingual wordlists. The method by Turchin et al. (2010) employs sound classes as proposed by Dolgopolsky (1964) and assigns words that match in their first two consonant classes to the same cognate set. The NED method calculates the normalized edit distance between words and groups them into cognate sets using a flat cluster algorithm.[6] The SCA and the LexStat methods (List, 2012a) use the same strategy for clustering, but the distances for the SCA method are calculated with help of the SCA alignment method (List, 2012b), and the distances for the LexStat method are derived from previously identified regular sound correspondences. Table 4 shows a small section of the results from the LexStat analysis of the Dogon data. As shown, LingPy follows the STARLING approach in displaying cognate judgments by assigning cognate words the same cognate ID (COGID). In Table 4, the words judged to be cognate are shaded in the same color. The full results are posted on the LingPy website.

2.5 Automatic Borrowing Detection

Automatic approaches for borrowing detection are still in their infancy in historical linguistics. LingPy provides a full reimplementation (along with specifically linguistic modifications) of the minimal lateral network (MLN) approach (Nelson-Sathi et al., 2011). This approach searches for cognate sets which are not compatible with a given reference tree topology. Incompatible (patchy) cognate sets often point to either borrowings or wrong cognate assessments in the data. The results can be visualized by connecting all taxa of the reference tree for which patchy cognate sets can be inferred with lateral links. In Figure 3, the method has been applied again to the Dogon dataset. Cognate judgments for this analysis were carried out with help of LingPy's LexStat method. The tree topology was calculated using MrBayes.

ID	CONCEPT	WORD	TAXON	COGID
...	...	...	...	...
1239	file (tool)	kí:rà	Toro_Tegu	68
1240	file (tool)	dì:sî:	Ben_Tey	69
1241	file (tool)	kírâl	Bankan_Tey	68
1242	file (tool)	dì:jú	Jamsay	69
...	...	...	...	...
1249	file (tool)	bìmbú	Tommo_So	70
1250	file (tool)	bìmbú	Dogul_Dom	70
1251	file (tool)	dì:zù	Yanda_Dom	69
1252	file (tool)	bí:mbyé	Mombo	70
...	...	...	...	...

Table 4: Cognate Detection in LingPy

2.6 Output Formats

The output formats supported by LingPy can be divided into three different classes. The first class consists of text-based formats that can be used for manual correction and inspection by importing the data into spreadsheet programs, or simply editing and reviewing the results in a text editor. The second class consists of specific formats for third-party toolkits, such as PHYLIP, SplitsTree, MrBayes, or STARLING. LingPy currently offers support for PHYLIP's distance calculations (DST-format), for tree-representation (Newick-format), for complex representations of character data (Nexus-format), and for the import into STARLING databases (CSV with STARLING markup). The third class consists of new approaches to the visualization of phonetic alignments, cognate sets, and phylogenetic networks. In fact, all plots in this paper were created with LingPy's output formats.

3 Evaluation

In order to improve the performance of quantitative approaches, it is of crucial importance to test and evaluate them. Evaluation is usually done by comparing how well a given approach performs on a reference dataset, i.e. a gold standard, where the results of the analysis are known in advance. LingPy comes with a module for the evaluation of

[6] The normalized edit distance is calculated by dividing the edit distance (Levenshtein, 1966) by the length of the smaller sequence, see Holman et al. (2011) for details.

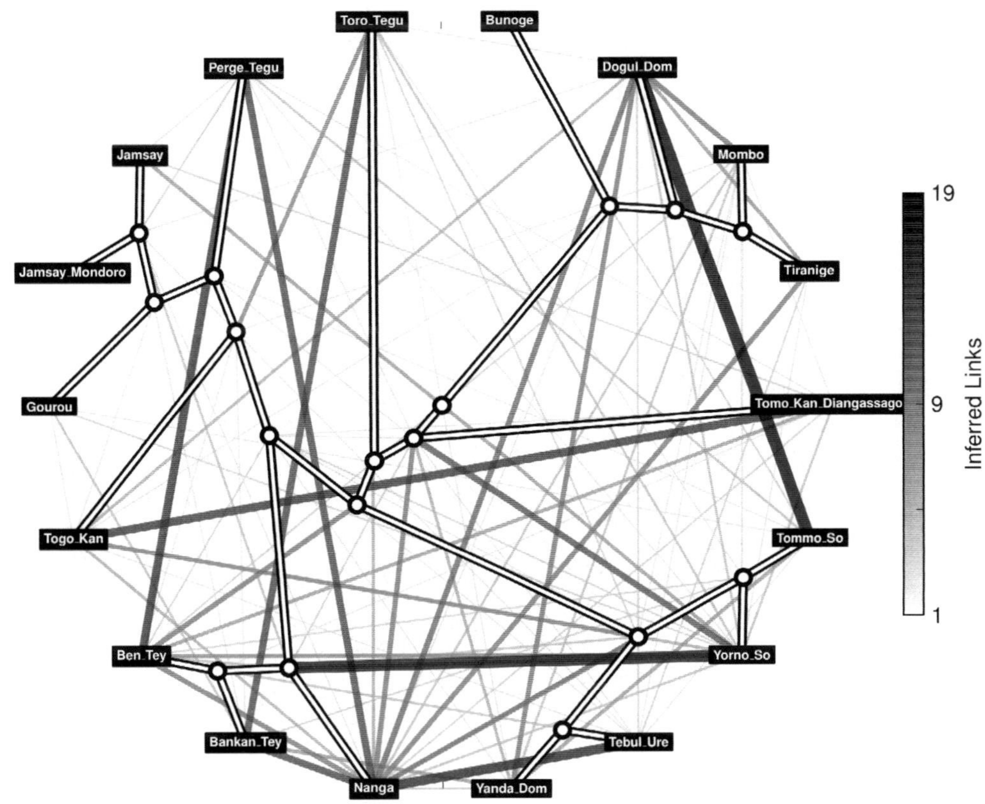

Figure 3: Borrowing Detection in LingPy

basic tasks in historical linguistics, such as phonetic alignment and cognate detection. This module offers both common evaluation measures that are used to assess the accuracy of the respective methods and gold standard datasets encoded in the LingPy input format.

In Figure 4, the performance of the four abovementioned approaches to automatic cognate detection are compared with the gold standard cognate judgments of a dataset covering 207 concepts translated into 20 Indo-European languages taken from the Indo-European Lexical Cognacy (IELex) database (Bouckaert et al., 2012).[7] The pair scores, implemented in LingPy after the description in Bouchard-Côté et al. (2013), were used as an evaluation measure. For all approaches we chose the respective thresholds that tend to yield the best results on all of the gold standards. As shown in Figure, both the SCA and LexStat methods show a higher accuracy than the Turchin and NED methods, with LexStat slightly outperforming SCA. However, the generally bad performance of all approaches on this dataset shows that there is a clear need for improving automatic cognate detection approaches, especially in cases of remote relationship, such as Indo-European.

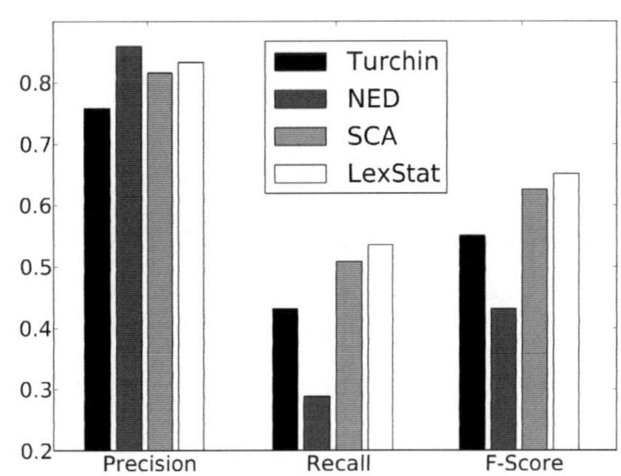

Figure 4: Evaluating Cognate Detection Methods

4 Conclusion

Quantitative approaches in historical linguistics are still in their infancy, far away from being able to compete with the intuition of trained historical

[7]Gold standard here means that the cognate judgments were carried out manually by the compilers of the IELex database.

linguists. The toolkit we presented is a first attempt to close the gap between quantitative and traditional methods by providing a homogeneous framework that serves as an interface between existing packages and at the same time provides high-quality implementations of new approaches.

References

A. Bouchard-Côté, D. Hall, T. L. Griffiths, and D. Klein. 2013. Automated reconstruction of ancient languages using probabilistic models of sound change. *PNAS*, 110(11):4224–4229.

R. Bouckaert, P. Lemey, M. Dunn, S. J. Greenhill, A. V. Alekseyenko, A. J. Drummond, R. D. Gray, M. A. Suchard, and Q. D. Atkinson. 2012. Mapping the origins and expansion of the Indo-European language family. *Science*, 337(6097):957–960, Aug.

A. B. Dolgopolsky. 1964. Gipoteza drevnejšego rodstva jazykovych semej Severnoj Evrazii s verojatnostej točky zrenija [A probabilistic hypothesis concerning the oldest relationships among the language families of Northern Eurasia]. *Voprosy Jazykoznanija*, 2:53–63.

J. Felsenstein. 2005. Phylip (phylogeny inference package) version 3.6. Distributed by the author. Department of Genome Sciences, University of Washington, Seattle.

J. Heath, S Moran, K. Prokhorov, L. McPherson, and B. Canslter. 2013. Dogon comparative lexicon. URL: `http://www.dogonlanguages.org`.

E. W. Holman, C. H. Brown, S. Wichmann, A. Müller, V. Velupillai, H. Hammarström, S. Sauppe, H. Jung, D. Bakker, P. Brown, O. Belyaev, M. Urban, R. Mailhammer, J.-M. List, and D. Egorov. 2011. Automated dating of the world's language families based on lexical similarity. *Current Anthropology*, 52(6):841–875.

D. H. Huson. 1998. SplitsTree. Analyzing and visualizing evolutionary data. *Bioinformatics*, 14(1):68–73.

B. Kessler. 2001. *The significance of word lists. Statistical tests for investigating historical connections between languages*. CSLI Publications, Stanford.

P. Kleiweg. 2009. RuG/L^{04}. Software for dialectometrics and cartography. Distributed by the Author. Rijksuniversiteit Groningen. Faculteit der Letteren, September.

R. Knight, P. Maxwell, A. Birmingham, J. Carnes, J. G. Caporaso, B. Easton, M. Eaton, M. Hamady, H. Lindsay, Z. Liu, C. Lozupone, D. McDonald, M. Robeson, R. Sammut, S. Smit, M. Wakefield, J. Widmann, S. Wikman, S. Wilson, H. Ying, and G. Huttley. 2007. PyCogent. A toolkit for making sense from sequence. *Genome Biology*, 8(8):R171.

G. Kondrak. 2000. A new algorithm for the alignment of phonetic sequences. In *Proceedings of the 1st North American chapter of the Association for Computational Linguistics conference*, NAACL 2000, pages 288–295, Stroudsburg, PA, USA. Association for Computational Linguistics.

V. I. Levenshtein. 1966. Binary codes capable of correcting deletions, insertions, and reversals. *Soviet Physics Doklady*, 10(8):707–710.

J.-M. List. 2012a. LexStat. Automatic detection of cognates in multilingual wordlists. In *Proceedings of the EACL 2012 Joint Workshop of LINGVIS & UNCLH*, pages 117–125. Association for Computational Linguistics.

J.-M. List. 2012b. SCA. Phonetic alignment based on sound classes. In M. Slavkovik and D. Lassiter, editors, *New directions in logic, language, and computation*, number 7415 in LNCS, pages 32–51. Springer, Berlin and Heidelberg.

S. Moran. 2012. *Phonetics information base and lexicon*. Ph.D. thesis, University of Washington.

S. B. Needleman and C. D. Wunsch. 1970. A gene method applicable to the search for similarities in the amino acid sequence of two proteins. *Journal of Molecular Biology*, 48:443–453, July.

S. Nelson-Sathi, J.-M. List, H. Geisler, H. Fangerau, R. D. Gray, W. Martin, and T. Dagan. 2011. Networks uncover hidden lexical borrowing in Indo-European language evolution. *Proceedings of the Royal Society B*, 278(1713):1794–1803.

J. Prokić, M. Wieling, and J. Nerbonne. 2009. Multiple sequence alignments in linguistics. In *Proceedings of the EACL 2009 Workshop on Language Technology and Resources for Cultural Heritage, Social Sciences, Humanities, and Education*, pages 18–25. Association for Computational Linguistics.

F. Ronquist and J. P. Huelsenbeck. 2003. MrBayes 3. Bayesian phylogenetic inference under mixed models. *Bioinformatics*, 19(12):1572–1574.

T. F. Smith and M. S. Waterman. 1981. Identification of common molecular subsequences. *Journal of Molecular Biology*, 1:195–197.

S. A. Starostin. 2000. The STARLING database program. URL: `http://starling.rinet.ru`.

L. Steiner, P. F. Stadler, and M. Cysouw. 2011. A pipeline for computational historical linguistics. *Language Dynamics and Change*, 1(1):89–127.

R. L. Trask. 2000. *The dictionary of historical and comparative linguistics*. Edinburgh University Press, Edinburgh.

P. Turchin, I. Peiros, and M. Gell-Mann. 2010. Analyzing genetic connections between languages by matching consonant classes. *Journal of Language Relationship*, 3:117–126.

AnnoMarket: An Open Cloud Platform for NLP

Valentin Tablan, Kalina Bontcheva
Ian Roberts, Hamish Cunningham
University of Sheffield,
Department of Computer Science
211 Portobello, Sheffield, UK
Initial.Surname@dcs.shef.ac.uk

Marin Dimitrov
Ontotext AD
47A Tsarigradsko Shosse, Sofia, Bulgaria
marin.dimitrov@ontotext.com

Abstract

This paper presents AnnoMarket, an open cloud-based platform which enables researchers to deploy, share, and use language processing components and resources, following the data-as-a-service and software-as-a-service paradigms. The focus is on multilingual text analysis resources and services, based on an open-source infrastructure and compliant with relevant NLP standards. We demonstrate how the AnnoMarket platform can be used to develop NLP applications with little or no programming, to index the results for enhanced browsing and search, and to evaluate performance. Utilising AnnoMarket is straightforward, since cloud infrastructural issues are dealt with by the platform, completely transparently to the user: load balancing, efficient data upload and storage, deployment on the virtual machines, security, and fault tolerance.

1 Introduction

Following the Software-as-a-Service (SaaS) paradigm from cloud computing (Dikaiakos et al., 2009), a number of text processing services have been developed, e.g. OpenCalais[1] and Alchemy API[2]. These provide information extraction services, accessible programmatically and charged per number of documents processed.

However, they suffer from two key technical drawbacks. Firstly, document-by-document processing over HTTP is inefficient on large datasets and is also limited to within-document text processing algorithms. Secondly, the text processing algorithms are pre-packaged: it is not possible for researchers to extend the functionality (e.g. adapt such a service to recognise new kinds of entities). Additionally, these text processing SaaS sites come with daily rate limits, in terms of number of API calls or documents that can be processed. Consequently, using these services for research is not just limited in terms of text processing functionality offered, but also quickly becomes very expensive on large-scale datasets. A moderately-sized collection of tweets, for example, comprises small but numerous documents, which can lead to unfeasibly high processing costs.

Platform-as-a-Service (PaaS) (Dikaiakos et al., 2009) are a type of cloud computing service which insulates developers from the low-level issues of utilising cloud infrastructures effectively, while providing facilities for efficient development, testing, and deployment of software over the Internet, following the SaaS model. In the context of traditional NLP research and development, and pre-dating cloud computing, similar needs were addressed through NLP infrastructures, such as GATE (Cunningham et al., 2013) and UIMA (Ferrucci and Lally, 2004). These infrastructures accelerated significantly the pace of NLP research, through reusable algorithms (e.g. rule-based pattern matching engines, machine learning algorithms), free tools for low-level NLP tasks, and support for multiple input and output document formats (e.g. XML, PDF, DOC, RDF, JSON).

This demonstration introduces the AnnoMarket[3] open, cloud-based platform, which has been developed following the PaaS paradigm. It enables researchers to deploy, share, and use language processing components and resources, following the Data-as-a-Service (DaaS) and Software-as-a-Service (SaaS) paradigms. It gives researchers access to an open, standard-compliant NLP infrastructure and enables them

[1] http://www.opencalais.com
[2] http://www.alchemyapi.com

[3] At the time of writing, a beta version of AnnoMarket is available at http://annomarket.com

to carry out large-scale NLP experiments by harnessing the vast, on-demand compute power of the Amazon cloud. It supports not only NLP algorithm development and execution, but also on-demand collaborative corpus annotation and performance evaluation. Important infrastructural issues are dealt with by the platform, completely transparently for the researcher: load balancing, efficient data upload and storage, deployment on the virtual machines, security, and fault tolerance.

AnnoMarket differs from previous work (e.g. (Zhou et al., 2010; Ramakrishnan et al., 2010)) in that it requires no programming in order to run a GATE-compliant NLP application on a large dataset. In that sense, it combines the ease of use of an NLP SaaS with the openness and comprehensive facilities of the GATE NLP infrastructure. AnnoMarket offers a growing number of pre-packaged services, in multiple languages. Additionally, as a specialised NLP PaaS, it also supports a *bring-your-own-pipeline* option, which can be built easily by reusing pre-existing GATE-compatible NLP components and adding some new ones. Moreover, in addition to offering entity extraction services like OpenCalais, our NLP PaaS also supports manual corpus annotation, semantic indexing and search, and performance evaluation.

The contributions of this paper are as follows:

1. A demonstration of running AnnoMarket multilingual NLP services on large datasets, without programming. The new service deployment facilities will also be shown, including how services can optionally be shared with others.
2. A demonstration on shared research corpora via the AnnoMarket platform, following the data-as-a-service model (the sharer is responsible for ensuring no copyright violations).
3. A demonstration of the large-scale search and browsing interface, which uses the results of the NLP SaaS to offer enhanced, semantic-based functionality.

2 The AnnoMarket NLP PaaS

This section first discusses the methodology underpinning the AnnoMarket platform, then presents its architecture and key components.

2.1 Development and Deployment Methodology

The development of text analysis algorithms and pipelines typically follows a certain methodological pattern, or lifecycle. A central problem is to define the NLP task, such that human annotators can perform it with a high level of agreement and to create high quality training and evaluation datasets. It is common to use double or triple annotation, where several people perform the annotation task independently and we then measure their level of agreement (*Inter-Annotator Agreement*, or IAA) to quantify and control the quality of this data (Hovy, 2010).

The AnnoMarket platform was therefore designed to offer full methodological support for all stages of the text analysis development lifecycle:

1. Create an initial prototype of the NLP pipeline, testing on a small document collection, using the desktop-based GATE user interface (Cunningham et al., 2002);
2. If required, collect a gold-standard corpus for evaluation and/or training, using the GATE Teamware collaborative corpus annotation service (Bontcheva et al., 2013), running in AnnoMarket;
3. Evaluate the performance of the automatic pipeline on the gold standard (either locally in the GATE development environment or on the cloud). Return to step 1 for further development and evaluation cycles, as needed.
4. Upload the large datasets and deploy the NLP pipeline on the AnnoMarket PaaS;
5. Run the large-scale NLP experiment and download the results as XML or a standard linguistic annotation format (Ide and Romary, 2004). AnnoMarket also offers scalable semantic indexing and search over the linguistic annotations and document content.
6. Analyse any errors, and if required, iterate again over the earlier steps.

AnnoMarket is fully compatible with the GATE open-source architecture (Cunningham et al., 2002), in order to benefit from GATE's numerous reusable and multilingual text processing components, and also from its infrastructural support for linguistic standards and diverse input formats.

2.2 Architecture

The architecture of the AnnoMarket PaaS comprises of four layers (see Figure 1), combining

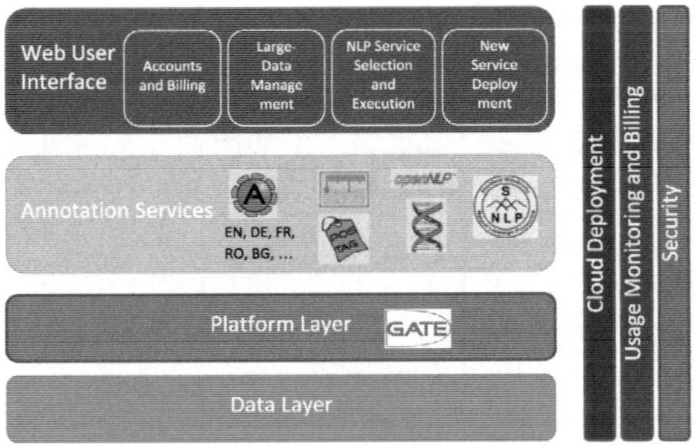

Figure 1: The AnnoMarket Architecture

components with related capabilities. Additionally, we have identified three aspects, which span across multiple layers.

The Data Layer is described in Section 2.3, the Platform Layer – in Section 2.4, and the Annotation Services – in Section 2.5.

The fourth, web user interface layer, contains a number of UI components that allow researchers to use the AnnoMarket platform in various ways, e.g. to run an already deployed text annotation service on a large dataset, to deploy and share a new service on the platform, or to upload (and optionally share) a document collection (i.e. a corpus). There is also support for finding relevant services, deployed on the AnnoMarket platform. Lastly, due to the platform running on the Amazon cloud infrastructure, there are account management interfaces, including billing information, payments, and usage reports.

The first vertical aspect is cloud deployment on Amazon. This covers support for automatic up and down-scaling of the allocated Amazon resources, detection of and recovery from Amazon infrastructure failures and network failures, and data backup.

Usage monitoring and billing is the second key vertical aspect, since fine-grained pay-as-you-go ability is essential. Even in the case of freely-available annotations services, Amazon usage charges are incurred and thus such functionality is needed. Various usage metrics are monitored and metered so that proper billing can be guaranteed, including: storage space required by language resources and data sets; CPU utilisation of the annotation services; number and size of documents processed.

Security aspects also have impact on all the layers of the AnnoMarket platform:

- Data Layer – data encryption and access control;
- Platform Layer – data encryption, authentication and access control;
- Service layer – authentication and transport level encryption;
- User Interface layer – authentication and transport level encryption.

In addition, we have implemented a REST programming API for AnnoMarket, so that data upload and download and running of annotation services can all be done automatically, outside of the web interface. This allows tighter integration within other applications, as well as support for synchronous (i.e. document-by-document) calling of the annotation services.

2.3 The Data Layer

The Data Layer stores various kinds of content, e.g. crawled web content, users' own corpora (private or shared with others), results from running the annotation services, etc.

Input documents can be in all major formats (e.g., XML, HTML, JSON, PDF, DOC), based on GATE's comprehensive format support. In all cases, when a document is being processed by AnnoMarket, the format is analysed and converted into a single unified, graph-based model of *annotation*: the one of the GATE NLP framework (Cunningham et al., 2002). Then this internal annotation format is also used by the collaborative corpus annotation web tool, and for annotation indexing and search. Annotations produced can be exported as in-line or stand-off XML, including XCES (Ide and Romary, 2004).

In implementation terms, Amazon S3 is used to store content on the platform. S3 provides a REST service for content access, as well as direct HTTP access, which provides an easy way for AnnoMarket users to upload and download content.

While stored on the cloud, data is protected by Amazon's security procedures. All transfers between the cloud storage, the annotation services, and the user's computer are done via an encrypted channel, using SSL.

2.4 The Platform Layer

The AnnoMarket platform provides an environment where text processing applications can be deployed as annotation services on the cloud. It allows processing pipelines that were produced on a

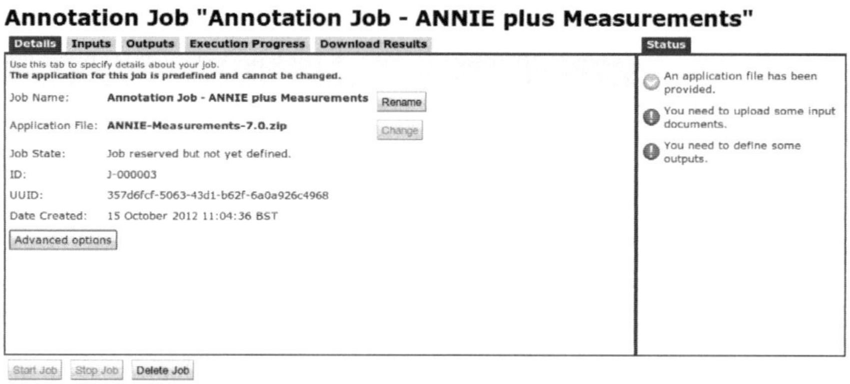

Figure 2: Web-based Job Editor

developer's stand-alone computer to be deployed seamlessly on distributed hardware resources (the compute cloud) with the aim of processing large amounts of data in a timely fashion. This process needs to be resilient in the face of failures at the level of the cloud infrastructure, the network communication, errors in the processing pipeline and in the input data.

The platform layer determines the optimal number of virtual machines for running a given NLP application, given the size of the document collection to be processed and taking into account the overhead in starting up new virtual machines on demand. The implementation is designed to be robust in the face of hardware failures and processing errors. For technical details on the way this was implemented on Amazon EC2 see (Tablan et al., 2013).

The GATE plugin-based architecture (Cunningham et al., 2002) is the basis for the platform environment. Users can upload any pipelines compliant with the GATE Processing Resource (PR) model and these are automatically deployed as annotation services on the AnnoMarket platform.

2.5 Annotation Services

As discussed above, the platform layer in AnnoMarket addresses most of the technical and methodological requirements towards the NLP PaaS, making the deployment, execution, and sharing of annotation services (i.e. pipelines and algorithms) a straightforward task. From a researcher's perspective, executing an annotation service on a dataset involves a few simple steps:

- Upload the document collection to be processed or point the system to a shared dataset on the platform;
- Upload a GATE-based processing pipeline to be used (or choose an already deployed annotation service);
- Set any required parameter values;
- Press the '*Start*' button.

While the job is running, a regularly updated execution log is made available in the user's dashboard. Upon job completion, an email notification is also sent. Most of the implementation details are hidden away from the user, who interacts with the system through a web-based job editor, depicted in Figure 2, or through a REST API.

The number of already deployed annotation services on the platform is growing continuously. Figure 3 shows a subset of them, as well as the metadata tags associated with these services, so that users can quickly restrict which types of services they are after and then be shown only the relevant subset. At the time of writing, there are services of the following kinds:

- Part-of-Speech-Taggers for English, German, Dutch, and Hungarian.
- Chunking: the GATE NP and VP chunkers and the OpenNLP ones;
- Parsing: currently the Stanford Parser [4], but more are under integration;
- Stemming in 15 languages, via the Snowball stemmer;
- Named Entity Recognition: in English, German, French, Arabic, Dutch, Romanian, and Bulgarian;
- Biomedical taggers: the PennBio[5] and the AbGene (Tanabe and Wilbur, 2002) taggers;
- Twitter-specific NLP: language detection, tokenisation, normalisation, POS tagging, and

[4]http://nlp.stanford.edu/software/lex-parser.shtml

[5]http://www.seas.upenn.edu/~strctlrn/BioTagger/BioTagger.html

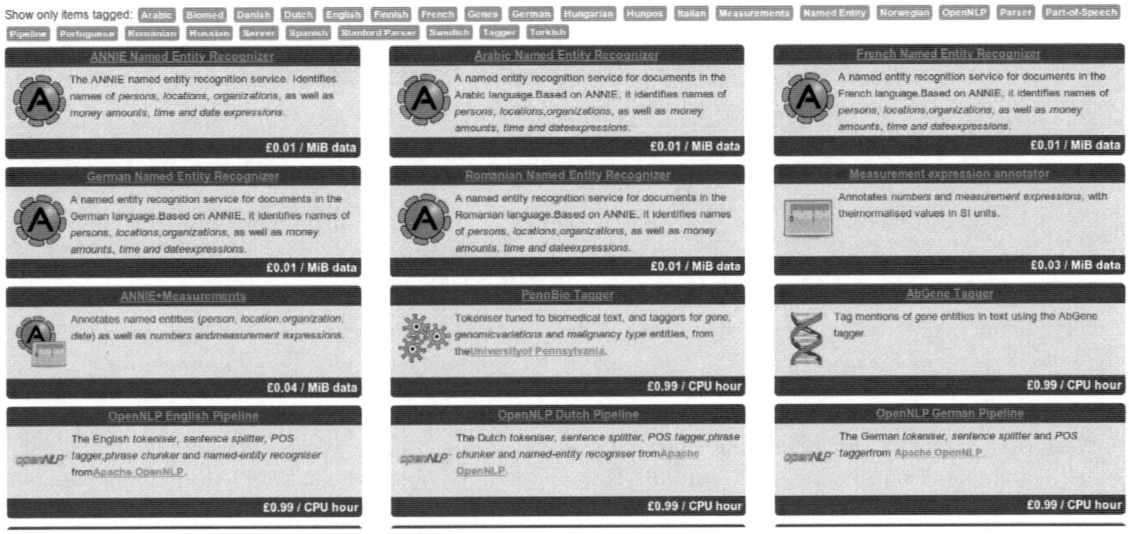

Figure 3: Pre-deployed Text Annotation Services

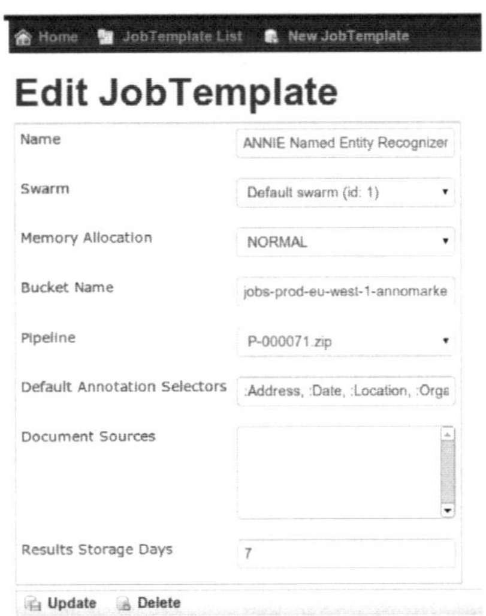

Figure 4: Creating a New Annotation Service

NER.

The deployment of new annotation services is done via a web interface (see Figure 4), where an administrator needs to configure some basic details related to the utilisation of the platform layer and provide a self-contained GATE-compatible application. Platform users can only publish their own annotation services by contacting an administrator, who can validate the provided pipeline before making it publicly available to the other users. This step is intended to protect the users community from malicious or poor quality pipelines.

3 Search and Browsing of Annotated Corpora

The AnnoMarket platform also includes a service for indexing and searching over a collection of semantically annotated documents. The output of an annotation service (see Figure 2) can be fed directly into a search index, which is created as the service is run on the documents. This provides facilities for searching over different views of document text, for example one can search the document's words, the part-of-speech of those words, or their morphological roots. As well as searching the document text, we also support searches over the documents' semantic annotations, e.g. named entity types or semantic roles.

Figure 5 shows a semantic search over 80,000 news web pages from the BBC. They have first been pre-processed with the POS tagging, morphological analysis, and NER services on the platform and the output indexed automatically. The search query is for documents, where entities of type Person are followed by any morphological form of the verb say, i.e. `{Person} root:say`.

4 Conclusion

This paper described a cloud-based open platform for text mining, which aims to assist the development and deployment of robust, large-scale text processing applications. By supporting the sharing of annotation pipelines, AnnoMarket also pro-

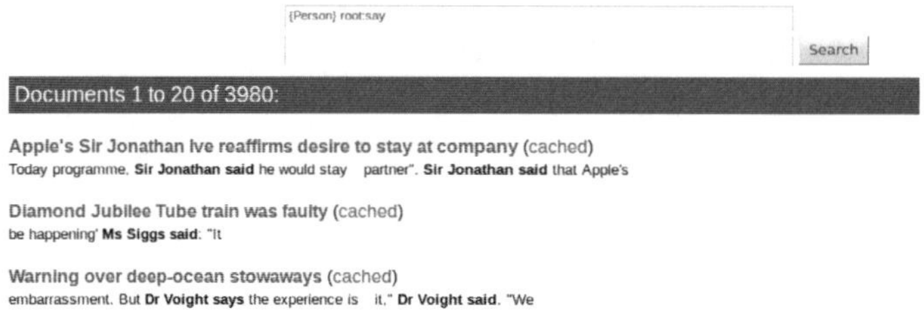

Figure 5: Example Semantic Search Results

motes reuse and repeatability of experiments.

As the number of annotation services offered by the platform has grown, we identified a need for service search, so that users can locate useful NLP services more effectively. We are currently developing a new UI, which offers search and browsing functionality, alongside various criteria, such as functionality (e.g. POS tagger, named entity recogniser), user ratings, natural language supported). In the medium- to long-term we have also planned to support UIMA-based pipelines, via GATE's UIMA compatibility layer.

A beta version is currently open to researchers for experimentation. Within the next six months we plan to to solicit more shared annotation pipelines to be deployed on the platform by other researchers.

Acknowledgments

This work was supported by the European Union under grant agreement No. 296322 AnnoMarket,[6] and a UK EPSRC grant No. EP/I004327/1.

References

Kalina Bontcheva, Hamish Cunningham, Ian Roberts, Angus. Roberts, Valentin. Tablan, Niraj Aswani, and Genevieve Gorrell. 2013. GATE Teamware: A Web-based, Collaborative Text Annotation Framework. *Language Resources and Evaluation*.

Hamish Cunningham, Diana Maynard, Kalina Bontcheva, and Valentin Tablan. 2002. Gate: an architecture for development of robust hlt applications. In *Proceedings of the 40th Annual Meeting on Association for Computational Linguistics, 7–12 July 2002*, ACL '02, pages 168–175, Stroudsburg, PA, USA. Association for Computational Linguistics.

Hamish Cunningham, Valentin Tablan, Angus Roberts, and Kalina Bontcheva. 2013. Getting more out of biomedical documents with gate's full lifecycle open source text analytics. *PLoS Computational Biology*, 9(2):e1002854, 02.

Marios D Dikaiakos, Dimitrios Katsaros, Pankaj Mehra, George Pallis, and Athena Vakali. 2009. Cloud computing: Distributed internet computing for IT and scientific research. *IEEE Internet Computing*, 13(5):10–13.

David Ferrucci and Adam Lally. 2004. UIMA: An Architectural Approach to Unstructured Information Processing in the Corporate Research Environment. *Natural Language Engineering*, 10(3-4):327–348.

Eduard Hovy. 2010. Annotation. In *Tutorial Abstracts of ACL*.

Nancy Ide and Laurent Romary. 2004. Standards for language resources. *Natural Language Engineering*, 10:211–225.

C. Ramakrishnan, W. A. Baumgartner, J. A. Blake, G. A. P. C. Burns, K. Bretonnel Cohen, H. Drabkin, J. Eppig, E. Hovy, C. N. Hsu, L. E. Hunter, T. Ingulfsen, H. R. Onda, S. Pokkunuri, E. Riloff, C. Roeder, and K. Verspoor. 2010. Building the scientific knowledge mine (SciKnowMine): a community-driven framework for text mining tools in direct service to biocuration. In *New Challenges for NLP Frameworks (NLPFrameworks 2010)*, LREC 2010, pages 9–14, Valletta, Malta, May. ELRA.

Valentin Tablan, Ian Roberts, Hamish Cunningham, and Kalina Bontcheva. 2013. GATECloud.net: a Platform for Large-Scale, Open-Source Text Processing on the Cloud. *Philosophical Transactions of the Royal Society A: Mathematical, Physical & Engineering Sciences*, 371(1983):20120071.

Lorraine Tanabe and W. John Wilbur. 2002. Tagging Gene and Protein Names in Full Text Articles. In *Proceedings of the ACL-02 workshop on Natural Language Processing in the biomedical domain, 7–12 July 2002*, volume 3, pages 9–13, Philadelphia, PA. Association for Computational Linguistics.

Bin Zhou, Yan Jia, Chunyang Liu, and Xu Zhang. 2010. A distributed text mining system for online web textual data analysis. In *Cyber-Enabled Distributed Computing and Knowledge Discovery (CyberC), 2010 International Conference on*, pages 1–4, Los Alamitos, CA, USA, October. IEEE Computer Society.

[6] See `http://www.annomarket.eu/`.

Detecting Event-Related Links and Sentiments from Social Media Texts

Alexandra Balahur and **Hristo Tanev**
European Commission Joint Research Centre
Via E. Fermi 2749, T.P. 267
21027 Ispra (VA), Italy
{alexandra.balahur, hristo.tanev}@jrc.ec.europa.eu

Abstract

Nowadays, the importance of Social Media is constantly growing, as people often use such platforms to share mainstream media news and comment on the events that they relate to. As such, people no loger remain mere spectators to the events that happen in the world, but become part of them, commenting on their developments and the entities involved, sharing their opinions and distributing related content. This paper describes a system that links the main events detected from clusters of newspaper articles to tweets related to them, detects complementary information sources from the links they contain and subsequently applies sentiment analysis to classify them into positive, negative and neutral. In this manner, readers can follow the main events happening in the world, both from the perspective of mainstream as well as social media and the public's perception on them.

This system will be part of the EMM media monitoring framework working live and it will be demonstrated using Google Earth.

1 Introduction

In the context of the Web 2.0, the importance of Social Media has been constantly growing in the past years. People use Twitter, Facebook, LinkedIn, Pinterest, blogs and Web forums to give and get advice, share information on products, opinions and real-time information about ongoing and future events. In particular Twitter, with its half a billion active members, was used during disasters, protests, elections, and other events to share updates, opinions, comments and post links to online resources (e.g. news, videos, pictures, blog posts, etc.). As such, Twitter can be used as a complementary source of information, from which we can retrieve additional facts, but also learn about the attitude of the people towards certain events. On the one hand, news from the traditional media focus on the factual side of events, important for the society or at least large groups of people. On the other hand, social media reflects subjective interpretations of facts, with different levels of relevance (societal or only individual). Therefore, the events reported in online news can be considered a point of intersection for both types of media, which are able to offer complementary views on these events.

In this context, we describe a system that we developed as an additonal component to the EMM (Europe Media Monitor)[1] news monitoring framework, linking mainstream news to related texts from social media and detecting the opinion (sentiment) users express on these topics.

In the EMM news monitoring system, the different news sites are monitored and new articles are scraped from them, with a refresh rate of 10 minutes. Subsequently, news items are clustered and the most important ones are displayed (top 10). These are called "stories". Our system subsequently links these stories to messages from Twitter (tweets) and extracts the related URLs they contain. Finally, it analyzes the sentiments expressed in the tweets by using a hybrid knowledge-based and statistical sentiment detection module. The overview of the system is depicted in Figure

[1]http://emm.jrc.it/NewsBrief/clusteredition/en/latest.html

1.

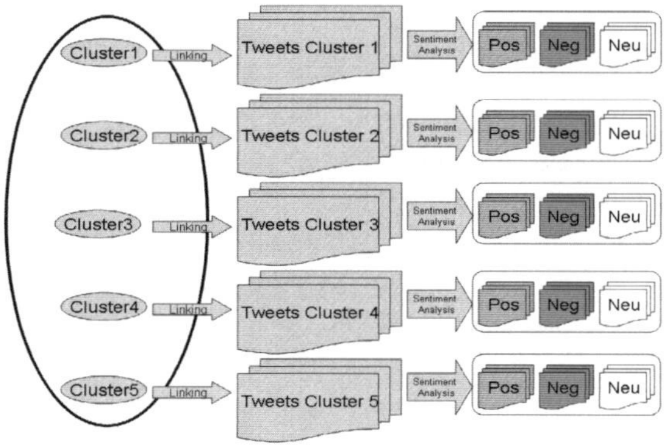

Figure 1: Overview of the news clusters-Twitter linking and sentiment analysis system.

The system will be demonstrated using the Google Earth interface (Figure 2), presenting the characteristics of the event described in the story (type, date, location, the first words in the article that is the centroid of the news cluster for that story). In addition, we present new information that we extract from Twitter - links (URLs) that we find from the tweets we retrieved linked to the story and positive, negative and neutral sentiment, respectively, as a proportion of the total number of tweets retrieved.

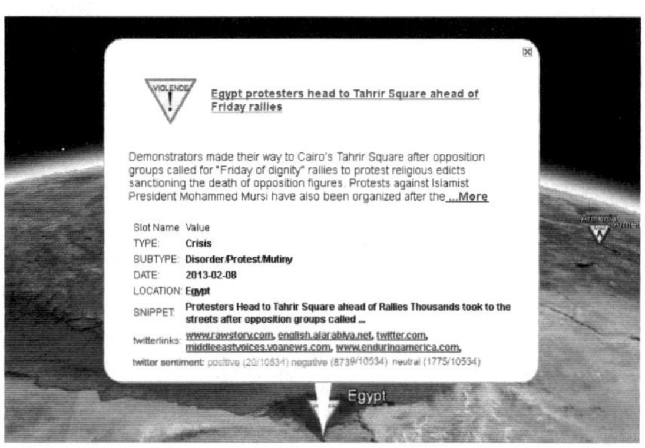

Figure 2: Demo interface for the event-Twitter linking and sentiment analysis.

2 Related Work and Contribution

The work presented herein is mostly related to the linking of events with social media texts and sentiment analysis from Twitter.

Although Twitter was used as an information source in the context of different crisis events, relatively little work focused on linking and extracting content about events which are known *a priori*, e.g., Becker et al. [2011].

In this context, the main challenge is to determine relevant keywords to search for event-related tweets and rank them according to their relevance. Related approaches (e.g., Verma et al. [2011]) report on the use of semantic features (e.g., objectivity, impersonality, formality, etc.) for detecting tweets with content relevant to situational awareness during mass emergencies. Other approaches elaborate on machine learning-based techniques for Named Entity Recognition (NER) from tweets, which are subsequently employed as search query terms (Ritter et al. [2011], Liu et al. [2011]).

Related research on sentiment analysis from Twitter was done by Alec Go and Huang [2009], Pak and Paroubek [2010] and Agarwal et al. [2011]. Alec Go and Huang [2009] and Pak and Paroubek [2010] exploit the presence of emoticons that represent positive or negative feelings to build a training set of tweets with sentiment labels, using which they build models based on n-gram features and part-of-speech tags. Agarwal et al. [2011] employ emoticons dictionaries and replace certain elements such as URLs and topics with predefinded labels. They employ syntactic features and specialized tree kernels and obtain around 75% to 80% accuracy for the sentiment classification.

The main contributions of our system reside in the linking of mainstream news to the complementary content found in social media (tweets and, through them, to the links to additional information sources like blogs, flickr, youtube, etc.) and the analysis of sentiment on these important news. For events such as "The Arab Spring", protests, financial news (e.g. the fluctuations of the Euro, the bailout of different European countries, the rise in unemployment rate, etc.), it was seen that the sentiment expressed in social media has a high impact on the subsequent development of the story[2] (Saif et al. [2012], Bollen et al. [2011]). The impact of sentiment expressed in social media is also visible for topics which apparently have an apriori valence (e.g. disasters, crisis, etc.). Nevertheless, in these cases, people communicate using the social media platforms not only to express their negative feelings, but also their will to help, their situation, their messages of encouragement, their gratefulness for the help and so on.

[2]http://cs229.stanford.edu/proj2011/ChenLazer-SentimentAnalysisOfTwitterFeedsForThePredictionOfStockMarketMovement.pdf

Secondly, the methods employed in our system are simple, work fast and efficient and can be easily adapted to other languages.

Finally, the methods presented take into account the specificity of social media languages, applying methods to normalize the language and adapting the features considered for the supervised learning process.

3 Linking News Clusters to Twitter

The first step in our system involves linking the news stories detected by EMM to related tweets. The linking system employs the Twitter Search API[3]. For each news story, our application detects relevant URLs by finding tweets that are lexically similar to the news story, represented by a cluster of news, and are mentioned frequently in Twitter. In Figure 3, we provide an example of the top six stories on the afternoon of April 2nd, 2013.

Figure 3: Top six clusters of news in the afternoon of April 2nd, 2013.

In order to detect lexically similar tweets, we use vector similarity: We build a term vector for both the news story and the tweet and then we consider as a similarity measure the projection of the tweet vector on the story vector. We do not calculate cosine similarity, since this would give an advantage to short tweets. We experimentally set a similarity threshold above which the tweets with URL are accepted. To define the similarity threshold and the coefficients in the URL ranking formula, we used a development set of about 100 randomly selected English-language news clusters, downloaded during a week. The threshold and the coefficients were derived empirically. We consider experimenting with SVM and other machine-learning approaches to define these parameters in a more consistent way.

Once the tweets that relate to the news story are retrieved, we evaluate each URL taking into account the following parameters:

- Number of mentions, which we will designate as $Mentions$.
- Number of retweets, designated $Retweet$.
- Number of mentions in conversations, designated $InConv$.
- Number of times the URL was favortited, designated $Favorited$.
- Number of tweets which replied to tweets, mentioning the URL, designated $ReplyTo$.

The score of the URL is calculated using the following empirically derived formula. The coefficients were defined based on the empirical analysis described above.

$$score(URL) = ((Mentions{-}1) + Retweets.1,3$$
$$+ Favorited * 4).(InConv + 2 * ReplyTo + 1)$$

In this formula we give slight preference to the retweets with respect to the mentions. We made this choice, since retweets happen inside Twitter and reflect the dynamics of the information spread inside this social media. On the other hand, multiple mentions of news-related tweets (which are not retweeted) are due to clicking the "Share in Twitter" button, which nowadays is present on most of the news sites. In this way, news from visited web sites appear more often in Twitter. This phenomena is to be further explored. It should also be noted that our formula boosts significantly URLs, which are mentioned inside a conversation thread and even more the ones, to which there were "reply to" tweets. Conversations tend to be centered around topics which are of interest to Twitter users and in this way they are a good indicator of how interesting an URL is. Replying to a tweet requires more time and attention than just pressing the "Retweet" button, therefore conversations show more interest to an URL, with respect to retweeting. Examples of tweets extracted that complement information from mainstream media are presented in Figure 4.

[3]https://dev.twitter.com/docs/api/1/get/search

@a - RT @photojournalism: More North Korean army camouflage. This is stealth! MT @patrickwitty KCNA via @AFP http://t.co/jRXrN0iFUp

@h - #Cuba #EEUU #USA North Korea Vows to Restart Nuclear Reactor in Weapons Bid: http://t.co/6kA9v3LX4E

@s - North Korea nuke crisis has 'gone too far' – UN chief http://t.co/M37wbKmNkh

@r - North Korea Leader Kim Jung Un Body Language Shows Fear in Midst of Threats As He Is Controlled By Father's Old... http://t.co/4GIhggi8pp

Figure 4: Examples of tweets extracted on the North Korea crisis (anonimized).

4 Sentiment Analysis on Tweets Related to Events Reported in News

After extracting the tweets related to the main news clusters detected by the media monitoring system, we pass them onto the sentiment analysis system, where they are classified according to their polarity (into positive, negative and neutral).

In order to classify the tweet's sentiment, we employ a hybrid approach based on supervised learning with a Support Vector Machines Sequential Minimal Optimization (SVM SMO - Platt [1998]) linear kernel, on unigram and bigram features, but exploiting as features sentiment dictionaries, emoticon lists, slang lists and other social media-specific features. We do not employ any specific language analysis software. The aim is to be able to apply, in a straightforward manner, the same approach to as many languages as possible. The approach can be extended to other languages by using similar dictionaries that have been created in our team.

The sentiment analysis process contains two stages: preprocessing and sentiment classification.

4.1 Tweet Preprocessing

The language employed in Social Media sites is different from the one found in mainstream media and the form of the words employed is sometimes not the one we may find in a dictionary. Further on, users of Social Media platforms employ a special "slang" (i.e. informal language, with special expressions, such as "lol", "omg"), emoticons, and often emphasize words by repeating some of their letters. Additionally, the language employed in Twitter has specific characteristics, such as the markup of tweets that were reposted by other users with "RT", the markup of topics using the "#" (hash sign) and of the users using the "@" sign.

All these aspects must be considered at the time of processing tweets. As such, before applying supervised learning to classify the sentiment of the tweets, we preprocess them, to normalize the language they contain. The preprocessing stage contains the following steps:

- ***Repeated punctuation sign normalization.*** In the first step of the preprocessing, we detect repetitions of punctuation signs (".", "!" and "?"). Multiple consecutive punctuation signs are replaced with the labels "multistop", for the fullstops, "multiexclamation" in the case of exclamation sign and "multiquestion" for the question mark and spaces before and after.

- ***Emoticon replacement.*** In the second step of the preprocessing, we employ the annotated list of emoticons from SentiStrength[4] and match the content of the tweets against this list. The emoticons found are replaced with their polarity ("positive" or "negative") and the "neutral" ones are deleted.

- ***Lower casing and tokenization.*** Subsequently, the tweets are lower cased and split into tokens, based on spaces and punctuation signs.

- ***Slang replacement.*** The next step involves the normalization of the language employed. In order to be able to include the semantics of the expressions frequently used in Social Media, we employed the list of slang from a specialized site [5].

- ***Word normalization.*** At this stage, the tokens are compared to entries in Roget's Thesaurus. If no match is found, repeated letters are sequentially reduced to two or one until a match is found in the dictionary (e.g. "perrrrrrrrrrrrrrrrrrfeeect" becomes "perrfeect", "perfeect", "perrfect" and subsequently "perfect"). The words used in this form are maked as "stressed".

- ***Affect word matching.*** Further on, the tokens in the tweet are matched against three different sentiment lexicons: General Inquirer, LIWC and MicroWNOp, which were previously split into four different categories

[4]http://sentistrength.wlv.ac.uk/

[5]http://www.chatslang.com/terms/social_media

("positive", "high positive", "negative" and "high negative"). Matched words are replaced with their sentiment label - i.e. "positive", "negative", "hpositive" and "hnegative".

- ***Modifier word matching.*** Similar to the previous step, we employ a list of expressions that negate, intensify or diminish the intensity of the sentiment expressed to detect such words in the tweets. If such a word is matched, it is replaced with "negator", "intensifier" or "diminisher", respectively.

- ***User and topic labeling.*** Finally, the users mentioned in the tweet, which are marked with "@", are replaced with "PERSON" and the topics which the tweet refers to (marked with "#") are replaced with "TOPIC".

4.2 Sentiment Classification of Tweets

Once the tweets are preprocessed, they are passed on to the sentiment classification module. We employed supervised learning using SVM SMO with a linear kernel, employing boolean features - the presence or absence of unigrams and bigrams determined from the training data (tweets that were previousely preprocessed as described above) that appeared at least twice. Bigrams are used especially to spot the influence of modifiers (negations, intensifiers, diminishers) on the polarity of the sentiment-bearing words. We tested the approach on different datasets and dataset splits, using the Weka data mining software [6]. The training models are built on a cluster of computers (4 cores, 5000MB of memory each).

5 Evaluation and Discussion

5.1 Evaluation of the News-Twitter Linking Component

The algorithm employed to retrieve tweets similar to news clusters was evaluated by Tanev et al. [2012]. The precision attained was 75%. Recall cannot be computed, as the use of the Twitter API allows only the retrieval of a subset of tweets.

In order to evaluate the link extraction component, we randomly chose 68 URLs, extracted from 10 different news stories. For each URL, we evaluated its relevance to the news story in the following way: A URL is considered relevant only if it reports about the same news story or talks about facts, like effects, post developments and motivations, directly related to this news story. It turned out that 66 out of the 68 were relevant, which gives accuracy of 97%.

5.2 Evaluation of the Sentiment Analysis System

In order to evaluate the sentiment analysis system on external resources, we employed the data provided for training in the SemEval 2013 Task 2 "Sentiment Analysis from Twitter" [7]. The initial training data has been provided in two stages: 1) sample datasets for the first task and the second task and 2) additional training data for the two tasks. We employ the joint sample datasets as test data (denoted as $t*$) and the data released subsequently as training data (denoted as $T*$). We employ the union of these two datasets to perform cross-validation experiments (the joint dataset is denoted as $T * +t*$. The characteristics of the dataset are described in Table 1. On the last column, we also include the baseline in terms of accuracy, which is computed as the number of examples of the majoritary class over the total number of examples. The results of the experiments are presented in Table 2. Given the difficulty of language in social media, the results are good and

Data	#Tweet	#Pos	#Neg	#Neu	B%
T*	19241	4779	2343	12119	62
t*	2597	700	393	1504	57
T*+t*	21838	5479	2736	13623	62

Table 1: Characteristics of the training (T*), testing (t*) and joint training and testing datasets.

Measure	Train(T*) & test(t*)	10-fold CV
Acc.	0.74	0.93
P_{pos}	0.66	0.91
R_{pos}	0.88	0.69
P_{neg}	0.94	0.62
R_{neg}	0.81	0.49
P_{neu}	0.93	0.80
R_{neg}	0.97	0.82

Table 2: Results in terms of accuracy and precision and recall per polarity class on training and test sets evaluation and 10-fold cross-validation.

[6]http://www.cs.waikato.ac.nz/ml/weka/

[7]http://www.cs.york.ac.uk/semeval-2013/task2/

useful in the context of our application (Figure 2).

6 Conclusions and Future Work

In this demo paper, we presented a system that links mainstream media stories to tweets that comment on the events covered. The system retrieves relevant tweets, extracts the links they contain and subsequently performs sentiment analysis. The system works at a good level, giving an accurate picture of the social media reaction to the mainstream media stories.

As future work, we would like to extend the system to more languages and analyze and include new features that are particular to social media to improve the performance of both the retrieval and sentiment analysis components.

Acknowledgements

We would like to thank the EMM team of the OPTIMA action at the European Commission Joint Research Centre for the technical support.

References

Apoorv Agarwal, Boyi Xie, Ilia Vovsha, Owen Rambow, and Rebecca Passonneau. Sentiment analysis of twitter data. In *Proceedings of LSM 2011*, LSM '11, pages 30–38, 2011.

Richa Bhayani Alec Go and Lei Huang. Twitter sentiment classication using distant supervision. Technical report, Technical report, Stanford University, 2009.

Hila Becker, Feiyang Chen, Dan Iter, Mor Naaman, and Luis Gravano. Automatic identification and presentation of twitter content for planned events. In *Proceedings of ICWSM 2011*, 2011.

J. Bollen, H. Mao, and X. Zeng. Twitter mood predicts the stock market. *Journal of Computational Science*, 2011.

Xiaohua Liu, Shaodian Zhang, Furu Wei, and Ming Zhou. Recognizing Named Entities in Tweets. In *Proceedings of ACL 2011*, pages 359–367, Stroudsburg, PA, USA, 2011.

Alexander Pak and Patrick Paroubek. Twitter based system: Using twitter for disambiguating sentiment ambiguous adjectives. In *Proceedings of SemEval 2010*, SemEval '10, pages 436–439, 2010.

John C. Platt. Sequential minimal optimization: A fast algorithm for training support vector machines. Technical report, Advances in Kernel Methods - Support Vector Learning, 1998.

Alan Ritter, Sam Clark, Mausam, and Oren Etzioni. Named Entity Recognition in Tweets: An Experimental Study. In *Proceedings of EMNLP 2011*, pages 1524–1534, Edinburgh, Scotland, UK., 2011.

Hassan Saif, Yulan He, and Harith Alani. Alleviating data sparsity for twitter sentiment analysis. In *Making Sense of Microposts (#MSM2012)*, pages 2–9, 2012.

Hristo Tanev, Maud Ehrmann, Jakub Piskorski, and Vanni Zavarella. Enhancing event descriptions through twitter mining. In John G. Breslin, Nicole B. Ellison, James G. Shanahan, and Zeynep Tufekci, editors, *ICWSM*. The AAAI Press, 2012.

Sudha Verma, Sarah Vieweg, William Corvey, Leysia Palen, James Martin, Martha Palmer, Aaron Schram, and Kenneth Anderson. Natural Language Processing to the Rescue? Extracting "Situational Awareness"' Tweets During Mass Emergency. In *Proceedings of ICWSM 2011*, pages 385–392. AAAI, 2011.

DISSECT - *DIS*tributional *SE*mantics *C*omposition *T*oolkit

Georgiana Dinu and **Nghia The Pham** and **Marco Baroni**
Center for Mind/Brain Sciences (University of Trento, Italy)
`(georgiana.dinu|thenghia.pham|marco.baroni)@unitn.it`

Abstract

We introduce DISSECT, a toolkit to build and explore computational models of word, phrase and sentence meaning based on the principles of distributional semantics. The toolkit focuses in particular on compositional meaning, and implements a number of composition methods that have been proposed in the literature. Furthermore, DISSECT can be useful to researchers and practitioners who need models of word meaning (without composition) as well, as it supports various methods to construct distributional semantic spaces, assessing similarity and even evaluating against benchmarks, that are independent of the composition infrastructure.

1 Introduction

Distributional methods for meaning similarity are based on the observation that similar words occur in similar contexts and measure similarity based on patterns of word occurrence in large corpora (Clark, 2012; Erk, 2012; Turney and Pantel, 2010). More precisely, they represent words, or any other target linguistic elements, as high-dimensional vectors, where the dimensions represent context features. Semantic relatedness is assessed by comparing vectors, leading, for example, to determine that *car* and *vehicle* are very similar in meaning, since they have similar contextual distributions. Despite the appeal of these methods, modeling words in isolation has limited applications and ideally we want to model semantics *beyond word level* by representing the meaning of phrases or sentences. These combinations are infinite and compositional methods are called for to derive the meaning of a larger construction from the meaning of its parts. For this reason, the question of compositionality within the distributional paradigm has received a lot of attention in recent years and a number of compositional frameworks have been proposed in the distributional semantic literature, see, e.g., Coecke et al. (2010) and Mitchell and Lapata (2010). For example, in such frameworks, the distributional representations of *red* and *car* may be combined, through various operations, in order to obtain a vector for *red car*.

The DISSECT toolkit (`http://clic.cimec.unitn.it/composes/toolkit`) is, to the best of our knowledge, the first to provide an easy-to-use implementation of many compositional methods proposed in the literature. As such, we hope that it will foster further work on compositional distributional semantics, as well as making the relevant techniques easily available to those interested in their many potential applications, e.g., to context-based polysemy resolution, recognizing textual entailment or paraphrase detection. Moreover, the DISSECT tools to construct distributional semantic spaces from raw co-occurrence counts, to measure similarity and to evaluate these spaces might also be of use to researchers who are not interested in the compositional framework. DISSECT is freely available under the GNU General Public License.

2 Building and composing distributional semantic representations

The pipeline from corpora to compositional models of meaning can be roughly summarized as consisting of three stages:[1]

1. Extraction of co-occurrence counts from corpora In this stage, an input corpus is used to extract counts of target elements co-occurring with some contextual features. The target elements can vary from words (for lexical similarity), to pairs of words (e.g., for relation categorization),

[1] See Turney and Pantel (2010) for a technical overview of distributional methods for semantics.

to paths in syntactic trees (for unsupervised paraphrasing). Context features can also vary from shallow window-based collocates to syntactic dependencies.

2. Transformation of the raw counts This stage may involve the application of weighting schemes such as Pointwise Mutual Information, feature selection, dimensionality reduction methods such as Singular Value Decomposition, etc. The goal is to eliminate the biases that typically affect raw counts and to produce vectors which better approximate similarity in meaning.

3. Application of composition functions Once meaningful representations have been constructed for the atomic target elements of interest (typically, words), various methods, such as vector addition or multiplication, can be used for combining them to derive context-sensitive representations or for constructing representations for larger phrases or even entire sentences.

DISSECT can be used for the second and third stages of this pipeline, as well as to measure similarity among the resulting word or phrase vectors. The first step is highly language-, task- and corpus-annotation-dependent. We do not attempt to implement all the corpus pre-processing and co-occurrence extraction routines that it would require to be of general use, and expect instead as input a matrix of raw target-context co-occurrence counts.[2] DISSECT provides various methods to re-weight the counts with association measures, dimensionality reduction methods as well as the composition functions proposed by Mitchell and Lapata (2010) (*Additive*, *Multiplicative* and *Dilation*), Baroni and Zamparelli (2010)/Coecke et al. (2010) (*Lexfunc*) and Guevara (2010)/Zanzotto et al. (2010) (*Fulladd*). In DISSECT we define and implement these in a unified framework and in a computationally efficient manner. The focus of DISSECT is to provide an intuitive interface for researchers and to allow easy extension by adding other composition methods.

3 DISSECT overview

DISSECT is written in Python. We provide many standard functionalities through a set of powerful command-line tools, however users with basic Python familiarity are encouraged to use the Python interface that DISSECT provides. This section focuses on this interface (see the online documentation on how to perform the same operations with the command-line tools), that consists of the following top-level packages:

```
#DISSECT packages
composes.matrix
composes.semantic_space
composes.transformation
composes.similarity
composes.composition
composes.utils
```

Semantic spaces and transformations The concept of a semantic space (`composes.semantic_space`) is at the core of the DISSECT toolkit. A semantic space consists of co-occurrence values, stored as a matrix, together with strings associated to the rows of this matrix (by design, the target linguistic elements) and a (potentially empty) list of strings associated to the columns (the context features). A number of transformations (`composes.transformation`) can be applied to semantic spaces. We implement weighting schemes such as positive Pointwise Mutual Information (*ppmi*) and Local Mutual Information, feature selection methods, dimensionality reduction (Singular Value Decomposition (*SVD*) and Nonnegative Matrix Factorization (*NMF*)), and new methods can be easily added.[3] Going from raw counts to a transformed space is accomplished in just a few lines of code (Figure 1).

```
#create a semantic space from counts in
#dense format("dm"): word freq1 freq2 ..
ss = Space.build(data="counts.txt",
                 format="dm")

#apply transformations
ss = ss.apply(PpmiWeighting())
ss = ss.apply(Svd(300))

#retrieve the vector of a target element
print ss.get_row("car")
```

Figure 1: Creating a semantic space.

[2]These counts can be read from a text file containing two strings (the target and context items) and a number (the corresponding count) on each line (e.g., `maggot food 15`) or from a matrix in format `word freq1 freq2 ...`

[3]The complete list of transformations currently supported can be found at `http://clic.cimec.unitn.it/composes/toolkit/spacetrans.html#spacetrans`.

```
#load a previously saved space
ss = io_utils.load("ss.pkl")

#compute cosine similarity
print ss.get_sim("car", "book",
                 CosSimilarity())

#the two nearest neighbours of "car"
print ss.get_neighbours("car", 2,
                        CosSimilarity())
```

Figure 2: Similarity queries in a semantic space.

Furthermore DISSECT allows the possibility of adding new data to a semantic space in an online manner (using the `semantic_space.peripheral_space` functionality). This can be used as a way to efficiently expand a co-occurrence matrix with new rows, without re-applying the transformations to the entire space. In some other cases, the user may want to represent phrases that are specialization of words already existing in the space (e.g., *slimy maggot* and *maggot*), without distorting the computation of association measures by counting the same context twice. In this case, adding *slimy maggot* as a "peripheral" row to a semantic space that already contains *maggot* implements the desired behaviour.

Similarity queries Semantic spaces are used for the computation of similarity scores. DISSECT provides a series of similarity measures such as cosine, inverse Euclidean distance and Lin similarity, implemented in the `composes.similarity` package. Similarity of two elements can be computed within one semantic space or across two spaces that have the same dimensionality. Figure 2 exemplifies (word) similarity computations with DISSECT.

Composition functions Composition functions in DISSECT (`composes.composition`) take as arguments a list of element pairs to be composed, and one or two spaces where the elements to be composed are represented. They return a semantic space containing the distributional representations of the composed items, which can be further transformed, used for similarity queries, or used as inputs to another round of composition, thus scaling up beyond binary composition. Figure 3 shows a Multiplicative composition example. See Table 1 for the currently available composition models, their definitions and parameters.

Model	Composition function	Parameters
Add.	$w_1\vec{u} + w_2\vec{v}$	$w_1(=1), w_2(=1)$
Mult.	$\vec{u} \odot \vec{v}$	-
Dilation	$\|\|\vec{u}\|\|_2^2\vec{v} + (\lambda - 1)\langle\vec{u}, \vec{v}\rangle\vec{u}$	$\lambda(=2)$
Fulladd	$W_1\vec{u} + W_2\vec{v}$	$W_1, W_2 \in \mathbf{R}^{m\times m}$
Lexfunc	$A_u\vec{v}$	$A_u \in \mathbf{R}^{m\times m}$

Table 1: Currently implemented composition functions of inputs (u, v) together with parameters and their default values in parenthesis, where defined. Note that in Lexfunc each functor word corresponds to a separate matrix or tensor A_u (Baroni and Zamparelli, 2010).

Parameter estimation All composition models except Multiplicative have parameters to be estimated. For simple models with few parameters, such as as Additive, the parameters can be passed by hand. However, DISSECT supports automated parameter estimation from training examples. In particular, we extend to all composition methods the idea originally proposed by Baroni and Zamparelli (2010) for Lexfunc and Guevara (2010) for Fulladd, namely to use corpus-extracted example vectors of both the input (typically, words) and output elements (typically, phrases) in order to optimize the composition operation parameters. The problem can be generally stated as:

$$\boldsymbol{\theta}^* = \arg\min_{\boldsymbol{\theta}} ||P - fcomp_{\boldsymbol{\theta}}(U, V)||_F$$

where U, V and P are matrices containing input and output vectors respectively. For example U may contain adjective vectors such as *red*, *blue*, V noun vectors such as *car*, *sky* and P corpus-extracted vectors for the corresponding phrases *red car*, *blue sky*. $fcomp_{\boldsymbol{\theta}}$ is a composition function and $\boldsymbol{\theta}$ stands for a list of parameters that this composition function is associated with.[4] We implement standard least-squares estimation methods as well as Ridge regression with the option for generalized cross-validation, but other methods such as partial least-squares regression can be easily added. Figure 4 exemplifies the Fulladd model.

Composition output examples DISSECT provides functions to evaluate (compositional) distributional semantic spaces against benchmarks in the `composes.utils` package. However, as a more qualitatively interesting example of what can be done with DISSECT, Table 2 shows the nearest

[4]Details on the extended corpus-extracted vector estimation method in DISSECT can be found in Dinu et al. (2013).

```
#instantiate a multiplicative model
mult_model = Multiplicative()

#use the model to compose words from input space input_space
comp_space = mult_model.compose([("red", "book", "my_red_book"),
                                 ("red", "car", "my_red_car")],
                                input_space)

#compute similarity of: 1) two composed phrases and 2) a composed phrase and a word
print comp_space.get_sim("my_red_book", "my_red_car", CosSimilarity())
print comp_space.get_sim("my_red_book", "book", CosSimilarity(), input_space)
```

Figure 3: Creating and using Multiplicative phrase vectors.

```
#training data for learning an adjective-noun phrase model
train_data = [("red","book","red_book"), ("blue","car","blue_car")]

#train a fulladd model
fa_model = FullAdditive()
fa_model.train(train_data, input_space, phrase_space)

#use the model to compose a phrase from new words and retrieve its nearest neighb.
comp_space = fa_model.compose([("yellow", "table", "my_yellow_table")], input_space)
print comp_space.get_neighbours("my_yellow_table", 10, CosSimilarity())
```

Figure 4: Estimating a Fulladd model and using it to create phrase vectors.

Target	Method	Neighbours
florist	Corpus	Harrod, wholesaler, stockist
flora + -ist	Fulladd	flora, fauna, ecologist
	Lexfunc	ornithologist, naturalist, botanist
	Additive	flora, fauna, ecosystem

Table 3: Compositional models for morphology. Top 3 neighbours of *florist* using its (low-frequency) corpus-extracted vector, and when the vector is obtained through composition of *flora* and *-ist* with Fulladd, Lexfunc and Additive.

neighbours of *false belief* obtained through composition with the Fulladd, Lexfunc and Additive models. In Table 3, we exemplify a less typical application of compositional models to derivational morphology, namely obtaining a representation of *florist* compositionally from distributional representations of *flora* and *-ist* (Lazaridou et al., 2013).

4 Main features

Support for dense and sparse representations Co-occurrence matrices, as extracted from text, tend to be very sparse structures, especially when using detailed context features which include syntactic information, for example. On the other hand, dimensionality reduction operations, which are often used in distributional models, lead to smaller, dense structures, for which sparse representations are not optimal. This is our motivation for supporting both dense and sparse representations. The choice of dense vs. sparse is initially determined by the input format, if a space is created from co-occurrence counts. By default, DISSECT switches to dense representations after dimensionality reduction, however the user can freely switch from one representation to the other, in order to optimize computations. For this purpose DISSECT provides wrappers around matrix operations, as well as around common linear algebra operations, in the `composes.matrix` package. The underlying Python functionality is provided by `numpy.array` and `scipy.sparse`.

Efficient computations DISSECT is optimized for speed since most operations are cast as matrix operations, that are very efficiently implemented in Python's `numpy` and `scipy` modules[5]. Tables 4 and 5 show running times for typical DISSECT operations: application of the *ppmi* weighting scheme, nearest neighbour queries and estimation of composition function parameters (on a 2.1

[5]For SVD on sparse structures, we use `sparsesvd` (`https://pypi.python.org/pypi/sparsesvd/`). For NMF, we adapted `http://www.csie.ntu.edu.tw/~cjlin/nmf/` (Lin, 2007).

Target	Method	Neighbours
belief	Corpus	moral, dogma, worldview, religion, world-view, morality, theism, tenet, agnosticism, dogmatic
false belief	Fulladd	pantheist, belief, agnosticism, religiosity, dogmatism, pantheism, theist, fatalism, deism, mind-set
	Lexfunc	self-deception, untruth, credulity, obfuscation, misapprehension, deceiver, disservice, falsehood
	Additive	belief, assertion, falsity, falsehood, truth, credence, dogma, supposition, hearsay, denial

Table 2: Top nearest neighbours of *belief* and of *false belief* obtained through composition with the Fulladd, Lexfunc and Additive models.

Method	Fulladd	Lexfunc	Add.	Dilation
Time (s.)	2864	787	46	68

Table 4: Composition model parameter estimation times (in seconds) for 1 million training points in 300-dimensional space.

Matrix size (nnz)	Ppmi	Query
100Kx300 (30M)	5.8	0.5
100Kx100K (250M)	52.6	9.5

Table 5: Running times (in seconds) for 1) application of *ppmi* weighting and 2) querying for the top neighbours of a word (cosine similarity) for different matrix sizes (nnz: number of non-zero entries, in millions).

GHz machine). The price to pay for fast computations is that data must be stored in main memory. We do not think that this is a major inconvenience. For example, a typical symmetric co-occurrence matrix extracted from a corpus of several billion words, defining context in terms of 5-word windows and considering the top 100K$\times$100K most frequent words, contains $\approx$ 250 million entries and requires only 2GB of memory for (double precision) storage.

Simple design We have opted for a very simple and intuitive design as the classes interact in very natural ways: A semantic space stores the actual data matrix and structures to index its rows and columns, and supports similarity queries and transformations. Transformations take one semantic space as input to return another, transformed, space. Composition functions take one or more input spaces and yield a composed-elements space, which can further undergo transformations and be used for similarity queries. In fact, DISSECT semantic spaces also support higher-order tensor representations, not just vectors. Higher-order representations are used, for example, to represent transitive verbs and other multi-argument functors by Coecke et al. (2010) and Grefenstette et al. (2013). See `http://clic.cimec.unitn.it/composes/toolkit/composing.html` for an example of using DISSECT for estimating such tensors.

Extensive documentation The DISSECT documentation can be found at `http://clic.cimec.unitn.it/composes/toolkit`. We provide a tutorial which guides the user through the creation of some toy semantic spaces, estimation of the parameters of composition models and similarity computations in semantic spaces. We also provide a full-scale example of intransitive verb-subject composition. We show how to go from co-occurrence counts to composed representations and make the data used in the examples available for download.

Comparison to existing software In terms of design choices, DISSECT most resembles the Gensim toolkit (Řehůřek and Sojka, 2010). However Gensim is intended for topic modeling, and therefore diverges considerably from DISSECT in its functionality. The SSpace package of Jurgens and Stevens (2010) also overlaps to some degree with DISSECT in terms of its intended use, however, like Gensim, it does not support compositional operations that, as far as we know, are an unique feature of DISSECT.

5 Future extensions

We implemented and are currently testing DISSECT functions supporting other composition methods, including the one proposed by Socher et al. (2012). Adding further methods is our top-priority goal. In particular, several distributional models of word meaning in context share important similarities with composition models, and we plan to add them to DISSECT. Dinu et al. (2012) show, for example, that well-performing, simplified variants of the method in Thater et al. (2010), Thater et al. (2011) and Erk and Padó (2008) can be reduced to relatively simple matrix operations, making them particularly suitable for a DISSECT implementation.

DISSECT is currently optimized for the composition of many phrases of the same type. This is in line with most of the current evaluations of compositional models, which focus on specific phenomena, such as adjectival modification, noun-noun compounds or intransitive verbs, to name a few. In the future we plan to provide a module for composing entire sentences, taking syntactic trees as input and returning composed representations for each node in the input trees.

Finally, we intend to make use of the existing Python plotting libraries to add a visualization module to DISSECT.

6 Acknowledgments

We thank Angeliki Lazaridou for helpful discussions. This research was supported by the ERC 2011 Starting Independent Research Grant n. 283554 (COMPOSES).

References

Marco Baroni and Roberto Zamparelli. 2010. Nouns are vectors, adjectives are matrices: Representing adjective-noun constructions in semantic space. In *Proceedings of EMNLP*, pages 1183–1193, Boston, MA.

Stephen Clark. 2012. Vector space models of lexical meaning. In Shalom Lappin and Chris Fox, editors, *Handbook of Contemporary Semantics, 2nd edition*. Blackwell, Malden, MA. In press.

Bob Coecke, Mehrnoosh Sadrzadeh, and Stephen Clark. 2010. Mathematical foundations for a compositional distributional model of meaning. *Linguistic Analysis*, 36:345–384.

Georgiana Dinu, Stefan Thater, and Sören Laue. 2012. A comparison of models of word meaning in context. In *Proceedings of NAACL HLT*, pages 611–615, Montreal, Canada.

Georgiana Dinu, Nghia The Pham, and Marco Baroni. 2013. A general framework for the estimation of distributional composition functions. In *Proceedings of ACL Workshop on Continuous Vector Space Models and their Compositionality*, Sofia, Bulgaria. In press.

Katrin Erk and Sebastian Padó. 2008. A structured vector space model for word meaning in context. In *Proceedings of EMNLP*, pages 897–906, Honolulu, HI.

Katrin Erk. 2012. Vector space models of word meaning and phrase meaning: A survey. *Language and Linguistics Compass*, 6(10):635–653.

Edward Grefenstette, Georgiana Dinu, Yao-Zhong Zhang, Mehrnoosh Sadrzadeh, and Marco Baroni. 2013. Multi-step regression learning for compositional distributional semantics. In *Proceedings of IWCS*, pages 131–142, Potsdam, Germany.

Emiliano Guevara. 2010. A regression model of adjective-noun compositionality in distributional semantics. In *Proceedings of GEMS*, pages 33–37, Uppsala, Sweden.

David Jurgens and Keith Stevens. 2010. The S-Space package: an open source package for word space models. In *Proceedings of the ACL 2010 System Demonstrations*, pages 30–35, Uppsala, Sweden.

Angeliki Lazaridou, Marco Marelli, Roberto Zamparelli, and Marco Baroni. 2013. Compositional-ly derived representations of morphologically complex words in distributional semantics. In *Proceedings of ACL*, Sofia, Bulgaria. In press.

Chih-Jen Lin. 2007. Projected gradient methods for Nonnegative Matrix Factorization. *Neural Computation*, 19(10):2756–2779.

Jeff Mitchell and Mirella Lapata. 2010. Composition in distributional models of semantics. *Cognitive Science*, 34(8):1388–1429.

Radim Řehůřek and Petr Sojka. 2010. Software framework for topic modelling with large corpora. In *Proceedings of the LREC 2010 Workshop on New Challenges for NLP Frameworks*, pages 45–50, Valletta, Malta.

Richard Socher, Brody Huval, Christopher Manning, and Andrew Ng. 2012. Semantic compositionality through recursive matrix-vector spaces. In *Proceedings of EMNLP*, pages 1201–1211, Jeju Island, Korea.

Stefan Thater, Hagen Fürstenau, and Manfred Pinkal. 2010. Contextualizing semantic representations using syntactically enriched vector models. In *Proceedings of ACL*, pages 948–957, Uppsala, Sweden.

Stefan Thater, Hagen Fürstenau, and Manfred Pinkal. 2011. Word meaning in context: A simple and effective vector model. In *Proceedings of IJCNLP*, pages 1134–1143, Chiang Mai, Thailand.

Peter Turney and Patrick Pantel. 2010. From frequency to meaning: Vector space models of semantics. *Journal of Artificial Intelligence Research*, 37:141–188.

Fabio Zanzotto, Ioannis Korkontzelos, Francesca Falucchi, and Suresh Manandhar. 2010. Estimating linear models for compositional distributional semantics. In *Proceedings of COLING*, pages 1263–1271, Beijing, China.

DKPro WSD – A Generalized UIMA-based Framework for Word Sense Disambiguation

Tristan Miller[1] **Nicolai Erbs**[1] **Hans-Peter Zorn**[1] **Torsten Zesch**[1,2] **Iryna Gurevych**[1,2]
(1) Ubiquitous Knowledge Processing Lab (UKP-TUDA)
Department of Computer Science, Technische Universität Darmstadt
(2) Ubiquitous Knowledge Processing Lab (UKP-DIPF)
German Institute for Educational Research and Educational Information
http://www.ukp.tu-darmstadt.de/

Abstract

Implementations of word sense disambiguation (WSD) algorithms tend to be tied to a particular test corpus format and sense inventory. This makes it difficult to test their performance on new data sets, or to compare them against past algorithms implemented for different data sets. In this paper we present DKPro WSD, a freely licensed, general-purpose framework for WSD which is both modular and extensible. DKPro WSD abstracts the WSD process in such a way that test corpora, sense inventories, and algorithms can be freely swapped. Its UIMA-based architecture makes it easy to add support for new resources and algorithms. Related tasks such as word sense induction and entity linking are also supported.

1 Introduction

Word sense disambiguation, or WSD (Agirre and Edmonds, 2006)—the task of determining which of a word's senses is the one intended in a particular context—has been a core research problem in computational linguistics since the very inception of the field. Despite the task's importance and popularity as a subject of study, tools and resources supporting WSD have seen relatively little generalization and standardization. That is, most prior implementations of WSD systems have been hard-coded for particular algorithms, sense inventories, and data sets. This makes it difficult to compare systems or to adapt them to new scenarios without extensive reimplementation.

In this paper we present DKPro WSD, a general-purpose framework for word sense disambiguation which is both modular and extensible. Its *modularity* means that it makes a logical separation between the *data sets* (e.g., the corpora to be annotated, the answer keys, manually annotated training examples, etc.), the *sense inventories* (i.e., the lexical-semantic resources enumerating the senses to which words in the corpora are assigned), and the *algorithms* (i.e., code which actually performs the sense assignments and prerequisite linguistic annotations), and provides a standard interface for each of these component types. Components which provide the same functionality can be freely swapped, so that one can easily run the same algorithm on different data sets (irrespective of which sense inventory they use), or test several different algorithms on the same data set.

While DKPro WSD ships with support for a number of common WSD algorithms, sense inventories, and data set formats, its *extensibility* means that it is easy to adapt to work with new methods and resources. The system is written in Java and is based on UIMA (Lally et al., 2009), an industry-standard architecture for analysis of unstructured information. Support for new corpus formats, sense inventories, and WSD algorithms can be added by implementing new UIMA components for them, or more conveniently by writing UIMA wrappers around existing code. The framework and all existing components are released under the Apache License 2.0, a permissive free software licence.

DKPro WSD was designed primarily to support the needs of WSD researchers, who will appreciate the convenience and flexibility it affords in tuning and comparing algorithms and data sets. However, as a general-purpose toolkit it could also be used to implement a WSD module for a real-world natural language processing application. Its support for interactive visualization of the disambiguation process also makes it a powerful tool for learning or teaching the principles of WSD.

The remainder of this paper is organized as follows: In §2 we review previous work in WSD file formats and implementations. In §3 we describe our system and further explain its capabilities and advantages. Finally, in §4 we discuss our plans for further development of the framework.

2 Background

In the early days of WSD research, electronic dictionaries and sense-annotated corpora tended to be small and hand-crafted on an ad-hoc basis. It was not until the growing availability of large-scale lexical resources and corpora in the 1990s that the need to establish a common platform for the evaluation of WSD systems was recognized. This led to the founding of the Senseval (and later SemEval) series of competitions, the first of which was held in 1998. Each competition defined a number of tasks with prescribed evaluation metrics, sense inventories, corpus file formats, and human-annotated test sets. For each task it was therefore possible to compare algorithms against each other. However, sense inventories and file formats still vary across tasks and competitions. There are also a number of increasingly popular resources used outside Senseval and SemEval, each with their own formats and structures: examples of sense-annotated corpora include SemCor (Miller et al., 1994), MASC (Ide et al., 2010), and WebCAGe (Henrich et al., 2012), and sense inventories include VerbNet (Kipper et al., 2008), FrameNet (Ruppenhofer et al., 2010), DANTE (Kilgarriff, 2010), BabelNet (Navigli and Ponzetto, 2012), and online community-produced resources such as Wiktionary and Wikipedia. So despite attempts at standardization, the canon of WSD resources remains quite fragmented.

The few publically available implementations of individual disambiguation algorithms, such as SenseLearner (Mihalcea and Csomai, 2005), SenseRelate::TargetWord (Patwardhan et al., 2005), UKB (Agirre and Soroa, 2009), and IMS (Zhong and Ng, 2010), are all tied to a particular corpus and/or sense inventory, or define their own custom formats into which existing resources must be converted. Furthermore, where the algorithm depends on linguistic annotations such as part-of-speech tags, the users are expected to supply these themselves, or else must use the annotators built into the system (which may not always be appropriate for the corpus language or domain).

One alternative to coding WSD algorithms from scratch is to use general-purpose NLP toolkits such as NLTK (Bird, 2006) or DKPro (Gurevych et al., 2007). Such toolkits provide individual components potentially useful for WSD, such as WordNet-based measures of sense similarity and readers for the odd corpus format. However, these toolkits are not specifically geared towards development and evaluation of WSD systems; there is no unified type system or architecture which allows WSD-specific components to be combined or substituted orthogonally.

The only general-purpose dedicated WSD system we are aware of is I Can Sense It (Joshi et al., 2012), a Web-based interface for running and evaluating various WSD algorithms. It includes I/O support for several corpus formats and implementations of a number of baseline and state-of-the-art disambiguation algorithms. However, as with previous single-algorithm systems, it is not possible to select the sense inventory, and the user is responsible for pre-annotating the input text with POS tags. The usability and extensibility of the system are greatly restricted by the fact that it is a proprietary, closed-source application fully hosted by the developers.

3 DKPro WSD

Our system, DKPro WSD, is implemented as a framework of UIMA components (type systems, collection readers, annotators, CAS consumers, resources) which the user combines into a data processing pipeline. We can best illustrate this with an example: Figure 1 shows a pipeline for running two disambiguation algorithms on the Estonian all-words task from Senseval-2. UIMA components are the solid, rounded boxes in the lower half of the diagram, and the data and algorithms they encapsulate are the light grey shapes in the upper half. The first component of the pipeline is a collection reader which reads the text of the XML-formatted corpus into a CAS (a UIMA data structure for storing layers of data and stand-off annotations) and marks the words to be disambiguated (the "instances") with their IDs. The next component is an annotator which reads the answer key—a separate file which associates each instance ID with a sense ID from the Estonian EuroWordNet—and adds the gold-standard sense annotations to their respective instances in the CAS. Processing then passes to another annotator—in this case a UIMA wrapper for TreeTagger (Schmid, 1994)—which adds POS and lemma annotations to the instances.

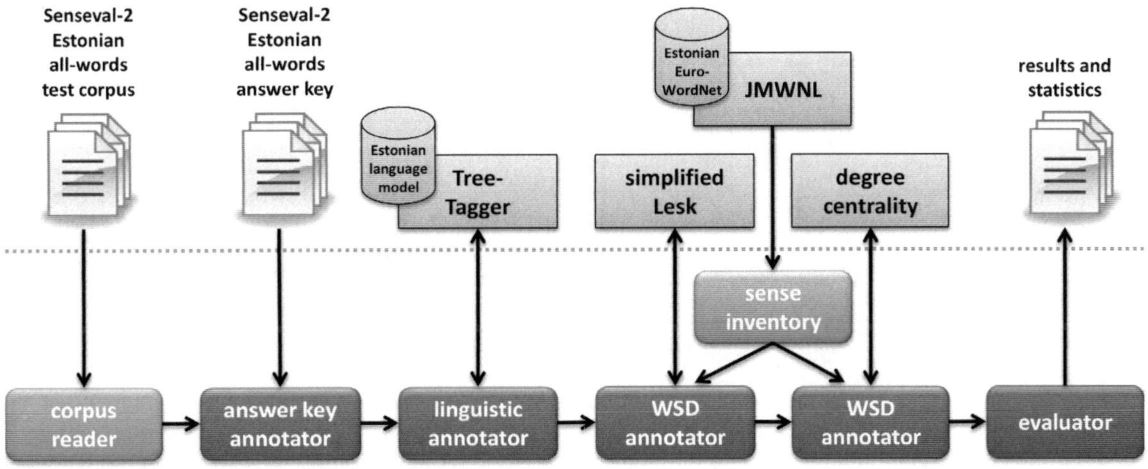

Figure 1: A sample DKPro WSD pipeline for the Estonian all-words data set from Senseval-2.

Then come the two disambiguation algorithms, also modelled as UIMA annotators wrapping non-UIMA-aware algorithms. Each WSD annotator iterates over the instances in the CAS and annotates them with sense IDs from EuroWordNet. (EuroWordNet itself is accessed via a UIMA resource which wraps JMWNL (Pazienza et al., 2008) and which is bound to the two WSD annotators.) Finally, control passes to a CAS consumer which compares the WSD algorithms' sense annotations against the gold-standard annotations produced by the answer key annotator, and outputs these sense annotations along with various evaluation metrics (precision, recall, etc.).

A pipeline of this sort can be written with just a few lines of code: one or two to declare each component and if necessary bind it to the appropriate resources, and a final one to string the components together into a pipeline. Moreover, once such a pipeline is written it is simple to substitute functionally equivalent components. For example, with only a few small changes the same pipeline could be used for Senseval-3's English lexical sample task, which uses a corpus and sense inventory in a different format and language. Specifically, we would substitute the collection reader with one capable of reading the Senseval lexical sample format, we would pass an English instead of Estonian language model to TreeTagger, and we would substitute the sense inventory resource exposing the Estonian EuroWordNet with one for WordNet 1.7.1. Crucially, none of the WSD algorithms need to be changed.

The most important features of our system are as follows:

Corpora and data sets. DKPro WSD currently has collection readers for all Senseval and SemEval all-words and lexical sample tasks, the AIDA CoNLL-YAGO data set (Hoffart et al., 2011), the TAC KBP entity linking tasks (McNamee and Dang, 2009), and the aforementioned MASC, SemCor, and WebCAGe corpora. Our prepackaged corpus analysis modules can compute statistics on monosemous terms, average polysemy, terms absent from the sense inventory, etc.

Sense inventories. Sense inventories are abstracted into a system of types and interfaces according to the sort of lexical-semantic information they provide. There is currently support for WordNet (Fellbaum, 1998), WordNet++ (Ponzetto and Navigli, 2010), EuroWordNet (Vossen, 1998), the Turk Bootstrap Word Sense Inventory (Biemann, 2013), and UBY (Gurevych et al., 2012), which provides access to WordNet, Wikipedia, Wiktionary, GermaNet, VerbNet, FrameNet, OmegaWiki, and various alignments between them. The system can automatically convert between various versions of WordNet using the UPC mappings (Daudé et al., 2003).

Algorithms. As with sense inventories, WSD algorithms have a type and interface hierarchy according to what knowledge sources they require. Algorithms and baselines already implemented include the analytically calculated random sense baseline; the most frequent sense baseline; the original, simplified, extended, and lexically expanded Lesk variants (Miller et al., 2012); various graph connectivity approaches from Navigli and Lapata (2010); Personalized PageRank (Agirre and Soroa, 2009); the supervised TWSI system (Biemann, 2013); and IMS (Zhong and Ng, 2010). Our open API permits users to program support for further knowledge-based and supervised algorithms.

Linguistic annotators. Many WSD algorithms require linguistic annotations from segmenters, lemmatizers, POS taggers, parsers, etc. Off-the-shelf UIMA components for producing such annotations, such as those provided by DKPro Core (Gurevych et al., 2007), can be used in a DKPro WSD pipeline with little or no adaptation.

Visualization tools. We have enhanced some families of algorithms with animated, interactive visualizations of the disambiguation process. For example, Figure 2 shows part of a screenshot from the interactive running of the degree centrality algorithm (Navigli and Lapata, 2010). The system is disambiguating the three content words in the sentence "I drink milk with a straw." Red, green, and blue nodes represent senses (or more specifically, WordNet sense keys) of the words *drink*, *milk*, and *straw*, respectively; grey nodes are senses of other words discovered by traversing semantic relations (represented by arcs) in the sense inventory. The current traversal (toast%2:34:00:: to fuddle%2:34:00::) is drawn in a lighter colour. Mouseover tooltips provide more detailed information on senses. We have found such visualizations to be invaluable for understanding and debugging algorithms.

Parameter sweeping. The behaviour of many components (or entire pipelines) can be altered according to various parameters. For example, for the degree centrality algorithm one must specify the maximum search depth, the minimum vertex degree, and the context size. DKPro WSD can perform a parameter sweep, automatically running the pipeline once for every possible combination of parameters in user-specified ranges and concatenating the results into a table from which the optimal system configurations can be identified.

Reporting tools. There are several reporting tools to support evaluation and error analysis. Raw sense assignments can be output in a variety of formats (XML, HTML, CSV, Senseval answer key, etc.), some of which support colour-coding to

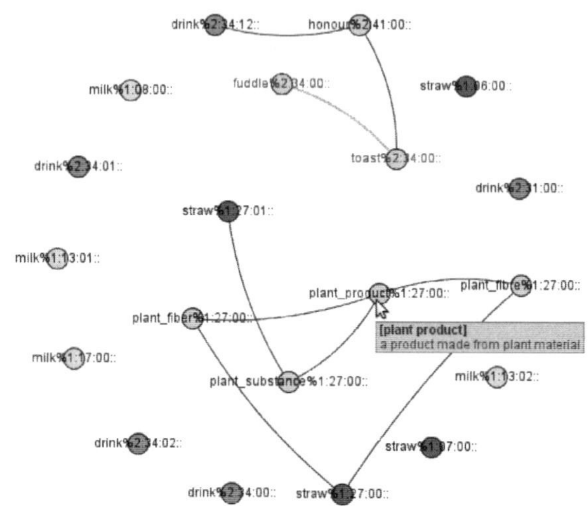

Figure 2: DKPro WSD's interactive visualization of a graph connectivity WSD algorithm.

highlight correct and incorrect assignments. The system can also compute common evaluation metrics (Agirre and Edmonds, 2006, pp. 76–80) and plot precision–recall curves for each algorithm in the pipeline, as well as produce confusion matrices for algorithm pairs. Users can specify backoff algorithms, and have the system compute results with and without the backoff. Results can also be broken down by part of speech. Figure 3 shows an example of an HTML report produced by the system—on the left is the sense assignment table, in the upper right is a table of evaluation metrics, and in the lower right is a precision–recall graph.

DKPro WSD also has support for tasks closely related to word sense disambiguation:

Entity linking. Entity linking (EL) is the task of linking a named entity in a text (e.g., *Washington*) to its correct representation in some knowledge base (e.g., either *George Washington* or *Washington, D.C.* depending on the context). EL is very similar to WSD in that both tasks involve connecting ambiguous words in a text to entries in some inventory. DKPro WSD supports EL-specific sense inventories such as the list of Wikipedia articles used in the Knowledge Base Population workshop of the Text Analysis Conference (TAC KBP). This workshop, held annually since 2009, provides a means for comparing different EL systems in a controlled setting. DKPro WSD contains a reader for the TAC KBP data set, components for mapping other sense inventories to the TAC KBP inventory, and evaluation components for the

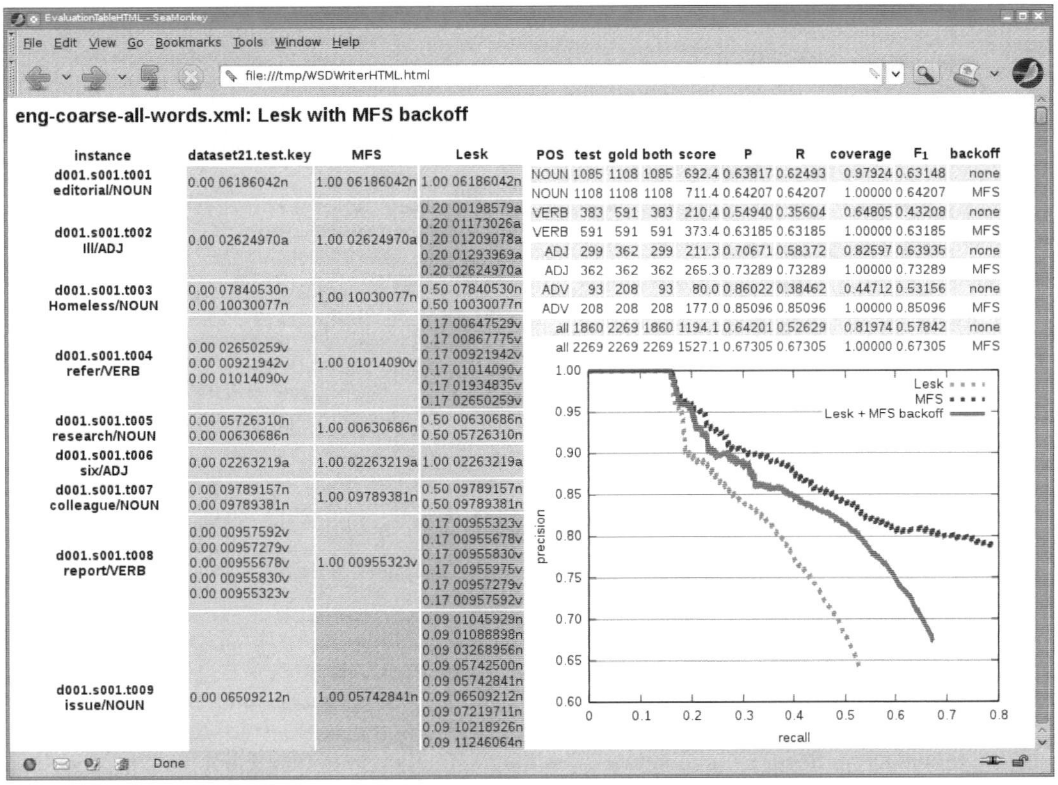

Figure 3: An HTML report produced by DKPro WSD.

official metrics. Researchers can therefore mitigate the entry barrier for their first participation at TAC KBP and experienced participants can extend their systems by making use of further WSD algorithms.

Word sense induction. WSD is usually performed with respect to manually created sense inventories such as WordNet. In word sense induction (WSI) a sense inventory for target words is automatically constructed from an unlabelled corpus. This can be useful for search result clustering, or for general applications of WSD for languages and domains for which a sense inventory is not yet available. It is usually necessary to perform WSD at some point in the evaluation of WSI. DKPro WSD supports WSI by providing state-of-the art WSD algorithms capable of using arbitrary sense inventories, including induced ones. It also includes readers and writers for the SemEval-2007 and -2013 WSI data sets.

4 Conclusions and future work

In this paper we introduced DKPro WSD, a Java- and UIMA-based framework for word sense disambiguation. Its primary advantages over existing tools are its modularity, its extensibility, and its free licensing. By segregating and providing layers of abstraction for code, data sets, and sense inventories, DKPro WSD greatly simplifies the comparison of WSD algorithms in heterogeneous scenarios. Support for a wide variety of commonly used algorithms, data sets, and sense inventories has already been implemented.

The framework is under active development, with work on several new features planned or in progress. These include implementations or wrappers for further algorithms and for the DANTE and BabelNet sense inventories. A Web interface is in the works and should be operational by the time of publication. Source code, binaries, documentation, tutorials, FAQs, an issue tracker, and community mailing lists are available on the project's website at `https://code.google.com/p/dkpro-wsd/`.

Acknowledgments

This work has been supported by the Volkswagen Foundation as part of the Lichtenberg Professorship Program under grant № I/82806.

References

Eneko Agirre and Philip Edmonds, editors. 2006. *Word Sense Disambiguation: Algorithms and Applications*. Springer.

Eneko Agirre and Aitor Soroa. 2009. Personalizing PageRank for word sense disambiguation. In *Proc. EACL*, pages 33–41.

Chris Biemann. 2013. Creating a system for lexical substitutions from scratch using crowdsourcing. *Lang. Resour. and Eval.*, 47(1):97–122.

Steven Bird. 2006. NLTK: The natural language toolkit. In *Proc. ACL-COLING (Interactive Presentation Sessions)*, pages 69–72.

Jordi Daudé, Lluís Padró, and German Rigau. 2003. Validation and tuning of WordNet mapping techniques. In *Proc. RANLP*, pages 117–123.

Christiane Fellbaum, editor. 1998. *WordNet: An Electronic Lexical Database*. MIT Press.

Iryna Gurevych, Max Mühlhäuser, Christof Müller, Jürgen Steimle, Markus Weimer, and Torsten Zesch. 2007. Darmstadt Knowledge Processing Repository Based on UIMA. In *Proc. UIMA Workshop at GLDV*.

Iryna Gurevych, Judith Eckle-Kohler, Silvana Hartmann, Michael Matuschek, Christian M. Meyer, and Christian Wirth. 2012. UBY – A large-scale unified lexical-semantic resource. In *Proc. EACL*, pages 580–590.

Verena Henrich, Erhard Hinrichs, and Tatiana Vodolazova. 2012. WebCAGe – A Web-harvested corpus annotated with GermaNet senses. In *Proc. EACL*, pages 387–396.

Johannes Hoffart, Mohamed Amir Yosef, Ilaria Bordino, Hagen Fürstenau, Manfred Pinkal, Marc Spaniol, Bilyana Taneva, Stefan Thater, and Gerhard Weikum. 2011. Robust disambiguation of named entities in text. In *Proc. EMNLP*, pages 782–792.

Nancy Ide, Christiane Fellbaum, Collin Baker, and Rebecca Passonneau. 2010. The Manually Annotated Sub-Corpus: A community resource for and by the people. In *Proc. ACL (Short Papers)*, pages 68–73.

Salil Joshi, Mitesh M. Khapra, and Pushpak Bhattacharyya. 2012. I Can Sense It: A comprehensive online system for WSD. In *Proc. COLING (Demo Papers)*, pages 247–254.

Adam Kilgarriff. 2010. A detailed, accurate, extensive, available English lexical database. In *Proc. NAACL-HLT*, pages 21–24.

Karin Kipper, Anna Korhonen, Neville Ryant, and Martha Palmer. 2008. A large-scale classification of English verbs. *Lang. Resour. and Eval.*, 42(1):21–40.

Adam Lally, Karin Verspoor, and Eric Nyberg, editors. 2009. *Unstructured Information Management Architecture (UIMA) Version 1.0*. OASIS.

Paul McNamee and Hoa Trang Dang. 2009. Overview of the TAC 2009 knowledge base population track. In *Proc. TAC*.

Rada Mihalcea and Andras Csomai. 2005. SenseLearner: Word sense disambiguation for all words in unrestricted text. In *Proc. ACL (System Demos)*, pages 53–56.

George A. Miller, Martin Chodorow, Shari Landes, Claudio Leacock, and Robert G. Thomas. 1994. Using a semantic concordance for sense identification. In *Proc. HLT*, pages 240–243.

Tristan Miller, Chris Biemann, Torsten Zesch, and Iryna Gurevych. 2012. Using distributional similarity for lexical expansion in knowledge-based word sense disambiguation. In *Proc. COLING*, pages 1781–1796.

Roberto Navigli and Mirella Lapata. 2010. An experimental study of graph connectivity for unsupervised word sense disambiguation. *IEEE Trans. on Pattern Anal. and Machine Intel.*, 32(4):678–692.

Roberto Navigli and Simone Paolo Ponzetto. 2012. An overview of BabelNet and its API for multilingual language processing. In Iryna Gurevych and Jungi Kim, editors, *The People's Web Meets NLP: Collaboratively Constructed Language Resources*. Springer.

Siddharth Patwardhan, Satanjeev Banerjee, and Ted Pedersen. 2005. SenseRelate::TargetWord – A generalized framework for word sense disambiguation. In *Proc. ACL (System Demos)*, pages 73–76.

Maria Teresa Pazienza, Armando Stellato, and Alexandra Tudorache. 2008. JMWNL: An extensible multilingual library for accessing wordnets in different languages. In *Proc. LREC*, pages 28–30.

Simone Paolo Ponzetto and Roberto Navigli. 2010. Knowledge-rich word sense disambiguation rivaling supervised systems. In *Proc. ACL*, pages 1522–1531.

Josef Ruppenhofer, Michael Ellsworth, Miriam R. L. Petruck, Christopher R. Johnson, and Jan Scheffczyk. 2010. *FrameNet II: Extended Theory and Practice*. International Computer Science Institute.

Helmud Schmid. 1994. Probabilistic part-of-speech tagging using decision trees. In *Proc. NeMLaP*.

Piek Vossen, editor. 1998. *EuroWordNet: A Multilingual Database with Lexical Semantic Networks*. Springer.

Zhi Zhong and Hwee Tou Ng. 2010. It Makes Sense: A wide-coverage word sense disambiguation system for free text. In *Proc. ACL (System Demos)*, pages 78–83.

Extending an interoperable platform to facilitate the creation of multilingual and multimodal NLP applications

Georgios Kontonatsios*, Paul Thompson*, Riza Theresa Batista-Navarro*, Claudiu Mihăilă*, Ioannis Korkontzelos and Sophia Ananiadou
The National Centre for Text Mining,
School of Computer Science, The University of Manchester
131 Princess Street, Manchester M1 7DN, UK
{kontonag,batistar,thompsop,mihailac,
korkonti,ananiads}@cs.man.ac.uk

Abstract

U-Compare is a UIMA-based workflow construction platform for building natural language processing (NLP) applications from heterogeneous language resources (LRs), without the need for programming skills. U-Compare has been adopted within the context of the META-NET Network of Excellence, and over 40 LRs that process 15 European languages have been added to the U-Compare component library. In line with META-NET's aims of increasing communication between citizens of different European countries, U-Compare has been extended to facilitate the development of a wider range of applications, including both multilingual and multimodal workflows. The enhancements exploit the UIMA *Subject of Analysis* (*Sofa*) mechanism, that allows different facets of the input data to be represented. We demonstrate how our customised extensions to U-Compare allow the construction and testing of NLP applications that transform the input data in different ways, e.g., machine translation, automatic summarisation and text-to-speech.

1 Introduction

Currently, there are many repositories that contain a range of NLP components, e.g., OpenNLP[1], Stanford CoreNLP[2], JULIE NLP Toolsuite[3] and NaCTeM software tools[4]. The ability to chain components from these repositories into pipelines is a prerequisite to facilitate the development of complex NLP applications. Combining together heterogeneous components is not, however, always straightforward. The various components used in a pipeline may be implemented using different programming languages, may have incompatible input/output formats, e.g., stand-off or inline annotations, or may require or produce incompatible data types, e.g., a particular named entity recogniser (NER) may require specific types of syntactic constituents as input, making it important to choose the right type of syntactic parser to run prior to the NER. Thus, the tools required to build a new application may not be *interoperable* with each other, and considerable extra work may be required to make the tools talk to each other.

The Unstructured Information Management Architecture (UIMA) (Ferrucci and Lally, 2004) was created as a means to alleviate such problems. It is a framework that facilitates the straightforward combination of LRs, i.e., tools and corpora, into workflow applications. UIMA is an OASIS standard that enables interoperability of LRs by defining a standard workflow metadata format and standard input/output representations.

U-Compare (Kano et al., 2011) is a graphical NLP workflow construction platform built on top of UIMA. It facilitates the rapid construction, testing and evaluation of NLP workflows using drag-and-drop actions within its graphical user interface (GUI). U-Compare enhances interoperability among UIMA-compliant LRs, by defining a common and sharable *Type System*, i.e., a hierarchy of annotation types, which models a wide range of NLP data types, e.g., sentence, token, part-of-speech tag, named entity and discourse annotations. The aim is for all components in U-Compare's library to be compliant with this type system. In the context of META-NET, U-Compare's library has been extended with 46 new LRs supporting 15 European languages, all of which are compliant with the same type system.

*The authors have contributed equally to the development of this work and production of the manuscript.

[1] http://opennlp.sourceforge.net/projects.html
[2] http://nlp.stanford.edu/software/corenlp.shtml
[3] http://www.julielab.de/Resources/Software/NLP_Tools.html
[4] http://nactem.ac.uk/software.php

This makes U-Compare the world's largest repository of type system-compatible LRs, allowing users to seamlessly combine together resources to create a range of NLP applications.

Previously, U-Compare was able to support the development of a wide range of monolingual lexical, syntactic and semantic processing tasks applications that enriched textual input documents by adding annotations of various types. However, not all NLP applications operate in this way; some workflows *transform* the input data to create new "views" of the input data. The META-NET project aims to ensure equal access to information by all European citizens. This aim implies the development of both multilingual applications, which transform input data from one language into another, or multimodal applications, in which text may be transformed into speech, or vice versa.

U-Compare has been extended in several ways to support the construction of these more complex workflow types. Specifically, information about both the original and transformed data, together with annotations associated with each view, can now be visualised in a straightforward manner. The changes support two new categories of workflow. Firstly, workflows that produce two or more textual views of an input text are useful not only for multilingual applications, such as those that carry out machine translation, but also applications that transform the input text in other ways, such as those that produce a summary of an input text. Secondly, workflows that output audio as well as textual views, e.g., text-to-speech applications, are also supported.

2 Related work

Over the past few years, an increasing numbers of researchers have begun to create and distribute their own workflow construction architectures (Ferrucci and Lally, 2004; Cunningham et al., 2002; Grishman et al., 1997; Schäfer, 2006) or platforms (Kano et al., 2011; Rak et al., 2012; Ogrodniczuk and Karagiozov, 2011; Savova et al., 2010) that allow the rapid development of NLP applications.

GATE (Cunningham et al., 2002) is a workflow construction framework that has been used to develop several types of NLP applications, including summarisation systems. It facilitates the development of a wide range of NLP applications by providing a collection of components that can process various languages, together with Java libraries that handle character encoding for approximately 100 languages. However, GATE does not formally define any standards to model multilingual or multimodal applications, but rather aims to boost the development process of NLP applications.

TIPSTER (Grishman et al., 1997) is a generic framework for the development of NLP applications. TIPSTER provides multilingual functionalities by associating text segments of a parallel document with one or more languages. This allows language-dependent NLP components to process only the appropriate mono-lingual subdocuments. However, TIPSTER does not provide explicit guidelines regarding the annotation types and attributes that are produced by components. This lack of a common and sharable system of annotation types discourages interoperability between LRs. However, TIPSTER does not provide a mechanism that facilitates the development of multilingual or multimodal NLP applications.

Heart of Gold (Schäfer, 2006) is an XML-based workflow construction architecture that enables interoperability of tools developed in different programming languages to be combined into pipelines. Heart of Gold contains a rich library of shallow and deep parsing components supporting several languages, e.g., English, German, Japanese and Greek. Nonetheless, Heart of Gold does not specifically support the construction of multilingual or multimodal workflows.

In contrast to the other frameworks introduced above, UIMA (Ferrucci and Lally, 2004) provides an abstract-level mechanism that can be used to support the development of workflows that carry out transformations of the input data. This mechanism is called the *Subject of Analysis* or *Sofa*. Multiple Sofas can be linked with an input file, each of which stores different data and associated annotations. This mechanism can thus be exploited to represent alternative "views" of the input data, such as a source text and its translation. The data stored in different Sofas is not restricted to textual information; it can also correspond to other modalities, such as audio data. This makes the Sofa mechanism equally suitable for storing the output of text-to-speech workflows. Our extensions to U-Compare are thus implemented by reading and displaying the contents of different types of Sofas.

The Sofa mechanism has previously been

under-exploited by UIMA developers, despite its power in allowing more complex NLP workflows to be constructed. Indeed, no other existing UIMA-based platform (Kano et al., 2011; Rak et al., 2012; Savova et al., 2010; Hahn et al., 2008) has demonstrated the use of Sofas to construct multilingual or multimodal applications. Thus, to our knowledge, our enhancements to U-Compare constitute the first attempt to make the construction of workflows that carry out transformations of input data more readily available to UIMA users, without the need for programming skills.

3 METANET4U Components in U-Compare

The two dozen national and many regional languages of Europe present linguistic barriers that can severely limit the free flow of goods, information and services. The META-NET Network of Excellence was created to respond to this issue. Consisting of 60 research centres from 34 countries, META-NET has aimed to stimulate a concerted, substantial and continent-wide effort to push forward language technology research and engineering, in order to ensure equal access to information and knowledge for all European citizens.

META-NET's aims are dependent on the ready availability of LRs that can carry out NLP and text mining (TM) on a range of European languages. Such resources constitute the building blocks for constructing language technology applications that can help European citizens to gain easy access to the information they require. One of the major outcomes of META-NET has been the development of META-SHARE, an open, distributed facility for sharing and exchange of LRs in a large number of European languages.

Within the context of META-NET, interoperability of LRs is clearly of utmost importance, to expedite the process of developing new NLP applications. In order to provide a concrete demonstration of the utility and power of promoting interoperability within META-SHARE, one of the sub-projects of META-NET, i.e., METANET4U, has carried out a pilot study on interoperability, making use of the UIMA framework and the U-Compare platform. It is in this context that a set of 46 new LRs, available in META-SHARE, were wrapped as UIMA components and made available in U-Compare. Of these components, 37 operate on one or more specific languages other than English and 4 are language-independent. Table 1 shows the full set of categories of UIMA components created during the METANET4U project, together with the languages supported.

Several of these new components output multiple Sofas, i.e., two machine translation components, two automatic summarisation components and a text-to-speech component. It is hoped that our U-Compare extensions will help to stimulate the development of a greater number of related UIMA components, and thus promote a new level of complexity for future UIMA workflows.

Component Function	Supported Languages
Language Identifier	54 modern languages
Paragraph breaker	pt, mt
Sentence splitter	en, pt ,mt, es, ca, ast, cy, gl, it
Tokeniser	en, pt, mt, es, ca, ast, cy, gl, it, fr
Morph. Analyser	en, pt, es, ca, ast, cy, gl, it, ro, eu, fr
POS Tagger	en, es, ca, cy, gl, it, pt, ro, eu, fr, mt
Syntactic chunker	en, es, ca, gl, ast, ro, fr
NP chunker	ro
Segmenter	ro, en
FDG Parser	ro
Dependency Parser	en, es, ca, gl, ast
Discourse Parser	ro
NER	Language independent
Summariser	ro, en
Machine translation	es$\leftrightarrow${gl,pt,ca} en$\leftrightarrow$es, eu$\rightarrow$es

Table 1: METANET4U UIMA components

4 Enhancements to U-Compare

In UIMA, an artefact, i.e., raw text, audio, image, video, and its annotations, e.g., part-of-speech tags, are represented in a standard format, namely the *Common Analysis Structure* (CAS). A CAS can contain any number of smaller sub-CASes, i.e., Sofas, that carry different artefacts with their linked annotations. Figure 1 illustrates the different types of Sofas that are created by the three types of workflows that we will demonstrate. Firstly, for a machine translation workflow, at least

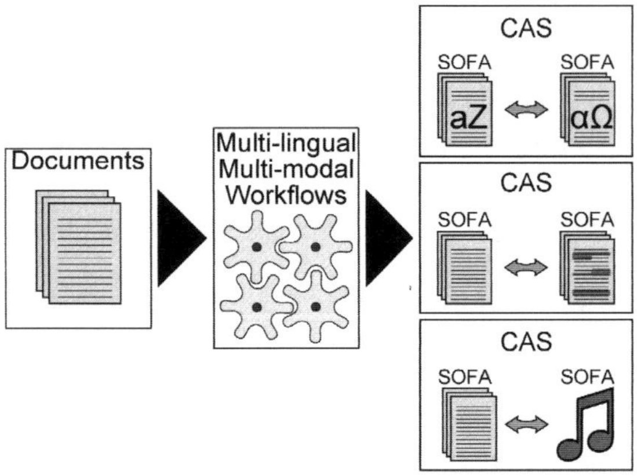

Figure 1: UIMA based multilingual and multimodal workflow architecture

two CAS views, i.e., Sofas, are created, the first corresponding to the text in the source language, and the other Sofas corresponding to the translation(s) of the source text into target language(s). The second type of workflow, i.e., automatic summarisation, is related to the former workflow, in that the two Sofas produced by the workflow are both textual, one containing the input text and one containing a summary of the original text. The third type of workflow is different, in that a Sofa containing audio data is used to represent the output of a multimodal workflow.

Two specific extensions have been made to U-Compare to handle both textual and audio Sofas. When the output of a workflow consists of multiple textual views (Sofas), the default annotation viewer is automatically split to allow multiple views of the text to be displayed and side-by-side. This can be useful, e.g., to allow careful comparison of a source text and target translation in a machine translation workflow. To handle audio Sofas, we have developed a new, customised viewer that can visualise and play audio data. The visualisation consists of a graphical display of the waveform, power information and spectrogram, as well as segmentation of the audio data into regions (such as individual tokens) and transcriptions, if such information is present in the audio Sofa. The viewer makes use the open-source library Java Speech Toolkit (JSTK)[5].

5 Workflow applications

In order to provide a practical demonstration of the enhanced capabilities of U-Compare, we show three different workflows that transform the input data in different ways, namely translation, automatic summarisation and speech synthesis. In this section, we provide brief details of these workflows.

5.1 Machine translation

The University of Manchester has created UIMA wrapper components corresponding to different modules of Apertium (Corbí-Bellot et al., 2005), a free rule-based machine translation engine. These components consist of a morphological analyser, POS tagger and translator. The three components must be run in sequence to carry out translation, although the first two components can be used in other workflows to carry out monolingual analyses. The UIMA components currently handle a subset of the 27 languages dealt with by the complete Apertium system, corresponding to the languages of the METANET4U partners, i.e., English↔Spanish, Galician↔Spanish, Portuguese↔Spanish, Catalan↔Spanish and Basque→Spanish. However, additional language pairs can be added straightforwardly. Our sample workflow includes as its initial component the Language Identifier from the Romanian Academy Research Institute for Artificial Intelligence (RACAI), to automatically detect the language of the text in the input Sofa. The subsequent components in the workflow are the Apertium modules. The workflow demonstrates how heterogeneous components from different research groups can be combined into workflows to create new NLP applications. A sample output from running the workflow is shown in Figure 2. The input text was detected as English by the RACAI Language Identifier. The English text was subsequently analysed by the morphological analyser and POS Tagger, and translated to Spanish by the translator. Figure 2 illustrates the side-by-side display of the contents of the two Sofas.

5.2 Automatic summarisation

Automatic summarisation for Romanian text can be carried out by creating a workflow consisting of two components developed by the Universitatea "Alexandru Ioan Cuza" din Iaşi (UAIC). Firstly, a segmenter (UAICSeg) splits the input text into fragments, which are in turn used as input to the summariser component (UAICSum). The length of the output summary (percentage of the whole document) is parameterised. As can be seen in

[5]http://code.google.com/p/jstk

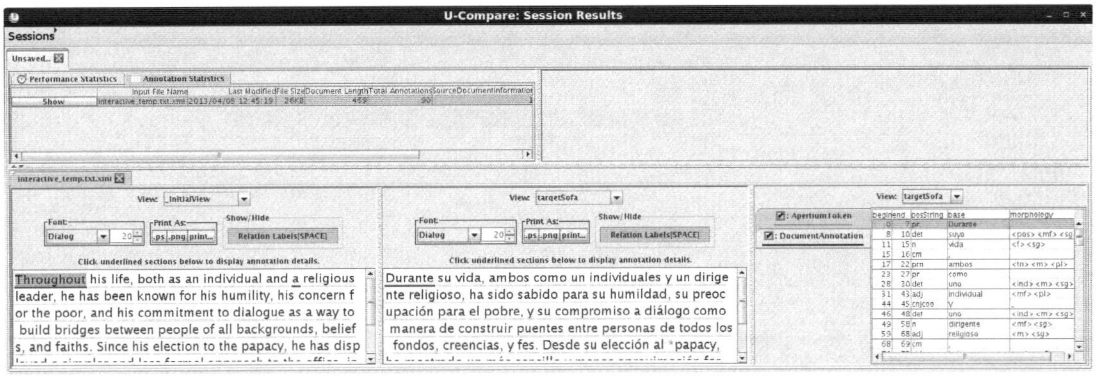

Figure 2: Translation of English text to Spanish

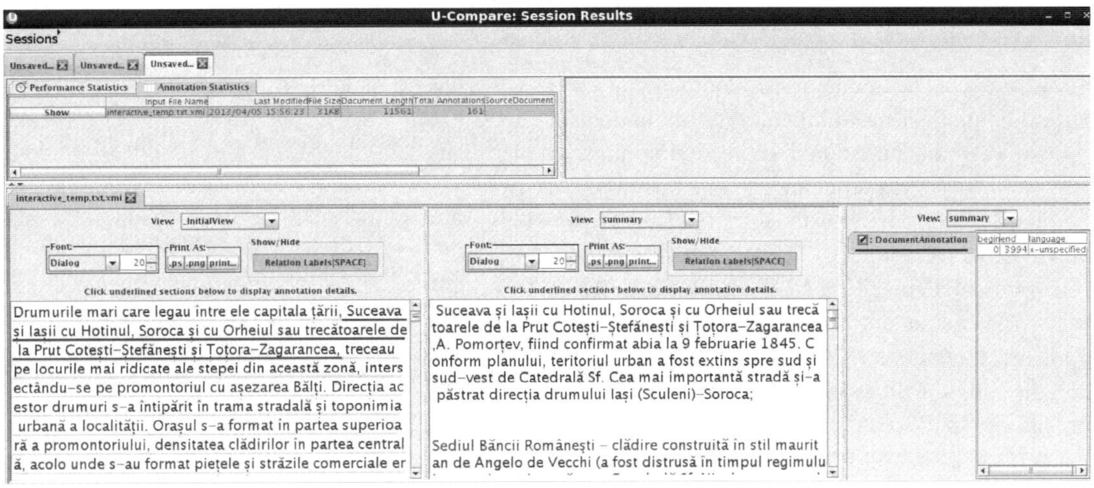

Figure 3: Summarisation of Romanian text

Figure 3, the output of this workflow is displayed using the same parallel Sofa viewer. In this case, the full text is displayed in the left-hand pane and the summary is shown in the right-hand pane.

5.3 Speech synthesis

The Universitat Politècnica de Catalunya (UPC) developed a speech synthesiser component that is based around their Ogmios text-to-speech system (Bonafonte et al., 2006). The UIMA component version of this tool generates separate text and audio Sofas; the former stores the textual tokens and textual representations of their pronunciations, whilst the latter stores the start and end time offsets of each of the tokens in the audio file, together with their transcriptions. Fig. 4 shows how the textual Sofa information is displayed in U-Compare's default annotation viewer, whilst the audio Sofa information is shown in the new audio visualiser mentioned above. The three different types of visual information are displayed below each other, and the segments (tokens) of the audio file, together with their transcriptions, are displayed at the bottom of the window. A "Play" button allows either the complete file or a selected segment to be played.

6 Conclusions

The requirements of META-NET have motivated several new enhancements to the U-Compare platform, which, to our knowledge, make it the first UIMA-based workflow construction platform that is fully geared towards the development of NLP applications that support a wide range of European languages. The 46 new UIMA-wrapped LRs that have been made available through U-Compare, supporting 15 different European languages and all compliant with the same type system, mean that the improved U-Compare is essentially a hub of multilingual resources, which can be freely and flexibly combined to create new workflows. In

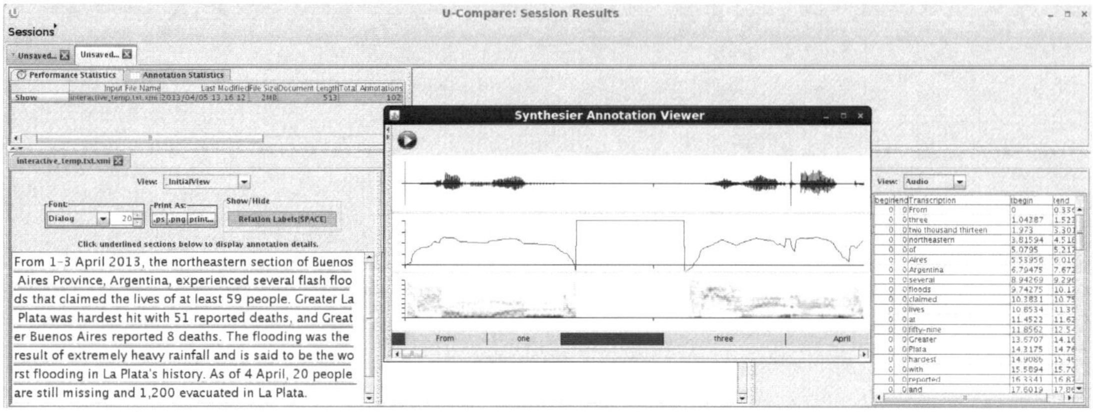

Figure 4: Speech Synthesis

addition, our enhancements to U-Compare mean that various types of multilingual and multimodal workflows can now be created with the minimum effort. These enhancements are intended to make U-Compare more attractive to users, and to help stimulate the development of a new generation of more complex UIMA-based NLP applications. As future work, we intend to extend the library of components that output multiple Sofas, and further extend the functionalities of U-Compare to handle other data modalities, e.g., video.

Acknowledgements

This work was partially funded by the European Community's Seventh Framework Program (FP7/2007-2013) [grant number 318736 (OSSMETER)]; MetaNet4U project (ICT PSP Programme) [grant number 270893]; and Engineering and Physical Sciences Research Council [grant numbers EP/P505631/1, EP/J50032X/1].

References

A. Bonafonte, P. Agüero, J. Adell, J. Pérez, and A. Moreno. 2006. Ogmios: The upc text-to-speech synthesis system for spoken translation. In *TC-STAR Workshop on Speech-to-Speech Translation*, pages 199–204.

A. Corbí-Bellot, M. Forcada, S. Ortiz-Rojas, J. Pérez-Ortiz, G. Ramírez-Sánchez, F. Sánchez-Martínez, I. Alegria, A. Mayor, and K. Sarasola. 2005. An open-source shallow-transfer machine translation engine for the romance languages of Spain. In *Proceedings of the 10th Conference of the EAMT*, pages 79–86.

H. Cunningham, D. Maynard, K. Bontcheva, and V. Tablan. 2002. GATE: an architecture for development of robust HLT applications.

D. Ferrucci and A. Lally. 2004. Building an example application with the unstructured information management architecture. *IBM Systems Journal*, 43(3):455–475.

R. Grishman, B. Caid, J. Callan, J. Conley, H. Corbin, J. Cowie, K. DiBella, P. Jacobs, M. Mettler, B. Ogden, et al. 1997. TIPSTER text phase ii architecture design version 2.1 p 19 june 1996.

U. Hahn, E. Buyko, R. Landefeld, M. Mühlhausen, M. Poprat, K. Tomanek, and J. Wermter. 2008. An overview of JCoRe, the JULIE lab UIMA component repository. In *LREC'08 Workshop 'Towards Enhanced Interoperability for Large HLT Systems: UIMA for NLP'*, pages 1–7, Marrakech, Morocco, May.

Y. Kano, M. Miwa, K. Cohen, L. Hunter, S. Ananiadou, and J. Tsujii. 2011. U-compare: A modular nlp workflow construction and evaluation system. *IBM Journal of Research and Development*, 55(3):11.

M. Ogrodniczuk and D. Karagiozov. 2011. Atlas - the multilingual language processing platform. *Procesamiento de Lenguaje Natural*, 47(0):241–248.

R. Rak, A. Rowley, W. Black, and S. Ananiadou. 2012. Argo: an integrative, interactive, text mining-based workbench supporting curation. *Database: The Journal of Biological Databases and Curation*, 2012.

G. Savova, J. Masanz, P. Ogren, J. Zheng, S. Sohn, K. Kipper-Schuler, and C. Chute. 2010. Mayo clinical text analysis and knowledge extraction system (ctakes): architecture, component evaluation and applications. *Journal of the American Medical Informatics Association*, 17(5):507–513.

U. Schäfer. 2006. Middleware for creating and combining multi-dimensional nlp markup. In *Proceedings of the 5th Workshop on NLP and XML: Multi-Dimensional Markup in Natural Language Processing*, pages 81–84. ACL.

FudanNLP: A Toolkit for Chinese Natural Language Processing

Xipeng Qiu, Qi Zhang, Xuanjing Huang
Fudan University, 825 Zhangheng Road, Shanghai, China
xpqiu@fudan.edu.cn, qz@fudan.edu.cn, xjhuang@fudan.edu.cn

Abstract

The growing need for Chinese natural language processing (NLP) is largely in a range of research and commercial applications. However, most of the currently Chinese NLP tools or components still have a wide range of issues need to be further improved and developed. FudanNLP is an open source toolkit for Chinese natural language processing (NLP), which uses statistics-based and rule-based methods to deal with Chinese NLP tasks, such as word segmentation, part-of-speech tagging, named entity recognition, dependency parsing, time phrase recognition, anaphora resolution and so on.

1 Introduction

Chinese is one of the most widely used languages in this world, and the proportion that Chinese language holds on the Internet is also quite high. Under the current circumstances, there are greater and greater demands for intelligent processing and analyzing of the Chinese texts.

Similar to English, the main tasks in Chinese NLP include word segmentation (CWS), part-of-speech (POS) tagging, named entity recognition (NER), syntactic parsing, anaphora resolution (AR), and so on. Although the general ways are essentially the same for English and Chinese, the implementation details are different. It is also non-trivial to optimize these methods for Chinese NLP tasks.

There are also some toolkits to be used for NLP, such as Stanford CoreNLP[1], Apache OpenNLP[2], Curator[3] and NLTK[4]. But these toolkits are developed mainly for English and not optimized for Chinese.

In order to customize an optimized system for Chinese language process, we implement an open source toolkit, FudanNLP[5], which is written in Java. Since most of the state-of-the-art methods for NLP are based on statistical learning, the whole framework of our toolkit is established around statistics-based methods, supplemented by some rule-based methods. Therefore, the quality of training data is crucial for our toolkit. However, we find that there are some drawbacks in currently most commonly used corpora, such as CTB (Xia, 2000) and CoNLL (Hajič et al., 2009) corpora. For example, in CTB corpus, the set of POS tags is relative small and some categories are derived from the perspective of English grammar. And in CoNLL corpus, the head words are often interrogative particles and punctuations, which are unidiomatic in Chinese. These drawbacks bring more challenges to further analyses, such as information extraction and semantic understanding. Therefore, we first construct a corpus with a modified guideline, which is more in accordance with the common understanding for Chinese grammar.

In addition to the basic Chinese NLP tasks

[1] http://nlp.stanford.edu/software/corenlp.shtml

[2] http://incubator.apache.org/opennlp/

[3] http://cogcomp.cs.illinois.edu/page/software_view/Curator

[4] http://www.nltk.org/

[5] http://fudannlp.googlecode.com

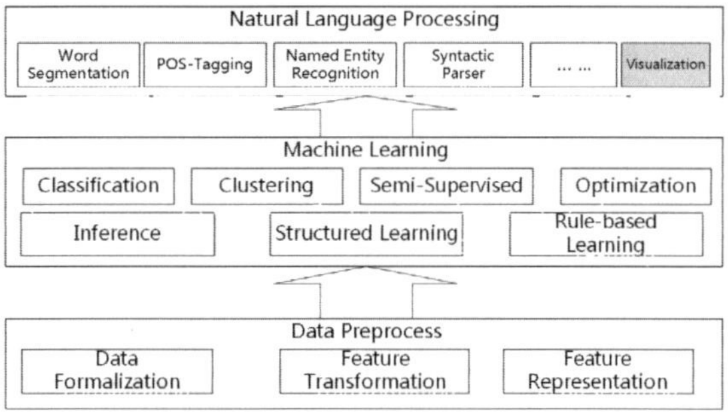

Figure 1: System Structure of FudanNLP

mentioned above, the toolkit also provides many minor functions, such as text classification, dependency tree kernel, tree pattern-based information extraction, keywords extraction, translation between simplified and traditional Chinese, and so on.

Currently, our toolkit has been used by many universities and companies for various applications, such as the dialogue system, social computing, recommendation system and vertical search.

The rest of the demonstration is organized as follows. We first briefly describe our system and its main components in section 2. Then we show system performances in section 3. Section 4 introduces three ways to use our toolkit. In section 5, we summarize the paper and give some directions for our future efforts.

2 System Overview

The components of our system have three layers of structure: data preprocessing, machine learning and natural language processing, which is shown in Figure 1. We will introduce these components in detail in the following subsections.

2.1 Data Preprocessing Component

In the natural language processing system, the original input is always text. However, the statistical machine learning methods often deal with data with vector-based representation. So we firstly need to preprocess the input texts and transform them to the required format. Due to the fact that text data is usually discrete and sparse, the sparse vector structure is largely used. Similar to Mallet (McCallum, 2002), we use the pipeline structure for a flexible transformation of various data. The pipeline consists of several serial or parallel modules. Each module, called "pipe", is aimed at a single and simple function.

For example, when we transform a sentence into a vector with "bag-of-words", the transformation process would involve the following serial pipes:

1. String2Token Pipe: to transform a string into word tokens.

2. Token2Index Pipe: to look up the word alphabet to get the indices of the words.

3. WeightByFrequency Pipe: to calculate the vector weight for each word according to its frequency of occurrence.

With the pipeline structure, the data preprocessing component has good flexibility, extensibility and reusability.

2.2 Machine Learning Component

The outputs of NLP are often structured, so the structured learning is our core module. Structured learning is the task of assigning a structured label $\mathbf{y}$ to an input $\mathbf{x}$. The label $\mathbf{y}$ can be a discrete variable, a sequence, a tree or a more complex structure.

To illustrate by a sample $\mathbf{x}$, we define the feature as $\Phi(\mathbf{x}, \mathbf{y})$. Thus, we can label $\mathbf{x}$ with a score function,

$$\hat{\mathbf{y}} = \arg\max_{\mathbf{y}} F(\mathbf{w}, \Phi(\mathbf{x}, \mathbf{y})), \qquad (1)$$

where $\mathbf{w}$ is the parameter of function $F(\cdot)$. The feature vector $\Phi(\mathbf{x}, \mathbf{y})$ consists of lots of overlapping features, which is the chief benefit of a discriminative model.

For example, in sequence labeling, both $\mathbf{x} = x_1, \ldots, x_L$ and $\mathbf{y} = y_1, \ldots, y_L$ are sequences. For first-order Markov sequence labeling, the feature can be denoted as $\phi_k(y_{i-1}, y_i, \mathbf{x}, i)$, where i is the position in the sequence. Then the score function can be rewritten as

$$\hat{\mathbf{y}} = \arg\max_{\mathbf{y}} F(\sum_{i=1}^{L} \sum_{k} w_k \phi_k(y_{i-1}, y_i, \mathbf{x}, i)), \qquad (2)$$

where L is the length of $\mathbf{x}$.

Different algorithms vary in the definition of $F(\cdot)$ and the corresponding objective function.

$F(\cdot)$ is usually defined as a linear or exponential family function. For example, in conditional random fields (CRFs) (Lafferty et al., 2001), $F(\cdot)$ is defined as:

$$P_{\mathbf{w}}(\mathbf{y}|\mathbf{x}) = \frac{1}{Z_{\mathbf{w}}} \exp(\mathbf{w}^T \Phi(\mathbf{x}, \mathbf{y})), \quad (3)$$

where $Z_{\mathbf{w}}$ is the normalization constant such that it makes the sum of all the terms one.

In FudanNLP, the linear function is universally used as the objective function. Eq. (1) is written as:

$$\hat{\mathbf{y}} = \arg\max_{\mathbf{y}} < \mathbf{w}, \Phi(\mathbf{x}, \mathbf{y}) > . \quad (4)$$

2.2.1 Training

In the training stage, we use the passive-aggressive algorithm to learn the model parameters. Passive-aggressive (PA) algorithm (Crammer et al., 2006) was proposed for normal multi-class classification and can be easily extended to structure learning (Crammer et al., 2005). Like Perceptron, PA is an online learning algorithm.

2.2.2 Inference

For consistency with statistical machine learning, we call the process to calculate the Eq.(1) as "inference". In structured learning, the number of possible solutions is very huge, so dynamic programming or approximate approaches are often used for efficiency. For NLP tasks, the most popular structure is sequence. To label the sequence, we use Viterbi dynamic programming to solve the inference problem in Eq. (4).

Our system can support any order of Viterbi decoding. In addition, we also implement a constrained Viterbi algorithm to reduce the number of possible solutions by pre-defined rules. For example, when we know the probable labels, we delete the unreachable states from state transition matrix. It is very useful for CWS and POS tagging with sequence labeling. When we have a word dictionary or know the POS for some words, we can get more accurate results.

2.2.3 Other Algorithms

Apart from the core modules of structured learning, our system also includes several traditional machine learning algorithms, such as Perceptron, Adaboost, kNN, k-means, and so on.

2.3 Natural Language Processing Components

Our toolkit provides the basic NLP functions, such as word segmentation, part-of-speech tagging, named entity recognition, syntactic parsing, temporal phrase recognition, anaphora resolution, and so on. These functions are trained on our developed corpus. We also develop a visualization module to displaying the output. Table 1 shows the output representation of our toolkit.

2.3.1 Chinese Word Segmentation

Different from English, Chinese sentences are written in a continuous sequence of characters without explicit delimiters such as the blank space. Since the meanings of most Chinese characters are not complete, words are the basic syntactic and semantic units. Therefore, it is indispensable step to segment the sentence into words in Chinese language processing.

We use character-based sequence labeling (Peng et al., 2004) to find the boundaries of words. Besides the carefully chosen features, we also use the meaning of character drawn from HowNet(Dong and Dong, 2006), which improves the performance greatly. Since unknown words detection is still one of main challenges of Chinese word segmentation. We implement a constrained Viterbi algorithm to allow users to add their own word dictionary.

2.3.2 POS tagging

Chinese POS tagging is very different from that in English. There are no morphological changes for a word among its different POS tags. Therefore, most of Chinese words may have multiple POS tags. For example, there are different morphologies in English for the word "毁灭 (destroy)", such as "destroyed", "destroying" and "destruction". But in Chinese, there is just one same form(Xia, 2000).

There are two popular guidelines to tag the word's POS: CTB (Xia, 2000) and PKU (Yu et al., 2001). We take into account both the weaknesses and the strengths of these two guidelines, and propose our guideline for better subsequent analyses, such as parser and named entity recognition. For example, the proper name is labeled as "NR" in CTB, while we label it with one of four categories: person,

Input:
约翰来自华盛顿，他生于 1980 年。
John is from Washington, and he was born in 1980.

Output:

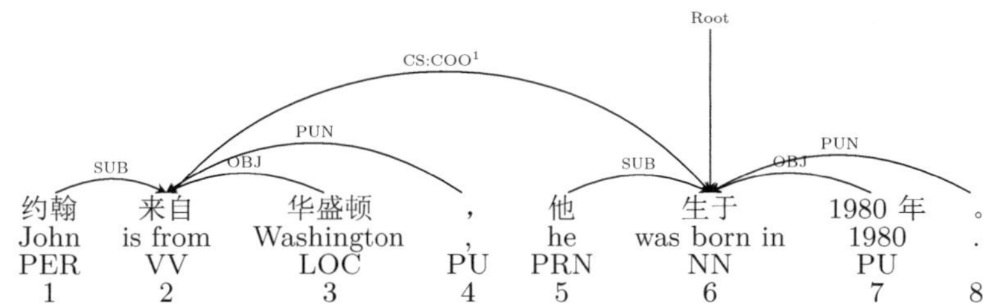

NER:		
1	→	PER
3	→	LOC
AR:		
5	→	1
TIME:		
7	→	1980

[1] CS:COO means the coordinate complex sentence.

Table 1: Example of the output representation of our toolkit

location, organization and other proper name. Conversely, we merge the "VC" and "VE" into "VV" since there is no link verb in Chinese. Finally, we use a tag set with 39 categories in total.

Since a POS tag is assigned to each word, not to each character, Chinese POS tagging has two ways: pipeline method or joint method. Currently, the joint method is more popular and effective because it uses more flexible features and can reduce the error propagation (Ng and Low, 2004). In our system, we implement both methods for POS tagging. Besides, we also use some knowledge to improve the performance, such as Chinese surname and the common suffixes of the names of locations and organizations.

2.3.3 Named Entity Recognition

In Chinese named entity recognition (NER), there are usually three kinds of named entities (NEs) to be dealt with: names of persons (PER) , locations (LOC) and organizations (ORG). Unlike English, there is no obvious identification for NEs, such as initial capitals. The internal structures are also different for different kinds of NEs, so it is difficult to build a unified model for named entity recognition.

Our NER is based on the results of POS tagging and uses some customize features to detect NEs. First, the number of NEs is very large and the new NEs are endlessly emerging, so it is impossible to store them in dictionary. Since the internal structures are relatively more important, we use language models to capture the internal structures. Second, we merge the continuous NEs with some rule-based strategies. For example, we combine the continuous words "人民/NN 大会堂/NN" into " 人民大会堂/LOC".

2.3.4 Dependency parsing

Our syntactic parser is currently a dependency parser, which is implemented with the shift-reduce deterministic algorithm based on the work in (Yamada and Matsumoto, 2003). The syntactic structure of Chinese is more complex than that of English, and semantic meaning is more dominant than syntax in Chinese sentences. So we select the dependency parser to avoid the minutiae in syntactic constituents and wish to pay more attention to the subsequent semantic analysis. Since the structure of the Chinese language is quite different from that of English, we use more effective features according to the characteristics of Chinese sentences.

The common used corpus for Chinese dependency parsing is CoNLL corpus (Hajič et al., 2009). However, there are some illogical cases in CoNLL corpus. For example, the head words are often interrogative particles and punctuations. Our guideline is based on common understanding for Chinese grammar. The Chinese syntactic components usually include subject, predicate, object, attribute, adverbial modifier and complement. Figure 2 and 3 show the differences between the trees of CoNLL and our Corpus. Table 2 shows some primary dependency relations in our guideline.

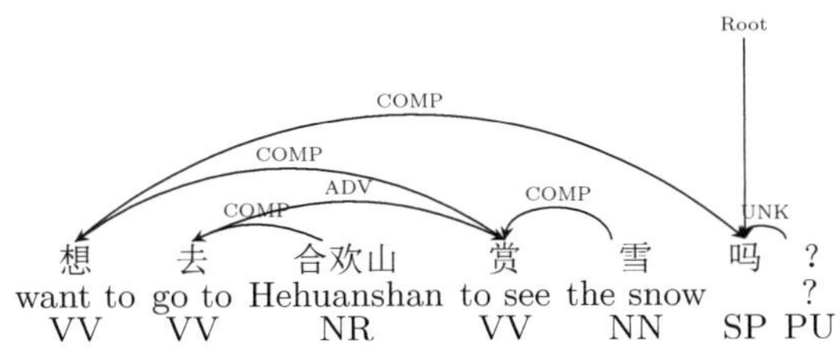

Figure 2: Dependency Tree in CoNLL Corpus

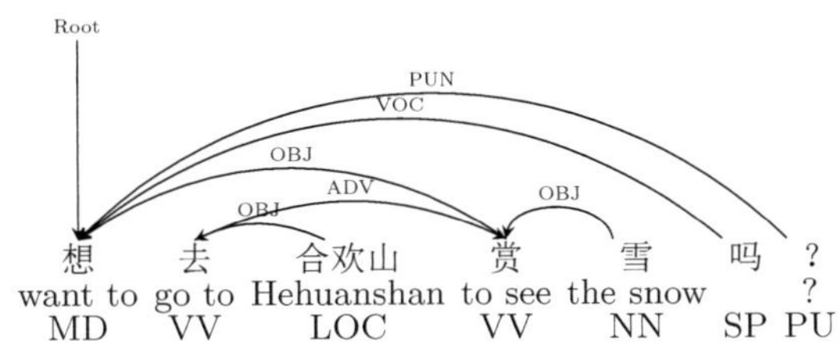

Figure 3: Dependency Tree in Our Corpus

Relations	Chinese	Definitions
SUB	主语	Subject
PRED	谓语	Predicate
OBJ	宾语	Object
ATT	定语	Attribute
ADV	状语	Adverbial Modifier
COMP	补语	Complement
SVP	连动	Serial Verb Phrases
SUB-OBJ	兼语	Pivotal Construction
VOC	语态	Voice
TEN	时态	Tense
PUN	标点	Punctuation

Table 2: Some primary dependency relations

2.3.5 Temporal Phrase Recognition and Normalization

Chinese temporal phrases is more flexible than English. Firstly, there are two calendars: Gregorian and lunar calendars. Both of them are frequently used. Secondly, the forms of same temporal phrase are various, which often consists of Chinese characters, Arabic numerals and English letters, such as "早上 10 点" and "10:00 PM".

Different from the general process based on machine learning, we implement the time phrase recognizer with a rule-based method. These rules include 376 regular expressions and nearly a hundred logical judgments.

After recognizing the temporal phrases, we normalize them with a standard time format. For a phrase indicating a relative time , such as "一年后" and " 一小时后", we first find the base time in the context. If no base time is found, or there is also no temporal phrase to indicate the base time (such as "明天"), we set the base time to the current system time. Table 3 gives examples for our temporal phrase recognition module.

Input:
08 年北京举行奥运会，8 月 8 号开幕。四年后的七月二十七日，伦敦奥运开幕。
The Beijing Olympic Games took place from August 8, 2008. Four years later, the London Olympic Games took place from July 21.

今天我很忙，晚上 9 点才能下班。周日也要加班。
I'm busy today, and have to come off duty after 9:00 PM. And I also have to work this Sunday.

Output:	
08 年 (2008)	2008
8 月 8 号 (August 8)	2008-8-8
七月二十七日 (July 21)	2012-7-27
今天 (today)	2012-2-22[1]
晚上 9 点 (9:00 PM)	2012-2-22 21:00
周日 (this Sunday)	2012-2-26

[1] The base time is 2012-02-22 10:00AM.

Table 3: Examples for Temporal Phrase Recognition

2.3.6 Anaphora Resolution

Anaphora resolution is to detect the pronouns and find what they are referring to. We first find all pronouns and entity names, then use a classifier to predict whether there is a relation between each pair of pronoun and entity name. Table 4 gives examples for our anaphora resolution module.

Input:
牛津大学创建于 1167 年。它位于英国牛津城。这个大学培育了好多优秀的学生。
Oxford University is founded in 1167. It is located in Oxford, UK. The university has nurtured a lot of good students.

Output:	
它 (It)	牛津大学
这 个 大 学 (The university)	牛津大学 (Oxford University)

Table 4: Examples for Anaphora Resolution

3 System Performances

In this section, we investigate the performances for the six tasks: Chinese word segmentation (CWS), POS tagging (POS), named entity recognition (NER) and dependency parser(DePar), Temporal Phrase Recognition (TPR) and Anaphora Resolution (AR). We use 5-fold cross validation on our developed corpus. The corpus includes $65,745$ sentences and $959,846$ words. The performances are shown in Table 5.

Task	Accuracy	Speed[1]	Memory
CWS	97.5%	98.9K	66M
POS	93.4%	44.5K	110M
NER	98.40%	38K	30M
DePar	85.3%	21.1	80M
TPR	95.16%	22.9k	237K
AR	70.3%	35.7K	52K

[1] characters per second. Test environment: CPU 2.67GHz, JRE 7.

Table 5: System Performances

4 Usages

We provide three ways to use our toolkit.

Firstly, our toolkit can be used as library. Users can call application programming interfaces (API) in their own applications.

Secondly, users can also invoke the main NLP modules to process the inputs (strings or files) from the command line directly.

Thirdly, the web services are provided for platform-independent and language-independent use. We use a REST (Representational State Transfer) architecture, in which the web services are viewed as resources and can be identified by their URLs.

5 Conclusions

In this demonstration, we have described the system, FudanNLP, which is a Java-based open source toolkit for Chinese natural language processing. In the future, we will add more functions, such as semantic parsing. Besides, we will also optimize the algorithms and codes to improve the system performances.

Acknowledgments

We would like to thank all the people[6] involved with our FudanNLP project. This work was funded by NSFC (No.61003091 and No.61073069) and 973 Program (No.2010CB327900).

[6] `https://code.google.com/p/fudannlp/wiki/People`

References

K. Crammer, R. McDonald, and F. Pereira. 2005. Scalable large-margin online learning for structured classification. In *NIPS Workshop on Learning With Structured Outputs*. Citeseer.

Koby Crammer, Ofer Dekel, Joseph Keshet, Shai Shalev-Shwartz, and Yoram Singer. 2006. Online passive-aggressive algorithms. *Journal of Machine Learning Research*, 7:551–585.

Z. Dong and Q. Dong. 2006. *Hownet And the Computation of Meaning*. World Scientific Publishing Co., Inc. River Edge, NJ, USA.

J. Hajič, M. Ciaramita, R. Johansson, D. Kawahara, M.A. Martí, L. Màrquez, A. Meyers, J. Nivre, S. Padó, J. Štěpánek, et al. 2009. The CoNLL-2009 shared task: Syntactic and semantic dependencies in multiple languages. In *Proceedings of the Thirteenth Conference on Computational Natural Language Learning: Shared Task*, pages 1–18. Association for Computational Linguistics.

John D. Lafferty, Andrew McCallum, and Fernando C. N. Pereira. 2001. Conditional random fields: Probabilistic models for segmenting and labeling sequence data. In *Proceedings of the Eighteenth International Conference on Machine Learning*.

Andrew Kachites McCallum. 2002. Mallet: A machine learning for language toolkit. http://mallet.cs.umass.edu.

H.T. Ng and J.K. Low. 2004. Chinese part-of-speech tagging: one-at-a-time or all-at-once? word-based or character-based. In *Proceedings of EMNLP*, volume 4.

F. Peng, F. Feng, and A. McCallum. 2004. Chinese segmentation and new word detection using conditional random fields. *Proceedings of the 20th international conference on Computational Linguistics*.

F. Xia, 2000. *The part-of-speech tagging guidelines for the penn chinese treebank (3.0)*.

H. Yamada and Y. Matsumoto. 2003. Statistical dependency analysis with support vector machines. In *Proceedings of the International Workshop on Parsing Technologies (IWPT)*, volume 3.

S. Yu, J. Lu, X. Zhu, H. Duan, S. Kang, H. Sun, H. Wang, Q. Zhao, and W. Zhan. 2001. Processing norms of modern chinese corpus. Technical report, Technical report.

ICARUS – An Extensible Graphical Search Tool for Dependency Treebanks

Markus Gärtner Gregor Thiele Wolfgang Seeker Anders Björkelund Jonas Kuhn
Institut für Maschinelle Sprachverarbeitung
University of Stuttgart
firstname.lastname@ims.uni-stuttgart.de

Abstract

We present ICARUS, a versatile graphical search tool to query dependency treebanks. Search results can be inspected both quantitatively and qualitatively by means of frequency lists, tables, or dependency graphs. ICARUS also ships with plugins that enable it to interface with tool chains running either locally or remotely.

1 Introduction

In this paper we present **ICARUS**[1] a search and visualization tool that primarily targets dependency syntax. The tool has been designed such that it requires minimal effort to get started with searching a treebank or system output of an automatic dependency parser, while still allowing for flexible queries. It enables the user to search dependency treebanks given a variety of constraints, including searching for particular subtrees. Emphasis has been placed on a functionality that makes it possible for the user to switch back and forth between a high-level, aggregated view of the search results and browsing of particular corpus instances, with an intuitive visualization of the way in which it matches the query. We believe this to be an important prerequisite for accessing annotated corpora, especially for non-expert users.

Search queries in ICARUS can be constructed either in a graphical or a text-based manner. Building queries graphically removes the overhead of learning a specialized query language and thus makes the tool more accessible for a wider audience. ICARUS provides a very intuitive way of breaking down the search results in terms of frequency statistics (such as the distribution of part-of-speech on one child of a particular verb against the lemma of another child). The dimensions for the frequency break-down are simply specified by using grouping operators in the query. The frequency tables are filled and updated in real time as the search proceeds through the corpus – allowing for a quick detection of misassumptions in the query.

ICARUS uses a plugin-based architecture that permits the user to write his own plugins and integrate them into the system. For example, it comes with a plugin that interfaces with an external parser that can be used to parse a sentence from within the user interface. The constraints for the query can then be copy-pasted from the resulting parse visualization. This facilitates example-based querying, which is particularly helpful for inexperienced users – they do not have to recall details of the annotation conventions outside of their focus of interests but can go by what the parser provides.[2]

ICARUS is written entirely in Java and runs out of the box without requiring any installation of the tool itself or additional libraries. This makes it platform independent and the only requirement is that a Java Runtime Environment (JRE) is installed on the host system. It is open-source and freely available for download.[3]

As parsers and other Natural Language Processing (NLP) tools are starting to find their way into other sciences such as (digital) humanities or social sciences, it gets increasingly important to provide intuitive visualization tools that integrate seamlessly with existing NLP tools and are easy to use also for non-linguists. ICARUS interfaces readily with NLP tools provided as web services by CLARIN-D,[4] the German incarnation of the European Infrastructure initiative CLARIN.

[1] Interactive platform for Corpus Analysis and Research tools, University of Stuttgart

[2] This is of course only practical with rather reliable automatic parsers, but in our experience, the state-of-the-art quality is sufficient.

[3] www.ims.uni-stuttgart.de/forschung/ressourcen/werkzeuge/icarus.en.html

[4] http://de.clarin.eu

The remainder of this paper is structured as follows: In Section 2 we elaborate on the motivation for the tool and discuss related work. Section 3 presents a running example of how to build queries and how results are visualized. In Section 4 we outline the details of the architecture. Section 5 discusses ongoing work, and Section 6 concludes.

2 Background

Linguistically annotated corpora are among the most important sources of knowledge for empirical linguistics as well as computational modeling of natural language. Moreover, for most users the only way to develop a systematic understanding of the phenomena in the annotations is through a process of continuous exploration, which requires suitable and intuitive tools.

As automatic analysis tools such as syntactic parsers have reached a high quality standard, exploration of large collections of auto-parsed corpus material becomes more and more common. Of course, the querying problem is the same no matter whether some target annotation was added manually, as in a treebank, or automatically. Yet, the strategy changes, as the user will try to make sure he catches systematic parsing errors and develops an understanding of how the results he is dealing with come about. While there is no guaranteed method for avoiding erroneous matches, we believe that an easy-to-use transparent querying mechanism that allows the user to look at the same or similar results from various angles is the best possible basis for an informed usage: frequency tables breaking down the corpus distributions in different dimensions are a good high-level hint, and the actual corpus instances should be only one or two mouse clicks away, presented with a concise visualization of the respective instantiation of the query constraints.

Syntactic annotations are quite difficult to query if one is interested in specific constructions that are not directly encoded in the annotation labels (which is the case for most interesting phenomena). Several tools have been developed to enable researchers to do this. However, many of these tools are designed for constituent trees only.

Dependency syntax has become popular as a framework for treebanking because it lends itself naturally to the representation of free word order phenomena and was thus adopted in the creation of treebanks for many languages that have less strict word order, such as the Prague Dependency Treebank for Czech (Hajič et al., 2000) or SynTagRus for Russian (Boguslavsky et al., 2000).

A simple tool for visualization of dependency trees is *What's wrong with my NLP?* (Riedel, 2008). Its querying functionality is however limited to simple string-searching on surface forms. A somewhat more advanced tool is *MaltEval* (Nilsson and Nivre, 2008), which offers a number of predefined search patterns ranging from part-of-speech tag to branching degree.

On the other hand, powerful tools such as *PML-TQ* (Pajas and Štěpánek, 2009) or *INESS* (Meurer, 2012) offer expressive query languages and can facilitate cross-layer queries (e.g., involving both syntactic and semantic structures). They also accommodate both constituent and dependency structures.

In terms of complexity in usage and expressivity, we believe ICARUS constitutes a middle way between highly expressive and very simple visualization tools. It is easy to use, requires no installation, while still having rich query and visualization capabilities. ICARUS is similar to PML-TQ in that it also allows the user to create queries graphically. It is also similar to the search tool *GrETEL* (Augustinus et al., 2012) as it interfaces with a parser, allowing the user to create queries starting from an automatic parse. Thus, queries can be created without any prior knowledge of the treebank annotation scheme.

As for searching constituent treebanks, there is a plethora of existing search tools, such as *TGrep2* (Rohde, 2001), *TigerSearch* (Lezius, 2002), *MonaSearch* (Maryns, 2009), and *Fangorn* (Ghodke and Bird, 2012), among others. They implement different query languages with varying efficiency and expressiveness.

3 Introductory Example

Before going into the technical details, we show an example of what you can do with ICARUS. Assume that a user is interested in passive constructions in English, but does not know exactly how this is annotated in a treebank. As a first step, he can use a provided plugin that interfaces with a tool chain[5] to parse a sentence that contains a passive construction (thus adopting the example-based querying approach laid out in the introduc-

[5]using mate-tools by Bohnet (2010); available at http://code.google.com/p/mate-tools

tion). Figure 1 shows the parser interface. In the lower field, the user entered the sentence. The other two fields show the output of the parser, once as a graph and once as a feature value description.

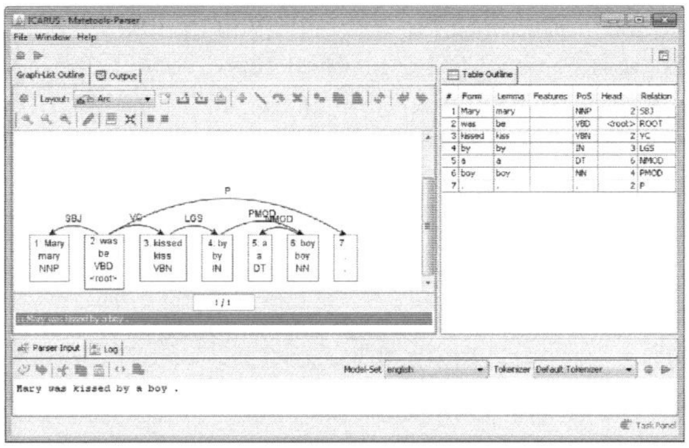

Figure 1: Parsing the sentence *"Mary was kissed by a boy."* with a predefined tool chain.

In the second step, the user can then mark parts of the output graph by selecting some nodes and edges, and have ICARUS construct a query structure from it, following the drag-and-drop scheme users are familiar with from typical office software. The automatically built query can be manually adjusted by the user (relaxing constraints) and then be used to search for similar structures in a treebank. The parsing step can of course be skipped altogether, and a query can be constructed by hand right away. Figure 2 shows the query builder, where the user can define or edit search graphs graphically in the main window, or enter them as a query string in the lower window.

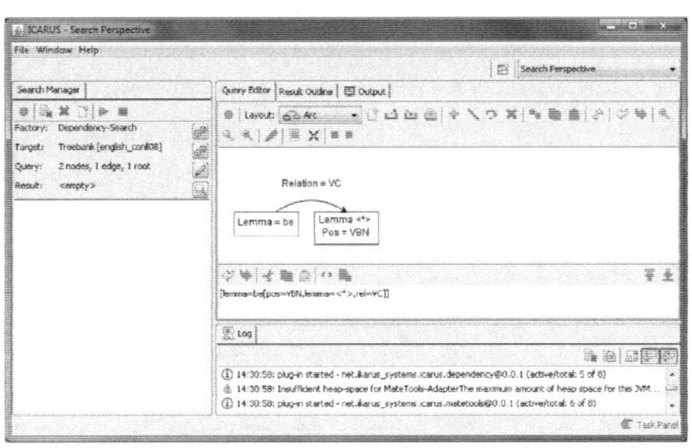

Figure 2: Query builder for constructing queries.

For the example, Figure 3 shows the query as it is automatically constructed by ICARUS from the partial parse tree (3a), and what it might look like after the user has changed it (3b). The modified query matches passive constructions in English, as annotated in the CoNLL 2008 Shared Task data set (Surdeanu et al., 2008), which we use here.

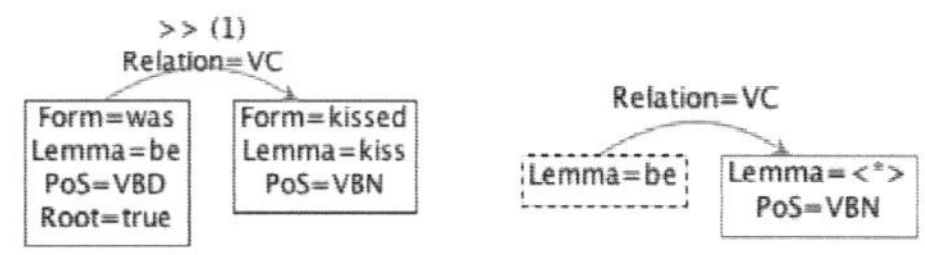

(a) automatically extracted (b) manually edited

Figure 3: Search graphs for finding passive constructions. (a) was constructed automatically from the parsed sentence, (b) is a more general version.

The search returns 6,386 matches. Note that the query (Figure 3b) contains a <*>-expression. This grouping operator groups the results according to the specified dimension, in this case by the lemma of the passivized verb. Figure 4 shows the result view. On the left, a list of lemmas is presented, sorted by frequency. Clicking on the lemma displays the list of matches containing that particular lemma on the right side. The matching sentences can then be browsed, with the active sentence also being shown as a tree. Note that the instantiation of the query constraints is highlighted in the tree display.

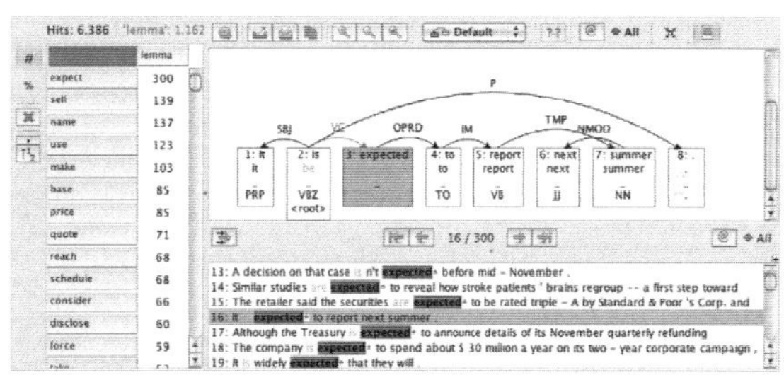

Figure 4: Passive constructions in the treebank grouped by lemma and sorted by frequency.

The query could be further refined to restrict it to passives with an overt logical subject, using a more complex search graph for the *by*-phrase and a second instance of the grouping operator. The results will then also be grouped by the lemma of the logical subject, and are therefore presented as a two-dimensional table. Figure 5 shows the new query and the resulting view. The user is presented with a frequency table, where each cell contains the number of hits for this particular combination of verb lemma and logical subject. Clicking on the cell opens up a view similar to the right part of Figure 4 where the user can then again browse the actual trees.

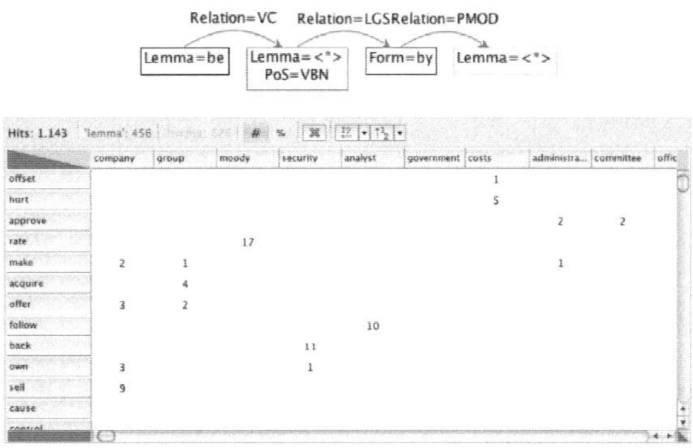

Figure 5: Search graph and result view for passive constructions with overt logical subjects, grouped by lemma of the verb and the lemma of the logical subject.

Finally, we can add a third grouping operator. Figure 6 shows a further refined query for passives with an overt logical subject and an object. In the results, the user is presented with a list of values for the first grouping operator to the left. Clicking on one item in that list opens up a table on the right presenting the other two dimensions of the query.

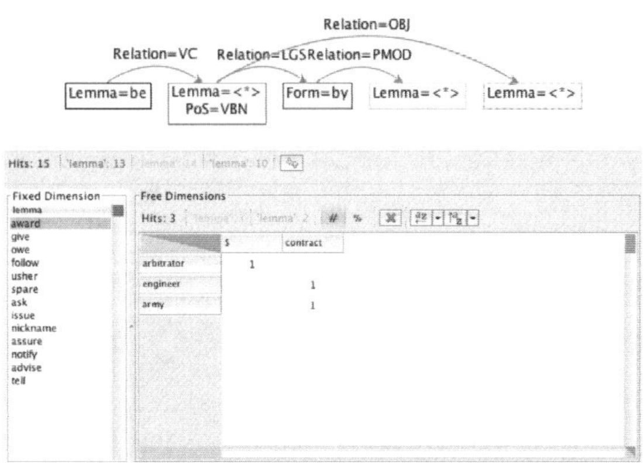

Figure 6: Search graph and result view for passive constructions with an overt logical subject and an object, grouped by lemma of the verb, the logical subject, and the object.

This example demonstrates a typical use case for a user that is interested in certain linguistic constructions in his corpus. Creating the search graph and interpreting the results does not require any specialized knowledge other than familiarity with the annotation of the corpus being searched. It especially does not require any programming skills, and the possibility to graphically build a query obviates the need to learn a specialized query language.

4 Architecture

This section goes into more details about the inner workings of ICARUS. A main component is the search engine, which enables the user to quickly search treebanks for whatever he is interested in. A second important feature of ICARUS is the plugin-based architecture, which allows for the definition of custom extensions. Currently, ICARUS can read the commonly used CoNLL dependency formats, and it is easy to write extensions in order to add additional formats.

4.1 Search Engine and Query Builder

ICARUS has a tree-based search engine for treebanks, and includes a graphical query builder. Structure and appearance of search graphs are similar to the design used for displaying dependency trees (cf. Figure 1), which is realized with the open-source library JGraph.[6] Queries and/or their results can be saved to disk and later reloaded for further processing.

Defining a query graphically basically amounts to drawing a partial graph structure that defines the type of structure that the user is interested in. In practice, this is done by creating nodes in the query builder and connecting them by edges. The nodes correspond to words in the dependency trees of the treebank. Several features like word identity, lemma, part of speech, etc. can be specified for each node in the search graph in order to restrict the query. Dominance and precedence constraints over a set of nodes can be defined by simply linking nodes with the appropriate edge type. Edges can be further specified for relation type, distance, direction, projectivity, and transitivity. A simple example is shown in Figures 2 and 3. The search engine supports regular expressions for all string-properties (form, lemma, part of speech, relation). It also supports negation of (existence of) nodes and edges, and their properties.

As an alternative to the search graph, the user can also specify the query in a text-based format by constructing a comma separated collection of constraints in the form of *key=value* pairs for a single node contained within square brackets. Hierarchical structures are expressed by nesting their textual representation. Figure 7 shows the text-based form of the three queries used in the examples in Section 3.

[6]http://www.jgraph.com/

```
Query 1:  [lemma=be[pos=VBN,lemma=<*>,rel=VC]]
Query 2:  [lemma=be[pos=VBN,lemma=<*>,rel=VC[form=by,rel=LGS[lemma=<*>,rel=PMOD]]]]
Query 3:  [lemma=be[pos=VBN,lemma=<*>,rel=VC[form=by,rel=LGS[lemma=<*>,rel=PMOD]]
                                         [lemma=<*>,rel=OBJ]]]
```

Figure 7: Text representation of the three queries used in the example in Section 3.

A central feature of the query language is the **grouping operator** (<*>), which will match any value and cause the search engine to group result entries by the actual instance of the property declared to be grouped. The results of the search will then be visualized as a list of instances together with their respective frequencies. Results can be sorted alphabetically or by frequency (absolute or relative counts) . Depending on the number of grouping operators used (up to a maximum of three) the result is structured as a list of frequencies (cf. Figure 4), a table of frequencies for pairs of instances (cf. Figure 5), or a list where each item then opens up a table of frequency results (cf. Figure 6). In the search graph and the result view, different colors are used to distinguish between different grouping operators.

The ICARUS search engine offers three different search modes:

Sentence-based. Sentence based search stops at the first successful hit in a sentence and returns every sentence on a list of results at most once.

Exhaustive sentence-based. The exhaustive sentence-based search mode extends the sentence based search by the possibility of processing multiple hits within a single sentence. Every sentence with at least one hit is returned exactly once. In the result view, the user can then browse the different hits found in one sentence.

Hit-based. Every successful hit is returned separately on the corresponding list of results.

When a query is issued, the search results are displayed on the fly as the search engine is processing the treebank. The sentences can be rendered in one of two ways: either as a tree, where nodes are arranged vertically by depth in the tree, or horizontally with all the nodes arranged side-by-side. If a tree does not fit on the screen, part of it is automatically collapsed but can be expanded again by the user.

4.2 Extensibility

ICARUS relies on the Java Plugin Framework,[7] which provides a powerful XML-based framework for defining plugins similarly to the engine used by the popular Eclipse IDE project. The **plugin-based architecture** makes it possible for anybody to write extensions to ICARUS that are specialized for a particular task. The parser integration of mate-tools demonstrated in Section 3 is an example for such an extension.

The plugin system facilitates custom extensions that make it possible to intercept certain stages of an ongoing search process and interact with it. This makes it possible for external tools to preprocess search data and apply additional annotations and/or filtering, or even make use of existing indices by using search constraints to limit the amount of data passed to the search engine. With this general setup, it is for example possible to easily extend ICARUS to work with constituent trees.

ICARUS comes with a dedicated plugin that enables access to web services provided by CLARIN-D. The project aims to provide tools and services for language-centered research in the humanities and social sciences. In contrast to the integration of, e.g., mate-tools, where the tool chain is executed locally, the user can define a tool chain by chaining several web services (e.g., lemmatizers, part-of-speech taggers etc.) together and apply them to his own data. To do this, ICARUS is able to read and write the TCF exchange format (Heid et al., 2010) that is used by CLARIN-D web services. The output can then be inspected and searched using ICARUS. As new NLP tools are added as CLARIN-D web services they can be immediately employed by ICARUS.

5 Upcoming Extensions

An upcoming release includes the following extensions:

- Currently, treebanks are assumed to fit into the executing computer's main memory. The new implementation will support asynchronous loading of data, with notifications passed to the query engine or a plugin when required data is available. Treebanks with millions of entries can then be loaded in less

[7] http://jpf.sourceforge.net/

memory consuming chunks, thus keeping the system responsive when access is requested.

- The search engine is being extended with an operator that allows disjunctions of queries. This will enable the user to aggregate frequency output over multiple queries.

6 Conclusion

We have presented ICARUS, a versatile and user-friendly search and visualization tool for dependency trees. It is aimed not only at (computational) linguists, but also at people from other disciplines, e.g., the humanities or social sciences, who work with language data. It lets the user create queries graphically and returns results (1) quantitatively by means of frequency lists and tables as well as (2) qualitatively by connecting the statistics to the matching sentences and allowing the user to browse them graphically. Its plugin-based architecture enables it to interface for example with external processing pipelines, which lets the user apply processing tools directly from the user interface.

In the future, specialized plugins are planned to work with different linguistic annotations, e.g. cross-sentence annotations as used to annotate coreference chains. Additionally, a plugin is intended that interfaces the search engine with a database.

Acknowledgments

This work was funded by the Deutsche Forschungsgemeinschaft (DFG) via the SFB 732 "Incremental Specification in Context", project D8, and by the Bundesministerium für Bildung und Forschung (BMBF) via project No. 01UG1120F, CLARIN-D center Stuttgart. The authors are also indebted to André Blessing and Heike Zinsmeister for reading an earlier draft of this paper.

References

Liesbeth Augustinus, Vincent Vandeghinste, and Frank Van Eynde. 2012. Example-based Treebank Querying. In *Proceedings of the Eight International Conference on Language Resources and Evaluation (LREC'12)*, Istanbul, Turkey. ELRA.

Igor Boguslavsky, Svetlana Grigorieva, Nikolai Grigoriev, Leonid Kreidlin, and Nadezhda Frid. 2000. Dependency Treebank for Russian: Concept, Tools, Types of Information. In *COLING 2000*, pages 987–991, Saarbrücken, Germany.

Bernd Bohnet. 2010. Top Accuracy and Fast Dependency Parsing is not a Contradiction. In *COLING 2010*, pages 89–97, Beijing, China.

Sumukh Ghodke and Steven Bird. 2012. Fangorn: A System for Querying very large Treebanks. In *COLING 2012: Demonstration Papers*, pages 175–182, Mumbai, India.

Jan Hajič, Alena Böhmová, Eva Hajičová, and Barbora Vidová-Hladká. 2000. The Prague Dependency Treebank: A Three-Level Annotation Scenario. In *Treebanks: Building and Using Parsed Corpora*, pages 103–127. Amsterdam:Kluwer.

Ulrich Heid, Helmut Schmid, Kerstin Eckart, and Erhard Hinrichs. 2010. A Corpus Representation Format for Linguistic Web Services: The D-SPIN Text Corpus Format and its Relationship with ISO Standards. In *Proceedings of the Seventh International Conference on Language Resources and Evaluation (LREC'10)*, Valletta, Malta. ELRA.

Wolfgang Lezius. 2002. *Ein Suchwerkzeug für syntaktisch annotierte Textkorpora*. Ph.D. thesis, IMS, University of Stuttgart.

Hendrik Maryns. 2009. MonaSearch – A Tool for Querying Linguistic Treebanks. In *Proceedings of TLT 2009*, Groningen.

Paul Meurer. 2012. INESS-Search: A Search System for LFG (and Other) Treebanks. In Miriam Butt and Tracy Holloway King, editors, *Proceedings of the LFG2012 Conference*. CSLI Publications.

Jens Nilsson and Joakim Nivre. 2008. MaltEval: an Evaluation and Visualization Tool for Dependency Parsing. In *Proceedings of the Sixth International Conference on Language Resources and Evaluation (LREC'08)*, Marrakech, Morocco. ELRA.

Petr Pajas and Jan Štěpánek. 2009. System for Querying Syntactically Annotated Corpora. In *Proceedings of the ACL-IJCNLP 2009 Software Demonstrations*, pages 33–36, Suntec, Singapore. Association for Computational Linguistics.

Sebastian Riedel. 2008. What's Wrong With My NLP? `http://code.google.com/p/whatswrong/`.

Douglas L.T. Rohde. 2001. TGrep2 the next-generation search engine for parse trees. `http://tedlab.mit.edu/~dr/Tgrep2/`.

Mihai Surdeanu, Richard Johansson, Adam Meyers, Lluís Màrquez, and Joakim Nivre. 2008. The CoNLL 2008 Shared Task on Joint Parsing of Syntactic and Semantic Dependencies. In *CoNLL 2008*, pages 159–177, Manchester, England.

Meet EDGAR, a tutoring agent at MONSERRATE

Pedro Fialho, Luísa Coheur, Sérgio Curto, Pedro Cláudio
Ângela Costa, Alberto Abad, Hugo Meinedo and Isabel Trancoso
Spoken Language Systems Lab (L2F), INESC-ID
Rua Alves Redol 9
1000-029 Lisbon, Portugal
name.surname@l2f.inesc-id.pt

Abstract

In this paper we describe a platform for embodied conversational agents with tutoring goals, which takes as input written and spoken questions and outputs answers in both forms. The platform is developed within a game environment, and currently allows speech recognition and synthesis in Portuguese, English and Spanish. In this paper we focus on its understanding component that supports in-domain interactions, and also small talk. Most in-domain interactions are answered using different similarity metrics, which compare the perceived utterances with questions/sentences in the agent's knowledge base; small-talk capabilities are mainly due to AIML, a language largely used by the chatbots' community. In this paper we also introduce EDGAR, the butler of MONSERRATE, which was developed in the aforementioned platform, and that answers tourists' questions about MONSERRATE.

1 Introduction

Several initiatives have been taking place in the last years, targeting the concept of Edutainment, that is, education through entertainment. Following this strategy, virtual characters have animated several museums all over the world: the 3D animated Hans Christian Andersen is capable of establishing multimodal conversations about the writer's life and tales (Bernsen and Dybkjr, 2005), Max is a virtual character employed as guide in the Heinz Nixdorf Museums Forum (Pfeiffer et al., 2011), and Sergeant Blackwell, installed in the Cooper-Hewitt National Design Museum in New York, is used by the U.S. Army Recruiting Command as a hi-tech attraction and information source (Robinson et al., 2008). DuARTE Digital (Mendes et al., 2009) and EDGAR are also examples of virtual characters for the Portuguese language with the same edutainment goal: DuARTE Digital answers questions about Custódia de Belém, a famous work of the Portuguese jewelry; EDGAR is a virtual butler that answers questions about MONSERRATE (Figure 1).

Figure 1: EDGAR at MONSERRATE.

Considering the previous mentioned agents, they all cover a specific domain of knowledge (although a general Question/Answering system was integrated in Max (Waltinger et al., 2011)). However, as expected, people tend also to make small talk when interacting with these agents. Therefore, it is important that these systems properly deal with it. Several strategies are envisaged to this end and EDGAR is of no exception. In this paper, we describe the platform behind EDGAR, which we developed aiming at the fast insertion of in-domain knowledge, and to deal with small talk. This platform is currently in the process of being industrially applied by a company known for its expertise in building and deploying kiosks. We will provide the hardware and software required to demonstrate EDGAR, both on a computer and on a tablet.

This paper is organized as follows: in Section 2 we present EDGAR's development platform

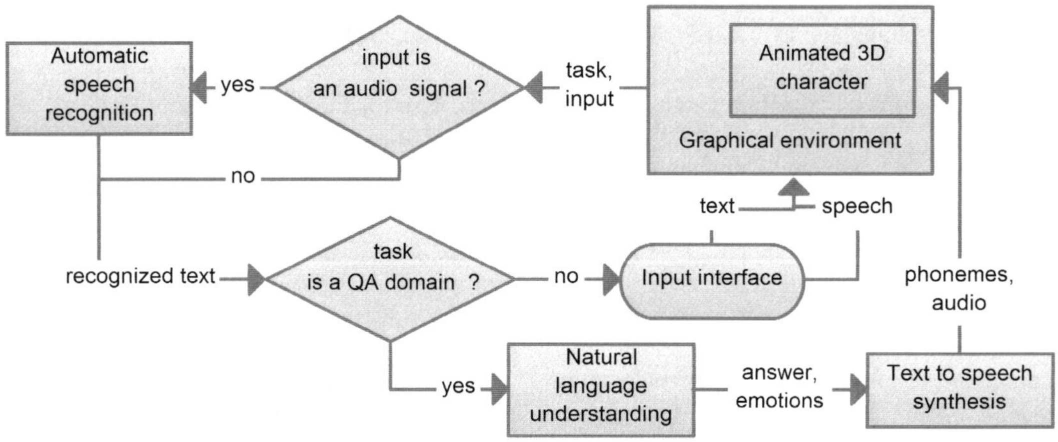

Figure 2: EDGAR architecture

and describe typical interactions, in Section 3 we show how we move from in-domain interactions to small talk, and in Section 4 we present an analysis on collected logs and their initial evaluation results. Finally, in Section 5 we present some conclusions and point to future work.

2 The Embodied Conversational Agent platform

2.1 Architecture overview

The architecture of the platform, generally designed for the development of Embodied Conversational Agents (ECAs) (such as EDGAR), is shown in Figure 2. In this platform, several modules intercommunicate by means of well defined protocols, thus leveraging the capabilities of independent modules focused on specific tasks, such as speech recognition or 3D rendering/animation. This independence allows us to use subsets of this platform modules in scenarios with different requirements (for instance, we can record characters uttering a text).

Design and deployment of the front end of EDGAR is performed in a game engine, which has enabled the use of computer graphics technologies and high quality assets, as seen in the video game industry.

2.2 Multimodal components

The game environment, where all the interaction with EDGAR takes place, is developed in the Unity[1] platform, being composed of one highly detailed character, made and animated by Rocketbox studios[2], a virtual keyboard and a push-while-talking button.

In this platform, Automatic Speech Recognition (ASR) is performed by AUDIMUS (Meinedo et al., 2003) for all languages, using generic acoustic and language models, recently compiled from broadcast news data (Meinedo et al., 2010). Language models were interpolated with all the domain questions defined in the Natural Language Understanding (NLU) framework (see below), while ASR includes features such as speech/non-speech (SNS) detection and automatic gain control (AGC). Speech captured in a public space raises several ASR robustness issues, such as loudness variability of spoken utterances, which is particularly bound to happen in a museological environment (such as MONSERRATE) where silence is usually incited. Thus, we have added a bounded amplication to the captured signal, despite the AGC mechanism, ensuring that too silent sounds are not discarded by the SNS mechanism.

Upon a spoken input, AUDIMUS translates it into a sentence, with a confidence value. An empty recognition result, or one with low confidence, triggers a control tag ("_REPEAT_") to the NLU module, which results in a request for the user to repeat what was said. The answer returned by the NLU module is synthesized in a language dependent Text To Speech (TTS) system, with DIXI (Paulo et al., 2008) being used for Portuguese, while a recent version of FESTIVAL (Zen et al., 2009) covers both English and Spanish. The

[1] http://unity3d.com/

[2] http://www.rocketbox-libraries.com/

synthesized audio is played while the corresponding phonemes are mapped into visemes, represented as skeletal animations, being synchronized according to phoneme durations, available in all the employed TTS engines.

Emotions are declared in the knowledge sources of the agent. As shown in Figure 3, they are coordinated with viseme animations.

Figure 3: The EDGAR character in a joyful state.

2.3 Interacting with EDGAR

In a typical interaction, the user enters a question with a virtual keyboard or says it to the microphone while pressing a button (Figure 4), in the language chosen in the interface (as previously said, Portuguese, English or Spanish).

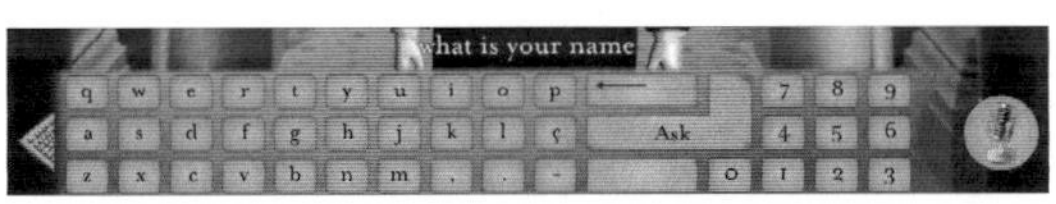

Figure 4: A question written in the EDGAR interface.

Then, the ASR will transcribe it and the NLU module will process it. Afterwards, the answer, chosen by the NLU module, is heard through the speakers, due to the TTS, and sequentially written in a talk bubble, according to the produced speech. The answer is accompanied with visemes, represented by movements of the character's mouth/lips, and by facial emotions as marked in the answers of the NLU knowledge base. A demo of EDGAR, only for English interactions, can be tested in `https://edgar.l2f.inesc-id.pt/m3/edgar.php`.

3 The natural language understanding component

3.1 In-domain knowledge sources

The in-domain knowledge sources of the agent are XML files, hand-crafted by domain experts. This XML files have multilingual pairs constituted by different paraphrases of the same question and possible answers. The main reason to follow this approach (and contrary to other works where grammars are used), is to ease the process of creating/enriching the knowledge sources of the agent being developed, which is typically done by non experts in linguistics or computer science. Thus, we opted for following a similar approach of the work described, for instance, in (Leuski et al., 2006), where the agents knowledge sources are easy to create and maintain. An example of a questions/answers pair is:

```
<questions>
 <q en="How is everything?"
      es="Todo bien?">
       Tudo bem?</q>
</questions>
<answers>
  <a en="I am ok, thank you."
  es="Estoy bien, gracias."
  emotion="smile_02">
  Estou bem, obrigado.</a>
</answers>
```

As it can been see from this example, emotions are defined in these files, associated to each question/answer pair (emotion="smile" in the example, one of the possible smile emotions).

These knowledge sources can be (automatically) extended with "synonyms". We call them "synonyms", because they do not necessarily fit in the usual definition of synonyms. Here we follow a broader approach to this concept and if two words, within the context of a sentence from the knowledge source, will lead to the same answer, then we consider them to be "synonyms". For instance "palace" or "castle" are not synonyms. However, people tend to refer to MONSERRATE in both forms. Thus, we consider them to be "synonyms" and if one of these is used in the original knowledge sources, the other is used to expand them. It should be clear that we will generate many incorrect questions with this procedure, but empirical tests (out of the scope of this paper) show that these questions do not hurt the system performance. Moreover, they are useful for ASR language model interpolation, which is based on N-grams.

3.2 Out-of-domain knowledge sources

The same format of the previously described knowledge sources can be used to represent out-of-domain knowledge. Here, we extensively used the "synonyms" approach. For instance, words *wife* and *girlfriend* are considered to be "synonyms" as all the personal questions with these words should be answered with the same sentence: *I do not want to talk about my private life.*

Nevertheless, and taking into consideration the work around small talk developed by the chatbots community (Klwer, 2011), we decided to use the most popular language to build chatbots: the "Artificial Intelligence Markup Language", widely known as AIML, a derivative of XML. With AIML, knowledge is coded as a set of rules that will match the user input, associated with templates, the generators of the output. A detailed description of AIML syntax can be found in `http://www.alicebot.org/aiml.html`. In what respects AIML interpreters, we opted to use Program D (java), which we integrated in our platform. Currently, we use AIML to deal with slang and to answer questions that have to do with cinema and compliments.

As a curiosity, we should explain that we deal with slang when input came from the keyboard, and not when it is speech, as the language models are not trained with this specific lexicon. The reason we do that is because if the language models were trained with slang, it would be possible to erroneously detect it in utterances and then answer them accordingly, which could be extremely unpleasant. Therefore, EDGAR only deals with slang when the input is the keyboard.

The current knowledge sources have 152 question/answer pairs, corresponding to 763 questions and 206 answers. For Portuguese, English and Spanish the use of 226, 219 and 53 synonym relations, led to the generation of 22 194, 16 378 and 1 716 new questions, respectively.

3.3 Finding the appropriate answer

The NLU module is responsible for the answer selection process. It has three main components.

The first one, STRATEGIES, is responsible to choose an appropriate answer to the received interaction. Several strategies are implemented, including the ones based on string matching, string distances (as for instance, Levenshtein, Jaccard and Dice), N-gram Overlap and support vector machines (seeing the answer selection as a classification problem). Currently, best results are attained using a combination of Jaccard and bigram Overlap measures and word weight through the use of tf-idf statistic. In this case, Jaccard takes into account how many words are shared between the user's interaction and the knowledge source entry, bigram Overlap gives preference to the shared sequences of words and tf-idf contributes to the results attained by previous measures, by given weight to unfrequent words, which should have more weight on the decision process (for example, the word MONSERRATE occurs in the majority of the questions in the corpus, so it is not very informative and should not have the same weight as, for instance, the word *architect* or *owner*).

The second component, PLUGINS, deals with two different situations. First, it accesses Program D when interactions are not answered by the STRATEGIES component. That is, when the technique used by STRATEGIES returns a value that is lower than a threshold (dependent of the used technique), the PLUGIN component runs Program D in order to try to find an answer to the posed question. Secondly, when the ASR has no confidence of the attained transcription (and returns the "_REPEAT_" tag) or Program D is not able to find an answer, the PLUGINS component does the following (with the goal of taking the user again to the agent topic of expertise):

- In the first time that this occurs, a sentence such as *Sorry, I did not understand you.* is chosen as the answer to be returned.
- The second time this occurs, EDGAR asks the user *I did not understand you again. Why don't you ask me X?*, being X generated in run time and being a question from a subset of the questions from the knowledge sources. Obviously, only in-domain (not expanded) questions are considered for replacing X.
- The third time there is a misunderstanding, EDGAR says *We are not understanding each other, let me talk about* MONSERRATE. And it randomly choses some answer to present to the user.

The third component is the HISTORY-TRACKER, which handles the agent knowledge about previous interactions (kept until a default time without interactions is reached).

4 Preliminary evaluation

Edgar is more a domain-specific Question Answering (QA) than a task-oriented dialogue system. Therefore, we evaluated it with the metrics typically used in QA. The mapping of the different situations in true/false positives/negatives is explained in the following.

We have manually transcribed 1086 spoken utterances (in Portuguese), which were then labeled with the following tags, some depending on the answer given by EDGAR:

- 0: in-domain question incorrectly answered, although there was information in the knowledge sources (excluding Program D) to answer it;
- 1: out-of-domain question, incorrectly answered;
- 2: question correctly answered by Program D;
- 3: question correctly answered by using knowledge sources (excluding Program D);
- 4: in-domain question, incorrectly answered. There is no information in the knowledge source to answer it, but it should be;
- 5: multiple questions, partially answered;
- 6: multiple questions, unanswered;
- 7: question with implicit information (there, him, etc.), unanswered;
- 8: question which is not "ipsis verbis" in the knowledge source, but has a paraphrase there and was not correctly answered;
- 9: question with a single word (*garden*, *palace*), unanswered;
- 10: question that we do not want the system to answer (some were answered, some were not).

The previous tags were mapped into:

- true positives: questions marked with 2, 3 and 5;
- true negatives: questions marked with 0 and 10 (the ones that were not answered by the system);
- false positives: questions marked with 0 and 10 (the ones that were answered by the system);
- false negatives: questions marked with 4, 6, 7, 8 and 9.

Then, two experiments were conducted: in the first, the NLU module was applied to the manual transcriptions; in the second, directly to the output of the ASR. Table 1 shows the results.

NLU input = manual transcriptions		
Precision	Recall	F-measure
0.92	0.60	0.72
acNLU input = ASR		
Precision	Recall	F-measure
0.71	0.32	0.45

Table 1: NLU results

The ASR Word Error Rate (WER) is of 70%. However, we detect some problems in the way we were collecting the audio, and in more recent evaluations (by using 363 recent logs where previous problems were corrected), that error decreased to a WER of 52%, including speech from 111 children, 21 non native Portuguese speakers (thus, with a different pronunciation), 23 individuals not talking in Portuguese and 27 interactions where multiple speakers overlap. Here, we should refer the work presented in (Traum et al., 2012), where an evaluation of two virtual guides in a museum is presented. They also had to deal with speakers from different ages and with question off-topic, and report a ASR with 57% WER (however they majority of their user are children: 76%).

We are currently preparing a new corpus for evaluating the NLU module, however, the following results remain: in the best scenario, if transcription is perfect, the NLU module behaves as indicated in Table 1 (manual transcriptions).

5 Conclusions and Future Work

We have described a platform for developing ECAs with tutoring goals, that takes both speech and text as input and output, and introduced EDGAR, the butler of MONSERRATE, which was developed in that platform. Special attention was given to EDGAR's NLU module, which couples techniques that try to find distances between the user input and sentences in the existing knowledge sources, with a framework imported from the chatbots community (AIML plus Program D). EDGAR has been tested with real users for the last year and we are currently performing a detailed evaluation of it. There is much work to be done, including to be able to deal with language varieties, which is an important source of recognition errors. Moreover, the capacity of dealing with out-of-domain questions is still a hot research topic and one of our priorities in the near future. We have testified that people are delighted when EDGAR answers out-of-domain questions (*Do you like soccer?/I rather have a tea and read a good criminal book*) and we cannot forget that entertainment is also one of this Embodied Conversational Agent (ECA)'s goal.

Acknowledgments

This work was supported by national funds through FCT – Fundação para a Ciência e a Tecnologia, under project PEst-OE/EEI/LA0021/2013. Pedro Fialho, Sérgio Curto and Pedro Cláudio scholarships were supported under project FALACOMIGO (ProjectoVII em co-promoção, QREN n 13449).

References

N. O. Bernsen and L. Dybkjr. 2005. Meet hans christian andersen. In *In Proceedings of Sixth SIGdial Workshop on Discourse and Dialogue*, pages 237–241.

Tina Klwer. 2011. "i like your shirt" – dialogue acts for enabling social talk in conversational agents. In *Proceedings of the 11th International Conference on Intelligent Virtual Agents. International Conference on Intelligent Virtual Agents (IVA), 11th, September 17-19, Reykjavik, Iceland*. Springer.

Anton Leuski, Ronakkumar Patel, David Traum, and Brandon Kennedy. 2006. Building effective question answering characters. In *7th SIGdial Workshop on Discourse and Dialogue*, Sydney, Australia.

Hugo Meinedo, Diamantino Caseiro, João Neto, and Isabel Trancoso. 2003. Audimus.media: a broadcast news speech recognition system for the european portuguese language. In *Proceedings of the 6th international conference on Computational processing of the Portuguese language*, PROPOR'03, pages 9–17, Berlin, Heidelberg. Springer-Verlag.

H. Meinedo, A. Abad, T. Pellegrini, I. Trancoso, and J. P. Neto. 2010. The l2f broadcast news speech recognition system. In *Proceedings of Fala2010*, Vigo, Spain.

Ana Cristina Mendes, Rui Prada, and Luísa Coheur. 2009. Adapting a virtual agent to users' vocabulary and needs. In *Proceedings of the 9th International Conference on Intelligent Virtual Agents*, IVA '09, pages 529–530, Berlin, Heidelberg. Springer-Verlag.

Sérgio Paulo, Luís C. Oliveira, Carlos Mendes, Luís Figueira, Renato Cassaca, Céu Viana, and Helena Moniz. 2008. Dixi — a generic text-to-speech system for european portuguese. In *Proceedings of the 8th international conference on Computational Processing of the Portuguese Language*, PROPOR '08, pages 91–100, Berlin, Heidelberg. Springer-Verlag.

Thies Pfeiffer, Christian Liguda, Ipke Wachsmuth, and Stefan Stein. 2011. Living with a virtual agent: Seven years with an embodied conversational agent at the heinz nixdorf museumsforum. In *Proceedings of the International Conference Re-Thinking Technology in Museums 2011 - Emerging Experiences*, pages 121 – 131. thinkk creative & the University of Limerick.

Susan Robinson, David Traum, Midhun Ittycheriah, and Joe Henderer. 2008. What would you ask a conversational agent? observations of human-agent dialogues in a museum setting. In *International Conference on Language Resources and Evaluation (LREC)*, Marrakech, Morocco.

David Traum, Priti Aggarwal, Ron Artstein, Susan Foutz, Jillian Gerten, Athanasios Katsamanis, Anton Leuski, Dan Noren, and William Swartout. 2012. Ada and grace: Direct interaction with museum visitors. In *The 12th International Conference on Intelligent Virtual Agents (IVA)*, Santa Cruz, CA, September.

Ulli Waltinger, Alexa Breuing, and Ipke Wachsmuth. 2011. Interfacing virtual agents with collaborative knowledge: Open domain question answering using wikipedia-based topic models. In *IJCAI*, pages 1896–1902.

Heiga Zen, Keiichiro Oura, Takashi Nose, Junichi Yamagishi, Shinji Sako, Tomoki Toda, Takashi Masuko, Alan W. Black, and Keiichi Tokuda. 2009. Recent development of the HMM-based speech synthesis system (HTS). In *Proc. 2009 Asia-Pacific Signal and Information Processing Association (APSIPA)*, Sapporo, Japan, October.

PAL: A Chatterbot System for Answering Domain-specific Questions

Yuanchao Liu[1] **Ming Liu**[1] **Xiaolong Wang**[1] **Limin Wang**[2] **Jingjing Li**[1]

[1] School of Computer Science and Technology, Harbin Institute of Technology, Harbin, China
[2.] School of public health, Harbin Medical University, Harbin, China
{lyc,mliu,wangxl,jjl}@insun.hit.edu.cn, wanglimin2008@163.com

Abstract

In this paper, we propose PAL, a prototype chatterbot for answering non-obstructive psychological domain-specific questions. This system focuses on providing primary suggestions or helping people relieve pressure by extracting knowledge from online forums, based on which the chatterbot system is constructed. The strategies used by PAL, including semantic-extension-based question matching, solution management with personal information consideration, and XML-based knowledge pattern construction, are described and discussed. We also conduct a primary test for the feasibility of our system.

1 Introduction

A wide variety of chatterbots and question-and-answer (Q&A) systems have been proposed over the past decades, each with strengths that make them appropriate for particular applications. With numerous advances in information construction, people increasingly aim to communicate with computers using natural language. For example, chatterbots in some e-commerce Web sites can interact with customers and provide help similar to a real-life secretary (DeeAnna Merz Nagel, 2011; Yvette Colón, 2011).

In this paper, we propose PAL (Psychologist of Artificial Language), a chatterbot system for answering non-obstructive psychological questions. Non-obstructive questions refer to problems on family, human relationships, marriage, life pressure, learning, work and so on. In these cases, we expect the chatterbot to play an active role by providing tutoring, solution, support, advice, or even sympathy depending on the help needed by its users.

The difference of PAL from existing chatterbots lies not only in the specific research focus of this paper but also in the strategies we designed, such as P-XML templates for storing a knowledge base, comprehensive question matching method by considering both index and semantic similarities, and solution management by considering personal information. In the following sections, we will briefly discuss related work and then introduce our system and its main features.

2 Related Work

A number of research work on chatterbots (Rafael E. Banchs, Haizhou Li, 2012; Ai Ti Aw and Lian Hau Lee, 2012), Q&A systems (Shilin Ding, Gao Cong, Chin-Yew Lin, 2008; Leila Kosseim, 2008; Tiphaine Dalmas, 2007), and related natural language understanding technologies have recently been conducted (Walid S. Saba, 2007; Jing dong, 2009). Several studies on the application of natural language processing technologies for non-obstructive psychological Q&A systems have also been published (Hai-hu Shi, 2005).

Several online psychology counselling Web sites with service provided by human experts have also been established recently (DeeAnna Merz Nagel, 2011; Yvette Colón, 2011). For these Web sites, when the visitors ask similar questions, the expert may provide the same or very similar answers repeatedly. Based on this observation and consideration, we collected a large number of counselling Q&A pairs to extract common knowledge for the construction of a chatterbot system. Advances in automatic language analysis and processing are used as the bases for the emergence of a complex, task-oriented chatterbot system.

3 Basic Framework of PAL

A running screenshot of PAL is shown in Figure 1, and its basic system structure is demonstrated in Figure 2. As shown in Figure 2, the basic principles of PAL are as follows:

1) All interactions between system and users are scheduled by control logic;
2) When the user inputs a question, the system will search through its knowledge base for the matching entry, and then
3) The system will respond with an appropriate answer by analysing both the matched entry and the dialogue history.

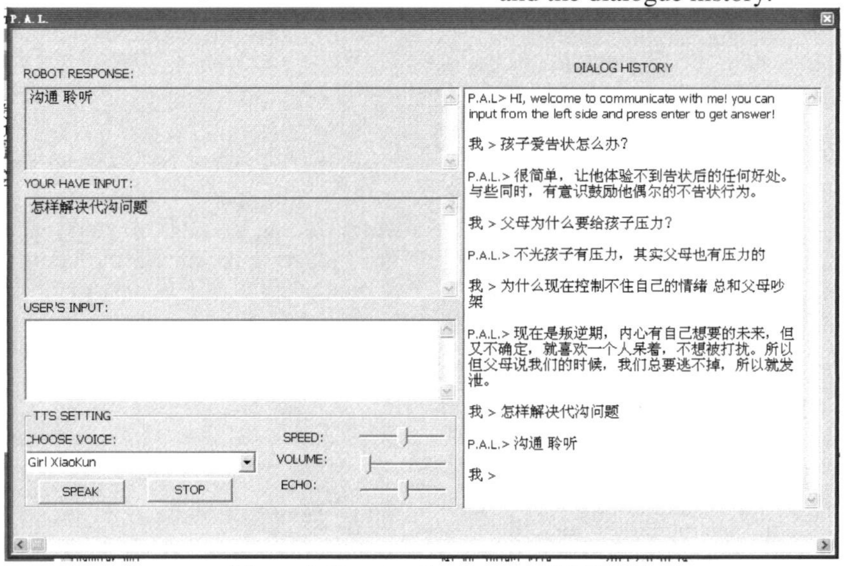

Figure 1. Running Screenshot of PAL

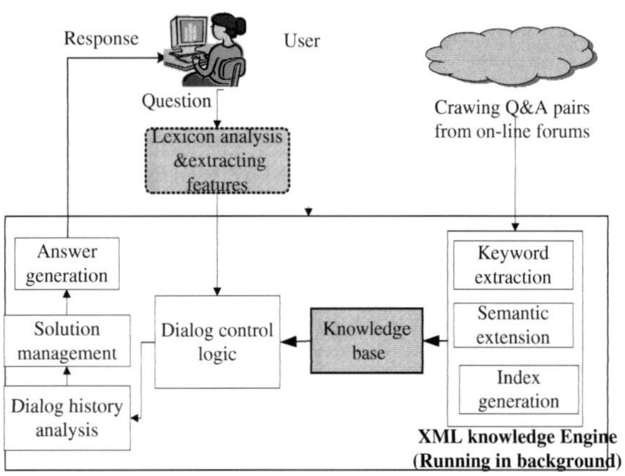

Figure 2. Basic Framework of PAL

4 Conversation Control Strategy of PAL

The Q&A process of the PAL system is coordinated by control logic to communicate with users effectively. The basic control logic strategy is shown in Figure 3.

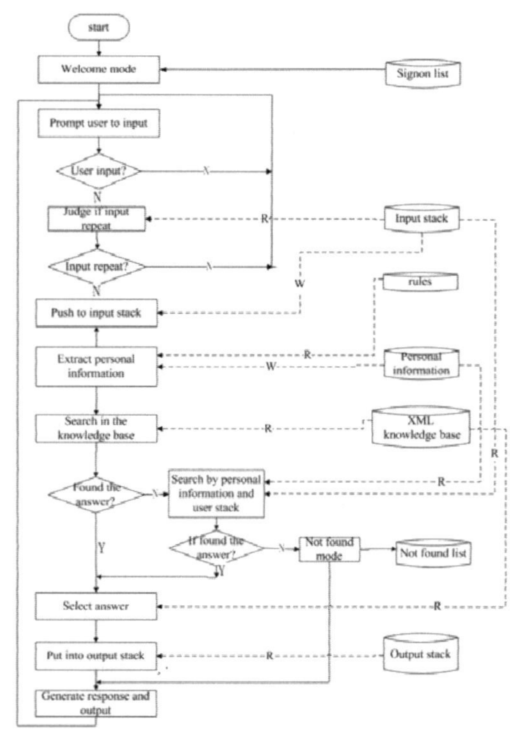

Figure 3. Basic Control Logic of PAL

As shown in Figure 3, the initial state is set to welcome mode, and the system can select a sentence from the "sign on" list, which will then provide a response. When users enter a question, the system will conduct the necessary analysis. The system's knowledge base is indexed by Clucene[1] beforehand. Thus, the knowledge index will be used to search the matched records quickly. If the system can find the matched patterns directly and the answer is suitable for the current user, one answer will be randomly selected to generate the response. Historical information and personal information will be analysed when necessary. We mainly adopted the method of ELIZA[2], which is an open-source program, to consider the historical information. A "not found" response list is also set to deal with situations when no suitable answers can be identified. Both system utterance and user input will be pushed into the stack as historical information. Given that user questions are at times very simple, the combination with historical input may also be required to determine its meaning. This step can also avoid the duplication of utterances.

5 Knowledge Construction and Question Matching Method

We design P-XML to store the knowledge base for PAL, as shown in Figure 4. The knowledge base for PAL is mainly derived from the Q&A pairs in the BAIDU ZHIDAO community[3]. One question usually has many corresponding answers.

```
<?xml version="1.0" encoding="GB2312"?>
<domain name="*"> <qapair speaker="*">
<zhidao_question_title>*</zhidao_question_t
itle>
<zhidao_question_content>*</zhidao_question
_content><zhidao_other_answer
intersection_number="4">*
<entity_and_problemword>*</entity_and_probl
emword> <peopleword>*</peopleword>
</zhidao_other_answer>
<title_extension>*</title_extension>
</qapair>
...
</domain>
```

Figure 4. The Structure of P-XML

1 http://sourceforge.net/projects/clucene/
2 http://www.codeforge.cn/article/191554
3 http://Zhidao.baidu.com

An effective method of capturing the user's meaning accurately is to create an extension for questions in the knowledge base. In this paper, the extension is primarily a synonym expansion of the keywords of questions, with CILIN (Wanxiang Che, 2010) as extension knowledge source.

The questions are indexed by Clucene to improve the retrieval efficiency of the search for a matched entry in the knowledge base. During the knowledge base searching step, both the index of the original form and the extension form of the problem are used to find the most possible matched record for the user's question, as shown in algorithm 1. Algorithm 1 is used to examine the similarity between user input and the record returned by Clucene, including traditional and extension similarities.

Algorithm 1. Problem-matching method

Begin

1) User inputs question Q;
2) Search from the index of original questions and obtain the returned record set RS1;
3) For the highest ranked record R1 in RS1,
    a) compute the similarity sim1 between question R1 and Q;
    b) compute the extension similarity sim2 between the question extensions of R1 and Q;
4) If sim1 is greater than the threshold value T1 or sim2 is greater than the threshold value T2, go to the solution management stage and obtain the answers of R1, and then find the candidate answer using algorithm 2;
5) Otherwise, a "not found" prompt is given.

End

6 Response Management Method

One question usually has many corresponding answers in the knowledge base, and these answers differ in explanation quality. Thus, the basic strategy employed by solution management is to select a reliable answer from the matched record as response, as shown in algorithm 2.

Personalised information includes name entity, gender, marital status and age information. PAL maintains some heuristics rules to help recognize such information. Based on these rules, if one answer contains personal information, it will be selected as the candidate answer only when the personal information is consistent with that of the current user. Very concise answers that do not contain personal information can generally be selected as a candidate answer.

Algorithm 2. Answer-selection method
Begin
1) User inputs one question Q;
2) The system extracts the speaker role S and personal information from Q;
3) Use Q as query to conduct information retrieval from the index and knowledge base and obtain the top matched record set R;
4) For each matched question Q' in R, test the following conditions:
   a) (condition 1) extract the speaker role S' in Q', and examine if S' is equal to S;
   b) (condition 2) extract personal information in Q', and examine if they are equal to that of in Q;
   c) For each answer A' of Q'
      i. If no personal information is found in A', A' will be pushed into response list;
      ii. If personal information is contained in A' and if both conditions 1 and 2 are true, A' will be pushed into response list;
   d) End for
5) End for
End

7 Experiments

For the current implementation of PAL, the size of the knowledge base is approximately 1.2G and contains six different topics: "Husband and wife", "Family relations", "Love affairs", "Adolescence", "Feeling and Mood", and "Mental tutors". Dialogue data collection used in PAL is mainly crawled from http://zhidao.baidu.com, which is one of the largest Chinese online communities. The criterion for choosing these six categories is also because they are the main topics in BAIDU communities about psychological problems. Some information on the knowledge base is given in Table 1, in which "Percent of questions matched" denotes the number of similar questions found when 100 open questions are input (we suppose that if the similarity threshold is bigger than 0.5, then a similar question will be deemed as "hit" in the knowledge base).

In 7.1, we examine the feasibility of using downloaded dialogue collection for constructing the knowledge base. Some dialogue examples are given in 7.2.

Domain	Avg. ques. length	Num. of unique Terms in ques.	Avg. ans. length	Num. of unique terms in ans.	Percent of questions matched (similarity threshold: 0.5)	Size(MB)
QS1	58.69	11571	64.13	27312	25	125
QS2	54.96	10918	64.92	25185	24	292
QS3	59.66	13530	49.52	13664	15	53
QS4	42.41	8607	47.11	23492	22	224
QS5	63.57	11915	48.86	26860	26	276
QS6	31.82	10009	98.55	20896	25	216

Table 1. Information of the knowledge base

7.1 System Performance Evaluation

Additional questions and their corresponding answers beyond the knowledge base are also used as a test set to evaluate system performance. Concretely, suppose question Q has |A| answers in the test set. Q is then input into the system. Suppose the system output is O, we examine if one best answer exists among |A| answers that are very similar to O (the similarity is greater than threshold T3). If yes, we then assume that one suitable answer has been found. In this way, precision can be calculated as the number of questions that have very similar answers in the system divided by the number of all input questions.

The performance evaluation results are shown in Figure 5. The horizon axis denotes the similarity threshold (T1 for sim1 and T2 for sim2) between a user's input and the questions in the knowledge base. Sim1 is the original similarity, whereas sim2 is the semantic extension similarity. Different thresholds were used (0.5 to 0.9). The similarity threshold T3 denotes the similarity between the answer in the test set and system output O. From Figures 5 (A) and (B), different T3 values were used (0.5 to 0.8).

Some observations can be made from Figure 5. The average system precision is approximately 0.5, and the range is from 0.2 to 0.9. Basically, when T3 is bigger, the system's performance tends to decrease because a high T3 value denotes a strict evaluation standard. Performance also differs between different areas, such that D4, D5 and D6 outperform than D1, D2 and D3.

When only index is used and both sim1 and sim2 are below the corresponding threshold T1 or T2, the system can still return record set RS2, but the returned answer may be inconsistent with user's question. Thus, incorporating semantic search shown in algorithm 1 is necessary.

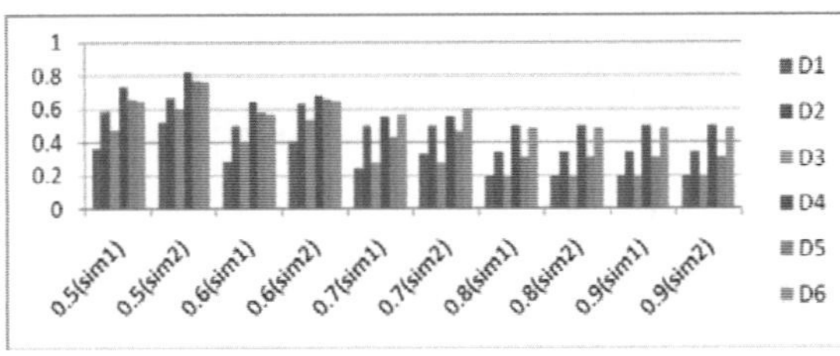

(A) (Sim. Thres. T3=0.5)

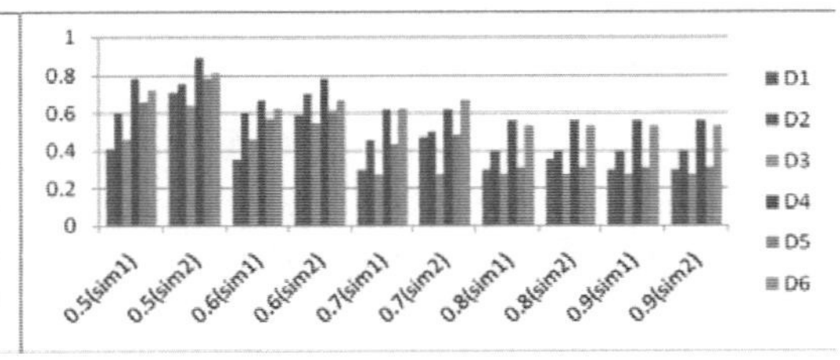

(B) (Sim. Thres. T3=0.6)

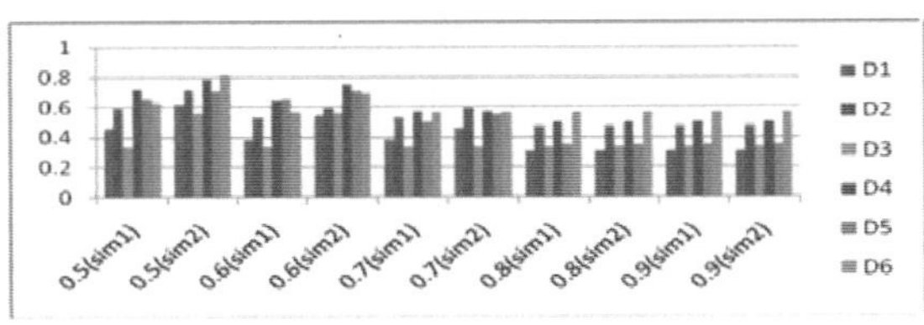

(C) (Sim. Thres. T3=0.7)

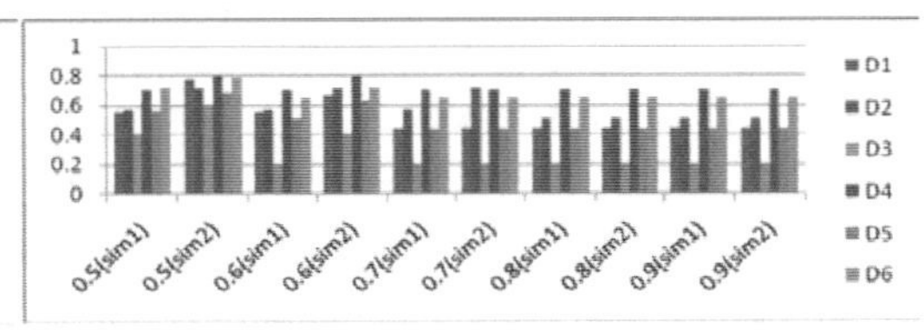

(D) (Sim. Thres. T3=0.8)

Figure 5. Precision of PAL with different similarity thresholds T3 (The X axis denotes different thresholds for sim1 (T1) and sim2 (T2). For example, 0.5(sim1) indicates that the threshold for sim1 is 0.5, whereas 0.5(sim2) suggests that the threshold for sim2 is 0.5. The Y axis stands for the precision value of different T1, T2 and T3 values for different areas).

7.2. Some Interaction Examples

Table 2 provides an interaction example of PAL in English. As users input their questions, the system can output the corresponding responses. The entire dialogue history can also be displayed. Basically, when users describe their troubles, PAL can provide some explanation or even try to console the user.

Compared to other chatterbots like Eliza, PAL is domain-specific and may provide help to some extent. Many different answers can usually be identified. Thus, the user could input the same question many times, with the system providing suggestions from different angles. PAL can also output voice by using Xiao-kun and Microsoft Anna as the text-to-speech (TTS) engine. The speed, volume and echo properties of the voice can be adjusted.

Dialog for Figure 1 (in English)
PAL> Hello, you are welcome to communicate with me! You can input from the left side and press enter to get answer!
I> How do I deal with the children who like to complain very frequently?
PAL>Very simple. Don't' let him experience the benefits of complaining very frequently.
I> Why do parents give children so much pressure
PAL> Children have pressure indeed; but parents also have a lot of pressure.
I> Why am I unable to control my emotions, and often quarrel with my parents?
PAL.> Now you may be in the stage of treason. And have your own uncertain plan for the future, want to be yourself, and do not want to be disturbed. So when parents criticize, you will be unhappy.
I> How to solve the gap problem?
PAL.> Communication, and listening .

Table 2. Example of an interaction with PAL (in English)

8 Conclusions

In this paper, we introduce a simple chatterbot for answering non-obstructive psychological questions. The knowledge behind the chatterbot is learned from the Q&A pairs derived from an online forum using several extraction strategies. The historical and personal information from the dialogues are also incorporated to output an appropriate answer.

For future work, we expect to add more features to PAL, e.g., enabling the system to ask questions actively and further improving P-XML to form richer patterns for storing Q&A knowledge. Another interesting aspect would be to add speech input as well as TTS and to transform PAL into a mobile platform for widespread use.

Acknowledgments

This research was supported by the project of The National High Technology Research and Development Program (863 program) of PR China under a research Grant No.2007AA01Z172, Youth Funds of China social & humanity science (10YJCZH099), and Key Laboratory Opening Funding of China MOE—MS Key Laboratory of Natural Language Processing and Speech (HIT.KLOF.2009022).

References

Ai Ti Aw and Lian Hau Lee. Personalized Normalization for a Multilingual Chat System. *Proceedings of the 50th Annual Meeting of the Association for Computational Linguistics,* Jeju, Republic of Korea, 8-14 July 2012, pages 31–36,

DeeAnna Merz Nagel, Kate Anthony. Text-based Online Counseling Chat. *Online Counseling (Second Edition)*, 2011, Pages 169-182

Hai-hu Shi, Yan Feng, LI Dong-mei, HU Ying-fei. Research on on-line psychology consultation expert system based on man-machine interaction technique. *Computer Engineering and Design.* 2005, 26(12):3307-3309

Jing dong. Research of sentiment model based on HMM and its application in psychological consulting expert system. *Master's thesis. Capital normal university (china),* 2009.

Leila Kosseim, Jamileh Yousefi. Improving the performance of question answering with semantically equivalent answer patterns. *Data & Knowledge Engineering*, 2008, 66(1):53-67

Rafael E. Banchs, Haizhou Li. IRIS: a Chat-oriented Dialogue System based on the Vector Space Model. *Proceedings of the 50th Annual Meeting of the Association for Computational Linguistics,* Jeju, Republic of Korea, 8-14 July 2012. pages 37–42

Shilin Ding, Gao Cong, Chin-Yew Lin, Xiaoyan Zhu. Using Conditional Random Fields to Extract Contexts and Answers of Questions from Online Forums. *Proceedings of 2008 Association for Computational Linguistics*, Columbus, Ohio, USA, June 2008. pages 710–718

Tiphaine Dalmas, Bonnie Webber. Answer comparison in automated question answering. *Journal of Applied Logic*, Volume 5, Issue 1, March 2007, Pages 104-120

Walid S. Saba. Language, logic and ontology: Uncovering the structure of commonsense knowledge. *International Journal of Human-Computer Studies*, Volume 65, Issue 7, July 2007, Pages 610-623

Wanxiang Che, Zhenghua Li, Ting Liu. LTP: A Chinese Language Technology Platform. *In Proceedings of the Coling 2010:Demonstrations.* August 2010, pp13-16, Beijing, China.

Yvette Colón, Stephanie Stern. Counseling Groups Online: Theory and Framework. *Online Counseling (Second Edition),* 2011, Pages 183-202.

PhonMatrix: Visualizing co-occurrence constraints of sounds

Thomas Mayer
Research Unit
Quantitative Language Comparison
Philipps University of Marburg
thomas.mayer@uni-marburg.de

Christian Rohrdantz
Data Analysis and Visualization Group
University of Konstanz
christian.rohrdantz
@uni-konstanz.de

Abstract

This paper describes the online tool *PhonMatrix*, which analyzes a word list with respect to the co-occurrence of sounds in a specified context within a word. The co-occurrence counts from the user-specified context are statistically analyzed according to a number of association measures that can be selected by the user. The statistical values then serve as the input for a matrix visualization where rows and columns represent the relevant sounds under investigation and the matrix cells indicate whether the respective ordered pair of sounds occurs more or less frequently than expected. The usefulness of the tool is demonstrated with three case studies that deal with vowel harmony and similar place avoidance patterns.

1 Introduction

In this paper, we introduce the *PhonMatrix*[1] tool, which is designed to visualize co-occurrence constraints of sounds within words given a reasonably sized word list of the language. It is a web-based implementation of the visualization method proposed in (Mayer et al., 2010a), including some further development such as an interactive component and a range of association measures and sorting methods to choose from. The original motivation for this tool is to give linguists the opportunity to upload their own word lists in order to visually explore co-occurrence constraints in languages. The basic idea behind the visual component of the tool is to provide for a first, at-a-glance mode of analysis which can be used to generate hypotheses about the data by simply looking at the visualization matrices.

Phonotactic constraints in languages abound. One of the most well-known and wide-spread constraints is commonly referred to as vowel harmony (van der Hulst and van de Weijer, 1995). In vowel harmony languages, vowels are separated into groups where vowels of the same group tend to co-occur within words, while vowels from different groups rarely co-occur. Likewise, in some languages there are patterns of consonant harmony (Hansson, 2010) that show a similar behavior with respect to consonants. Less common are cases of "synharmonism" (Trubetzkoy, 1967, p. 251) where both vowels and consonants form such groups and words usually only contain sounds from the same group (e.g., only front vowels and palatalized consonants). Whereas vowel harmony patterns are easily detectable in many harmonic languages due to the harmonic alternants in affixes, other co-occurrence constraints are less obvious. This is especially true for disharmonic patterns, the most famous of which is the principle of Similar Place Avoidance (SPA) in Semitic consonantal roots (Greenberg, 1950). Recent studies have shown that this principle is not only active in Semitic languages, where it was already known by grammarians in the Middle Ages, but is a more widespread tendency among the languages of the world (Pozdniakov and Segerer, 2007; Mayer et al., 2010b). One of the reasons why statistical constraints like SPA are more difficult to detect is the fact that they exhibit many frequent counterexamples and are therefore less easily spotted as a general (albeit statistical) tendency.

In our view, there are many more phonotactic constraints that wait to be discovered by linguists. With the availability of language data in electronic format such tendencies can be automatically processed and presented to the user in a form that allows for an easy exploration of the results in a short period of time. Thus a larger number of phonotactic contexts can be explored in order to

[1] http://paralleltext.info/phonmatrix/

find potential patterns in the data. The *PhonMatrix* tool is part of an ongoing effort to integrate methods and techniques from the field of visual analytics (Thomas and Cook, 2005) into linguistic research. The present tool will be gradually augmented with further functionalities in order to enhance its usefulness.

2 Related work

A related tool that quantifies the co-occurrence of sounds in a given corpus is the *Vowel Harmony Calculator* (Harrison et al., 2004). The major difference between *PhonMatrix* and the *Vowel Harmony Calculator* is that the latter is restricted to the context of vowel harmony and requires the user to input the harmony classes beforehand whereas *PhonMatrix* is designed to detect these classes by making potential harmonic patterns more easily perceptible to the user. The *Vowel Harmony Calculator* quantifies the notion of vowel harmony for the input corpus by giving the percentage of harmonic words and the harmony threshold. The harmony threshold is the percentage of words that would be expected to be harmonic purely by chance. The output of the Vowel Harmony Calculator consists of a list of values (number of polysyllabic words, harmony threshold, percentage of harmonic words, harmony index, among other things) but does not give any information about the harmonic strength of individual vowel pairs. In short, the *Vowel Harmony Calculator* is a way to quantify the notion of harmony given the harmony classes of the language whereas *PhonMatrix* is intended to help detect such patterns.

3 System overview

PhonMatrix is a web-based visualization tool that statistically analyzes sound co-occurrences within words and displays the result in a symmetric sound matrix. The statistical components are written in Python whereas the visualization part is in Javascript, using the D3 library (Bostock et al., 2011). Before discussing the individual steps of the system in more detail we will give a brief overview of the overall processing pipeline (see Figure 1).

In the first step, the user has to upload the text file containing the word list that serves as the input to the analysis process. Text files have to be encoded in UTF-8 and list only one word per line. For a meaningful analysis the words should be given in some phonemic transcription (e.g., using IPA).[2]

After the file has been uploaded to the server all symbols in the word list are analyzed according to their unigram and bigram frequencies. These frequencies are used to infer an automatic distinction between vowels, consonants and infrequent symbols. Infrequent symbols are considered to be noise in the data and can be ignored for further processing. A distinction between vowels and consonants is automatically inferred from the word list by means of Sukhotin's algorithm (Sukhotin, 1962). The results of Sukhotin's algorithm are presented to the user together with the frequency counts of the individual symbols in the word list.

In the third step, the user can make changes to the automatic classification of symbols into vowels and consonants and exclude infrequent symbols from further consideration. The subsequent calculations of co-occurrence values are mostly based on the distinction of input symbols into consonants (C) and vowels (V). Users can choose among a number of options that define the context for the co-occurrence calculations.[3] Two of those options will be discussed in more detail in this paper (vowel co-occurrences in VCV and CC sequences). Depending on the user's choice, the co-occurrences in the selected context are calculated and analyzed with respect to a number of statistical association measures from which the user can choose one for the visualization.

In the last step, the results of the statistical analysis of the co-occurrence counts are displayed in a quadratic matrix of sounds. The rows and columns of the matrix represent the individual sounds that are relevant for the selected context (e.g., vowels in the context of VCV sequences). The rows thereby stand for the first members of the relevant sound pairs, whereas the columns contain the second members. Each cell of the matrix then shows the result for the pair of sounds in the respective row and column.

The final result is a visualization of the co-occurrence matrix with rows and columns sorted according to the similarity of the sound vectors and statistical values represented as colors in the matrix cells. The visualization features a number

[2] For more information on the minimum amount of data necessary see (Mayer et al., 2010a).

[3] It is also possible for users to define their own contexts with regular expressions.

Figure 1: The processing pipeline of the *PhonMatrix* visualization tool.

of interactive components that facilitate the detection of potential patterns in the results by the user.

4 PhonMatrix components

PhonMatrix consists of three main components: preprocessing (including vowel-consonant distinction), statistical analysis of co-occurrence counts and visualization. In what follows, we will describe each component in more detail, with special emphasis on the visualization component.

4.1 Vowel-consonant distinction

Most of the co-occurrence restrictions that might be of interest make reference to a distinction between vowels and consonants. Since a manual classification of all sounds in the input into vowels and consonants is a tedious task (especially with a larger number of symbols), the first component deals with an automatic inference of such a distinction. Many methods have been discussed in the literature on how to discriminate vowels from consonants on the basis of their distribution in texts. Many of them involve many lines of code and are computationally demanding. Yet there is a very simple and fast algorithm that yields reasonably good results (Sukhotin, 1962; Guy, 1991).

The basic idea of Sukhotin's algorithm is that vowels and consonants have the tendency not to occur in groups within words but to alternate. Based on the additional assumption that the most frequent symbol in the text is a vowel, the algorithm iteratively selects the symbol which occurs most frequently adjacent to a vowel and determines it to be a consonant. The algorithm stops if no more consonants can be selected because no co-occurrence counts with any remaining vowel are positive. Although the algorithm is quite old and very simple, it gives reasonably good results (Goldsmith and Xanthos, 2009; Guy, 1991; Sassoon, 1992). *PhonMatrix* makes use of Sukhotin's algorithm as a preprocessing step to give a first guess of the class for each symbol, which the user can then modify if it turns out to be wrong. It mainly serves to speed up the classification step.

4.2 Co-occurrence statistics

With the distinction of symbols into vowels and consonants at hand, the user can then select a relevant context for the co-occurrence counts. The relevant context can be chosen from a list of predefined options. Here we will illustrate the statistical analysis with the context of VCV sequences to investigate vowel harmony in Turkish. The input consists of 20,968 orthographic words from the Turkish New Testament.[4] The tool automatically extracts all VCV sequences in the words and counts the co-occurrences of sounds in these sequences. The counts are then summarized in a quadratic contingency table and can be used for further statistical analyses.

In our experiments, two measures turned out to be especially useful for the detection of potential patterns: the probability and ϕ values. The ϕ value is a normalized χ^2 measure which allows for an easier mapping of values to the color scale because it is always between -1 and 1.[5] The ϕ values for the vowels in the Turkish text are shown in Table 1. Apart from probability and ϕ values, the user can also choose among a number of other association measures such as pointwise mutual information, likelihood ratios or t-scores (Manning and Schütze, 1999).

4.3 Visualization component

The input to the visualization component is a matrix of association measures for each sound pair in the relevant context. Two additional steps have to be performed in order to arrive at the final matrix visualization: 1) the rows and columns of the matrix have to be sorted in a meaningful way; 2) the association measures have to be mapped to visual variables. For the matrix arrangement, we decided to have the same order of symbols for the rows and columns. The order of symbols is determined by a clustering of the

[4]Turkish orthography represents the modern pronunciation with a high degree of accuracy.

[5]Apart from this, ϕ makes good use of the off-diagonal cells in the contingency tables (Church and Gale, 1991).

	a	e	i	o	u	ö	ü	ı
a	0.53699	-0.49730	-0.54579	-0.30421	-0.38117	-0.03895	-0.36874	0.65791
e	-0.48371	0.54763	0.64548	-0.28216	-0.37907	-0.05792	-0.32882	-0.53454
i	-0.40334	0.37477	0.59682	0.30227	-0.33970	0.09038	-0.30307	-0.49651
o	0.20048	-0.28306	-0.31395	-0.14114	0.65493	-0.05532	-0.20696	-0.33238
u	0.28855	-0.34937	-0.38283	0.17629	0.73451	0.10011	-0.22066	-0.39304
ö	-0.28879	0.32352	-0.29843	-0.16465	-0.21329	-0.04885	0.65373	-0.29354
ü	-0.31709	0.33094	-0.34774	0.14995	-0.24351	-0.05829	0.75780	-0.35024
ı	0.30302	-0.40711	-0.46423	0.32671	-0.33210	-0.07607	-0.28459	0.58548

Table 1: ϕ values of VCV sequences in Turkish.

symbols based on the similarity of their row values. The clustering is performed with the Python `scipy.cluster.hierarchy` package from the SciPy library. As a default setting Ward's algorithm (Ward, 1963) is used but other clustering algorithms can also be easily integrated.

Whereas the preprocessing steps and the data-driven sorting of rows and columns have been written in Python, the actual visualization of the results in the browser is implemented in Javascript using the D3 library (Bostock et al., 2011). The association measures and the order of the symbols are referenced as Javascript variables in the visualization document. The data is then automatically bound to DOM elements of the HTML document through the D3 data operator. The mapping from association measures to color values is made with the linear scale method from the `d3.scale` package. Scale methods map from an input domain to an output range. The input domain for the ϕ values is the interval $[-1; 1]$, while the output range can be given as a color scale ranging from one color to the other. For the ϕ values we decided to use two unipolar scales, one from -1 to 0 (red) and the other from 0 to $+1$ (blue). In order to reserve a larger color range for the densely populated area of low values we did not linearly map the numerical association measures but used the square roots of the numerical values as the input for the scale function. Additionally, the sign of the ϕ value, which shows whether the co-occurrence of a certain symbol pair occurs more $(+)$ or less $(-)$ frequently than expected, is displayed in the matrix cell.[6] The result of the matrix visualization for the ϕ values of the vowels in Turkish VCV sequences is shown in Section 5.1.

[6]The algebraic sign is displayed in white and therefore stands out more clearly with higher absolute ϕ values.

The matrix visualization also features some interaction to explore the results in more detail. On mouse-over, the respective matrix cell shows the actual values that serve as the input for the data mapping process. Additionally, the row and column labels are highlighted in order to show more clearly which pair of symbols is currently selected (see Figure 2). The size of the matrix can also be adjusted to the user's needs with the help of a slider above the matrix. Next to the slider is a dropdown menu from which users can choose the association measure that they want to be displayed in the visualization.

5 Case studies

After the description of the *PhonMatrix* system we will illustrate the usefulness of the visualization of co-occurrence patterns in sounds with three case studies. They are presented as a proof of concept that the visualization component allows for an at-a-glance exploration of potential patterns. The visualization part is thereby not considered to be a replacement of more detailed linguistic investigations but rather serves as a way to explore a multitude of different contexts and data in a comparatively short period of time. After a suspicious pattern has been detected it is indispensable to look at the actual data to see whether the visualization result is an artifact of the method or data at hand or whether the detected pattern is an interesting phonotactic feature of the language under consideration.

5.1 Turkish vowel harmony

The first case study shows the results of the VCV sequences in Turkish described above. For this purpose the vowels *a, e, i, o, u, ö, ü, ı* are selected as the relevant sounds that are to be compared in

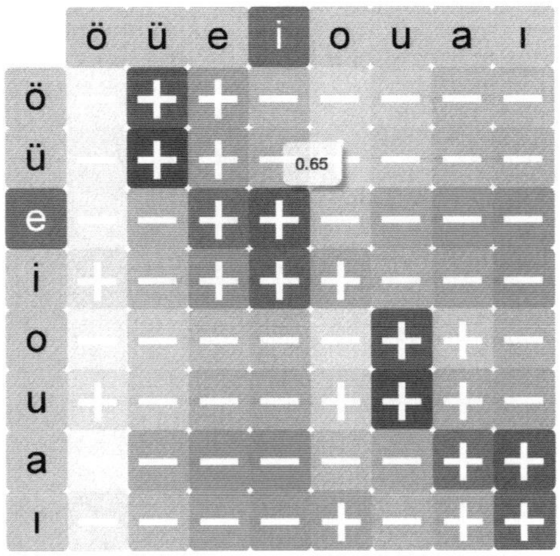

Figure 2: The visualization of the ϕ values of VCV sequences in the Turkish text.

Figure 3: The visualization of the probabilities of VCV sequences in the Finnish text.

the visualization. Figure 2 shows the results for the ϕ values that have been computed from the co-occurrence counts of the symbols in VCV sequences. The arrangement of the symbols in the matrix rows and columns already show a distinction between front (the first four vowels) and back (the last four vowels) vowels, reflecting the palatal harmony in Turkish. This distinction can best be seen when looking at the *e*- and *a*-columns where the top four vowels all have positive ϕ values for *e* and negative ϕ values for *a*, whereas the bottom four vowels show the opposite behavior. On closer inspection, the labial harmony for high vowels can also be seen in the matrix visualization. From top to bottom there are always pairs of vowels that take the same harmonic vowel, starting with (*ö*, *ü*) taking *ü* and followed by (*e*, *i*) taking *i*, (*o*, *u*) taking *u* and finally (*a*, *ı*) taking *ı*. The usefulness of the visualization component to detect such patterns can best be seen when comparing Figure 2 with Table 1, which contains the same information.

5.2 Finnish vowel harmony

The second case study shows that the harmonic patterns can also be detected in orthographic words of the Finnish Bible text. Finnish differs from Turkish in having only one type of harmony (palatal harmony) and neutral vowels, i.e., vowels that do not (directly) participate in the harmony process. As a different underlying association measure for the visualization consider the probability values in Figure 3. For probability values we have chosen a bipolar color scale ranging from white (for 0) over green (for 0.5) to blue (for 1). The probability matrix clearly shows the relevant blocks of vowels that mark the harmony groups.[7] The clustering algorithm separates the back vowels (first three vowels *o*, *a*, *u*) from the front vowels (vowels four to six, *ö*, *y*, *ä*) and the neutral vowels (*e*, *i*). The blocks along the main diagonal of the matrix show the harmonic pattern among the harmony groups, whereas the neutral vowels do not display any regular behavior.

5.3 Maltese verbal roots

PhonMatrix is not only useful to find vowel harmony patterns. The third case study shows that other co-occurrence constraints such as SPA can also be detected. To illustrate this, we show the visualization of CC patterns in a comprehensive list of Maltese verbal roots (Spagnol, 2011). The consonant matrix in Figure 4 shows two clusters, with one cluster (the first twelve consonants in the top row) containing labial and dorsal and the other cluster (the last eleven consonants) comprising only coronal consonants.[8] The visualization also reveals that, unlike in vowel harmony, consonants from the same cluster do not occur next to each other in the CC sequences, as shown by the red blocks in the top left and bottom right. This is exactly what SPA would predict.

[7] The +/− signs in the matrix are taken from the ϕ values.

[8] The consonants are given in their orthographic representation (Borg and Azzopardi-Alexander, 1997, p. 299).

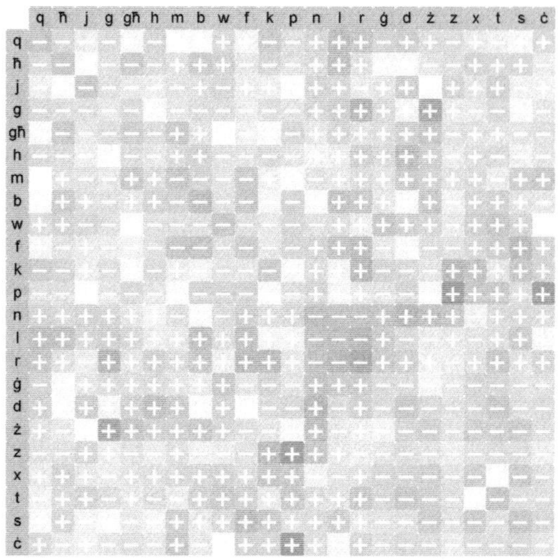

Figure 4: The visualization of the ϕ values of consonant sequences in Maltese verbal roots.

6 Conclusions

In this paper, we have presented *PhonMatrix*, a web-based, interactive visualization tool for investigating co-occurrence restrictions of sounds within words. The case studies of vowel harmony and SPA have shown that interesting patterns in the data can easily be seen only by looking at the matrix visualizations.

Acknowledgments

This work was partially funded by the DFG project "Algorithmic corpus-based approaches to typological comparison." We are grateful to two anonymous reviewers for their valuable comments and suggestions.

References

Albert Borg and Marie Azzopardi-Alexander. 1997. *Maltese*. Descriptive Grammar Series. London: Routledge.

Michael Bostock, Vadim Ogievetsky, and Jeffrey Heer. 2011. D3: Data-driven documents. *IEEE Transactions on Visualization & Computer Graphics (Proc. InfoVis)*, 17(12):2301–2309.

Kenneth W. Church and William A. Gale. 1991. Concordances for parallel text. In *Proceedings of the Seventh Annual Conference of the UW Centre for the New OED and Text Research*, pages 40–62.

John Goldsmith and Aris Xanthos. 2009. Learning phonological categories. *Language*, 85(1)(1):4–38.

Joseph H. Greenberg. 1950. The patterning of root morphemes in Semitic. *Word*, 6:161–182.

Jacques B. M. Guy. 1991. Vowel identification: an old (but good) algorithm. *Cryptologia*, 15(3):258–262, July.

Gunnar Ólafur Hansson. 2010. *Consonant Harmony*. Berkeley: University of California Press.

David Harrison, Emily Thomforde, and Michael O'Keefe. 2004. The vowel harmony calculator. `http://www.swarthmore.edu/SocSci/harmony/public_html/`.

Christopher D. Manning and Hinrich Schütze. 1999. *Foundations of Natural Language Processing*. Massachusetts Institute of Technology.

Thomas Mayer, Christian Rohrdantz, Miriam Butt, Frans Plank, and Daniel A Keim. 2010a. Visualizing vowel harmony. *Journal of Linguistic Issues in Language Technology (LiLT)*, 4(2):1–33.

Thomas Mayer, Christian Rohrdantz, Frans Plank, Peter Bak, Miriam Butt, and Daniel A. Keim. 2010b. Consonant co-occurrence in stems across languages: Automatic analysis and visualization of a phonotactic constraint. In *Proceedings of the ACL 2010 Workshop on NLP and Linguistics: Finding the Common Ground*, pages 67–75.

Konstantin Pozdniakov and Guillaume Segerer. 2007. Similar Place Avoidance: A statistical universal. *Linguistic Typology*, 11(2)(2):307–348.

George T. Sassoon. 1992. The application of Sukhotin's algorithm to certain Non-English languages. *Cryptologia*, 16(2)(2):165–173.

Michael Spagnol. 2011. *A tale of two morphologies. Verb structure and argument alternations in Maltese*. Ph.D. thesis, Germany: University of Konstanz dissertation.

Boris V. Sukhotin. 1962. Eksperimental'noe vydelenie klassov bukv s pomoşçju evm. *Problemy strukturnoj lingvistiki*, 234:189–206.

James J. Thomas and Kristin A. Cook. 2005. *Illuminating the Path: The Research and Development Agenda for Visual Analytics*. National Visualization and Analytics Ctr.

N. S. Trubetzkoy. 1967. *Grundzüge der Phonologie*. Göttingen: Vandenhoeck & Ruprecht. 4. Auflage.

Harry van der Hulst and Jeroen van de Weijer. 1995. Vowel harmony. In John Goldsmith, editor, *The Handbook of Phonological Theory*, chapter 14, pages 495–534. Basil Blackwell Ltd.

Joe H. Jr. Ward. 1963. Hierarchical grouping to optimize an objective function. *Journal of the American Statistical Association*, 58(1)(1):236–244.

QuEst - A translation quality estimation framework

Lucia Specia[§], **Kashif Shah**[§], **Jose G. C. de Souza**[†] and **Trevor Cohn**[§]
§Department of Computer Science
University of Sheffield, UK
{l.specia,kashif.shah,t.cohn}@sheffield.ac.uk

†Fondazione Bruno Kessler
University of Trento, Italy
desouza@fbk.eu

Abstract

We describe QuEst, an open source framework for machine translation quality estimation. The framework allows the extraction of several quality indicators from source segments, their translations, external resources (corpora, language models, topic models, etc.), as well as language tools (parsers, part-of-speech tags, etc.). It also provides machine learning algorithms to build quality estimation models. We benchmark the framework on a number of datasets and discuss the efficacy of features and algorithms.

1 Introduction

As Machine Translation (MT) systems become widely adopted both for gisting purposes and to produce professional quality translations, automatic methods are needed for predicting the quality of a translated segment. This is referred to as Quality Estimation (QE). Different from standard MT evaluation metrics, QE metrics do not have access to reference (human) translations; they are aimed at MT systems in use. QE has a number of applications, including:

- Deciding which segments need revision by a translator (quality assurance);
- Deciding whether a reader gets a reliable gist of the text;
- Estimating how much effort it will be needed to post-edit a segment;
- Selecting among alternative translations produced by different MT systems;
- Deciding whether the translation can be used for self-training of MT systems.

Work in QE for MT started in the early 2000's, inspired by the confidence scores used in Speech Recognition: mostly the estimation of word posterior probabilities. Back then it was called *confidence estimation*, which we believe is a narrower term. A 6-week workshop on the topic at John Hopkins University in 2003 (Blatz et al., 2004) had as goal to estimate automatic metrics such as BLEU (Papineni et al., 2002) and WER. These metrics are difficult to interpret, particularly at the sentence-level, and results of their very many trials proved unsuccessful. The overall quality of MT was considerably lower at the time, and therefore pinpointing the very few good quality segments was a hard problem. No software nor datasets were made available after the workshop.

A new surge of interest in the field started recently, motivated by the widespread used of MT systems in the translation industry, as a consequence of better translation quality, more user-friendly tools, and higher demand for translation. In order to make MT maximally useful in this scenario, a quantification of the quality of translated segments similar to "fuzzy match scores" from translation memory systems is needed. QE work addresses this problem by using more complex metrics that go beyond matching the source segment with previously translated data. QE can also be useful for end-users reading translations for gisting, particularly those who cannot read the source language.

QE nowadays focuses on estimating more interpretable metrics. "Quality" is defined according to the application: post-editing, gisting, etc. A number of positive results have been reported. Examples include improving post-editing efficiency by filtering out low quality segments which would require more effort or time to correct than translating from scratch (Specia et al., 2009; Specia, 2011), selecting high quality segments to be published as they are, without post-editing (Soricut and Echihabi, 2010), selecting a translation from either an MT system or a translation memory for post-editing (He et al., 2010), selecting the best translation from multiple MT systems (Specia et al.,

2010), and highlighting sub-segments that need revision (Bach et al., 2011).

QE is generally addressed as a supervised machine learning task using a variety of algorithms to induce models from examples of translations described through a number of features and annotated for quality. For an overview of various algorithms and features we refer the reader to the WMT12 shared task on QE (Callison-Burch et al., 2012). Most of the research work lies on deciding which aspects of quality are more relevant for a given task and designing feature extractors for them. While simple features such as counts of tokens and language model scores can be easily extracted, feature engineering for more advanced and useful information can be quite labour-intensive. Different language pairs or optimisation against specific quality scores (e.g., post-editing time vs translation adequacy) can benefit from very different feature sets.

QuEst, our framework for quality estimation, provides a wide range of feature extractors from source and translation texts and external resources and tools (Section 2). These go from simple, language-independent features, to advanced, linguistically motivated features. They include features that rely on information from the MT system that generated the translations, and features that are oblivious to the way translations were produced (Section 2.1). In addition, by integrating a well-known machine learning toolkit, `scikit-learn`,[1] and algorithms that are known to perform well on this task, QuEst provides a simple and effective way of experimenting with techniques for feature selection and model building, as well as parameter optimisation through grid search (Section 2.2). In Section 3 we present experiments using the framework with nine QE datasets.

In addition to providing a practical platform for quality estimation, by freeing researchers from feature engineering, QuEst will facilitate work on the learning aspect of the problem. Quality estimation poses several machine learning challenges, such as the fact that it can exploit a large, diverse, but often noisy set of information sources, with a relatively small number of annotated data points, and it relies on human annotations that are often inconsistent due to the subjectivity of the task (quality judgements). Moreover, QE is highly non-linear: unlike many other problems in language processing, considerable improvements can be achieved using non-linear kernel techniques. Also, different applications for the quality predictions may benefit from different machine learning techniques, an aspect that has been mostly neglected so far. Finally, the framework will also facilitate research on ways of using quality predictions in novel extrinsic tasks, such as self-training of statistical machine translation systems, and for estimating quality in other text output applications such as text summarisation.

2 The QuEst framework

QuEst consists of two main modules: a feature extraction module and a machine learning module. The first module provides a number of feature extractors, including the most commonly used features in the literature and by systems submitted to the WMT12 shared task on QE (Callison-Burch et al., 2012). More than 15 researchers from 10 institutions contributed to it as part of the QuEst project.[2] It is implemented in Java and provides abstract classes for features, resources and preprocessing steps so that extractors for new features can be easily added.

The basic functioning of the feature extraction module requires raw text files with the source and translation texts, and a few resources (where available) such as the source MT training corpus and language models of source and target. Configuration files are used to indicate the resources available and a list of features that should be extracted.

The machine learning module provides scripts connecting the feature files with the `scikit-learn` toolkit. It also uses `GPy`, a Python toolkit for Gaussian Processes regression, which outperformed algorithms commonly used for the task such as SVM regressors.

2.1 Feature sets

In Figure 1 we show the types of features that can be extracted in QuEst. Although the text unit for which features are extracted can be of any length, most features are more suitable for sentences. Therefore, a "segment" here denotes a sentence.

From the source segments QuEst can extract features that attempt to quantify the **complexity**

[1] `http://scikit-learn.org/`

[2] `http://www.dcs.shef.ac.uk/~lucia/projects/quest.html`

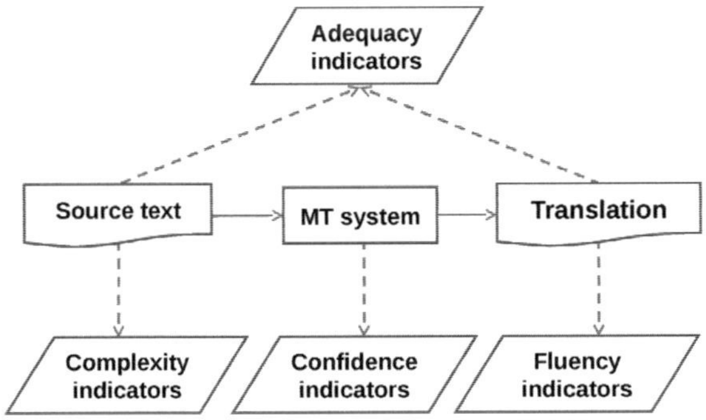

Figure 1: Families of features in QuEst.

of translating those segments, or how unexpected they are given what is known to the MT system. Examples of features include:

- number of tokens in the source segment;
- language model (LM) probability of source segment using the source side of the parallel corpus used to train the MT system as LM;
- percentage of source 1–3-grams observed in different frequency quartiles of the source side of the MT training corpus;
- average number of translations per source word in the segment as given by IBM 1 model with probabilities thresholded in different ways.

From the translated segments QuEst can extract features that attempt to measure the **fluency** of such translations. Examples of features include:

- number of tokens in the target segment;
- average number of occurrences of the target word within the target segment;
- LM probability of target segment using a large corpus of the target language to build the LM.

From the comparison between the source and target segments, QuEst can extract **adequacy** features, which attempt to measure whether the structure and meaning of the source are preserved in the translation. Some of these are based on word-alignment information as provided by GIZA++. Features include:

- ratio of number of tokens in source and target segments;
- ratio of brackets and punctuation symbols in source and target segments;
- ratio of percentages of numbers, content- / non-content words in the source & target segments;
- ratio of percentage of nouns/verbs/etc in the source and target segments;
- proportion of dependency relations between (aligned) constituents in source and target segments;
- difference between the depth of the syntactic trees of the source and target segments;
- difference between the number of PP/NP/VP/ADJP/ADVP/CONJP phrases in the source and target;
- difference between the number of person/location/organization entities in source and target sentences;
- proportion of person/location/organization entities in source aligned to the same type of entities in target segment;
- percentage of direct object personal or possessive pronouns incorrectly translated.

When available, information from the MT system used to produce the translations can be very useful, particularly for statistical machine translation (SMT). These features can provide an indication of the **confidence** of the MT system in the translations. They are called "glass-box" features, to distinguish them from MT system-independent, "black-box" features. To extract these features, QuEst assumes the output of Moses-like SMT systems, taking into account word- and phrase-alignment information, a dump of the decoder's standard output (search graph information), global model score and feature values, n-best lists, etc. For other SMT systems, it can also take an XML file with relevant information. Examples of glass-box features include:

- features and global score of the SMT system;
- number of distinct hypotheses in the n-best list;
- 1–3-gram LM probabilities using translations in the n-best to train the LM;
- average size of the target phrases;
- proportion of pruned search graph nodes;
- proportion of recombined graph nodes.

We note that some of these features are language-independent by definition (such as the confidence features), while others can be dependent on linguistic resources (such as POS taggers), or very language-specific, such as the incorrect translation of pronouns, which was designed for Arabic-English QE.

Some word-level features have also been implemented: they include standard word posterior probabilities and n-gram probabilities for each target word. These can also be averaged across the whole sentence to provide sentence-level value.

The complete list of features available is given as part of QUEST's documentation. At the current stage, the number of BB features varies from 80 to 123 depending on the language pair, while GB features go from 39 to 48 depending on the SMT system used (see Section 3).

2.2 Machine learning

QUEST provides a command-line interface module for the `scikit-learn` library implemented in Python. This module is completely independent from the feature extraction code and it uses the extracted feature sets to build QE models. The dependencies are the `scikit-learn` library and all its dependencies (such as NumPy[3] and SciPy[4]). The module can be configured to run different regression and classification algorithms, feature selection methods and grid search for hyper-parameter optimisation.

The pipeline with feature selection and hyper-parameter optimisation can be set using a configuration file. Currently, the module has an interface for Support Vector Regression (SVR), Support Vector Classification, and Lasso learning algorithms. They can be used in conjunction with the feature selection algorithms (Randomised Lasso and Randomised decision trees) and the grid search implementation of `scikit-learn` to fit an optimal model of a given dataset.

Additionally, QUEST includes Gaussian Process (GP) regression (Rasmussen and Williams, 2006) using the `GPy` toolkit.[5] GPs are an advanced machine learning framework incorporating Bayesian non-parametrics and kernel machines, and are widely regarded as state of the art for regression. Empirically we found the performance to be similar to SVR on most datasets, with slightly worse MAE and better RMSE.[6] In contrast to SVR, inference in GP regression can be expressed analytically and the model hyper-parameters optimised directly using gradient ascent, thus avoiding the need for costly grid search. This also makes the method very suitable for feature selection.

[3]http://www.numpy.org/

[4]http://www.scipy.org/

[5]https://github.com/SheffieldML/GPy

[6]This follows from the optimisation objective: GPs use a quadratic loss (the log-likelihood of a Gaussian) compared to SVR which penalises absolute margin violations.

Data	Training	Test
WMT12 (en-es)	1,832	422
EAMT11 (en-es)	900	64
EAMT11 (fr-en)	2,300	225
EAMT09-s_1-s_4 (en-es)	3,095	906
GALE11-s_1-s_2 (ar-en)	2,198	387

Table 1: Number of sentences used for training and testing in our datasets.

3 Benchmarking

In this section we benchmark QUEST on nine existing datasets using feature selection and learning algorithms known to perform well in the task.

3.1 Datasets

The statistics of the datasets used in the experiments are shown in Table 1.[7]

WMT12 English-Spanish sentence translations produced by an SMT system and judged for post-editing effort in 1-5 (worst-best), taking a weighted average of three annotators.

EAMT11 English-Spanish (EAMT11-en-es) and French-English (EAMT11-fr-en) sentence translations judged for post-editing effort in 1-4.

EAMT09 English sentences translated by four SMT systems into Spanish and scored for post-editing effort in 1-4. Systems are denoted by s_1-s_4.

GALE11 Arabic sentences translated by two SMT systems into English and scored for adequacy in 1-4. Systems are denoted by s_1-s_2.

3.2 Settings

Amongst the various learning algorithms available in QUEST, to make our results comparable we selected SVR with radial basis function (RBF) kernel, which has been shown to perform very well in this task (Callison-Burch et al., 2012). The optimisation of parameters is done with grid search using the following ranges of values:

- penalty parameter C: [1, 10, 10]
- γ: [0.0001, 0.1, 10]
- ϵ: [0.1, 0.2, 10]

where elements in list denote beginning, end and number of samples to generate, respectively.

For feature selection, we have experimented with two techniques: Randomised Lasso and

[7]The datasets can be downloaded from http://www.dcs.shef.ac.uk/~lucia/resources.html

Gaussian Processes. Randomised Lasso (Meinshausen and Bühlmann, 2010) repeatedly resamples the training data and fits a Lasso regression model on each sample. A feature is said to be selected if it was selected (i.e., assigned a non-zero weight) in at least 25% of the samples (we do this 1000 times). This strategy improves the robustness of Lasso in the presence of high dimensional and correlated inputs.

Feature selection with Gaussian Processes is done by fitting per-feature RBF widths (also known as the *automatic relevance determination* kernel). The RBF width denotes the importance of a feature, the narrower the RBF the more important a change in the feature value is to the model prediction. To make the results comparable with our baseline systems we select the 17 top ranked features and then train a SVR on these features.[8]

As feature sets, we select all features available in QuEst for each of our datasets. We differentiate between black-box (BB) and glass-box (GB) features, as only BB are available for all datasets (we did not have access to the MT systems that produced the other datasets). For the WMT12 and GALE11 datasets, we experimented with both BB and GB features. For each dataset we build four systems:

- **BL**: 17 baseline features that performed well across languages in previous work and were used as baseline in the WMT12 QE task.
- **AF**: All features available for dataset.
- **FS**: Feature selection for automatic ranking and selection of top features with:
  - **RL**: Randomised Lasso.
  - **GP**: Gaussian Process.

Mean Absolute Error (MAE) and Root Mean Squared Error (RMSE) are used to evaluate the models.

3.3 Results

The error scores for all datasets with BB features are reported in Table 2, while Table 3 shows the results with GB features, and Table 4 the results with BB and GB features together. For each table and dataset, bold-faced figures are significantly better than all others (paired t-test with $p \leq 0.05$).

It can be seen from the results that adding more BB features (systems **AF**) improves the results in most cases as compared to the baseline systems

[8]More features resulted in further performance gains on most tasks, with 25–35 features giving the best results.

Dataset	System	#feats.	MAE	RMSE
WMT12	BL	17	0.6802	0.8192
	AF	80	0.6703	0.8373
	FS(RL)	69	**0.6628**	**0.8107**
	FS(GP)	17	**0.6537**	**0.8014**
EAMT11(en-es)	BL	17	0.4867	0.6288
	AF	80	**0.4696**	0.5438
	FS(RL)	29	0.4657	0.5424
	FS(GP)	17	**0.4640**	**0.5420**
EAMT11(fr-en)	BL	17	0.4387	0.6357
	AF	80	0.4275	0.6211
	FS(RL)	65	0.4266	0.6196
	FS(GP)	17	**0.4240**	**0.6189**
EAMT09-s_1	BL	17	0.5294	0.6643
	AF	80	0.5235	0.6558
	FS(RL)	73	**0.5190**	0.6516
	FS(GP)	17	0.5195	**0.6511**
EAMT09-s_2	BL	17	0.4604	0.5856
	AF	80	0.4734	0.5973
	FS(RL)	59	**0.4601**	0.5837
	FS(GP)	17	0.4610	**0.5825**
EAMT09-s_3	BL	17	0.5321	0.6643
	AF	80	0.5437	0.6827
	FS(RL)	67	0.5338	0.6627
	FS(GP)	17	0.5320	0.6630
EAMT09-s_4	BL	17	0.3583	0.4953
	AF	80	0.3569	0.5000
	FS(RL)	40	0.3554	0.4995
	FS(GP)	17	0.3560	0.4949
GALE11-s_1	BL	17	0.5456	0.6905
	AF	123	0.5359	0.6665
	FS(RL)	56	**0.5358**	**0.6649**
	FS(GP)	17	0.5410	0.6721
GALE11-s_2	BL	17	0.5532	0.7177
	AF	123	0.5381	0.6933
	FS(RL)	54	**0.5369**	**0.6955**
	FS(GP)	17	0.5424	0.6999

Table 2: Results with BB features.

Dataset	System	#feats.	MAE	RMSE
WMT12	AF	47	0.7036	0.8476
	FS(RL)	26	**0.6821**	**0.8388**
	FS(GP)	17	**0.6771**	**0.8308**
GALE11-s_1	AF	39	0.5720	0.7392
	FS(RL)	46	**0.5691**	**0.7388**
	FS(GP)	17	0.5711	0.7378
GALE11-s_2	AF	48	0.5510	0.6977
	FS(RL)	46	0.5512	0.6970
	FS(GP)	17	0.5501	0.6978

Table 3: Results with GB features.

Dataset	System	#feats.	MAE	RMSE
WMT12	AF	127	0.7165	0.8476
	FS(RL)	26	**0.6601**	**0.8098**
	FS(GP)	17	**0.6501**	**0.7989**
GALE11-s_1	AF	162	0.5437	0.6741
	FS(RL)	69	**0.5310**	**0.6681**
	FS(GP)	17	0.5370	0.6701
GALE11-s_2	AF	171	0.5222	0.6499
	FS(RL)	82	**0.5152**	**0.6421**
	FS(GP)	17	**0.5121**	**0.6384**

Table 4: Results with BB and GB features.

BL, however, in some cases the improvements are not significant. This behaviour is to be expected as adding more features may bring more relevant information, but at the same time it makes the representation more sparse and the learning prone to overfitting. In most cases, feature selection with both or either RL and GP improves over all features (AF). It should be noted that RL automatically selects the number of features used for training while FS(GP) was limited to selecting the top 17 features in order to make the results comparable with our baseline feature set. It is interesting to note that system FS(GP) outperformed the other systems in spite of using fewer features. This technique is promising as it reduces the time requirements and overall computational complexity for training the model, while achieving similar results compared to systems with many more features.

Another interesting question is whether these feature selection techniques identify a common subset of features from the various datasets. The overall top ranked features are:

- LM perplexities and log probabilities for source and target;
- size of source and target sentences;
- average number of possible translations of source words (IBM 1 with thresholds);
- ratio of target by source lengths in words;
- percentage of numbers in the target sentence;
- percentage of distinct unigrams seen in the MT source training corpus.

Interestingly, not all top ranked features are among the baseline 17 features which are reportedly best in literature.

GB features on their own perform worse than BB features, but in all three datasets, the combination of GB and BB followed by feature selection resulted in significantly lower errors than using only BB features with feature selection, showing that the two features sets are complementary.

4 Remarks

The source code for the framework, the datasets and extra resources can be downloaded from `http://www.quest.dcs.shef.ac.uk/`. The project is also set to receive contribution from interested researchers using a GitHub repository: `https://github.com/lspecia/quest`.

The license for the Java code, Python and shell scripts is BSD, a permissive license with no restrictions on the use or extensions of the software for any purposes, including commercial. For pre-existing code and resources, e.g., *scikit-learn*, *GPy* and Berkeley parser, their licenses apply, but features relying on these resources can be easily discarded if necessary.

Acknowledgments

This work was supported by the QuEst (EU FP7 PASCAL2 NoE, Harvest program) and QT-LaunchPad (EU FP7 CSA No. 296347) projects.

References

N. Bach, F. Huang, and Y. Al-Onaizan. 2011. Goodness: a method for measuring machine translation confidence. In *ACL11*, pages 211–219, Portland.

J. Blatz, E. Fitzgerald, G. Foster, S. Gandrabur, C. Goutte, A. Kulesza, A. Sanchis, and N. Ueffing. 2004. Confidence Estimation for Machine Translation. In *Coling04*, pages 315–321, Geneva.

C. Callison-Burch, P. Koehn, C. Monz, M. Post, R. Soricut, and L. Specia. 2012. Findings of the 2012 workshop on statistical machine translation. In *WMT12*, pages 10–51, Montréal.

Y. He, Y. Ma, J. van Genabith, and A. Way. 2010. Bridging SMT and TM with Translation Recommendation. In *ACL10*, pages 622–630, Uppsala.

N. Meinshausen and P. Bühlmann. 2010. Stability selection. *Journal of the Royal Statistical Society: Series B (Statistical Methodology)*, 72:417–473.

K. Papineni, S. Roukos, T. Ward, and W. Zhu. 2002. BLEU: a method for automatic evaluation of machine translation. In *ACL02*, pages 311–318, Philadelphia.

C.E. Rasmussen and C.K.I. Williams. 2006. *Gaussian processes for machine learning*, volume 1. MIT Press, Cambridge.

R. Soricut and A. Echihabi. 2010. Trustrank: Inducing trust in automatic translations via ranking. In *ACL11*, pages 612–621, Uppsala.

L. Specia, M. Turchi, N. Cancedda, M. Dymetman, and N. Cristianini. 2009. Estimating the Sentence-Level Quality of Machine Translation Systems. In *EAMT09*, pages 28–37, Barcelona.

L. Specia, D. Raj, and M. Turchi. 2010. Machine translation evaluation versus quality estimation. *Machine Translation*, 24(1):39–50.

L. Specia. 2011. Exploiting objective annotations for measuring translation post-editing effort. In *EAMT11*, pages 73–80, Leuven.

SORT: An Interactive Source-Rewriting Tool for Improved Translation

Shachar Mirkin, Sriram Venkatapathy, Marc Dymetman, Ioan Calapodescu
Xerox Research Centre Europe
6 Chemin de Maupertuis
38240 Meylan, France
firstname.lastname@xrce.xerox.com

Abstract

The quality of automatic translation is affected by many factors. One is the divergence between the specific source and target languages. Another lies in the source text itself, as some texts are more complex than others. One way to handle such texts is to modify them prior to translation. Yet, an important factor that is often overlooked is the source *translatability* with respect to the specific translation system and the specific model that are being used. In this paper we present an interactive system where source modifications are induced by confidence estimates that are derived from the translation model in use. Modifications are automatically generated and proposed for the user's approval. Such a system can reduce post-editing effort, replacing it by cost-effective pre-editing that can be done by monolinguals.

1 Introduction

While Machine Translation (MT) systems are constantly improving, they are still facing many difficulties, such as out-of-vocabulary words (i.e. words unseen at training time), lack of sufficient in-domain data, ambiguities that the MT model cannot resolve, and the like. An important source of problems lies in the source text itself – some texts are more complex to translate than others.

Consider the following English-to-French translation by a popular service, BING TRANSLATOR:[1] *Head of Mali defense seeks more arms* → *Défense de la tête du Mali cherche bras plus.* There, apart from syntactic problems, both *head* and *arms* have been translated as if they were body parts (*tête* and *bras*). However, suppose that we express the same English meaning in the following way: *Chief of Mali defense wants more weapons.* Then BING produces a much better translation: *Chef d'état-major de la défense du Mali veut plus d'armes.*

The fact that the formulation of the source can strongly influence the quality of the translation has long been known, and there have been studies indicating that adherence to so-called "Controlled Language" guidelines, such as *Simplified Technical English*[2] can reduce the MT post-edition effort. However, as one such study (O'Brien, 2006) notes, it is unfortunately not sufficient to just "*apply the rules [i.e. guidelines] and press Translate. We need to analyze the effect that rules are having on different language pairs and MT systems, and we need to tune our rule sets and texts accordingly*".

In the software system presented here, SORT (*SOurce Rewriting Tool*), we build on the basic insight that formulation of the source needs to be geared to the specific MT model being used, and propose the following approach. First, we assume that the original source text in English (say) is not necessarily under the user's control, but may be given to her. While she is a fluent English speaker, she does not know at all the target language, but uses an MT system; crucially, this system is able *to provide estimates of the quality of its translations* (Specia et al., 2009). SORT then automatically produces a number of rewritings of each English sentence, translates them with the MT system, and displays to the user those rewritings for which the translation quality estimates are higher than the estimate for the original source. The user then interactively selects one such rewriting per sentence, checking that it does not distort the original meaning, and finally the translations of these

[1] http://www.bing.com/translator, accessed on 4/4/2013.

[2] http://www.asd-ste100.org

reformulations are made available.

One advantage of this framework is that the proposed rewritings are implicitly "aware" of the underlying strengths and limitations of the specific MT model. A good *quality estimation*[3] component, for instance, will feel more confident about the translation of an unambiguous word like *weapon* than about that of an ambiguous one such as *arm*, or about the translation of a known term in its domain than about a term not seen during training.

Such a tool is especially relevant for business situations where post-edition costs are very high, for instance because of lack of people both expert in the domain and competent in the target language. Post-edition must be reserved for the most difficult cases, while pre-edition may be easier to organize. While the setup cannot fully guarantee the accuracy of all translations, it can reduce the number of sentences that need to go through post-edition and the overall cost of this task.

2 The rewriting tool

In this section we describe SORT, our implementation of the aforementioned rewriting approach. While the entire process can in principle be fully automated, we focus here on an interactive process where the user views and approves suggested rewritings. The details of the rewriting methods and of the quality estimation used in the current implementation are described in Sections 3 and 4.

Figure 1 presents the system's interface, which is accessed as a web application. With this interface, the user uploads the document that needs to be translated. The translation confidence of each sentence is computed and displayed next to it. The confidence scores are color-coded to enable quickly focusing on the sentences that require more attention. Green denotes sentences for which the translation confidence is high, and are thus expected to produce good translations. Red marks sentences that are estimated to be poorly translated, and all those in between are marked with an orange label.

We attempt to suggest rewritings only for sentences that are estimated to be not so well translated. When we are able to propose rewriting(s) with higher translation confidence than the original, a magnifying glass icon is displayed next to the sentence. Clicking it displays, on the right side of the screen, an ordered list of the more confident rewritings, along with their corresponding confidence estimations. The first sentence on the list is always the original one, to let it be edited, and to make it easier to view the difference between the original and the rewritings. An example is shown on the right side of Figure 1, where we see a rewriting suggestion for the fourth sentence in the document. Here, the suggestion is simply to replace the word *captured* with the word *caught*, a rewriting that is estimated to improve the translation of the sentence.

The user can select one of the suggestions or choose to edit either the original or one of the rewritings. The current sentence which is being examined is marked with a different color and the alternative under focus is marked with a small icon (the bidirectional arrows). The differences between the alternatives and the original are highlighted. After the user's confirmation (with the check mark icon), the display of the document on the left-hand side is updated based on her selection, including the updated confidence estimation. At any time, the user (if she speaks the target language) can click on the cogwheel icon and view the translation of the source or of its rewritten version. When done, the user can save the edited text or its translation. Moses Release 1.0 of an English-Spanish Europarl-trained model[4] was used in this work to obtain English-Spanish translations.

2.1 System and software architecture

SORT is implemented as a web application, using an MVC (Model View Controller) software architecture. The *Model* part is formed by Java classes representing the application state (user input, selected text lines, associated rewriting propositions and scores). The *Controller* consists of several servlet components handling each user interaction with the backend server (file uploads, SMT tools calls via XML-RPC or use of the embedded Java library that handles the actual rewritings). Finally, the *View* is built with standard web technologies: HTML5, JavaScript (AJAX) and CSS style sheets. The application was developed and deployed on Linux (CentOS release 6.4), with a Java Runtime 6 (Java HotSpot 64-Bit Server VM), within a Tomcat 7.0 Application Server, and tested with Firefox as the web client both on Linux and Windows 7.

Figure 2 shows the system architecture of SORT,

[3]Also known as *confidence estimation*.

[4]http://www.statmt.org/moses/RELEASE-1.0/model/

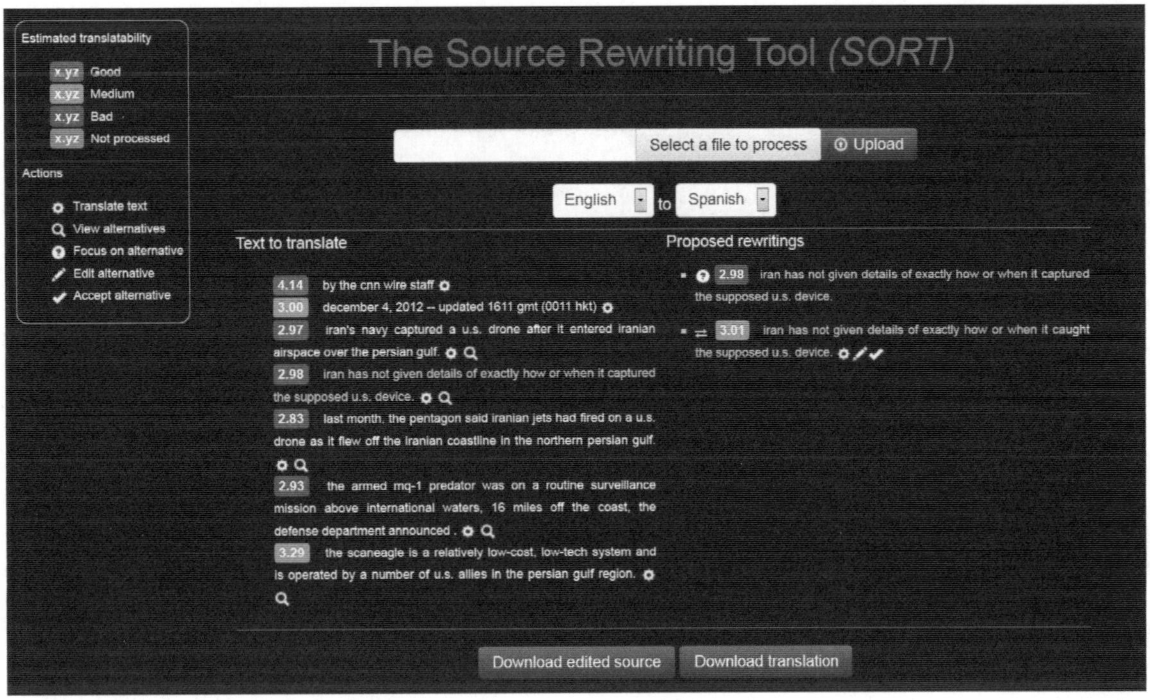

Figure 1: SORT's interface

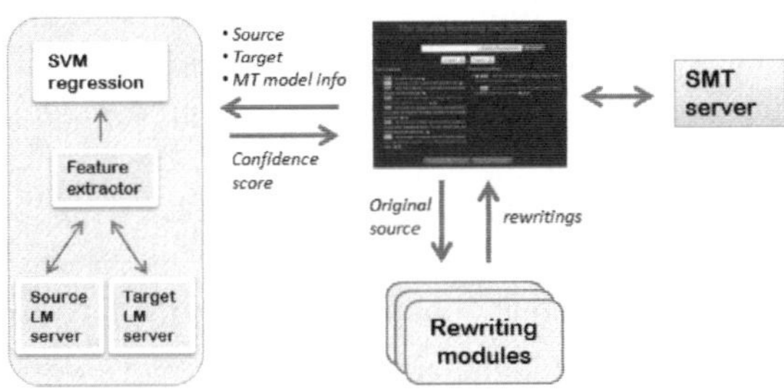

Figure 2: SORT's system architecture. For simplicity, only partial input-output details are shown.

with some details of the current implementation. The entire process is performed via a client-server architecture in order to provide responsiveness, as required in an interactive system. The user communicates with the system through the interface shown in Figure 1. When a document is loaded, its sentences are translated in parallel by an SMT Moses server (Koehn et al., 2007). Then, the source and the target are sent to the confidence estimator, and the translation model information is also made available to it. The confidence estimator extracts features from that input and returns a confidence score. Specifically, the language model features are computed with two SRILM servers (Stolcke, 2002), one for the source language and one for the target language. Rewritings are produced by the rewriting modules (see Section 3 for the implemented rewriting methods). For each rewriting, the same process of translation and confidence estimation is performed. Translations are cached during the session; thus, when the user wishes to view a translation or download the translations of the entire document, the response is immediate.

3 Source rewriting

Various methods can be used to rewrite a source text. In what follows we describe two rewriting methods, based on *Text Simplification* techniques, which we implemented and integrated in the current version of SORT. Simplification operations include the replacement of words by simpler ones, removal of complicated syntactic structures, shortening of sentences etc. (Feng, 2008). Our assumption is that simpler sentences are more likely to yield higher quality translations. Clearly, this is not always the case; yet, we leave this decision to the confidence estimation component.

Sentence-level simplification (Specia, 2010) has proposed to model text simplification as a Statistical Machine Translation (SMT) task where the goal is to translate sentences to their simplified version in the *same* language. In this approach, a simplification model is learnt from a parallel corpus of texts and their simplified versions. Applying this method, we train an SMT model from English to Simple English, based on the PWKP parallel corpus generated from Wikipedia (Zhu et al., 2010);[5] we use only alignments involving a single sentence on each side. This results in a phrase table containing many entries where source and target phrases are identical, but also phrase-pairs that are mapping complex phrases to their simplified counterparts, such as the following:

- *due to its location on → because it was on*
- *primarily dry and secondarily cold → both cold and dry*
- *the high mountainous alps → the alps*

Also, the language model is trained with Simple English sentences to encourage the generation of simpler texts. Given a source text, it is translated to its simpler version, and its n-best translations are assessed by the confidence estimation component.

Lexical simplification One of the primary operations for text-simplification is lexical substitution (Table 2 in (Specia, 2010)). Hence, in addition to rewriting a full sentence using the previous technique, we implemented a second method, addressing lexical simplification directly, and only modifying local aspects of the source sentence. The approach here is to extract relevant synonyms from our trained SMT model of English to Simplified English, and use them as substitutions to simplify new sentences. We extract all single token mappings from the phrase table of the trained model, removing punctuations, numbers and stop-words. We check whether their lemmas were synonyms in WordNet (Fellbaum, 1998) (with all possible parts-of-speech as this information was not available in the SMT model). Only those are left as valid substitution pairs. When a match of an English word is found in the source sentence it is replaced with its simpler synonym to generate an alternative for the source. For example, using this rewriting method for the source sentence "*Why the Galileo research program* **superseded rival** *programs,*" three rewritings of the sentence are generated when *rival* is substituted by *competitor* or *superseded* by *replaced*, and when both substitutions occur together.

[5]Downloaded from: `http://www.ukp.tu-darmstadt.de/data/sentence-simplification`

In the current version of SORT, both sentence-level and lexical simplification methods are used in conjunction to suggest rewritings for sentences with low confidence scores.

4 Confidence estimation

Our confidence estimator is based on the system and data provided for the 2012 *Quality estimation shared task* (Callison-Burch et al., 2012). In this task, participants were required to estimate the quality of automated translations. Their estimates were compared to human scores of the translation which referred to the suitability of the translation for post-editing. The scores ranged from 1 to 5, where 1 corresponded to translation that practically needs to be done from scratch, and 5 to translations that requires little to no editing.

The task's training set consisted of approximately 1800 source sentences in English, their Moses translations to Spanish and the scores given to the translations by the three judges. With this data we trained an SVM regression model using SVM^{light} (Joachims, 1999). Features were extracted with the task's feature-extraction baseline module. Two types of features are used in this module (i) *black-box* features, which do not assume access to the translation system, such as the length of the source and the target, number of punctuation marks and language model probabilities, and (ii) *glass-box* features, which are extracted from the translation model, such as the average number of translations per source word (Specia et al., 2009).

5 Initial evaluation and analysis

We performed an initial evaluation of our approach in an English to Spanish translation setting, using the 2008 News Commentary data.[6] First, two annotators who speak English but not Spanish used SORT to rewrite an English text. They reviewed the proposed rewritings for 960 sentences and were instructed to "trust the judgment" of the confidence estimator; that is, reviewing the suggestions from the most to the least confident one, they accepted the first rewriting that was fluent and preserved the meaning of the source document as a whole. 440 pairs of the original sentence and the selected alternative were then both translated to Spanish and were presented as competitors to

[6]Available at `http://www.statmt.org`

three native Spanish speakers. The sentences were placed within their context in the original document, taken from the Spanish side of the corpus. The order of presentation of the two competitors was random. In this evaluation, the translation of the original was preferred 20.6% of the cases, the rewriting 30.4% of them, and for 49% of the sentences, no clear winner was chosen.[7] Among the two rewriting methods, the sentence-level method more often resulted in preferred translations.

These results suggest that rewriting is estimated to improve translation quality. However, the amount of preferred original translations indicates that the confidence estimator is not always discriminative enough: by construction, for every rewriting that is displayed, the confidence component estimates the translation of the original to be less accurate than that of the rewriting; yet, this is not always reflected in the preferences of the evaluators. On a different dimension than translation quality, the large number of cases with no clear winner, and the analysis we conducted, indicate that the user's cognitive effort would be decreased if we only displayed those rewritings associated with a substantial improvement in confidence; due to the nature of our methods, frequently, identical or near-identical translations were generated, with only marginal differences in confidence, e.g., when two source synonyms were translated to the same target word. Also, often a wrong synonym was suggested as a replacement for a word (e.g. *Christmas air* for *Christmas atmosphere*). This was somewhat surprising as we had expected the language model features of the confidence estimator to help removing these cases. While they were filtered by the English-speaking users, and thus did not present a problem for translation, they created unnecessary workload. Putting more emphasis on context features in the confidence estimation or explicitly verifying context-suitability of a lexical substitutions could help addressing this issue.

6 Related work

Some related approaches focus on the authoring process and control *a priori* the range of possible texts, either by interactively enforcing lexical and syntactic constraints on the source that simplify the operations of a rule-based translation system (Carbonell et al., 1997), or by semantically guiding a monolingual author in the generation of multilingual texts (Power and Scott, 1998; Dymetman et al., 2000). A recent approach (Venkatapathy and Mirkin, 2012) proposes an authoring tool that consults the MT system itself to propose phrases that should be used during composition to obtain better translations. All these methods address the authoring of the source text from scratch. This is inherently different from the objective of our work where an existing text is modified to improve its translatability. Moving away from authoring approaches, (Choumane et al., 2005) propose an interactive system where the author helps a rule-based translation system disambiguate a source text inside a structured document editor. The techniques are generic and are not automatically adapted to a specific MT system or model. Closer to our approach of modifying the source text, one approach is to paraphrase the source or to generate sentences entailed by it (Callison-Burch et al., 2006; Mirkin et al., 2009; Marton et al., 2009; Aziz et al., 2010). These works, however, focus on handling out-of-vocabulary (OOV) words, do not assess the translatability of the source sentence and are not interactive.[8] The MonoTrans2 project (Hu et al., 2011) proposes monolingual-based editing for translation. Monolingual speakers of the source and target language collaborate to improve the translation. Unlike our approach, here both the feedback for poorly translated sentences and the actual modification of the source is done by humans. This contrasts with the automatic handling (albeit less accurate) of both these tasks in our work.

7 Conclusions and future work

We introduced a system for rewriting texts for translation under the control of a confidence estimator. While we focused on an interactive mode, where a monolingual user is asked to check the quality of the source reformulations, in an extension of this approach, the quality of the reformulations could also be assessed automatically, removing the interactive aspects at the cost of an increased risk of rewriting errors. For future work we wish to add more powerful rewriting techniques that are able to explore a larger space of possible reformulations, but compensate this ex-

[7] One should consider these figures with caution, as the numbers may be too small to be statistically meaningful.

[8] Another way to use paraphrases for improved translation has been proposed by (Max, 2010) who uses paraphrasing of the source text to increase the number of training examples for the SMT system.

panded space by robust filtering methods. Based on an evaluation of the quality of the generated alternatives as well as on user selection decisions, we may be able to learn a quality estimator for the rewriting operations themselves. Such methods could be useful both in an interactive mode, to minimize the effort of the monolingual source user, as well as in an automatic mode, to avoid misinterpretation. In this work we used an available baseline feature extraction module for confidence estimation. A better estimator could benefit our system significantly, as we argued above. Lastly, we wish to further improve the user interface of the tool, based on feedback from actual users.

References

[Aziz et al.2010] Wilker Aziz, Marc Dymetman, Shachar Mirkin, Lucia Specia, Nicola Cancedda, and Ido Dagan. 2010. Learning an expert from human annotations in statistical machine translation: the case of out-of-vocabularywords. In *Proceedings of EAMT*.

[Callison-Burch et al.2006] Chris Callison-Burch, Philipp Koehn, and Miles Osborne. 2006. Improved statistical machine translation using paraphrases. In *Proceedings of HLT-NAACL*.

[Callison-Burch et al.2012] Chris Callison-Burch, Philipp Koehn, Christof Monz, Matt Post, Radu Soricut, and Lucia Specia. 2012. Findings of the 2012 workshop on statistical machine translation. In *Proceedings of WMT*.

[Carbonell et al.1997] Jaime G Carbonell, Sharlene L Gallup, Timothy J Harris, James W Higdon, Dennis A Hill, David C Hudson, David Nasjleti, Mervin L Rennich, Peggy M Andersen, Michael M Bauer, et al. 1997. Integrated authoring and translation system. US Patent 5,677,835.

[Choumane et al.2005] Ali Choumane, Hervé Blanchon, and Cécile Roisin. 2005. Integrating translation services within a structured editor. In *Proceedings of the ACM symposium on Document engineering*. ACM.

[Dymetman et al.2000] Marc Dymetman, Veronika Lux, and Aarne Ranta. 2000. Xml and multilingual document authoring: Convergent trends. In *Proceedings of COLING*.

[Fellbaum1998] Christiane Fellbaum, editor. 1998. *WordNet: An Electronic Lexical Database (Language, Speech, and Communication)*. The MIT Press.

[Feng2008] Lijun Feng. 2008. Text simplification: A survey. Technical report, CUNY.

[Hu et al.2011] Chang Hu, Philip Resnik, Yakov Kronrod, Vladimir Eidelman, Olivia Buzek, and Benjamin B. Bederson. 2011. The value of monolingual crowdsourcing in a real-world translation scenario: simulation using haitian creole emergency sms messages. In *Proceedings of WMT*.

[Joachims1999] T. Joachims. 1999. Making large-scale SVM learning practical. In B. Schölkopf, C. Burges, and A. Smola, editors, *Advances in Kernel Methods - Support Vector Learning*, chapter 11, pages 169–184. MIT Press.

[Koehn et al.2007] Philipp Koehn, Hieu Hoang, Alexandra Birch, Chris Callison-Burch, Marcello Federico, Nicola Bertoldi, Brooke Cowan, Wade Shen, Christine Moran, Richard Zens, Chris Dyer, Ondrej Bojar, Alexandra Constantin, and Evan Herbst. 2007. Moses: Open source toolkit for statistical machine translation. In *Proceedings of ACL, Demo and Poster Sessions*.

[Marton et al.2009] Yuval Marton, Chris Callison-Burch, and Philip Resnik. 2009. Improved statistical machine translation using monolingually-derived paraphrases. In *Proceedings of EMNLP*.

[Max2010] Aurélien Max. 2010. Example-based paraphrasing for improved phrase-based statistical machine translation. In *Proceedings of EMNLP*.

[Mirkin et al.2009] Shachar Mirkin, Lucia Specia, Nicola Cancedda, Ido Dagan, Marc Dymetman, and Idan Szpektor. 2009. Source-language entailment modeling for translating unknown terms. In *Proceedings of ACL-IJCNLP*.

[O'Brien2006] Sharon O'Brien. 2006. Controlled Language and Post-Editing. *Multilingual*, 17(7):17–19.

[Power and Scott1998] Richard Power and Donia Scott. 1998. Multilingual authoring using feedback texts. In *Proceedings of ACL*.

[Specia et al.2009] Lucia Specia, Nicola Cancedda, Marc Dymetman, Marco Turchi, and Nello Cristianini. 2009. Estimating the sentence-level quality of machine translation systems. In *Proceedings of EAMT*.

[Specia2010] Lucia Specia. 2010. Translating from complex to simplified sentences. In *Proceedings of PROPOR*.

[Stolcke2002] Andreas Stolcke. 2002. SRILM - an extensible language modeling toolkit. In *INTERSPEECH*.

[Venkatapathy and Mirkin2012] Sriram Venkatapathy and Shachar Mirkin. 2012. An SMT-driven authoring tool. In *Proceedings of COLING 2012: Demonstration Papers*.

[Zhu et al.2010] Zhemin Zhu, Delphine Bernhard, and Iryna Gurevych. 2010. A monolingual tree-based translation model for sentence simplification. In *Proceedings of COLING*.

Travatar: A Forest-to-String Machine Translation Engine based on Tree Transducers

Graham Neubig
Graduate School of Information Science
Nara Institute of Science and Technology
8916-5 Takayama-cho, Ikoma-shi, Nara, Japan
neubig@is.naist.jp

Abstract

In this paper we describe Travatar, a forest-to-string machine translation (MT) engine based on tree transducers. It provides an open-source C++ implementation for the entire forest-to-string MT pipeline, including rule extraction, tuning, decoding, and evaluation. There are a number of options for model training, and tuning includes advanced options such as hypergraph MERT, and training of sparse features through online learning. The training pipeline is modeled after that of the popular Moses decoder, so users familiar with Moses should be able to get started quickly. We perform a validation experiment of the decoder on English-Japanese machine translation, and find that it is possible to achieve greater accuracy than translation using phrase-based and hierarchical-phrase-based translation. As auxiliary results, we also compare different syntactic parsers and alignment techniques that we tested in the process of developing the decoder.

Travatar is available under the LGPL at http://phontron.com/travatar

1 Introduction

One of the recent trends in statistical machine translation (SMT) is the popularity of models that use syntactic information to help solve problems of long-distance reordering between the source and target language text. These techniques can be broadly divided into pre-ordering techniques, which first parse and reorder the source sentence into the target order before translating (Xia and McCord, 2004; Isozaki et al., 2010b), and tree-based decoding techniques, which take a tree or forest as input and choose the reordering and translation jointly (Yamada and Knight, 2001; Liu et al., 2006; Mi et al., 2008). While pre-ordering is not able to consider both translation and reordering in a joint model, it is useful in that it is done before the actual translation process, so it can be performed with a conventional translation pipeline using a standard phrase-based decoder such as Moses (Koehn et al., 2007). For tree-to-string systems, on the other hand, it is necessary to have available or create a decoder that is equipped with this functionality, which becomes a bottleneck in the research and development process.

In this demo paper, we describe Travatar, an open-source tree-to-string or forest-to-string translation system that can be used as a tool for translation using source-side syntax, and as a platform for research into syntax-based translation methods. In particular, compared to other decoders which mainly implement syntax-based translation in the synchronous context-free grammar (SCFG) framework (Chiang, 2007), Travatar is built upon the tree transducer framework (Graehl and Knight, 2004), a richer formalism that can help capture important distinctions between parse trees, as we show in Section 2. Travatar includes a fully documented training and testing regimen that was modeled around that of Moses, making it possible for users familiar with Moses to get started with Travatar quickly. The framework of the software is also designed to be extensible, so the toolkit is applicable for other tree-to-string transduction tasks.

In the evaluation of the decoder on English-Japanese machine translation, we perform a comparison to Moses's phrase-based, hierarchical-phrase-based, and SCFG-based tree-to-string

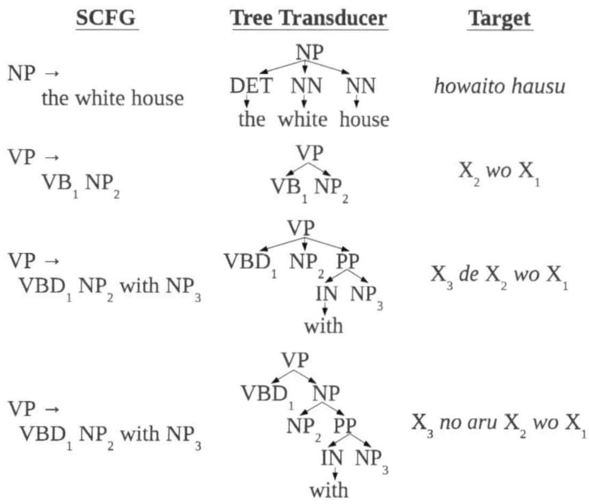

Figure 1: Tree-to-string translation rules for SCFGs and tree transducers.

translation. Based on the results, we find that tree-to-string, and particularly forest-to-string, translation using Travatar provides competitive or superior accuracy to all of these techniques. As auxiliary results, we also compare different syntactic parsers and alignment techniques that we tested in the process of developing the decoder.

2 Tree-to-String Translation

2.1 Overview

Tree-to-string translation uses syntactic information to improve translation by first parsing the source sentence, then using this source-side parse tree to decide the translation and reordering of the input. This method has several advantages, including efficiency of decoding, relatively easy handling of global reordering, and an intuitive representation of de-lexicalized rules that express general differences in order between the source and target languages. Within tree-to-string translation there are two major methodologies, synchronous context-free grammars (Chiang, 2007), and tree transducers (Graehl and Knight, 2004).

An example of tree-to-string translation rules supported by SCFGs and tree transducers is shown in Figure 1. In this example, the first rule is a simple multi-word noun phrase, the second example is an example of a delexicalized rule expressing translation from English SVO word order to Japanese SOV word order. The third and fourth examples are translations of a verb, noun phrase, and prepositional phrase, where the third rule has the preposition attached to the verb, and the fourth has the preposition attached to the noun.

For the SCFGs, it can be seen that on the source side of the rule, there are placeholders corresponding to syntactic phrases, and on the target side of the rule there corresponding placeholders that do not have a syntactic label. On the other hand in the example of the translation rules using tree transducers, it can be seen that similar rules can be expressed, but the source rules are richer than simple SCFG rules, also including the internal structure of the parse tree. This internal structure is important for achieving translation results faithful to the input parse. In particular, the third and fourth rules show an intuitive example in which this internal structure can be important for translation. Here the full tree structures demonstrate important differences in the attachment of the prepositional phrase to the verb or noun. While this is one of the most difficult and important problems in syntactic parsing, the source side in the SCFG is identical, losing the ability to distinguish between the very information that parsers are designed to disambiguate.

In traditional tree-to-string translation methods, the translator uses a single one-best parse tree output by a syntactic parser, but parse errors have the potential to degrade the quality of translation. An important advance in tree-to-string translation that helps ameliorate this difficulity is forest-to-string translation, which represents a large number of potential parses as a packed forest, allowing the translator to choose between these parses during the process of translation (Mi et al., 2008).

2.2 The State of Open Source Software

There are a number of open-source software packages that support tree-to-string translation in the SCFG framework. For example, Moses (Koehn et al., 2007) and NiuTrans (Xiao et al., 2012) support the annotation of source-side syntactic labels, and taking parse trees (or in the case of NiuTrans, forests) as input.

There are also a few other decoders that support other varieties of using source-side syntax to help improve translation or global reordering. For example, the cdec decoder (Dyer et al., 2010) supports the context-free-reordering/finite-state-translation framework described by Dyer and Resnik (2010). The Akamon decoder (Wu et al., 2012) supports translation using head-driven phrase structure grammars as described by Wu et al. (2010).

However, to our knowledge, while there is a general-purpose tool for tree automata in general (May and Knight, 2006), there is no open-source toolkit implementing the SMT pipeline in the tree transducer framework, despite it being a target of active research (Graehl and Knight, 2004; Liu et al., 2006; Huang et al., 2006; Mi et al., 2008).

3 The Travatar Machine Translation Toolkit

In this section, we describe the overall framework of the Travatar decoder, following the order of the training pipeline.

3.1 Data Preprocessing

This consists of parsing the source side sentence and tokenizing the target side sentences. Travatar can decode input in the bracketed format of the Penn Treebank, or also in forest format. There is documentation and scripts for using Travatar with several parsers for English, Chinese, and Japanese included with the toolkit.

3.2 Training

Once the data has been pre-processed, a tree-to-string model can be trained with the training pipeline included in the toolkit. Like the training pipeline for Moses, there is a single script that performs alignment, rule extraction, scoring, and parameter initialization. Language model training can be performed using a separate toolkit, and instructions are provided in the documentation.

For word alignment, the Travatar training pipeline is integrated with GIZA++ (Och and Ney, 2003) by default, but can also use alignments from any other aligner.

Rule extraction is performed using the GHKM algorithm (Galley et al., 2006) and its extension to rule extraction from forests (Mi and Huang, 2008). There are also a number of options implemented, including rule composition, attachment of null-aligned target words at either the highest point in the tree, or at every possible position, and left and right binarization (Galley et al., 2006; Wang et al., 2007).

Rule scoring uses a standard set of forward and backward conditional probabilities, lexicalized translation probabilities, phrase frequency, and word and phrase counts. Rule scores are stored as sparse vectors by default, which allows for scoring using an arbitrarily large number of feature functions.

3.3 Decoding

Given a translation model Travatar is able to decode parsed input sentences to generate translations. The decoding itself is performed using the bottom-up forest-to-string decoding algorithm of Mi et al. (2008). Beam-search implemented using cube pruning (Chiang, 2007) is used to adjust the trade-off between search speed and translation accuracy.

The source side of the translation model is stored using a space-efficient trie data structure (Yata, 2012) implemented using the marisa-trie toolkit.[1] Rule lookup is performed using left-to-right depth-first search, which can be implemented as prefix lookup in the trie for efficient search.

The language model storage uses the implementation in KenLM (Heafield, 2011), and particularly the implementation that maintains left and right language model states for syntax-based MT (Heafield et al., 2011).

3.4 Tuning and Evaluation

For tuning the parameters of the model, Travatar natively supports minimum error rate training (MERT) (Och, 2003) and is extension to hypergraphs (Kumar et al., 2009). This tuning can be performed for evaluation measures including BLEU (Papineni et al., 2002) and RIBES (Isozaki et al., 2010a), with an easily extendable interface that makes it simple to support other measures.

There is also a preliminary implementation of online learning methods such as the structured perceptron algorithm (Collins, 2002), and regularized structured SVMs trained using FOBOS (Duchi and Singer, 2009). There are plans to implement more algorithms such as MIRA or AROW (Chiang, 2012) in the near future.

The Travatar toolkit also provides an evaluation program that can calculate the scores of translation output according to various evaluation measures, and calculate the significance of differences between systems using bootstrap resampling (Koehn, 2004).

---

[1] `http://marisa-trie.googlecode.com`

4 Experiments

4.1 Experimental Setup

In our experiments, we validated the performance of the translation toolkit on English-Japanese translation of Wikipedia articles, as specified by the Kyoto Free Translation Task (KFTT) (Neubig, 2011). Training used the 405k sentences of training data of length under 60, tuning was performed on the development set, and testing was performed on the test set using the BLEU and RIBES measures. As baseline systems we use the Moses[2] implementation of phrase-based (MOSES-PBMT), hierarchical phrase-based (MOSES-HIER), and tree-to-string translation (MOSES-T2S). The phrase-based and hierarchical phrase-based models were trained with the default settings according to tutorials on each web site.

For all systems, we use a 5-gram Kneser-Ney smoothed language model. Alignment for each system was performed using either GIZA++[3] or Nile[4] with main results reported for the aligner that achieved the best accuracy on the dev set, and a further comparison shown in the auxiliary experiments in Section 4.3. Tuning was performed with minimum error rate training to maximize BLEU over 200-best lists. Tokenization was performed with the Stanford tokenizer for English, and the KyTea word segmenter (Neubig et al., 2011) for Japanese.

For all tree-to-string systems we use Egret[5] as an English parser, as we found it to achieve high accuracy, and it allows for the simple output of forests. Rule extraction was performed using one-best trees, which were right-binarized, and lower-cased post-parsing. For Travatar, composed rules of up to size 4 and a maximum of 2 non-terminals and 7 terminals for each rule were used. Null-aligned words were only attached to the top node, and no count normalization was performed, in contrast to Moses, which performs count normalization and exhaustive null word attachment. Decoding was performed over either one-best trees (TRAV-T2S), or over forests including all edges included in the parser 200-best list (TRAV-F2S), and a pop limit of 1000 hypotheses was used for cube pruning.

[2]http://statmt.org/moses/

[3]http://code.google.com/p/giza-pp/

[4]http://code.google.com/p/nile/ As Nile is a supervised aligner, we trained it on the alignments provided with the KFTT.

[5]http://code.google.com/p/egret-parser/

	BLEU	RIBES	Rules	Sent/s.
MOSES-PBMT	22.27	68.37	10.1M	5.69
MOSES-HIER	22.04	70.29	34.2M	1.36
MOSES-T2S	**23.81**	72.01	52.3M	1.71
TRAV-T2S	23.15	72.32	9.57M	3.29
TRAV-F2S	**23.97**	**73.27**	9.57M	1.11

Table 1: Translation results (BLEU, RIBES), rule table size, and speed in sentences per second for each system. Bold numbers indicate a statistically significant difference over all other systems (bootstrap resampling with $p > 0.05$) (Koehn, 2004).

4.2 System Comparison

The comparison between the systems is shown in Table 1. From these results we can see that the systems utilizing source-side syntax significantly outperform the PBMT and Hiero, validating the usefulness of source side syntax on the English-to-Japanese task. Comparing the two tree-to-string sytems, we can see that TRAV-T2S has slightly higher RIBES and slightly lower BLEU than MOSES-T2S. One reason for the slightly higher BLEU of MOSES-T2S is because Moses's rule extraction algorithm is more liberal in its attachment of null-aligned words, resulting in a much larger rule table (52.3M rules vs. 9.57M rules) and memory footprint. In this setting, TRAV-T2S is approximately two times faster than MOSES-T2S. When using forest based decoding in TRAV-F2S, we see significant gains in accuracy over TRAV-T2S, with BLEU slightly and RIBES greatly exceeding that of MOSES-T2S.

4.3 Effect of Alignment/Parsing

In addition, as auxiliary results, we present a comparison of Travatar's tree-to-string and forest-to-string systems using different alignment methods and syntactic parsers to examine the results on translation (Table 2).

For parsers, we compared Egret with the Stanford parser.[6] While we do not have labeled data to calculate parse accuracies with, Egret is a clone of the Berkeley parser, which has been reported to achieve higher accuracy than the Stanford parser on several domains (Kummerfeld et al., 2012). From the translation results, we can see that STAN-

[6]http://nlp.stanford.edu/software/lex-parser.shtml

	GIZA++		Nile	
	BLEU	RIBES	BLEU	RIBES
PBMT	22.28	68.37	22.37	68.43
HIER	22.05	70.29	21.77	69.31
STAN-T2S	21.47	70.94	22.44	72.02
EGRET-T2S	22.82	71.90	23.15	72.32
EGRET-F2S	23.35	71.77	**23.97**	**73.27**

Table 2: Translation results (BLEU, RIBES), for several translation models (PBMT, Hiero, T2S, F2S), aligners (GIZA++, Nile), and parsers (Stanford, Egret).

T2S significantly underperforms EGRET-T2S, confirming that the effectiveness of the parser plays a large effect on the translation accuracy.

Next, we compared the unsupervised aligner GIZA++, with the supervised aligner Nile, which uses syntactic information to improve alignment accuracy (Riesa and Marcu, 2010). We held out 10% of the hand aligned data provided with the KFTT, and found that GIZA++ achieves 58.32% alignment F-measure, while Nile achieves 64.22% F-measure. With respect to translation accuracy, we found that for translation that does not use syntactic information, improvements in alignment do not necessarily increase translation accuracy, as has been noted by Ganchev et al. (2008). However, for all tree-to-string systems, the improved alignments result in significant improvements in accuracy, showing that alignments are, in fact, important in our syntax-driven translation setup.

5 Conclusion and Future Directions

In this paper, we introduced Travatar, an open-source toolkit for forest-to-string translation using tree transducers. We hope this decoder will be useful to the research community as a test-bed for forest-to-string systems. The software is already sufficiently mature to be used as is, as evidenced by the competitive, if not superior, results in our English-Japanese evaluation.

We have a number of plans for future development. First, we plan to support advanced rule extraction techniques, such as fuller support for count regularization and forest-based rule extraction (Mi and Huang, 2008), and using the EM algorithm to choose attachments for null-aligned words (Galley et al., 2006) or the direction of rule binarization (Wang et al., 2007). We also plan to incorporate advances in decoding to improve search speed (Huang and Mi, 2010). In addition, there is a preliminary implementation of the ability to introduce target-side syntactic information, either through hard constraints as in tree-to-tree translation systems (Graehl and Knight, 2004), or through soft constraints, as in syntax-augmented machine translation (Zollmann and Venugopal, 2006). Finally, we will provide better support of parallelization through the entire pipeline to increase the efficiency of training and decoding.

Acknowledgements: We thank Kevin Duh and an anonymous reviewer for helpful comments. Part of this work was supported by JSPS KAKENHI Grant Number 25730136.

References

David Chiang. 2007. Hierarchical phrase-based translation. *Computational Linguistics*, 33(2).

David Chiang. 2012. Hope and fear for discriminative training of statistical translation models. *Journal of Machine Learning Research*, pages 1159–1187.

Michael Collins. 2002. Discriminative training methods for hidden Markov models: Theory and experiments with perceptron algorithms. In *Proc. EMNLP*, pages 1–8.

John Duchi and Yoram Singer. 2009. Efficient online and batch learning using forward backward splitting. *Journal of Machine Learning Research*, 10:2899–2934.

Chris Dyer and Philip Resnik. 2010. Context-free reordering, finite-state translation. In *Proc. HLT-NAACL*.

Chris Dyer, Adam Lopez, Juri Ganitkevitch, Jonathan Weese, Ferhan Ture, Phil Blunsom, Hendra Setiawan, Vladimir Eidelman, and Philip Resnik. 2010. cdec: A decoder, alignment, and learning framework for finite-state and context-free translation models. In *Proceedings of the ACL 2010 System Demonstrations*, pages 7–12.

Michel Galley, Jonathan Graehl, Kevin Knight, Daniel Marcu, Steve DeNeefe, Wei Wang, and Ignacio Thayer. 2006. Scalable inference and training of context-rich syntactic translation models. In *Proc. ACL*, pages 961–968.

Kuzman Ganchev, João V. Graça, and Ben Taskar. 2008. Better alignments = better translations? In *Proc. ACL*.

Jonathan Graehl and Kevin Knight. 2004. Training tree transducers. In *Proc. HLT*, pages 105–112.

Kenneth Heafield, Hieu Hoang, Philipp Koehn, Tetsuo Kiso, and Marcello Federico. 2011. Left language model state for syntactic machine translation. In *Proc. IWSLT*.

Kenneth Heafield. 2011. Kenlm: Faster and smaller language model queries. In *Proc. WMT*, pages 187–197.

Liang Huang and Haitao Mi. 2010. Efficient incremental decoding for tree-to-string translation. In *Proc. EMNLP*, pages 273–283.

Liang Huang, Kevin Knight, and Aravind Joshi. 2006. Statistical syntax-directed translation with extended domain of locality. In *Proceedings of AMTA*, pages 66–73.

Hideki Isozaki, Tsutomu Hirao, Kevin Duh, Katsuhito Sudoh, and Hajime Tsukada. 2010a. Automatic evaluation of translation quality for distant language pairs. In *Proc. EMNLP*, pages 944–952.

Hideki Isozaki, Katsuhito Sudoh, Hajime Tsukada, and Kevin Duh. 2010b. Head finalization: A simple reordering rule for SOV languages. In *Proc. WMT and MetricsMATR*.

Philipp Koehn, Hieu Hoang, Alexandra Birch, Chris Callison-Burch, Marcello Federico, Nicola Bertoldi, Brooke Cowan, Wade Shen, Christine Moran, Richard Zens, Chris Dyer, Ondrej Bojar, Alexandra Constantin, and Evan Herbst. 2007. Moses: Open source toolkit for statistical machine translation. In *Proc. ACL*, pages 177–180, Prague, Czech Republic.

Philipp Koehn. 2004. Statistical significance tests for machine translation evaluation. In *Proc. EMNLP*.

Shankar Kumar, Wolfgang Macherey, Chris Dyer, and Franz Och. 2009. Efficient minimum error rate training and minimum Bayes-risk decoding for translation hypergraphs and lattices. In *Proc. ACL*, pages 163–171.

Jonathan K Kummerfeld, David Hall, James R Curran, and Dan Klein. 2012. Parser showdown at the wall street corral: an empirical investigation of error types in parser output. In *Proc. EMNLP*, pages 1048–1059.

Yang Liu, Qun Liu, and Shouxun Lin. 2006. Tree-to-string alignment template for statistical machine translation. In *Proc. ACL*.

Jonathan May and Kevin Knight. 2006. Tiburon: A weighted tree automata toolkit. In *Implementation and Application of Automata*, pages 102–113. Springer.

Haitao Mi and Liang Huang. 2008. Forest-based translation rule extraction. In *Proc. EMNLP*, pages 206–214.

Haitao Mi, Liang Huang, and Qun Liu. 2008. Forest-based translation. In *Proc. ACL*, pages 192–199.

Graham Neubig, Yosuke Nakata, and Shinsuke Mori. 2011. Pointwise prediction for robust, adaptable Japanese morphological analysis. In *Proc. ACL*, pages 529–533, Portland, USA, June.

Graham Neubig. 2011. The Kyoto free translation task. `http://www.phontron.com/kftt`.

Franz Josef Och and Hermann Ney. 2003. A systematic comparison of various statistical alignment models. *Computational Linguistics*, 29(1):19–51.

Franz Josef Och. 2003. Minimum error rate training in statistical machine translation. In *Proc. ACL*.

Kishore Papineni, Salim Roukos, Todd Ward, and Wei-Jing Zhu. 2002. BLEU: a method for automatic evaluation of machine translation. In *Proc. ACL*, pages 311–318, Philadelphia, USA.

Jason Riesa and Daniel Marcu. 2010. Hierarchical search for word alignment. In *Proc. ACL*, pages 157–166.

Wei Wang, Kevin Knight, and Daniel Marcu. 2007. Binarizing syntax trees to improve syntax-based machine translation accuracy. In *Proc. EMNLP*, pages 746–754.

Xianchao Wu, Takuya Matsuzaki, and Jun'ichi Tsujii. 2010. Fine-grained tree-to-string translation rule extraction. In *Proc. ACL*, pages 325–334.

Xianchao Wu, Takuya Matsuzaki, and Jun'ichi Tsujii. 2012. Akamon: An open source toolkit for tree/forest-based statistical machine translation. In *Proceedings of the ACL 2012 System Demonstrations*, pages 127–132.

Fei Xia and Michael McCord. 2004. Improving a statistical MT system with automatically learned rewrite patterns. In *Proc. COLING*.

Tong Xiao, Jingbo Zhu, Hao Zhang, and Qiang Li. 2012. Niutrans: An open source toolkit for phrase-based and syntax-based machine translation. In *Proceedings of the ACL 2012 System Demonstrations*, pages 19–24.

Kenji Yamada and Kevin Knight. 2001. A syntax-based statistical translation model. In *Proc. ACL*.

Susumu Yata. 2012. Dictionary compression using nested prefix/Patricia tries (in Japanese). In *Proc. 17th NLP*.

Andreas Zollmann and Ashish Venugopal. 2006. Syntax augmented machine translation via chart parsing. In *Proc. WMT*.

PLIS: a Probabilistic Lexical Inference System

Eyal Shnarch[1], **Erel Segal-haLevi**[1], **Jacob Goldberger**[2], **Ido Dagan**[1]
[1]Computer Science Department, Bar-Ilan University, Israel
[2]Faculty of Engineering, Bar-Ilan University, Israel
{shey,erelsgl,dagan}@cs.biu.ac.il
goldbej@eng.biu.ac.il

Abstract

This paper presents PLIS, an open source Probabilistic Lexical Inference System which combines two functionalities: (i) a tool for integrating lexical inference knowledge from diverse resources, and (ii) a framework for scoring textual inferences based on the integrated knowledge. We provide PLIS with two probabilistic implementation of this framework. PLIS is available for download and developers of text processing applications can use it as an off-the-shelf component for injecting lexical knowledge into their applications. PLIS is easily configurable, components can be extended or replaced with user generated ones to enable system customization and further research. PLIS includes an online interactive viewer, which is a powerful tool for investigating lexical inference processes.

1 Introduction and background

Semantic Inference is the process by which machines perform reasoning over natural language texts. A semantic inference system is expected to be able to infer the meaning of one text from the meaning of another, identify parts of texts which convey a target meaning, and manipulate text units in order to deduce new meanings.

Semantic inference is needed for many Natural Language Processing (NLP) applications. For instance, a Question Answering (QA) system may encounter the following question and candidate answer (Example 1):

Q: *which explorer discovered the New World?*
A: *Christopher Columbus revealed America.*

As there are no overlapping words between the two sentences, to identify that A holds an answer for Q, background world knowledge is needed to link *Christopher Columbus* with *explorer* and *America* with *New World*. Linguistic knowledge is also needed to identify that *reveal* and *discover* refer to the same concept.

Knowledge is needed in order to bridge the gap between text fragments, which may be dissimilar on their surface form but share a common meaning. For the purpose of semantic inference, such knowledge can be derived from various resources (e.g. WordNet (Fellbaum, 1998) and others, detailed in Section 2.1) in a form which we denote as *inference links* (often called inference/entailment rules), each is an ordered pair of elements in which the first implies the meaning of the second. For instance, the link *ship*$\rightarrow$*vessel* can be derived from the *hypernym* relation of WordNet.

Other applications can benefit from utilizing inference links to identify similarity between language expressions. In Information Retrieval, the user's information need may be expressed in relevant documents differently than it is expressed in the query. Summarization systems should identify text snippets which convey the same meaning.

Our work addresses a generic, application independent, setting of lexical inference. We therefore adopt the terminology of Textual Entailment (Dagan et al., 2006), a generic paradigm for applied semantic inference which captures inference needs of many NLP applications in a common underlying task: given two textual fragments, termed hypothesis (H) and text (T), the task is to recognize whether T implies the meaning of H, denoted $T \rightarrow H$. For instance, in a QA application, H represents the question, and T a candidate answer. In this setting, T is likely to hold an answer for the question if it entails the question.

It is challenging to properly extract the needed inference knowledge from available resources, and to effectively utilize it within the inference process. The integration of resources, each has its own format, is technically complex and the quality

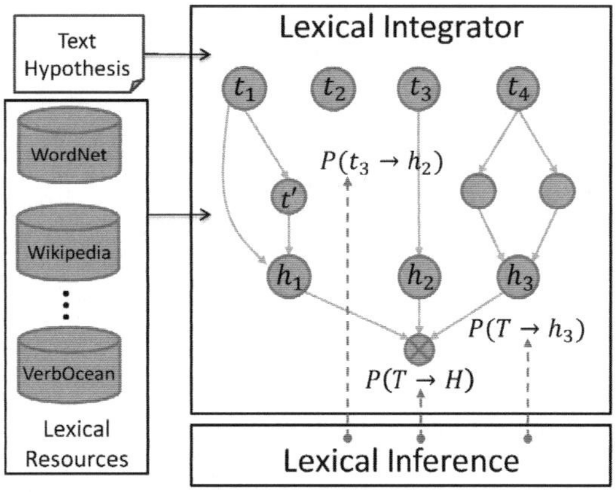

Figure 1: PLIS schema - a text-hypothesis pair is processed by the *Lexical Integrator* which uses a set of lexical resources to extract inference chains which connect the two. The *Lexical Inference* component provides probability estimations for the validity of each level of the process.

of the resulting inference links is often unknown in advance and varies considerably. For coping with this challenge we developed PLIS, a Probabilistic Lexical Inference System[1]. PLIS, illustrated in Fig 1, has two main modules: the *Lexical Integrator* (Section 2) accepts a set of lexical resources and a text-hypothesis pair, and finds all the lexical inference relations between any pair of text term t_i and hypothesis term h_j, based on the available lexical relations found in the resources (and their combination). The *Lexical Inference* module (Section 3) provides validity scores for these relations. These term-level scores are used to estimate the sentence-level likelihood that the meaning of the hypothesis can be inferred from the text, thus making PLIS a complete lexical inference system.

Lexical inference systems do not look into the structure of texts but rather consider them as bag of terms (words or multi-word expressions). These systems are easy to implement, fast to run, practical across different genres and languages, while maintaining a competitive level of performance.

PLIS can be used as a stand-alone efficient inference system or as the lexical component of any NLP application. PLIS is a flexible system, allowing users to choose the set of knowledge resources as well as the model by which inference is done. PLIS can be easily extended with new knowledge resources and new inference models. It comes with a set of ready-to-use plug-ins for many common lexical resources (Section 2.1) as well as two implementation of the scoring framework. These implementations, described in (Shnarch et al., 2011; Shnarch et al., 2012), provide probability estimations for inference. PLIS has an interactive online viewer (Section 4) which provides a visualization of the entire inference process, and is very helpful for analysing lexical inference models and lexical resources usability.

2 Lexical integrator

The input for the lexical integrator is a set of lexical resources and a pair of text T and hypothesis H. The lexical integrator extracts lexical inference links from the various lexical resources to connect each text term $t_i \in T$ with each hypothesis term $h_j \in H$[2]. A lexical inference link indicates a semantic relation between two terms. It could be a directional relation (*Columbus*$\rightarrow$*navigator*) or a bidirectional one (*car* $\longleftrightarrow$ *automobile*).

Since knowledge resources vary in their representation methods, the lexical integrator wraps each lexical resource in a common plug-in interface which encapsulates resource's inner representation method and exposes its knowledge as a list of inference links. The implemented plug-ins that come with PLIS are described in Section 2.1. Adding a new lexical resource and integrating it with the others only demands the implementation of the plug-in interface.

As the knowledge needed to connect a pair of terms, t_i and h_j, may be scattered across few resources, the lexical integrator combines inference links into *lexical inference chains* to deduce new pieces of knowledge, such as *Columbus* $\xrightarrow{resource1}$ *navigator* $\xrightarrow{resource2}$ *explorer*. Therefore, the only assumption the lexical integrator makes, regarding its input lexical resources, is that the inferential lexical relations they provide are transitive.

The lexical integrator generates lexical inference chains by expanding the text and hypothesis terms with inference links. These links lead to new terms (e.g. *navigator* in the above chain example and t' in Fig 1) which can be further expanded, as all inference links are transitive. A *transitivity*

[1]The complete software package is available at http://www.cs.biu.ac.il/nlp/downloads/PLIS.html and an online interactive viewer is available for examination at http://irsrv2.cs.biu.ac.il/nlp-net/PLIS.html.

[2]Where i and j run from 1 to the length of the text and hypothesis respectively.

limit is set by the user to determine the maximal length for inference chains.

The lexical integrator uses a graph-based representation for the inference chains, as illustrates in Fig 1. A node holds the lemma, part-of-speech and sense of a single term. The sense is the ordinal number of WordNet sense. Whenever we do not know the sense of a term we implement the most frequent sense heuristic.[3] An edge represents an inference link and is labeled with the semantic relation of this link (e.g. *cytokine→protein* is labeled with the WordNet relation *hypernym*).

2.1 Available plug-ins for lexical resources

We have implemented plug-ins for the following resources: the English lexicon WordNet (Fellbaum, 1998)(based on either JWI, JWNL or extJWNL java APIs[4]), CatVar (Habash and Dorr, 2003), a categorial variations database, Wikipedia-based resource (Shnarch et al., 2009), which applies several extraction methods to derive inference links from the text and structure of Wikipedia, VerbOcean (Chklovski and Pantel, 2004), a knowledge base of fine-grained semantic relations between verbs, Lin's distributional similarity thesaurus (Lin, 1998), and DIRECT (Kotlerman et al., 2010), a directional distributional similarity thesaurus geared for lexical inference.

To summarize, the lexical integrator finds all possible inference chains (of a predefined length), resulting from any combination of inference links extracted from lexical resources, which link any t, h pair of a given text-hypothesis. Developers can use this tool to save the hassle of interfacing with the different lexical knowledge resources, and spare the labor of combining their knowledge via inference chains.

The lexical inference model, described next, provides a mean to decide whether a given hypothesis is inferred from a given text, based on weighing the lexical inference chains extracted by the lexical integrator.

3 Lexical inference

There are many ways to implement an inference model which identifies inference relations between texts. A simple model may consider the number of hypothesis terms for which inference chains, originated from text terms, were found. In PLIS, the inference model is a plug-in, similar to the lexical knowledge resources, and can be easily replaced to change the inference logic.

We provide PLIS with two implemented baseline lexical inference models which are mathematically based. These are two Probabilistic Lexical Models (PLMs), *HN-PLM* and *M-PLM* which are described in (Shnarch et al., 2011; Shnarch et al., 2012) respectively.

A PLM provides probability estimations for the three parts of the inference process (as shown in Fig 1): the validity probability of each inference chain (i.e. the probability for a valid inference relation between its endpoint terms) $P(t_i \rightarrow h_j)$, the probability of each hypothesis term to be inferred by the entire text $P(T \rightarrow h_j)$ (term-level probability), and the probability of the entire hypothesis to be inferred by the text $P(T \rightarrow H)$ (sentence-level probability).

HN-PLM describes a generative process by which the hypothesis is generated from the text. Its parameters are the reliability level of each of the resources it utilizes (that is, the prior probability that applying an arbitrary inference link derived from each resource corresponds to a valid inference). For learning these parameters *HN-PLM* applies a schema of the EM algorithm (Dempster et al., 1977). Its performance on the recognizing textual entailment task, RTE (Bentivogli et al., 2009; Bentivogli et al., 2010), are in line with the state of the art inference systems, including complex systems which perform syntactic analysis. This model is improved by *M-PLM*, which deduces sentence-level probability from term-level probabilities by a Markovian process. PLIS with this model was used for a passage retrieval for a question answering task (Wang et al., 2007), and outperformed state of the art inference systems.

Both PLMs model the following prominent aspects of the lexical inference phenomenon: (i) considering the different reliability levels of the input knowledge resources, (ii) reducing inference chain probability as its length increases, and (iii) increasing term-level probability as we have more inference chains which suggest that the hypothesis term is inferred by the text. Both PLMs only need sentence-level annotations from which they derive term-level inference probabilities.

To summarize, the lexical inference module

[3]This disambiguation policy was better than considering all senses of an ambiguous term in preliminary experiments. However, it is a matter of changing a variable in the configuration of PLIS to switch between these two policies.

[4]http://wordnet.princeton.edu/wordnet/related-projects/

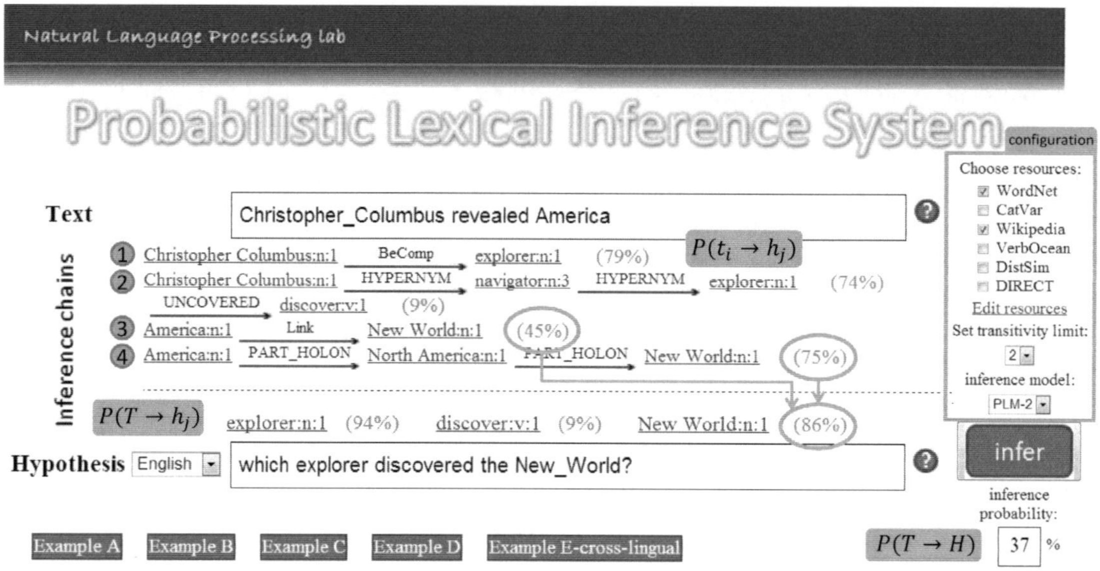

Figure 2: PLIS interactive viewer with Example 1 demonstrates knowledge integration of multiple inference chains and resource combination (additional explanations, which are not part of the demo, are provided in orange).

provides the setting for interfacing with the lexical integrator. Additionally, the module provides the framework for probabilistic inference models which estimate term-level probabilities and integrate them into a sentence-level inference decision, while implementing prominent aspects of lexical inference. The user can choose to apply another inference logic, not necessarily probabilistic, by plugging a different lexical inference model into the provided inference infrastructure.

4 The PLIS interactive system

PLIS comes with an online interactive viewer[5] in which the user sets the parameters of PLIS, inserts a text-hypothesis pair and gets a visualization of the entire inference process. This is a powerful tool for investigating knowledge integration and lexical inference models.

Fig 2 presents a screenshot of the processing of Example 1. On the right side, the user configures the system by selecting knowledge resources, adjusting their configuration, setting the transitivity limit, and choosing the lexical inference model to be applied by PLIS.

After inserting a text and a hypothesis to the appropriate text boxes, the user clicks on the *infer* button and PLIS generates all lexical inference chains, of length up to the transitivity limit, that connect text terms with hypothesis terms, as available from the combination of the selected input resources. Each inference chain is presented in a line between the text and hypothesis.

PLIS also displays the probability estimations for all inference levels; the probability of each chain is presented at the end of its line. For each hypothesis term, term-level probability, which weighs all inference chains found for it, is given below the dashed line. The overall sentence-level probability integrates the probabilities of all hypothesis terms and is displayed in the box at the bottom right corner.

Next, we detail the inference process of Example 1, as presented in Fig 2. In this QA example, the probability of the candidate answer (set as the text) to be relevant for the given question (the hypothesis) is estimated. When utilizing only two knowledge resources (WordNet and Wikipedia), PLIS is able to recognize that *explorer* is inferred by *Christopher Columbus* and that *New World* is inferred by *America*. Each one of these pairs has two independent inference chains, numbered 1–4, as evidence for its inference relation.

Both inference chains 1 and 3 include a single inference link, each derived from a different relation of the Wikipedia-based resource. The inference model assigns a higher probability for chain 1 since the *BeComp* relation is much more reliable than the *Link* relation. This comparison illustrates the ability of the inference model to learn how to differ knowledge resources by their reliability.

Comparing the probability assigned by the in-

[5] http://irsrv2.cs.biu.ac.il/nlp-net/PLIS.html

ference model for inference chain 2 with the probabilities assigned for chains 1 and 3, reveals the sophisticated way by which the inference model integrates lexical knowledge. Inference chain 2 is longer than chain 1, therefore its probability is lower. However, the inference model assigns chain 2 a higher probability than chain 3, even though the latter is shorter, since the model is sensitive enough to consider the difference in reliability levels between the two highly reliable *hypernym* relations (from WordNet) of chain 2 and the less reliable *Link* relation (from Wikipedia) of chain 3.

Another aspect of knowledge integration is exemplified in Fig 2 by the three circled probabilities. The inference model takes into consideration the multiple pieces of evidence for the inference of *New World* (inference chains 3 and 4, whose probabilities are circled). This results in a term-level probability estimation for *New World* (the third circled probability) which is higher than the probabilities of each chain separately.

The third term of the hypothesis, *discover*, remains uncovered by the text as no inference chain was found for it. Therefore, the sentence-level inference probability is very low, 37%. In order to identify that the hypothesis is indeed inferred from the text, the inference model should be provided with indications for the inference of *discover*. To that end, the user may increase the transitivity limit in hope that longer inference chains provide the needed information. In addition, the user can examine other knowledge resources in search for the missing inference link. In this example, it is enough to add VerbOcean to the input of PLIS to expose two inference chains which connect *reveal* with *discover* by combining an inference link from WordNet and another one from VerbOcean. With this additional information, the sentence-level probability increases to 76%. This is a typical scenario of utilizing PLIS, either via the interactive system or via the software, for analyzing the usability of the different knowledge resources and their combination.

A feature of the interactive system, which is useful for lexical resources analysis, is that each term in a chain is clickable and links to another screen which presents all the terms that are inferred from it and those from which it is inferred.

Additionally, the interactive system communicates with a server which runs PLIS, in a full-duplex WebSocket connection[6]. This mode of operation is publicly available and provides a method for utilizing PLIS, without having to install it or the lexical resources it uses.

Finally, since PLIS is a lexical system it can easily be adjusted to other languages. One only needs to replace the basic lexical text processing tools and plug in knowledge resources in the target language. If PLIS is provided with bilingual resources,[7] it can operate also as a cross-lingual inference system (Negri et al., 2012). For instance, the text in Fig 3 is given in English, while the hypothesis is written in Spanish (given as a list of lemma:part-of-speech). The left side of the figure depicts a cross-lingual inference process in which the only lexical knowledge resource used is a manually built English-Spanish dictionary. As can be seen, two Spanish terms, *jugador* and *casa* remain uncovered since the dictionary alone cannot connect them to any of the English terms in the text.

As illustrated in the right side of Fig 3, PLIS enables the combination of the bilingual dictionary with monolingual resources to produce cross-lingual inference chains, such as $\textit{footballer} \xrightarrow{hypernym} \textit{player} \xrightarrow{manual} \textit{jugador}$. Such inference chains have the capability to overcome monolingual language variability (the first link in this chain) as well as to provide cross-lingual translation (the second link).

5 Conclusions

To utilize PLIS one should gather lexical resources, obtain sentence-level annotations and train the inference model. Annotations are available in common data sets for task such as QA, Information Retrieval (queries are hypotheses and snippets are texts) and Student Response Analysis (reference answers are the hypotheses that should be inferred by the student answers).

For developers of NLP applications, PLIS offers a ready-to-use lexical knowledge integrator which can interface with many common lexical knowledge resources and constructs lexical inference chains which combine the knowledge in them. A developer who wants to overcome lexical language variability, or to incorporate background knowledge, can utilize PLIS to inject lex-

[6]We used the socket.io implementation.

[7]A bilingual resource holds inference links which connect terms in different languages (e.g. an English-Spanish dictionary can provide the inference link *explorer*→*explorador*).

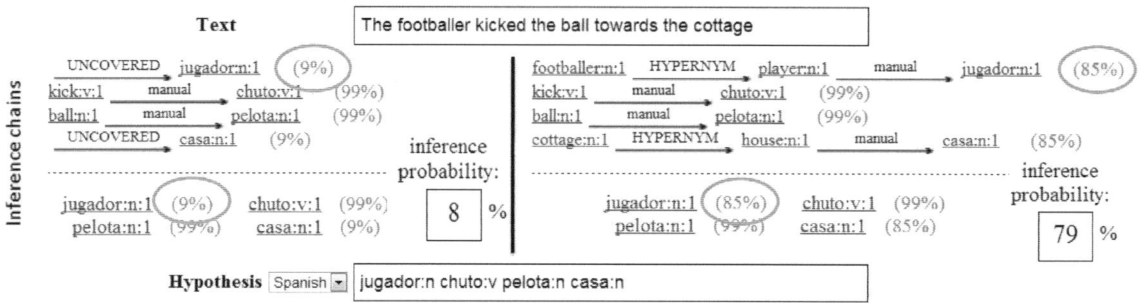

Figure 3: PLIS as a cross-lingual inference system. **Left**: the process with a single manual bilingual resource. **Right**: PLIS composes cross-lingual inference chains to increase hypothesis coverage and increase sentence-level inference probability.

ical knowledge into any text understanding application. PLIS can be used as a lightweight inference system or as the lexical component of larger, more complex inference systems.

Additionally, PLIS provides scores for inference chains and determines the way to combine them in order to recognize sentence-level inference. PLIS comes with two probabilistic lexical inference models which achieved competitive performance levels in the tasks of recognizing textual entailment and passage retrieval for QA.

All aspects of PLIS are configurable. The user can easily switch between the built-in lexical resources, inference models and even languages, or extend the system with additional lexical resources and new inference models.

Acknowledgments

The authors thank Eden Erez for his help with the interactive viewer and Miquel Esplà Gomis for the bilingual dictionaries. This work was partially supported by the European Community's 7th Framework Programme (FP7/2007-2013) under grant agreement no. 287923 (EXCITEMENT) and the Israel Science Foundation grant 880/12.

References

Luisa Bentivogli, Ido Dagan, Hoa Trang Dang, Danilo Giampiccolo, and Bernardo Magnini. 2009. The fifth PASCAL recognizing textual entailment challenge. In *Proc. of TAC*.

Luisa Bentivogli, Peter Clark, Ido Dagan, Hoa Trang Dang, and Danilo Giampiccolo. 2010. The sixth PASCAL recognizing textual entailment challenge. In *Proc. of TAC*.

Timothy Chklovski and Patrick Pantel. 2004. VerbOcean: Mining the web for fine-grained semantic verb relations. In *Proc. of EMNLP*.

Ido Dagan, Oren Glickman, and Bernardo Magnini. 2006. The PASCAL recognising textual entailment challenge. In *Lecture Notes in Computer Science*, volume 3944, pages 177–190.

A. P. Dempster, N. M. Laird, and D. B. Rubin. 1977. Maximum likelihood from incomplete data via the EM algorithm. *Journal of the royal statistical society, series [B]*, 39(1):1–38.

Christiane Fellbaum, editor. 1998. *WordNet: An Electronic Lexical Database*. MIT Press, Cambridge, Massachusetts.

Nizar Habash and Bonnie Dorr. 2003. A categorial variation database for English. In *Proc. of NAACL*.

Lili Kotlerman, Ido Dagan, Idan Szpektor, and Maayan Zhitomirsky-Geffet. 2010. Directional distributional similarity for lexical inference. *Natural Language Engineering*, 16(4):359–389.

Dekang Lin. 1998. Automatic retrieval and clustering of similar words. In *Proc. of COLOING-ACL*.

Matteo Negri, Alessandro Marchetti, Yashar Mehdad, Luisa Bentivogli, and Danilo Giampiccolo. 2012. Semeval-2012 task 8: Cross-lingual textual entailment for content synchronization. In *Proc. of SemEval*.

Eyal Shnarch, Libby Barak, and Ido Dagan. 2009. Extracting lexical reference rules from Wikipedia. In *Proc. of ACL*.

Eyal Shnarch, Jacob Goldberger, and Ido Dagan. 2011. Towards a probabilistic model for lexical entailment. In *Proc. of the TextInfer Workshop*.

Eyal Shnarch, Ido Dagan, and Jacob Goldberger. 2012. A probabilistic lexical model for ranking textual inferences. In *Proc. of *SEM*.

Mengqiu Wang, Noah A. Smith, and Teruko Mitamura. 2007. What is the Jeopardy model? A quasi-synchronous grammar for QA. In *Proc. of EMNLP*.

A Java Framework for Multilingual Definition and Hypernym Extraction

Stefano Faralli and **Roberto Navigli**
Dipartimento di Informatica
Sapienza Università di Roma
{faralli,navigli}@di.uniroma1.it

Abstract

In this paper we present a demonstration of a multilingual generalization of Word-Class Lattices (WCLs), a supervised lattice-based model used to identify textual definitions and extract hypernyms from them. Lattices are learned from a dataset of automatically-annotated definitions from Wikipedia. We release a Java API for the programmatic use of multilingual WCLs in three languages (English, French and Italian), as well as a Web application for definition and hypernym extraction from user-provided sentences.

1 Introduction

Electronic dictionaries and domain glossaries are definition repositories which prove very useful not only for lookup purposes, but also for automatic tasks such as Question Answering (Cui et al., 2007; Saggion, 2004), taxonomy learning (Navigli et al., 2011; Velardi et al., 2013), domain Word Sense Disambiguation (Duan and Yates, 2010; Faralli and Navigli, 2012), automatic acquisition of semantic predicates (Flati and Navigli, 2013), relation extraction (Yap and Baldwin, 2009) and, more in general, knowledge acquisition (Hovy et al., 2013). Unfortunately, constructing and updating such resources requires the effort of a team of experts. Moreover, they are of no help when dealing with new words or usages, or, even worse, new domains. Nonetheless, raw text often contains several definitional sentences, that is, it provides within itself formal explanations for terms of interest. Whilst it is not feasible to search texts manually for definitions in several languages, the task of extracting definitional information can be automatized by means of Machine Learning (ML) and Natural Language Processing (NLP) techniques.

Many approaches (Snow et al., 2004; Kozareva and Hovy, 2010, inter alia) build upon lexico-syntactic patterns, inspired by the seminal work of Hearst (1992). However, these methods suffer from two signifiicant drawbacks: on the one hand, low recall (as definitional sentences occur in highly variable syntactic structures), and, on the other hand, noise (because the most frequent definitional pattern – X is a Y – is inherently very noisy). A recent approach to definition and hypernym extraction, called Word-Class Lattices (Navigli and Velardi, 2010, WCLs), overcomes these issues by addressing the variability of definitional sentences and providing a flexible way of automatically extracting hypernyms from them. To do so, lattice-based classifiers are learned from a training set of textual definitions. Training sentences are automatically clustered by similarity and, for each such cluster, a lattice classifier is learned which models the variants of the definition template detected. A lattice is a directed acyclic graph, a subclass of non-deterministic finite state automata. The purpose of the lattice structure is to preserve (in a compact form) the salient differences among distinct sequences.

In this paper we present a demonstration of Word-Class Lattices by providing a Java API and a Web application for online usage. Since multilinguality is a key need in today's information society, and because WCLs have been tested overwhelmingly only with the English language, we provide experiments for three different languages, namely English, French and Italian. To do so, in contrast to Navigli and Velardi (2010), who created a manually annotated training set of definitions, we provide a heuristic method for the automatic acquisition of reliable training sets from Wikipedia, and use them to determine the robustness and generalization power of WCLs. We show high performance in definition and hypernym extraction for our three languages.

2 Word-Class Lattices

In this section we briefly summarize Word-Class Lattices, originally introduced by Navigli and Velardi (2010).

2.1 Definitional Sentence Generalization

WCL relies on a formal notion of textual definition. Specifically, given a definition, e.g.: "In computer science, a closure is a first-class function with free variables that are bound in the lexical environment", we assume that it contains the

[In geography, a **country**]$_{DF}$ [is]$_{VF}$ [a political *division*]$_{GF}$.
[In finance, a **bond**]$_{DF}$ [is]$_{VF}$ [a negotiable *certificate*]$_{GF}$ [that that acknowledges. . .]$_{REST}$.
[In poetry, a **foot**]$_{DF}$ [is]$_{VF}$ [a *measure*]$_{GF}$ [, consisting. . .]$_{REST}$.

Table 1: Example definitions (defined terms are marked in bold face, their hypernyms in italics).

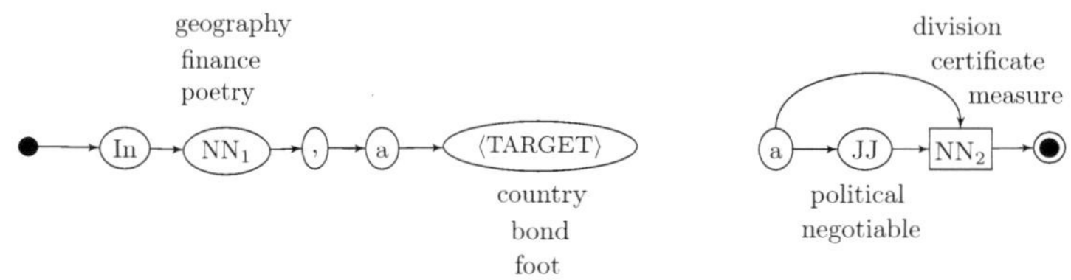

Figure 1: The DF and GF Word-Class Lattices for the sentences in Table 1.

following fields (Storrer and Wellinghoff, 2006): *definiendum* (DF), *definitor* (VF), *definiens* (GF) and *rest* (REST), where DF is the part of the definition including the word being defined (e.g., "In computer science, a closure"), VF is the verb phrase used to introduce the definition (e.g., "is"), GF usually includes the hypernym (e.g., "a first-class *function*", hypernym marked in italics) and RF includes additional clauses (e.g., "with free variables that are bound in the lexical environment").

Consider a set of training sentences T, each of which is automatically part-of-speech tagged and manually bracketed with the DF, VF, GF and REST fields (examples are shown in Table 1). We first identify the set of most frequent words F (e.g., *the*, *a*, *is*, *of*, *refer*, etc.). Then we add the symbol ⟨TARGET⟩ to F and replace in T the terms being defined with ⟨TARGET⟩. We then use the set of frequent words F to generalize words to "word classes".

We define a word class as either a word itself or its part of speech. Given a sentence $s = w_1, w_2, \ldots, w_{|s|}$, where w_i is the i-th word of s, we generalize its words w_i to word classes ω_i as follows:

$$\omega_i = \begin{cases} w_i & \text{if } w_i \in F \\ POS(w_i) & \text{otherwise} \end{cases}$$

that is, a word w_i is left unchanged if it occurs frequently in the training corpus (i.e., $w_i \in F$) or is transformed to its part of speech tag ($POS(w_i)$) otherwise. As a result, we obtain a generalized sentence $s' = \omega_1, \omega_2, \ldots, \omega_{|s|}$. For instance, given the first sentence in Table 1, we obtain the corresponding generalized sentence: "In NN, a ⟨TARGET⟩ is a JJ NN", where NN and JJ indicate the noun and adjective classes, respectively.

2.2 Learning

The WCL learning algorithm consists of 3 steps:

- **Star patterns:** each sentence in the training set is preprocessed and generalized to a star pattern by replacing with * all the words $w_i \notin F$, i.e., non-frequent words. For instance, "In geography, a country is a political division" is transformed to "In *, a ⟨TARGET⟩ is a *";
- **Sentence clustering:** the training sentences are then clustered based on the star patterns they belong to;
- **Word-Class Lattice construction:** for each sentence cluster, a WCL is created separately for each DF, VF and GF field by means of a greedy alignment algorithm. In Figure 1 we show the resulting lattices for the DF and GF fields built for the cluster of sentences of Table 1. Note that during the construction of the lattice the nodes associated with the hypernym words in the learning sentences (i.e., *division*, *certificate* and *measure*) are marked as hypernyms in order to determine the hypernym of a test sentence at classification time (see (Navigli and Velardi, 2010) for details).

2.3 Classification

Once the learning process is over, a set of WCLs is produced for the DF, VF and GF fields. Given a test sentence s, we consider all possible combinations of *definiendum*, *definitor* and *definiens* lattices and select the combination of the three WCLs that best fits the sentence, if such a combination exists. In fact, choosing the most appropriate combination of lattices impacts the performance of hypernym extraction. The best combination of WCLs is selected by maximizing the following confidence score: $score(s, l_{DF}, l_{VF}, l_{GF}) = coverage \cdot log(support + 1)$ where s is the candidate sentence, l_{DF}, l_{VF} and l_{GF} are three lattices one for each definition field, coverage is the fraction of words of the input sentence covered by the three lattices, and support is the sum of the number of sentences in the star patterns corresponding to the GF lattice. Finally, when a sentence is classified as a definition, its hypernym is extracted by

	# Wikipedia pages	# definitions extracted
English (EN)	3,904,360	1,552,493
French (FR)	1,617,359	447,772
Italian (IT)	1,008,044	291,259

Table 2: The number of Wikipedia pages and the resulting automatically annotated definitions.

selecting the words in the input sentence that are marked as hypernyms in the WCL selected for GF.

3 Multilingual Word-Class Lattices

In order to enable multilinguality, thereby extracting definitions and hypernyms in many languages, we provide here a heuristic method for the creation of multilingual training datasets from Wikipedia, that we apply to three languages: English, French and Italian. As a result, we are able to fully automatize the definition and hypernym extraction by utilizing collaboratively-curated encyclopedia content.

3.1 Automatic Learning of Multilingual WCLs

The method consists of four steps:

1. **candidate definition extraction:** we iterate through the collection of Wikipedia pages for the language of interest. For each article we extract the first paragraph, which usually, but not always, contains a definitional sentence for the concept expressed by the page title. We discard all those pages for which the title corresponds to a special page (i.e., title in the form "List of [...]", "Index of [...]", "[...] (disambiguation)" etc.).

2. **part-of-speech tagging and phrase chunking:** for each candidate definition we perform part-of-speech tagging and chunking, thus automatically identifying noun, verb, and prepositional phrases (we use TreeTagger (Schmid, 1997)).

3. **automatic annotation:** we replace all the occurrences in the candidate definition of the target term (i.e., the title of the page) with the marker ⟨TARGET⟩, we then tag as hypernym the words associated with the first hyperlink occurring to the right of ⟨TARGET⟩. Then we tag as VF (i.e., definitor field, see Section 2.1) the verb phrase found between ⟨TARGET⟩ and the hypernym, if such a phrase exists. Next we tag as GF (i.e., definiens field) the phrase which contains the hypernym and as DF (i.e., definiendum field) the phrase which starts at the beginning of the sentence and ends right before the start of the VP tag. Finally we mark as REST the remaining phrases after the phrase already tagged as GF. For example, given the sentence "Albert Einstein was a German-born theoretical physicist.", we produce the following sentence annotation: "[**Albert Einstein**]$_{DF}$ [was]$_{VF}$ [a German-born theoretical *physicist*]$_{GF}$." (target term marked in bold and hypernym in italics).

4. **filtering:** we finally discard all the candidate definitions for which not all fields could be found during the previous step (i.e., either the ⟨TARGET⟩, hypernym or any DF, VF, GF, REST tag is missing).

We applied the above four steps to the English, French and Italian dumps of Wikipedia[1]. The numbers are shown in Table 2: starting with 3,904,360 Wikipedia pages for English, 1,617,359 for French and 1,008,044 for Italian (first column), we obtained 1,552,493, 447,772, and 291,259 automatically tagged sentences, respectively, for the three languages (second column in the Table). Since we next had to use these sentences for training our WCLs, we took out a random sample of 1000 sentences for each language which we used for testing purposes. We manually annotated each of these sentences as definitional or non-definitional[2] and, in the case of the former, also with the correct hypernym.

3.2 Evaluation

We tested the newly acquired training dataset against two test datasets. The first dataset was our random sampling of 1000 Wikipedia test sentences which we had set aside for each language (no intersection with the training set, see previous section). The second dataset was the same one used in Navigli and Velardi (2010), made up of sentences from the ukWaC Web corpus (Ferraresi et al., 2008) and used to estimate the definition and hypernym extraction performance on an open text corpus.

3.3 Results

Table 3 shows the results obtained on definition (column 2-4) and hypernym extraction (column 5-7) in terms of precision (P), recall (R) and accuracy (A) on our first dataset. Note that accuracy also takes into account candidate definitions in the test set which were tagged as non-definitional (see Section 3.1). In the Table we compare the performance of our English WCL trained from Wikipedia sentences using our automatic procedure against the original performance of WCL

[1]We used the 21-09-2012 (EN), 17-09-2012 (FR), 21-09-2012 (IT) dumps.

[2]Note that the first sentence of a Wikipedia page might seldom be non-definitional, such as "Basmo fortress is located in the north-western part ...".

	Definition Extraction			Hypernym Extraction		
	P	R	A	P	R	A
EN	98.5	78.3	81.0	98.5	77.4	80.0
FR	98.7	83.3	84.0	98.6	78.0	79.0
IT	98.8	87.3	87.0	98.7	83.2	83.0
EN (2010)	100.0	59.0	66.0	100.0	58.3	65.0

Table 3: Precision (P), recall (R) and accuracy (A) of definition and hypernym extraction when testing on our dataset of 1000 randomly sampled Wikipedia first-paragraph sentences. EN (2010) refers to the WCL learned from the original manually-curated training set from Navigli and Velardi (2010), while EN, FR and IT refer to WCL trained, respectively, with one of the three training sets automatically acquired from Wikipedia.

	P	R
EN	98.9	57.6
EN (2010)	94.8	56.5

Table 4: Estimated WCL definition extraction precision (P) and recall (R), testing a sample of ukWaC sentences.

trained on 1,908 manually-selected training sentences[3]. It can be seen that the automatically acquired training set considerably improves the performance, as it covers higher variability. We note that the recall in both definition and hypernym extraction is higher for French and Italian. We attribute this behavior to the higher complexity and, again, variability of English Wikipedia pages, and specifically first-sentence definitions. We remark that the presented results were obtained without any human effort, except for the independent collaborative editing and hyperlinking of Wikipedia pages, and that the overall performances can be improved by manually checking the automatically annotated training datasets.

We also replicated the experiment carried out by Navigli and Velardi (2010), testing WCLs with a subset (over 300,000 sentences) of the ukWaC Web corpus. As can be seen in Table 4, the estimated precision and recall for WCL definition extraction with the 2010 training set were 94.8% and 56.5%, respectively, while with our automatically acquired English training set we obtained a higher precision of 98.9% and a recall of 57.6%. This second experiment shows that learning WCLs from hundreds of thousands of definition candidates does not overfit to Wikipedia-style definitional sentences.

After looking at the automatically acquired training datasets, we noted some erroneous annotations mainly due to the following factors: i) some Wikipedia pages do not start with definitional sentences; ii) they may contain more than one verbal phrase between the defined term and the hypernym; iii) the first link after the verbal phrase does not cover, or partially covers, the correct hypernym. The elimination of the above wrongly acquired definitional patterns can be implemented with some language-dependent heuristics or can be done by human annotators. In any case, given the presence of a high number of correct annotated sentences, these wrong definitional patterns have a very low impact on the definition and hypernym extraction precision as shown in the above experiments (see Table 3 and Table 4).

[3]Available from http://lcl.uniroma1.it/wcl

```
1  // select the language of interest
2  Language targetLanguage = Language.EN;
3  // open the training set
4  Dataset ts = new AnnotatedDataset(
5               trainingDatasetFile,
6               targetLanguage);
7  // obtain an instance of the WCL classifier
8  WCLClassifier c = new WCLClassifier(targetLanguage);
9  c.train(ts);
10 // create a sentence to be tested
11 Sentence sentence = Sentence.createFromString(
12              "WCL",
13              "WCL␣is␣a␣kind␣of␣classifier.",
14              targetLanguage);
15 // test the sentence
16 SentenceAnnotation sa = c.test(sentence);
17 // print the hypernym
18 if (sa.isDefinition())
19              System.out.println(sa.getHyper());
```

Figure 2: An example of WCL API usage.

4 Multilingual WCL API

Together with the training and test sets of the above experiments, we also release here our implementation of Word-Class Lattices, available as a Java API. As a result the WCL classifier can easily be used programmatically in any Java project. In Figure 2 we show an example of the API usage. After the selection of the target language (line 2), we load the training dataset for the target language (line 4). Then an instance of `WCLClassifier` is created (line 8) and the training phase is launched on the input training corpora (line 9). Now the classifier is ready to be tested on any given sentence in the target language (lines 11-16). If the classifier output is positive (line 18) we can print the extracted hypernym (line 19). The output of the presented code is the string "classifier" which corresponds to the hypernym extracted by WCL for the input sentence "WCL is a kind of classifier".

4.1 Web user interface

We also release a Web interface to enable online usage of our WCLs for the English, French and Italian languages. In Figure 3 we show a screenshot of our Web interface. The user can type the

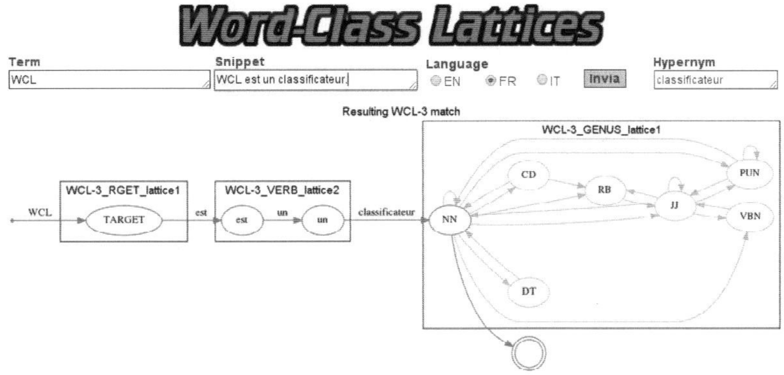

Figure 3: A screenshot of the WCL Web interface.

term of interest, the candidate definition, select the language of interest and, after submission, in the case of positive response from WCL, obtain the corresponding hypernym and a graphical representation of the lattices matching the given sentence, as shown in the bottom part of the Figure.

The graphical representation shows the concatenation of the learned lattices which match the DF, VF, GF parts of the given sentence (see Section 2). We also allow the user not to provide the term of interest: in this case all the nouns in the sentence are considered as candidate defined terms. The Web user interface is part of a client-server application, created with the JavaServer Pages technology. The server side produces an HTML page (like the one shown in Figure 3), using the WCL API (see Section 4) to process and test the submitted definition candidate.

5 Related Work

A great deal of work is concerned with the language independent extraction of definitions. Much recent work uses symbolic methods that depend on lexico-syntactic patterns or features, which are manually created or semi-automatically learned as recently done in (Zhang and Jiang, 2009; Westerhout, 2009). A fully automated method is, instead, proposed by Borg et al. (2009), where higher performance (around 60-70% F1-measure) is obtained only for specific domains and patterns. Velardi et al. (2008), in order to improve precision while keeping pattern generality, prune candidates using more refined stylistic patterns and lexical filters. Cui et al. (2007) propose the use of probabilistic lexico-semantic patterns, for definitional question answering in the TREC contest[4]. However, the TREC evaluation datasets cannot be considered true definitions, but rather text fragments providing some relevant fact about a target term.

Hypernym extraction methods vary from simple lexical patterns (Hearst, 1992; Oakes, 2005) to statistical and machine learning techniques (Agirre et al., 2000; Caraballo, 1999; Dolan et al., 1993; Sanfilippo and Poznanski, 1992; Ritter et al., 2009). Extraction heuristics can be adopted in many languages (De Benedictis et al., 2013), where given a definitional sentence the hypernym is identified as the first occuring noun after the defined term. One of the highest-coverage methods is proposed by Snow et al. (2004). They first search sentences that contain two terms which are known to be in a taxonomic relation (term pairs are taken from WordNet (Miller et al., 1990)); then they parse the sentences, and automatically extract patterns from the parse trees. Finally, they train a hypernym classifier based on these features. Lexico-syntactic patterns are generated for each sentence relating a term to its hypernym, and a dependency parser is used to represent them.

6 Conclusion

In this demonstration we provide three main contributions: 1) a general method for obtaining large training sets of annotated definitional sentences for many languages from Wikipedia, thanks to which we can release three new training sets for English, French and Italian; 2) an API to programmatically use WCLs in Java projects; 3) a Web application which enables online use of multilingual WCLs: `http://lcl.uniroma1.it/wcl/`.

Acknowledgments

The authors gratefully acknowledge the support of the ERC Starting Grant MultiJEDI No. 259234.

[4]Text REtrieval Conferences: `http://trec.nist.gov`

References

Eneko Agirre, Olatz Ansa, Eduard H. Hovy, and David Martínez. 2000. Enriching very large ontologies using the WWW. In *ECAI Workshop on Ontology Learning*, Berlin, Germany.

Claudia Borg, Mike Rosner, and Gordon Pace. 2009. Evolutionary algorithms for definition extraction. In *Proceedings of the 1st Workshop on Definition Extraction*, pages 26–32, Borovets, Bulgaria.

Sharon A. Caraballo. 1999. Automatic construction of a hypernym-labeled noun hierarchy from text. In *Proceedings of the* 37th *Annual Meeting of the Association for Computational Linguistics: Proceedings of the Conference*, pages 120–126, Maryland, USA.

Hang Cui, Min-Yen Kan, and Tat-Seng Chua. 2007. Soft pattern matching models for definitional question answering. *ACM Transactions on Information Systems*, 25(2):1–30.

Flavio De Benedictis, Stefano Faralli, and Roberto Navigli. 2013. GlossBoot: Bootstrapping Multilingual Domain Glossaries from the Web. In *Proceedings of 51st Annual Meeting of the Association for Computational Linguistics*, Sofia, Bulgaria.

William Dolan, Lucy Vanderwende, and Stephen D. Richardson. 1993. Automatically deriving structured knowledge bases from on-line dictionaries. In *Proceedings of the First Conference of the Pacific Association for Computational Linguistics*, pages 5–14, Vancouver, Canada.

Weisi Duan and Alexander Yates. 2010. Extracting glosses to disambiguate word senses. In *Proceedings of Human Language Technologies: The 11th Annual Conference of the North American Chapter of the Association for Computational Linguistics*, pages 627–635, Los Angeles, CA, USA.

Stefano Faralli and Roberto Navigli. 2012. A new minimally-supervised framework for Domain Word Sense Disambiguation. In *Proceedings of the 2012 Joint Conference on Empirical Methods in Natural Language Processing and Computational Natural Language Learning*, pages 1411–1422, Jeju, Korea.

Adriano Ferraresi, Eros Zanchetta, Marco Baroni, and Silvia Bernardini. 2008. Introducing and evaluating ukWaC, a very large web-derived corpus of English. In *Proceedings of the 4th Web as Corpus Workshop (WAC-4)*, pages 47–54, Marrakech, Morocco.

Tiziano Flati and Roberto Navigli. 2013. SPred: Large-scale Harvesting of Semantic Predicates. In *Proceedings of 51st Annual Meeting of the Association for Computational Linguistics*, Sofia, Bulgaria.

Marti A. Hearst. 1992. Automatic acquisition of hyponyms from large text corpora. In *Proceedings of the 15th International Conference on Computational Linguistics*, pages 539–545, Nantes, France.

Eduard Hovy, Roberto Navigli, and Simone Paolo Ponzetto. 2013. Collaboratively built semi-structured content and artificial intelligence: The story so far. *Artificial Intelligence*, 194:2–27.

Zornitsa Kozareva and Eduard Hovy. 2010. Learning arguments and supertypes of semantic relations using recursive patterns. In *Proceedings of the 48th Annual Meeting of the Association for Computational Linguistics (ACL), Uppsala, Sweden*, pages 1482–1491, Uppsala, Sweden.

George A. Miller, R.T. Beckwith, Christiane D. Fellbaum, D. Gross, and K. Miller. 1990. WordNet: an online lexical database. *International Journal of Lexicography*, 3(4):235–244.

Roberto Navigli and Paola Velardi. 2010. Learning Word-Class Lattices for definition and hypernym extraction. In *Proceedings of the 48th Annual Meeting of the Association for Computational Linguistics*, pages 1318–1327, Uppsala, Sweden.

Roberto Navigli, Paola Velardi, and Stefano Faralli. 2011. A graph-based algorithm for inducing lexical taxonomies from scratch. In *Proceedings of the 22th International Joint Conference on Artificial Intelligence*, pages 1872–1877, Barcelona, Spain.

Michael P. Oakes. 2005. Using Hearst's rules for the automatic acquisition of hyponyms for mining a pharmaceutical corpus. In *RANLP Text Mining Workshop'05*, pages 63–67, Borovets, Bulgaria.

Alan Ritter, Stephen Soderland, and Oren Etzioni. 2009. What is this, anyway: Automatic hypernym discovery. In *Proceedings of the 2009 AAAI Spring Symposium on Learning by Reading and Learning to Read*, pages 88–93, Palo Alto, California.

Horacio Saggion. 2004. Identifying definitions in text collections for question answering. In *Proceedings of the Fourth International Conference on Language Resources and Evaluation*, pages 1927–1930, Lisbon, Portugal.

Antonio Sanfilippo and Victor Poznanski. 1992. The acquisition of lexical knowledge from combined machine-readable dictionary sources. In *Proceedings of the third Conference on Applied Natural Language Processing*, pages 80–87, Trento, Italy.

Helmut Schmid. 1997. Probabilistic part-of-speech tagging using decision trees. In Daniel Jones and Harold Somers, editors, *New Methods in Language Processing*, Studies in Computational Linguistics, pages 154–164. UCL Press, London, GB.

Rion Snow, Daniel Jurafsky, and Andrew Y. Ng. 2004. Learning syntactic patterns for automatic hypernym discovery. In Lawrence K. Saul, Yair Weiss, and Léon Bottou, editors, *Proc. of NIPS 2004*, pages 1297–1304, Cambridge, Mass. MIT Press.

Angelika Storrer and Sandra Wellinghoff. 2006. Automated detection and annotation of term definitions in German text corpora. In *LREC 2006*, pages 275–295, Genoa, Italy.

Paola Velardi, Roberto Navigli, and Pierluigi D'Amadio. 2008. Mining the Web to create specialized glossaries. *IEEE Intelligent Systems*, 23(5):18–25.

Paola Velardi, Stefano Faralli, and Roberto Navigli. 2013. OntoLearn Reloaded: A graph-based algorithm for taxonomy induction. *Computational Linguistics*, 39(3).

Eline Westerhout. 2009. Definition extraction using linguistic and structural features. In *Proceedings of the RANLP 2009 Workshop on Definition Extraction*, page 61–67, Borovets, Bulgaria.

Willy Yap and Timothy Baldwin. 2009. Experiments on pattern-based relation learning. In *Proceedings of the 18th ACM Conference on Information and Knowledge Management (CIKM 2009)*, pages 1657–1660, Hong Kong, China, 2009.

Chunxia Zhang and Peng Jiang. 2009. Automatic extraction of definitions. In *Proceedings of 2nd IEEE International Conference on Computer Science and Information Technology*, pages 364–368, Beijing, China.

A Visual Analytics System for Cluster Exploration

Andreas Lamprecht[1], **Annette Hautli**[2], **Christian Rohrdantz**[1], **Tina Bögel**[2]
[1]Department of Computer Science, [2]Department of Linguistics
University of Konstanz, Germany
{firstname.lastname}@uni-konstanz.de

Abstract

This paper offers a new way of representing the results of automatic clustering algorithms by employing a Visual Analytics system which maps members of a cluster and their distance to each other onto a two-dimensional space. A case study on Urdu complex predicates shows that the system allows for an appropriate investigation of linguistically motivated data.

1 Motivation

In recent years, Visual Analytics systems have increasingly been used for the investigation of linguistic phenomena in a number of different areas, starting from literary analysis (Keim and Oelke, 2007) to the cross-linguistic comparison of language features (Mayer et al., 2010a; Mayer et al., 2010b; Rohrdantz et al., 2012a) and lexical semantic change (Rohrdantz et al., 2011; Heylen et al., 2012; Rohrdantz et al., 2012b). Visualization has also found its way into the field of computational linguistics by providing insights into methods such as machine translation (Collins et al., 2007; Albrecht et al., 2009) or discourse parsing (Zhao et al., 2012).

One issue in computational linguistics is the interpretability of results coming from machine learning algorithms and the lack of insight they offer on the underlying data. This drawback often prevents theoretical linguists, who work with computational models and need to see patterns on large data sets, from drawing detailed conclusions. The present paper shows that a Visual Analytics system facilitates "analytical reasoning [...] by an *interactive* visual interface" (Thomas and Cook, 2006) and helps resolving this issue by offering a customizable, in-depth view on the statistically generated result and simultaneously an at-a-glance overview of the overall data set.

In particular, we focus on the visual representation of automatically generated clusters, in itself not a novel idea as it has been applied in other fields like the financial sector, biology or geography (Schreck et al., 2009). But as far as the literature is concerned, *interactive* systems are still less common, particularly in computational linguistics, and they have not been designed for the specific needs of theoretical linguists. This paper offers a method of visually encoding clusters and their internal coherence with an interactive user interface, which allows users to adjust underlying parameters and their views on the data depending on the particular research question. By this, we partly open up the "black box" of machine learning.

The linguistic phenomenon under investigation, for which the system has originally been designed, is the varied behavior of nouns in N+V CP complex predicates in Urdu (e.g., memory+do = 'to remember') (Mohanan, 1994; Ahmed and Butt, 2011), where, depending on the lexical semantics of the noun, a set of different light verbs is chosen to form a complex predicate. The aim is an automatic detection of the different groups of nouns, based on their light verb distribution. Butt et al. (2012) present a static visualization for the phenomenon, whereas the present paper proposes an interactive system which alleviates some of the previous issues with respect to noise detection, filtering, data interaction and cluster coherence. For this, we proceed as follows: section 2 explains the proposed Visual Analytics system, followed by the linguistic case study in section 3. Section 4 concludes the paper.

2 The system

The system requires a plain text file as input, where each line corresponds to one data object.In our case, each line corresponds to one Urdu noun (data object) and contains its unique ID (the name of the noun) and its bigram frequencies with the four light verbs under investigation, namely *kar* 'do', *ho* 'be', *hu* 'become' and *rakH* 'put'; an exemplary input file is shown in Figure 1.

From a data analysis perspective, we have four-dimensional data objects, where each dimension corresponds to a bigram frequency previously extracted from a corpus. Note that more than four dimensions can be loaded and analyzed, but for the sake of simplicity we focus on the four-dimensional Urdu example for the remainder of this paper. Moreover, it is possible to load files containing absolute bigram frequencies and relative frequencies. When loading absolute frequencies, the program will automatically calculate the relative frequencies as they are the input for the clustering. The absolute frequencies, however, are still available and can be used for further processing (e.g. filtering).

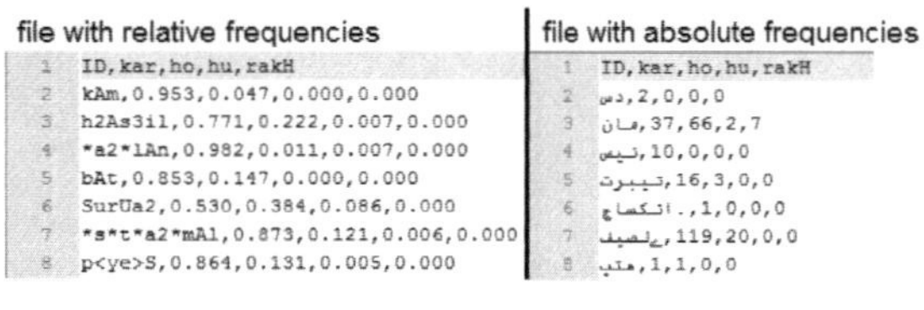
file with relative frequencies

```
1 ID,kar,ho,hu,rakH
2 kAm,0.953,0.047,0.000,0.000
3 h2As3il,0.771,0.222,0.007,0.000
4 *a2*lAn,0.982,0.011,0.007,0.000
5 bAt,0.853,0.147,0.000,0.000
6 SurUa2,0.530,0.384,0.086,0.000
7 *s*t*a2*mAl,0.873,0.121,0.006,0.000
8 p<ye>S,0.864,0.131,0.005,0.000
```

file with absolute frequencies

```
1 ID,kar,ho,hu,rakH
2 دس,2,0,0,0
3 مان,37,66,2,7
4 تیس,10,0,0,0
5 تیبرت,16,3,0,0
6 انکساع..,1,0,0,0
7 ےلصبف,119,20,0,0
8 متب,1,1,0,0
```

Figure 1: preview of appropriate file structures

2.1 Initial opening and processing of a file

It is necessary to define a metric distance function between data objects for both clustering and visualization. Thus, each data object is represented through a high dimensional (in our example four-dimensional) numerical vector and we use the Euclidean distance to calculate the distances between pairs of data objects. The smaller the distance between two data objects, the more similar they are.

For visualization, the high dimensional data is projected onto the two-dimensional space of a computer screen using a principal component analysis (PCA) algorithm[1]. In the 2D projection, the distances between data objects in the high-dimensional space, i.e. the dissimilarities of the bigram distributions, are preserved as accurately as possible. However, when projecting a high-dimensional data space onto a lower dimension, some distinctions necessarily level out: two data objects may be far apart in the high-dimensional space, but end up closely together in the 2D projection. It is important to bear in mind that the 2D visualization is often quite insightful, but interpretations have to be verified by interactively investigating the data.

The initial clusters are calculated (in the high-dimensional data space) using a default k-Means algorithm[2] with k being a user-defined parameter. There is also the option of selecting another clustering algorithm, called the Greedy Variance Minimization[3] (GVM), and an extension to include further algorithms is under development.

2.2 Configuration & Interaction

2.2.1 The main window

The main window in Figure 2 consists of three areas, namely the configuration area (a), the visualization area (b) and the description area (c). The visualization area is mainly built with the piccolo2d library[4] and initially shows data objects as colored circles with a variable diameter, where color indicates cluster membership (four clusters in this example). Hovering over a dot displays information on the particular noun, the cluster membership and the light verb distribution in the description area to the right. By using the mouse wheel, the user can zoom in and out of the visualization.

A very important feature for the task at hand is the possibility to select multiple data objects for further processing or for filtering, with a list of selected data objects shown in the description area. By right-clicking on these data objects, the user can assign a unique class (and class color) to them. Different clustering methods can be employed using the options item in the menu bar.

Another feature of the system is that the user can fade in the cluster centroids (illustrated by a larger dot in the respective cluster color in Figure 2), where the overall feature distribution of the cluster can be examined in a tooltip hovering over the corresponding centroid.

2.2.2 Visually representing data objects

To gain further insight into the data distribution based on the 2D projection, the user can choose between several ways to visualize the individual data objects, all of which are shown in Figure 3. The standard visualization type is shown on the left and consists of a **circle** which encodes cluster membership via color.

[1]http://workshop.mkobos.com/2011/java-pca-transformation-library/

[2]http://java-ml.sourceforge.net/api/0.1.7/ (From the JML library)

[3]http://www.tomgibara.com/clustering/fast-spatial/

[4]http://www.piccolo2d.org/

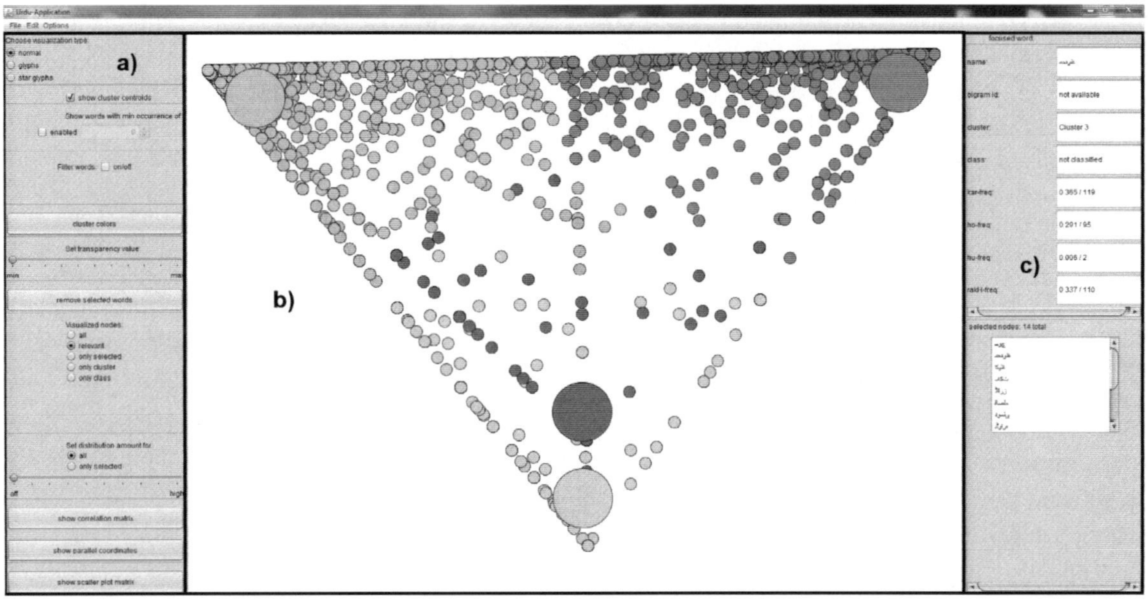

Figure 2: Overview of the main window of the system, including the configuration area (a), the visualization area (b) and the description area (c). Large circles are cluster centroids.

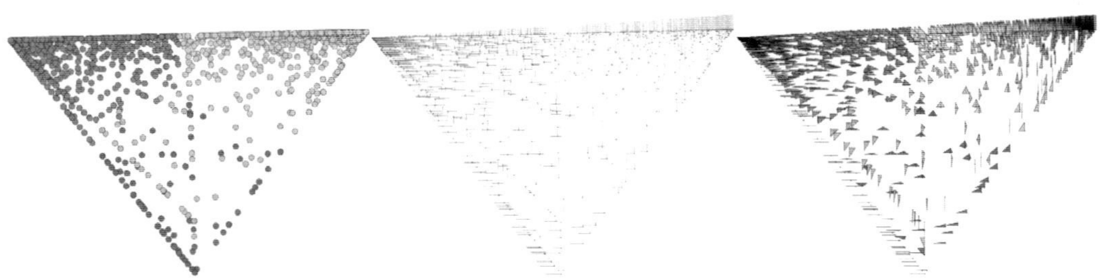

Figure 3: Different visualizations of data points

Alternatively, **normal glyphs** and **star glyphs** can be displayed. The middle part of Figure 3 shows the data displayed with **normal glyphs**. In this view, the relative frequency of each light verb is mapped onto the length of a line. The lines start in north position and are positioned clockwise around the center according to their occurrence in the input file. This view has the advantage that overall feature dominance in a cluster can be seen at-a-glance.

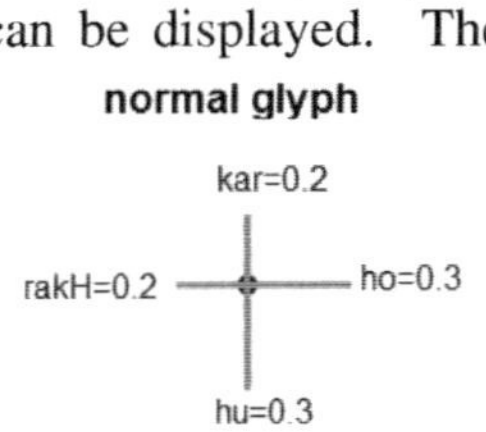

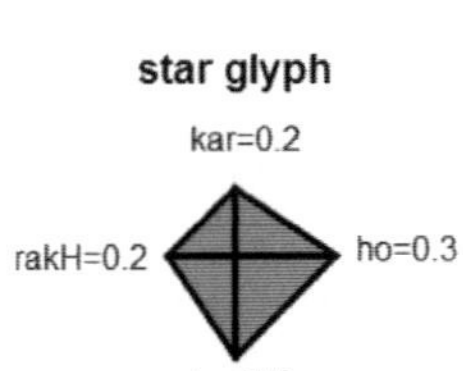

The visualization type on the right in Figure 3 is called the **star glyph**, an extension to normal glyphs. Here, the line endings are connected, forming a "star". As in the representation with the glyphs, this makes similar data objects easily recognizable and comparable with each other.

2.2.3 Filtering options

Our systems offers options for filtering data according to different criteria.

Filter by means of bigram occurrence By activating the bigram occurrence filtering, it is possible to only show those nouns, which occur in bigrams with a certain selected subset of all features (light verbs) only. This is especially useful when examining possible commonalities.

Filter selected words Another opportunity of showing only items of interest is to select and display them separately. The PCA is recalculated for these data objects and the visualization is stretched to the whole area.

Filter selected cluster Additionally, the user can visualize a specific cluster of interest. Again, the PCA is recalculated and the visualization stretched to the whole area. The cluster can then be manually fine-tuned and cleaned, for instance by removing wrongly assigned items.

2.2.4 Options to handle overplotting

Due to the nature of the data, much overplotting occurs. For example, there are many words, which only occur with one light verb. The PCA assigns the same position to these words and, as a consequence, only the top bigram can be viewed in the visualization. In order to improve visual access to overplotted data objects, several methods that allow for a more differentiated view of the data have been included and are described in the following paragraphs.

Change transparency of data objects By modifying the transparency with the given slider, areas with a dense data population can be readily identified, as shown in the following example:

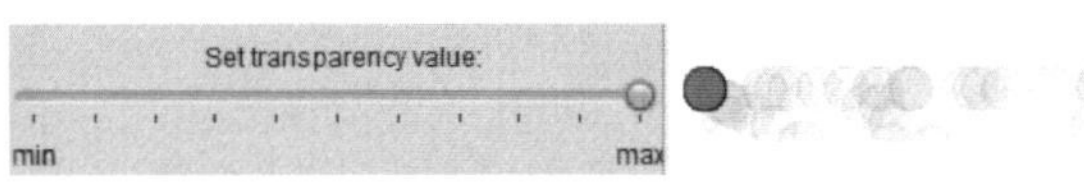

Repositioning of data objects To reduce the overplotting in densely populated areas, data objects can be repositioned randomly having a fixed deviation from their initial position. The degree of deviation can be interactively determined by the user employing the corresponding slider:

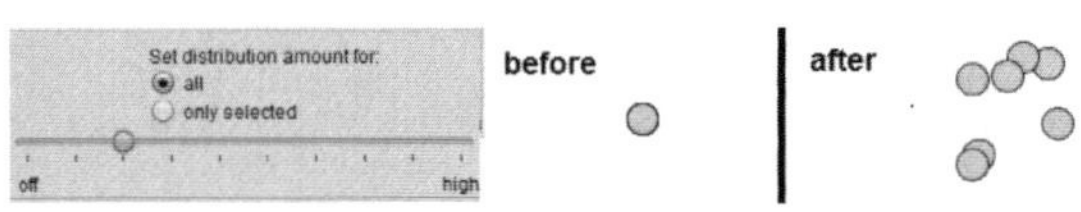

The user has the option to reposition either all data objects or only those that are selected in advance.

Frequency filtering If the initial data contains absolute bigram frequencies, the user can filter the visualized words by frequency. For example, many nouns occur only once and therefore have an observed probability of 100% for co-occurring with one of the light verbs. In most cases it is useful to filter such data out.

Scaling data objects If the user zooms beyond the maximum zoom factor, the data objects are scaled down. This is especially useful, if data objects are only partly covered by many other objects. In this case, they become fully visible, as shown in the following example:

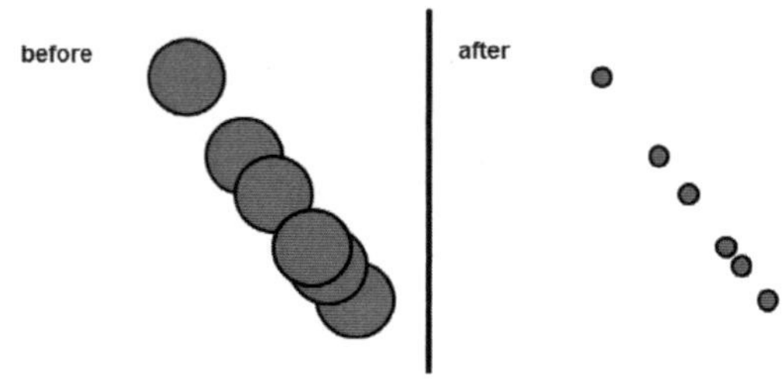

2.3 Alternative views on the data

In order to enable a holistic analysis it is often valuable to provide the user with different views on the data. Consequently, we have integrated the option to explore the data with further standard visualization methods.

2.3.1 Correlation matrix

The correlation matrix in Figure 4 shows the correlations between features, which are visualized by circles using the following encoding: The size of a circle represents the correlation strength and the color indicates whether the corresponding features are negatively (white) or positively (black) correlated.

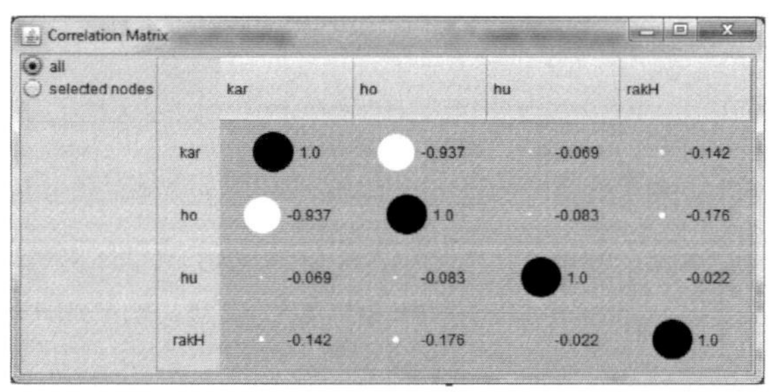

	kar	ho	hu	rakH
kar	1.0	-0.937	-0.069	-0.142
ho	-0.937	1.0	-0.083	-0.176
hu	-0.069	-0.083	1.0	-0.022
rakH	-0.142	-0.176	-0.022	1.0

Figure 4: example of a correlation matrix

2.3.2 Parallel coordinates

The parallel coordinates diagram shows the distribution of the bigram frequencies over the different dimensions (Figure 5). Every noun is represented with a line, and shows, when hovered over, a tooltip with the most important information. To filter the visualized words, the user has the option of displaying previously selected data objects, or s/he can restrict the value range for a feature and show only the items which lie within this range.

2.3.3 Scatter plot matrix

To further examine the relation between pairs of features, a scatter plot matrix can be used (Figure 6). The individual scatter plots give further insight into the correlation details of pairs of features.

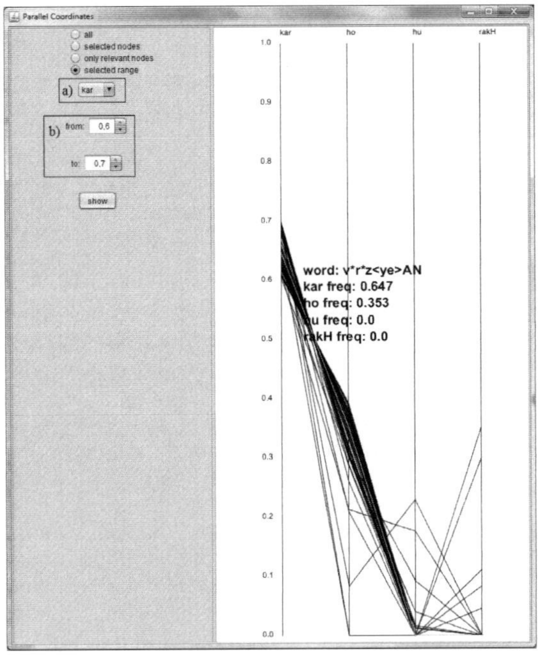

Figure 5: Parallel coordinates diagram

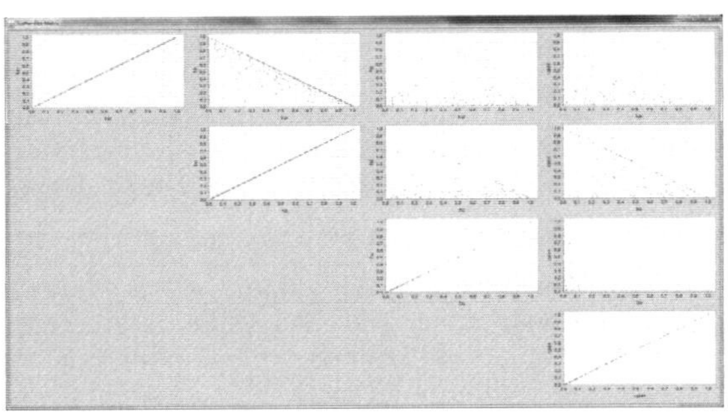

Figure 6: Example showing a scatter plot matrix.

3 Case study

In principle, the Visual Analytics system presented above can be used for any kind of cluster visualization, but the built-in options and add-ons are particularly designed for the type of work that linguists tend to be interested in: on the one hand, the user wants to get a quick overview of the overall patterns in the phenomenon, but on the same time, the system needs to allow for an in-depth data inspection. Both is given in the system: The overall cluster result shown in Figure 2 depicts the coherence of clusters and therefore the overall pattern of the data set. The different glyph visualizations in Figure 3 illustrate the properties of each cluster. Single data points can be inspected in the description area. The randomization of overplotted data points helps to see concentrated cluster patterns where light verbs behave very similarly in different noun+verb complex predicates.

The biggest advantage of the system lies in the ability for interaction: Figure 7 shows an example of the visualization used in Butt et al. (2012), the input being the same text file as shown in Figure 1. In this system, the relative frequencies of each noun with each light verb is correlated with color saturation — the more saturated the color to the right of the noun, the higher the relative frequency of the light verb occurring with it. The number of the cluster (here, 3) and the respective nouns (e.g. *kAm* 'work') is shown to the left. The user does not get information on the coherence of the cluster, nor does the visualization show prototypical cluster patterns.

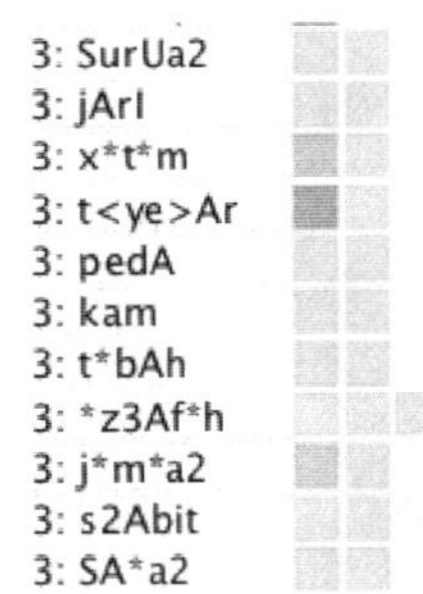

Figure 7: Cluster visualization in Butt et al. (2012)

Moreover, the system in Figure 7 only has a limited set of interaction choices, with the consequence that the user is not able to adjust the underlying data set, e.g. by filtering out noise. However, Butt et al. (2012) report that the Urdu data is indeed very noisy and requires a manual cleaning of the data set before the actual clustering. In the system presented here, the user simply marks conspicuous regions in the visualization panel and removes the respective data points from the original data set. Other filtering mechanisms, e.g. the removal of low frequency items which occur due to data sparsity issues, can be removed from the overall data set by adjusting the parameters.

A linguistically-relevant improvement lies in the display of cluster centroids, in other words the typical noun + light verb distribution of a cluster. This is particularly helpful when the linguist wants to pick out prototypical examples for the cluster in order to stipulate generalizations over the other cluster members.

4 Conclusion

In this paper, we present a novel visual analytics system that helps to automatically analyze bigrams extracted from corpora. The main purpose is to enable a more informed and steered cluster analysis than currently possible with standard methods. This includes rich options for interaction, e.g. display configuration or data manipulation. Initially, the approach was motivated by a concrete research problem, but has much wider applicability as any kind of high-dimensional numerical data objects can be loaded and analyzed. However, the system still requires some basic understanding about the algorithms applied for clustering and projection in order to prevent the user to draw wrong conclusions based on artifacts. Bearing this potential pitfall in mind when performing the analysis, the system enables a much more insightful and informed analysis than standard non-interactive methods.

In the future, we aim to conduct user experiments in order to learn more about how the functionality and usability could be further enhanced.

Acknowledgments

This work was partially funded by the German Research Foundation (DFG) under grant BU 1806/7-1 "Visual Analysis of Language Change and Use Patterns" and the German Federal Ministry of Education and Research (BMBF) under grant 01461246 "VisArgue" under research grant.

References

Tafseer Ahmed and Miriam Butt. 2011. Discovering Semantic Classes for Urdu N-V Complex Predicates. In *Proceedings of the international Conference on Computational Semantics (IWCS 2011)*, pages 305–309.

Joshua Albrecht, Rebecca Hwa, and G. Elisabeta Marai. 2009. The Chinese Room: Visualization and Interaction to Understand and Correct Ambiguous Machine Translation. *Comput. Graph. Forum*, 28(3):1047–1054.

Miriam Butt, Tina Bögel, Annette Hautli, Sebastian Sulger, and Tafseer Ahmed. 2012. Identifying Urdu Complex Predication via Bigram Extraction. In *In Proceedings of COLING 2012, Technical Papers*, pages 409 – 424, Mumbai, India.

Christopher Collins, M. Sheelagh T. Carpendale, and Gerald Penn. 2007. Visualization of Uncertainty in Lattices to Support Decision-Making. In *EuroVis 2007*, pages 51–58. Eurographics Association.

Kris Heylen, Dirk Speelman, and Dirk Geeraerts. 2012. Looking at word meaning. An interactive visualization of Semantic Vector Spaces for Dutch synsets. In *Proceedings of the EACL 2012 Joint Workshop of LINGVIS & UNCLH*, pages 16–24.

Daniel A. Keim and Daniela Oelke. 2007. Literature Fingerprinting: A New Method for Visual Literary Analysis. In *IEEE VAST 2007*, pages 115–122. IEEE.

Thomas Mayer, Christian Rohrdantz, Miriam Butt, Frans Plank, and Daniel A. Keim. 2010a. Visualizing Vowel Harmony. *Linguistic Issues in Language Technology*, 4(Issue 2):1–33, December.

Thomas Mayer, Christian Rohrdantz, Frans Plank, Peter Bak, Miriam Butt, and Daniel A. Keim. 2010b. Consonant Co-Occurrence in Stems across Languages: Automatic Analysis and Visualization of a Phonotactic Constraint. In *Proceedings of the 2010 Workshop on NLP and Linguistics: Finding the Common Ground*, pages 70–78, Uppsala, Sweden, July. Association for Computational Linguistics.

Tara Mohanan. 1994. *Argument Structure in Hindi*. Stanford: CSLI Publications.

Christian Rohrdantz, Annette Hautli, Thomas Mayer, Miriam Butt, Frans Plank, and Daniel A. Keim. 2011. Towards Tracking Semantic Change by Visual Analytics. In *ACL 2011 (Short Papers)*, pages 305–310, Portland, Oregon, USA, June. Association for Computational Linguistics.

Christian Rohrdantz, Michael Hund, Thomas Mayer, Bernhard Wälchli, and Daniel A. Keim. 2012a. The World's Languages Explorer: Visual Analysis of Language Features in Genealogical and Areal Contexts. *Computer Graphics Forum*, 31(3):935–944.

Christian Rohrdantz, Andreas Niekler, Annette Hautli, Miriam Butt, and Daniel A. Keim. 2012b. Lexical Semantics and Distribution of Suffixes - A Visual Analysis. In *Proceedings of the EACL 2012 Joint Workshop of LINGVIS & UNCLH*, pages 7–15, April.

Tobias Schreck, Jürgen Bernard, Tatiana von Landesberger, and Jörn Kohlhammer. 2009. Visual cluster analysis of trajectory data with interactive kohonen maps. *Information Visualization*, 8(1):14–29.

James J. Thomas and Kristin A. Cook. 2006. A Visual Analytics Agenda. *IEEE Computer Graphics and Applications*, 26(1):10–13.

Jian Zhao, Fanny Chevalier, Christopher Collins, and Ravin Balakrishnan. 2012. Facilitating Discourse Analysis with Interactive Visualization. *IEEE Trans. Vis. Comput. Graph.*, 18(12):2639–2648.

Development and Analysis of NLP Pipelines in Argo

Rafal Rak, Andrew Rowley, Jacob Carter, and Sophia Ananiadou
National Centre for Text Mining
School of Computer Science, University of Manchester
Manchester Institute of Biotechnology
131 Princess St, M1 7DN, Manchester, UK
{rafal.rak,andrew.rowley,jacob.carter,sophia.ananiadou}@manchester.ac.uk

Abstract

Developing sophisticated NLP pipelines composed of multiple processing tools and components available through different providers may pose a challenge in terms of their interoperability. The Unstructured Information Management Architecture (UIMA) is an industry standard whose aim is to ensure such interoperability by defining common data structures and interfaces. The architecture has been gaining attention from industry and academia alike, resulting in a large volume of UIMA-compliant processing components. In this paper, we demonstrate Argo, a Web-based workbench for the development and processing of NLP pipelines/workflows. The workbench is based upon UIMA, and thus has the potential of using many of the existing UIMA resources. We present features, and show examples, of facilitating the distributed development of components and the analysis of processing results. The latter includes annotation visualisers and editors, as well as serialisation to RDF format, which enables flexible querying in addition to data manipulation thanks to the semantic query language SPARQL. The distributed development feature allows users to seamlessly connect their tools to workflows running in Argo, and thus take advantage of both the available library of components (without the need of installing them locally) and the analytical tools.

1 Introduction

Building NLP applications usually involves a series of individual tasks. For instance, the extraction of relationships between named entities in text is preceded by text segmentation, part-of-speech recognition, the recognition of named entities, and dependency parsing. Currently, the availability of such atomic processing components is no longer an issue; the problem lies in ensuring their compatibility, as combining components coming from multiple repositories, written in different programming languages, requiring different installation procedures, and having incompatible input/output formats can be a source of frustration and poses a real challenge for developers.

Unstructured Information Management Architecture (UIMA) (Ferrucci and Lally, 2004) is a framework that tackles the problem of interoperability of processing components. Originally developed by IBM, it is currently an Apache Software Foundation open-source project[1] that is also registered at the Organization for the Advancement of Structured Information Standards (OASIS)[2]. UIMA has been gaining much interest from industry and academia alike for the past decade. Notable repositories of UIMA-compliant tools include U-Compare component library[3], DKPro (Gurevych et al., 2007), cTAKES (Savova et al., 2010), BioNLP-UIMA Component Repository (Baumgartner et al., 2008), and JULIE Lab's UIMA Component Repository (JCoRe) (Hahn et al., 2008).

In this work we demonstrate Argo[4], a Web-based (remotely-accessed) workbench for collaborative development of text-processing workflows. We focus primarily on the process of development and analysis of both individual processing components and workflows composed of such components.

The next section demonstrates general features of Argo and lays out several technical details about

[1] http://uima.apache.org
[2] http://www.oasis-open.org/committees/uima
[3] http://nactem.ac.uk/ucompare/
[4] http://argo.nactem.ac.uk

UIMA that will ease the understanding of the remaining sections. Sections 3–5 discuss selected features that are useful in the development and analysis of components and workflows. Section 6 mentions related efforts, and Section 7 concludes the paper.

2 Overview of Argo

Argo comes equipped with an ever-growing library of atomic processing components that can be put together by users to form meaningful pipelines or workflows. The processing components range from simple data serialisers to complex text analytics and include text segmentation, part-of-speech tagging, parsing, named entity recognition, and discourse analysis.

Users interact with the workbench through a graphical user interface (GUI) that is accessible entirely through a Web browser. Figure 1 shows two views of the interface: the main, resource management window (Figure 1(a)) and the workflow diagramming window (Figure 1(b)). The main window provides access to emphdocuments, *workflows*, and *processes* separated in easily accessible panels.

The *Documents* panel lists primarily user-owned files that are uploaded (through the GUI) by users into their respective personal spaces on the remote host. Documents may also be generated as a result of executing workflows (e.g., XML files containing annotations), in which case they are available for users to download.

The *Workflows* panel lists users' workflows, i.e., the user-defined arrangements of processing components together with their settings. Users compose workflows through a flexible, graphical diagramming editor by connecting the components (represented as blocks) with lines signifying the flow of data between components (see Figure 1(b)). The most common arrangement is to form a pipeline, i.e., each participating component has at most one incoming and at most one outgoing connection; however, the system also supports multiple branching and merging points in the workflow. An example is shown in Figure 2 discussed farther in text. For ease of use, components are categorized into readers, analytics, and consumers, indicating what role they are set to play in a workflow. Readers are responsible for delivering data for processing and have only an outgoing port (represented as a green triangle). The role of analytics is to modify incoming data structures and pass them onto following components in a workflow, and thus they have both incoming and outgoing ports. Finally, the consumers are responsible for serialising or visualising (selected or all) annotations in the data structures without modification, and so they have only an incoming port.

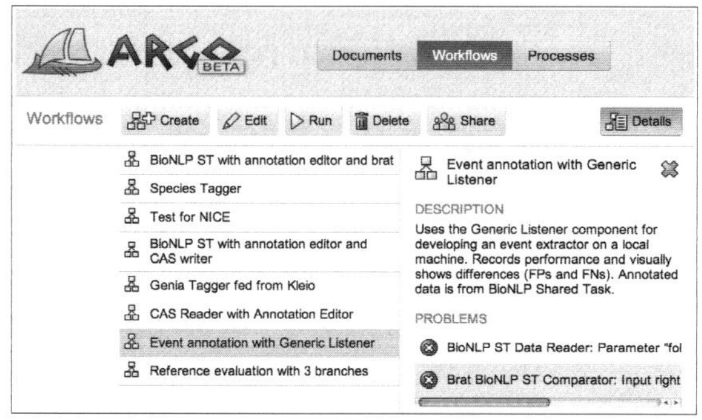

(a) Workflow management view

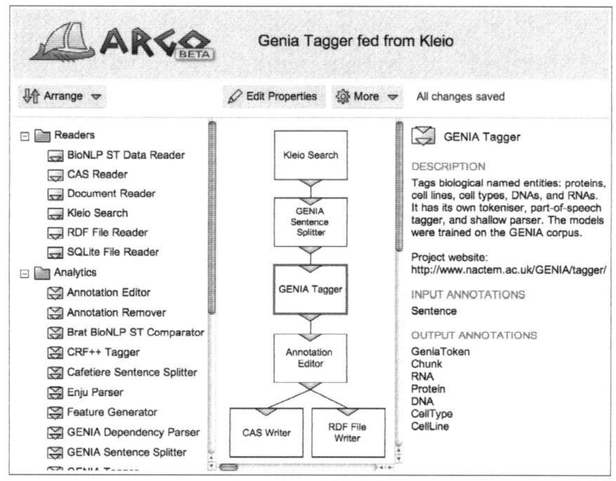

(b) Worflow diagram editor view

Figure 1: Screenshots of Argo Web browser content.

The *Processes* panel lists resources that are created automatically when workflows are submitted for execution by users. Users may follow the progress of the executing workflows (processes) as well as manage the execution from this panel. The processing of workflows is carried out on remote servers, and thus frees users from using their own processing resources.

2.1 Argo and UIMA

Argo supports and is based upon UIMA and thus can run any UIMA-compliant processing component. Each such component defines or imports *type systems* and modifies *common annotation structures* (CAS). A type system is the representation of a data model that is shared between components, whereas a CAS is the container of data whose structure complies with the type system. A CAS stores *feature structures*, e.g., a token with its text boundaries and a part-of-speech tag. Feature structures may, and often do, refer to a *subject of annotation* (Sofa), a structure that (in text-processing applications) stores the text. UIMA comes with built-in data types including primitive types (boolean, integer, string, etc.), arrays, lists, as well as several complex types, e.g., Annotation that holds a reference to a Sofa the annotation is asserted about, and two features, begin and end, for marking boundaries of a span of text. A developer is free to extend any of the complex types.

2.2 Architecture

Although the Apache UIMA project provides an implementation of the UIMA framework, Argo incorporates home-grown solutions, especially in terms of the management of workflow processing. This includes features such as workflow branching and merging points, user-interactive components (see Section 4), as well as distributed processing.

The primary processing is carried out on a multi-core server. Additionally, in order to increase computing throughput, we have incorporated cloud computing capabilities into Argo, which is designed to work with various cloud computing providers. As a proof of concept, the current implementation uses HTCondor, an open-source, high-throughput computing software framework. Currently, Argo is capable of switching the processing of workflows to a local cluster of over 3,000 processor cores. Further extensions to use the Microsoft Azure[5] and Amazon EC2[6] cloud platforms are also planned.

The Argo platform is available entirely using RESTful Web services (Fielding and Taylor, 2002), and therefore it is possible to gain access to all or selected features of Argo by implementing a compliant client. In fact, the "native" Web interface shown in Figure 1 is an example of such a client.

3 Distributed Development

Argo includes a Generic Listener component that permits execution of a UIMA component that is running externally of the Argo system. It is primarily intended to be used during the development of processing components, as it allows a developer to rapidly make any necessary changes, whilst continuing to make use of the existing components available within Argo, which may otherwise be unavailable if developing on the developer's local system. Any component that a user wishes to deploy on the Argo system has to undergo a verification process, which could lead to a slower development lifecycle without the availability of this component.

Generic Listener operates in a reverse manner to a traditional Web service; rather than Argo connecting to the developer's component, the component connects to Argo. This behaviour was deliberately chosen to avoid network-related issues, such as firewall port blocking, which could become a source of frustration to developers.

When a workflow, containing a Generic Listener, is executed within Argo, it will continue as normal until the point at which the Generic Listener receives its first CAS object. Argo will prompt the user with a unique URL, which must be supplied to the client component run by the user, allowing it to connect to the Argo workflow and continue its execution.

A skeleton Java project has been provided to assist in the production of such components. It contains a Maven structure, Eclipse IDE project files, and required libraries, in addition to a number of shell scripts to simplify the running of the component. The project provides both a command-line interface (CLI) and GUI runner applications that take, as arguments, the name of the class of the locally developed component and the URL provided by Argo, upon each run of a workflow containing the remote component.

An example of a workflow with a Generic Listener is shown in Figure 2. The workflow is designed for the analysis and evaluation of a solution (in this case, the automatic extraction of biological events) that is being developed locally by the user. The reader (BioNLP ST Data Reader) provides text documents together with gold (i.e., manually created) event annotations prepared for the BioNLP Shared Task[7]. The annotations are selectively removed with the Annotation Remover and the remaining data is sent onto the Generic Listener component, and consequently, onto the developer's machine. The developer's task is to

[5]http://www.windowsazure.com

[6]http://aws.amazon.com/ec2

[7]http://2013.bionlp-st.org/

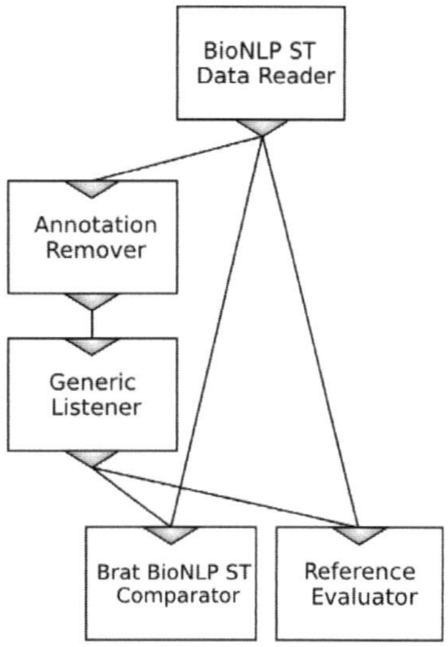

Figure 2: Example of a workflow for development, analysis, and evaluation of a user-developed solution for the BioNLP Shared Task.

connect to Argo, retrieve CASes from the running workflow, and for each CAS recreate the removed annotations as faithfully as possible. The developer can then track the performance of their solution by observing standard information extraction measures (precision, recall, etc.) computed by the Reference Evaluator component that compares the original, gold annotations (coming from the reader) against the developer's annotations (coming from the Generic Listener), and saves these measures for each document/CAS into a tabular-format file. Moreover, the differences can be tracked visually though the interactive Brat BioNLP ST Comparator component, discussed in the next section.

4 Annotation Analysis and Manipulation

Traditionally, NLP pipelines (including existing UIMA-supporting platforms), once set up, are executed without human involvement. One of the novelties in Argo is an introduction of *user-interactive components*, a special type of analytic that, if present in a workflow, cause the execution of the workflow to pause. Argo resumes the execution only after receiving input from a user. This feature allows for manual intervention in the otherwise automatic processing by, e.g., manipulating automatically created annotations. Examples of user-interactive components include Annotation Editor and Brat BioNLP ST Comparator.

The Brat BioNLP ST Comparator component

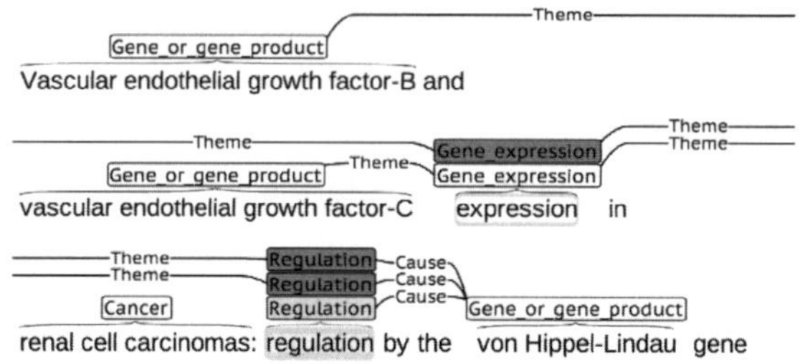

Figure 3: Example of an annotated fragment of a document visualised with the Brat BioNLP ST Comparator component. The component highlights (in red and green) differences between two sources of annotations.

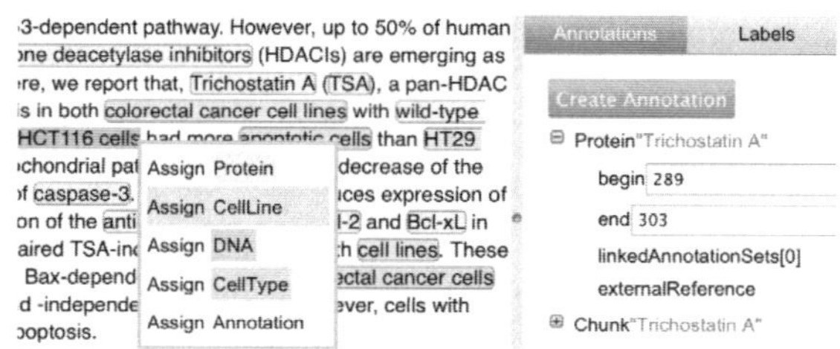

Figure 4: Example of manual annotation with the user-interactive Annotation Editor component.

expects two incoming connections from components processing the same subject of annotation. As a result, using brat visualisation (Stenetorp et al., 2012), it will show annotation structures by laying them out above text and mark differences between the two inputs by colour-coding missing or additional annotations in each input. A sample of visualisation coming from the workflow in Figure 2 is shown in Figure 3. Since in this particular workflow the Brat BioNLP ST Comparator receives gold annotations (from the BioNLP ST Data Reader) as one of its inputs, the highlighted differences are, in fact, false positives and false negatives.

Annotation Editor is another example of a user-interactive component that allows the user to add, delete or modify annotations. Figure 4 shows the editor in action. The user has an option to create a span-of-text annotation by selecting a text fragment and assigning an annotation type. More complex annotation types, such as tokens with part-of-speech tags or annotations that do not refer to the text (meta-annotations) can be created or modified using an expandable tree-like structure (shown on the right-hand side of the figure), which makes it possible to create any annotation

```
select ?neAText ?neACat ?neBText ?neBCat (count(*) as ?count)
{
  # retrieve sentence data
  { select ?sent ?sentBegin ?sentEnd ?sofa {
    ?sent a syn:Sentence ; b:sofa ?sofa ;
          t:begin ?sentBegin ; t:end ?sentEnd . } }

  # retrieve the 1st entity data
  { select ?ne1 ?ne1Cat ?ne1Begin ?ne1End ?sofa {
    ?ne1 rdf:type/rdfs:subClassOf* sem:NamedEntity ;
         a ?ne1Cat ; b:sofa ?sofa ;
         t:begin ?ne1Begin ; t:end ?ne1End . } }

  # retrieve the 2nd entity data
  { select ?ne2 ?ne2Cat ?ne2Begin ?ne2End ?sofa {
    ?ne2 rdf:type/rdfs:subClassOf* sem:NamedEntity ;
         a ?ne2Cat ; b:sofa ?sofa ;
         t:begin ?ne2Begin ; t:end ?ne2End . } }

  # the 2 entities must be enclosed in the sentence
  filter (?ne1Begin>=?sentBegin && ?ne1End<=?sentEnd
        && ?ne2Begin>=?sentBegin && ?ne2End<=?sentEnd)

  # extract covered text from the Sofa
  ?sofa s:sofaString ?text .
  bind (substr(?text, ?sentBegin+1, ?sentEnd-?sentBegin)
        as ?sentText) .
  bind (substr(?text, ?ne1Begin+1, ?ne1End-?ne1Begin)
        as ?ne1Text) .
  bind (substr(?text, ?ne2Begin+1, ?ne2End-?ne2Begin)
        as ?ne2Text) .

  # prevent symmetric duplicates
  filter(str(?ne1)<str(?ne2))
  bind(if(?ne1Text<?ne2Text, ?ne1Text, ?ne2Text) as ?neAText)
  bind(if(?ne1Text<?ne2Text, ?ne1Cat, ?ne2Cat) as ?neACat)
  bind(if(?ne1Text>=?ne2Text, ?ne1Text, ?ne2Text) as ?neBText)
  bind(if(?ne1Text>=?ne2Text, ?ne1Cat, ?ne2Cat) as ?neBCat)
}
group by ?neAText ?neACat ?neBText ?neBCat
order by desc(?count)
```

(a) Select query

neAText	neACat	neBText	neBCat	count
Ki-67	Protein	p53	Protein	85
DC	CellType	p53	Protein	61
DC	CellType	KCOT	Protein	47

(b) Results (fragment)

```
insert {
  _:relationship a sem:Relationship ;
             sem:Relationship:arg1 ?ne1 ;
             sem:Relationship:arg2 ?ne2 . }
{
  # retrieve sentence data
  { select ?sent ?sentBegin ?sentEnd ?sofa {
    ?sent a syn:Sentence ; b:sofa ?sofa ;
          t:begin ?sentBegin ; t:end ?sentEnd . } }

  # retrieve the 1st entity data
  { select ?ne1 ?ne1Begin ?ne1End ?sofa {
    ?ne1 rdf:type/rdfs:subClassOf* sem:NamedEntity ;
         b:sofa ?sofa ;
         t:begin ?ne1Begin ; t:end ?ne1End . } }

  # retrieve the 2nd entity data
  { select ?ne2 ?ne2Begin ?ne2End ?sofa {
    ?ne2 rdf:type/rdfs:subClassOf* sem:NamedEntity ;
         b:sofa ?sofa ;
         t:begin ?ne2Begin ; t:end ?ne2End . } }

  # the 2 entities must be enclosed in the sentence
  filter (?ne1Begin>=?sentBegin && ?ne1End<=?sentEnd
        && ?ne2Begin>=?sentBegin && ?ne2End<=?sentEnd)

  # prevent symmetric duplicates
  filter(str(?ne1)<str(?ne2))
}
```

(c) Insert query

Figure 5: Example of (a) a SPARQL query that returns biological interactions; (b) a fragment of retrieved results; and (c) a SPARQL query that creates new UIMA feature structures. Namespaces and data types are omitted for brevity.

structure permissible by a given type system.

5 Querying Serialised Data

Argo comes with several (de)serialisation components for reading and storing collections of data, such as a generic reader of text (Document Reader) or readers and writers of CASes in XMI format (CAS Reader and CAS Writer). One of the more useful in terms of annotation analysis is, however, the RDF Writer component as well as its counterpart, RDF Reader. RDF Writer serialises data into RDF files and supports several RDF formats such as RDF/XML, Turtle, and N-Triple. A resulting RDF graph consists of both the data model (type system) and the data itself (CAS) and thus constitutes a self-contained knowledge base. RDF Writer has an option to create a graph for each CAS or a single graph for an entire collection. Such a knowledge base can be queried with languages such as SPARQL[8], an official W3C Recommendation.

Figure 5 shows an example of a SPARQL query that is performed on the output of an RDF Writer in the workflow shown in Figure 1(b). This workflow results in several types of annotations including the boundaries of sentences, tokens with part-of-speech tags and lemmas, chunks, as well as biological entities, such as DNA, RNA, cell line and cell type. The SPARQL query is meant to retrieve pairs of seemingly interacting biological entities ranked according to their occurrence in the entire collection. The interaction here is (naïvely) defined as co-occurrence of two entities in the same sentence. The query includes patterns for retrieving the boundaries of sentences (`syn:Sentence`) and two biological entities (`sem:NamedEntity`) and then filters out the crossproduct of those by ensuring that the two en-

[8]http://www.w3.org/TR/2013/REC-sparql11-overview-20130321/

tities are enclosed in a sentence. As a result, the query returns a list of biological entity pairs accompanied by their categories and the number of appearances, as shown in Figure 5(b). Note that the query itself does not list the four biological categories; instead, it requests their common semantic ancestor `sem:NamedEntity`. This is one of the advantages of using semantically-enabled languages, such as SPARQL.

SPARQL also supports graph manipulation. Suppose a user is interested in placing the retrieved biological entity interactions from our running example into the UIMA structure Relationship that simply defines a pair of references to other structures of any type. This can be accomplished, without resorting to programming, by issuing a SPARQL insert query shown in Figure 5(c). The query will create triple statements compliant with the definition of Relationship. The resulting modified RDF graph can then be read back to Argo by the RDF Reader component that will convert the new RDF graph back into a CAS.

6 Related Work

Other notable examples of NLP platforms that provide graphical interfaces for managing workflows include GATE (Cunningham et al., 2002) and U-Compare (Kano et al., 2010). GATE is a standalone suite of text processing and annotation tools and comes with its own programming interface. In contrast, U-Compare—similarly to Argo—uses UIMA as its base interoperability framework. The key features of Argo that distinguish it from U-Compare are the Web availability of the platform, primarily remote processing of workflows, a multi-user, collaborative architecture, and the availability of user-interactive components.

7 Conclusions

Argo emerges as a one-stop solution for developing and processing NLP tasks. Moreover, the presented annotation viewer and editor, performance evaluator, and lastly RDF (de)serialisers are indispensable for the analysis of processing tasks at hand. Together with the distributed development support for developers wishing to create their own components or run their own tools with the help of resources available in Argo, the workbench becomes a powerful development and analytical NLP tool.

Acknowledgments

This work was partially funded by the MRC Text Mining and Screening grant (MR/J005037/1).

References

W A Baumgartner, K B Cohen, and L Hunter. 2008. An open-source framework for large-scale, flexible evaluation of biomedical text mining systems. *Journal of biomedical discovery and collaboration*, 3:1+.

H Cunningham, D Maynard, K Bontcheva, and V Tablan. 2002. GATE: A framework and graphical development environment for robust NLP tools and applications. In *Proceedings of the 40th Anniversary Meeting of the Association for Computational Linguistics*.

D Ferrucci and A Lally. 2004. UIMA: An Architectural Approach to Unstructured Information Processing in the Corporate Research Environment. *Natural Language Engineering*, 10(3-4):327–348.

R T Fielding and R N Taylor. 2002. Principled design of the modern Web architecture. *ACM Trans. Internet Technol.*, 2(2):115–150, May.

I Gurevych, M Mühlhäuser, C Müller, J Steimle, M Weimer, and T Zesch. 2007. Darmstadt knowledge processing repository based on uima. In *Proceedings of the First Workshop on Unstructured Information Management Architecture*, Tübingen, Germany.

U Hahn, E Buyko, R Landefeld, M Mühlhausen, M Poprat, K Tomanek, and J Wermter. 2008. An Overview of JCORE, the JULIE Lab UIMA Component Repository. In *Language Resources and Evaluation Workshop, Towards Enhanc. Interoperability Large HLT Syst.: UIMA NLP*, pages 1–8.

Y Kano, R Dorado, L McCrochon, S Ananiadou, and J Tsujii. 2010. U-Compare: An integrated language resource evaluation platform including a comprehensive UIMA resource library. In *Proceedings of the Seventh International Conference on Language Resources and Evaluation*, pages 428–434.

G K Savova, J J Masanz, P V Ogren, J Zheng, S Sohn, K C Kipper-Schuler, and C G Chute. 2010. Mayo clinical Text Analysis and Knowledge Extraction System (cTAKES): architecture, component evaluation and applications. *Journal of the American Medical Informatics Association*, 17(5):507–513.

P Stenetorp, S Pyysalo, G Topić, T Ohta, S Ananiadou, and J Tsujii. 2012. brat: a web-based tool for nlp-assisted text annotation. In *Proceedings of the 13th Conference of the European Chapter of the Association for Computational Linguistics*, pages 102–107, Avignon, France.

DKPro Similarity: An Open Source Framework for Text Similarity

Daniel Bär[†], **Torsten Zesch**[†‡], **and Iryna Gurevych**[†‡]
[†]Ubiquitous Knowledge Processing Lab (UKP-TUDA)
Department of Computer Science, Technische Universität Darmstadt
[‡]Ubiquitous Knowledge Processing Lab (UKP-DIPF)
German Institute for Educational Research and Educational Information
www.ukp.tu-darmstadt.de

Abstract

We present *DKPro Similarity*, an open source framework for text similarity. Our goal is to provide a comprehensive repository of text similarity measures which are implemented using standardized interfaces. DKPro Similarity comprises a wide variety of measures ranging from ones based on simple n-grams and common subsequences to high-dimensional vector comparisons and structural, stylistic, and phonetic measures. In order to promote the reproducibility of experimental results and to provide reliable, permanent experimental conditions for future studies, DKPro Similarity additionally comes with a set of full-featured experimental setups which can be run out-of-the-box and be used for future systems to built upon.

1 Introduction

Computing text similarity is key to several natural language processing applications such as automatic essay grading, paraphrase recognition, or plagiarism detection. However, only a few text similarity measures proposed in the literature are released publicly, and those then typically do not comply with any standardization. We are currently not aware of any designated text similarity framework which goes beyond simple lexical similarity or contains more than a small number of measures, even though related frameworks exist, which we discuss in Section 6. This fact was also realized by the organizers of the pilot *Semantic Textual Similarity Task* at SemEval-2012 (see Section 5), as they argue for the creation of an open source framework for text similarity (Agirre et al., 2012).

In order to fill this gap, we present DKPro Similarity, an open source framework for text similarity. DKPro Similarity is designed to complement DKPro Core[1], a collection of software components for natural language processing based on the Apache UIMA framework (Ferrucci and Lally, 2004). Our goal is to provide a comprehensive repository of text similarity measures which are implemented in a common framework using standardized interfaces. Besides the already available measures, DKPro Similarity is easily extensible and intended to allow for custom implementations, for which it offers various templates and examples. The Java implementation is publicly available at Google Code[2] under the Apache Software License v2 and partly under GNU GPL v3.

2 Architecture

DKPro Similarity is designed to operate in either of two modes: The *stand-alone mode* allows to use text similarity measures as independent components in any experimental setup, but does not offer means for further language processing, e.g. lemmatization. The *UIMA-coupled mode* tightly integrates similarity computation with full-fledged *Apache UIMA*-based language processing pipelines. That way, it allows to perform any number of languge processing steps, e.g. coreference or named-entitiy resolution, along with the text similarity computation.

Stand-alone Mode In this mode, text similarity measures can be used independently of any language processing pipeline just by passing them a pair of texts as (i) two strings, or (ii) two lists of strings (e.g. already lemmatized texts). We therefore provide an API module, which contains Java interfaces and abstract base classes for the measures. That way, DKPro Similarity allows for a maximum flexibility in experimental design, as the text similarity measures can easily be integrated with any existing experimental setup:

[1] code.google.com/p/dkpro-core-asl
[2] code.google.com/p/dkpro-similarity-asl

```
TextSimilarityMeasure m =
    new GreedyStringTiling();
double similarity =
    m.getSimilarity(text1, text2);
```

The above code snippet instantiates the *Greedy String Tiling* measure (Wise, 1996) and then computes the text similarity between the given pair of texts. The resulting similarity score is normalized into $[0, 1]$ where 0 means *not similar at all*, and 1 corresponds to *perfectly similar*.[3] By using the common `TextSimilarityMeasure` interface, it is easy to replace Greedy String Tiling with any measure of choice, such as *Latent Semantic Analysis* (Landauer et al., 1998) or *Explicit Semantic Analysis* (Gabrilovich and Markovitch, 2007). We give an overview of measures available in DKPro Similarity in Section 3.

UIMA-coupled Mode In this mode, DKPro Similarity allows text similarity computation to be directly integrated with any UIMA-based language processing pipeline. That way, it is easy to use text similarity components in addition to other UIMA-based components in the same pipeline. For example, an experimental setup may require to first compute text similarity scores and then to run a classification algorithm on the resulting scores.

In Figure 1, we show a graphical overview of the integration of text similarity measures (right) with a UIMA-based pipeline (left). The pipeline starts by reading a given dataset, then performs any number of pre-processing steps such as tokenization, sentence splitting, lemmatization, or stopword filtering, then runs the text similarity computation, before executing any subsequent post-processing steps and finally returning the processed texts in a suitable format for evaluation or manual inspection. As all text similarity measures in DKPro Similarity conform to standardized interfaces, they can be easily exchanged in the text similarity computation step.

With DKPro Similarity, we offer various subclasses of the generic UIMA components which are specifically tailored towards text similarity experiments, e.g. corpus readers for standard evaluation datasets as well as evaluation components for running typical evaluation metrics. By leveraging UIMA's architecture, we also define an

[3]Some string distance measures such as the *Levenshtein distance* (Levenshtein, 1966) return a raw distance score where less distance corresponds to higher similarity. However, the score can easily be normalized, e.g. by text length.

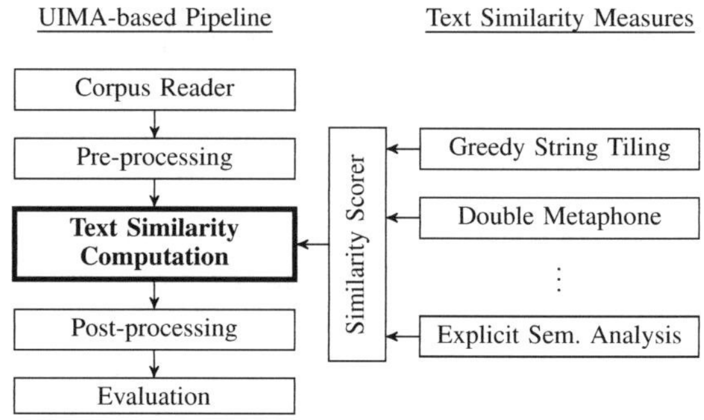

Figure 1: DKPro Similarity allows to integrate any text similarity measure (right) which conforms to standardized interfaces into a UIMA-based language processing pipeline (left) by means of a dedicated *Similarity Scorer* component (middle).

additional interface to text similarity measures: The `JCasTextSimilarityMeasure` inherits from `TextSimilarityMeasure`, and adds a method for two `JCas` text representations:[4]

```
double getSimilarity
    (JCas text1, JCas text2);
```

The additional interface allows to implement measures which have full access to UIMA's document structure. That way, it is possible to create text similarity measures which can use any piece of information that has been annotated in the processed documents, such as dependency trees or morphological information. We detail the new set of components offered by DKPro Similarity in Section 4.

3 Text Similarity Measures

In this section, we give an overview of the text similarity measures which are already available in DKPro Similarity. While we provide new implementations for a multitude of measures, we rely on specialized libraries such as the *S-Space Package* (see Section 6) if available. Due to space limitations and due to the fact that the framework is actively under development, we do not provide an exhaustive list here, but rather mention the most interesting and most popular measures.

3.1 Simple String-based Measures

DKPro Similarity includes text similarity measures which operate on string sequences and determine, for example, the longest common

[4]The `JCas` is an object-oriented Java interface to the *Common Analysis Structure* (Ferrucci and Lally, 2004), Apache UIMA's internal document representation format.

(non-)contiguous sequence of characters. It also contains *Greedy String Tiling* (Wise, 1996), a measure which allows to compare strings if parts have been reordered. The framework also offers measures which compute sets of character and word n-grams and compare them using different overlap coefficients, e.g. the Jaccard index. It further includes popular string distance metrics such as the *Jaro-Winkler* (Winkler, 1990), *Monge and Elkan (1997)* and *Levenshtein (1966)* distance measures.

3.2 Semantic Similarity Measures

DKPro Similarity also contains several measures which go beyond simple character sequences and compute text similarity on a semantic level.

Pairwise Word Similarity These measures are based on pairwise word similarity computations which are then aggregated for the complete texts. The measures typically operate on a graph-based representation of words and the semantic relations among them within a lexical-semantic resource. DKPro Similarity therefore contains adapters for WordNet, Wiktionary[5], and Wikipedia, while the framework can easily be extended to other data sources that conform to a common interface (Garoufi et al., 2008). Pairwise similarity measures in DKPro Similarity include *Jiang and Conrath (1997)* or *Resnik (1995)*. The aggregation for the complete texts can for example be done using the strategy by Mihalcea et al. (2006).

Vector Space Models These text similarity measures project texts onto high-dimensional vectors which are then compared. *Cosine similarity*, a basic measure often used in information retrieval, weights words according to their term frequencies or *tf-idf* scores, and computes the cosine between two text vectors. *Latent Semantic Analysis* (Landauer et al., 1998) alleviates the inherent sparseness of a high-dimensional term-document matrix by reducing it to one of reduced rank. *Explicit Semantic Analysis* (Gabrilovich and Markovitch, 2007) constructs the vector space on corpora where the documents are assumed to describe natural concepts such as *cat* or *dog*. Originally, Wikipedia was proposed as the document collection of choice.

DKPro Similarity goes beyond a single implementation of these measures and comes with highly customizable code which allows to set various parameters for the construction of the vector space and the comparison of the document vectors, and further allows to construct the vector space for arbitrary collections, e.g. domain-specific corpora.

3.3 Further Measures

Previous research (Bär et al., 2012b) has shown promising results for the inclusion of measures which go beyond textual content and compute similarity along other text characteristics. Thus, DKPro Similarity also includes measures for structural, stylistic, and phonetic similarity.

Structural Similarity Structural similarity between texts can be computed, for example, by comparing sets of *stopword n-grams* (Stamatatos, 2011). The idea here is that similar texts may preserve syntactic similarity while exchanging only content words. Other measures in DKPro Similarity allow to compare texts by *part-of-speech n-grams*, and *order* and *distance features* for pairs of words (Hatzivassiloglou et al., 1999).

Stylistic Similarity DKPro Similarity includes, for example, a measure which compares *function word frequencies* (Dinu and Popescu, 2009) between two texts. The framework also includes a set of measures which capture statistical properties of texts such as the *type-token ratio* (TTR) and the *sequential TTR* (McCarthy and Jarvis, 2010).

Phonetic Similarity DKPro Similarity also allows to compute text similarity based on pairwise phonetic comparisons of words. It therefore contains implementations of well-known phonetic algorithms such as *Double Metaphone* (Philips, 2000) and *Soundex* (Knuth, 1973), which also conform to the common text similarity interface.

4 UIMA Components

In addition to a rich set of text similarity measures as partly described above, DKPro Similarity includes components which allow to integrate text similarity measures with any UIMA-based pipeline, as outlined in Figure 1. In the following, we introduce these components along with their resources.

Readers & Datasets DKPro Similarity includes corpus readers specifically tailored towards combining the input texts in a number of ways, e.g. all possible combinations, or each text paired with n others by random. Standard datasets for which

[5] http://www.wiktionary.org

readers come pre-packaged include, among others, the SemEval-2012 STS data (Agirre et al., 2012), the METER corpus (Clough et al., 2002), or the RTE 1–5 data (Dagan et al., 2006). As far as license terms allow redistribution, the datasets themselves are integrated into the framework.

Similarity Scorer The *Similarity Scorer* allows to integrate any text similarity measure (which is decoupled from UIMA by default) into a UIMA-based pipeline. It builds upon the standardized text similarity interfaces and thus allows to easily exchange the text similarity measure as well as to specify the data types the measure should operate on, e.g. tokens or lemmas.

Machine Learning Previous research (Agirre et al., 2012) has shown that different text similarity measures can be combined using machine learning classifiers. Such a combination shows improvements over single measures due to the fact that different measures capture different text characteristics. DKPro Similarity thus provides adapters for the Weka framework (Hall et al., 2009) and allows to first pre-compute sets of text similarity scores which can then be used as features for various machine learning classifiers.

Evaluation Metrics In the final step of a UIMA pipeline, the processed data is read by a dedicated evaluation component. DKPro Similarity ships with a set of components which for example compute Pearson or Spearman correlation with human judgments, or apply task-specific metrics such as average precision as used in the RTE challenges.

5 Experimental Setups

DKPro Similarity further encourages the creation and publication of complete experimental setups. That way, we promote the reproducibility of experimental results, and provide reliable, permanent experimental conditions which can benefit future studies and help to stimulate the reuse of particular experimental steps and software modules.

The experimental setups are instantiations of the generic UIMA-based language processing pipeline depicted in Figure 1 and are designed to precisely match the particular task at hand. They thus come pre-configured with corpus readers for the relevant input data, with a set of pre- and post-processing as well as evaluation components, and with a set of text similarity measures which are well-suited for the particular task. The experimental setups are self-contained systems and can be run out-of-the-box without further configuration.[6]

DKPro Similarity contains two major types of experimental setups: (i) those for an *intrinsic evaluation* allow to evaluate the system performance in an isolated setting by comparing the system results with a human gold standard, and (ii) those for an *extrinsic evaluation* allow to evaluate the system with respect to a particular task at hand, where text similarity is a means for solving a concrete problem, e.g. recognizing textual entailment.

Intrinsic Evaluation DKPro Similarity contains the setup (Bär et al., 2012a) which participated in the *Semantic Textual Similarity (STS) Task* at SemEval-2012 (Agirre et al., 2012) and which has become one of the recommended baseline systems for the second task of this series.[7] The system combines a multitude of text similarity measures of varying complexity using a simple log-linear regression model. The provided setup allows to evaluate how well the system output resembles human similarity judgments on short texts which are taken from five different sources, e.g. paraphrases of news texts or video descriptions.

Extrinsic Evaluation Our framework includes two setups for an extrinsic evaluation: detecting text reuse, and recognizing textual entailment.

For detecting text reuse (Clough et al., 2002), the setup we provide (Bär et al., 2012b) combines a multitude of text similarity measures along different text characteristics. Thereby, it not only combines simple string-based and semantic similarity measures (see Sections 3.1 and 3.2), but makes extensive use of measures along structural and stylistic text characteristics (see Section 3.3). Across three standard evaluation datasets, the system consistently outperforms all previous work.

For recognizing textual entailment, we provide a setup which is similar in configuration to the one described above, but contains corpus readers and evaluation components precisely tailored towards the RTE challenge series (Dagan et al., 2006). We believe that our setup can be used for filtering those text pairs which need further analysis by a dedicated textual entailment system.

[6] A one-time setup of local lexical-semantic resources such as WordNet may be necessary, though.

[7] In 2013, the STS Task is a shared task of the Second Joint Conference on Lexical and Computational Semantics, `http://ixa2.si.ehu.es/sts`

6 Related Frameworks

To the best of our knowledge, only a few generalized similarity frameworks exist at all. In the following, we discuss them and give insights where DKPro Similarity uses implementations of these existing libraries. That way, DKPro Similarity brings together the scattered efforts by offering access to all measures through common interfaces. It goes far beyond the functionality of the original libraries as it generalizes the resources used, allows a tight integration with any UIMA-based pipeline, and comes with full-featured experimental setups which are pre-configured stand-alone text similarity systems that can be run out-of-the-box.

S-Space Package Even though no designated text similarity library, the S-Space Package (Jurgens and Stevens, 2010)[8] contains some text similarity measures such as Latent Semantic Analysis (LSA) and Explicit Semantic Analysis (see Section 3.2). However, it is primarily focused on word space models which operate on word distributions in text. Besides such algorithms, it offers a variety of interfaces, data structures, evaluation datasets and metrics, and global operation utilities e.g. for dimension reduction using Singular Value Decomposition or randomized projections, which are particularly useful with such distributional word space models. DKPro Similarity integrates LSA based on the S-Space Package.

Semantic Vectors The Semantic Vectors package is a package for distributional semantics (Widdows and Cohen, 2010)[9] that contains measures such as LSA and allows for comparing documents within a given vector space. The main focus lies on word space models with a number of dimension reduction techniques, and applications on word spaces such as automatic thesaurus generation.

WordNet::Similarity The open source package by Pedersen et al. (2004)[10] is a popular Perl library for the similarity computation on WordNet. It comprises six word similarity measures that operate on WordNet, e.g. *Jiang and Conrath (1997)* or *Resnik (1995)*. Unfortunately, no strategies have been added to the package yet which aggregate the word similarity scores for complete texts in a similar manner as described in Section 3.2. In DKPro Similarity, we offer native Java implementations of all measures contained in WordNet::Similarity, and allow to go beyond WordNet and use the measures with any lexical-semantic resource of choice, e.g. Wiktionary or Wikipedia.

SimMetrics Library The Java library by Chapman et al. (2005)[11] exclusively comprises text similarity measures which compute lexical similarity on string sequences and compare texts without any semantic processing. It contains measures such as the *Levenshtein (1966)* or *Monge and Elkan (1997)* distance metrics. In DKPro Similarity, some string-based measures (see Section 3.1) are based on implementations from this library.

SecondString Toolkit The freely available library by Cohen et al. (2003)[12] is similar to SimMetrics, and also implemented in Java. It also contains several well-known text similarity measures on string sequences, and includes many of the measures which are also part of the SimMetrics Library. Some string-based measures in DKPro Similarity are based on the SecondString Toolkit.

7 Conclusions

We presented DKPro Similarity, an open source framework designed to streamline the development of text similarity measures. All measures conform to standardized interfaces and can either be used as stand-alone components in any experimental setup (e.g. an already existing system which is not based on Apache UIMA), or can be tightly coupled with a full-featured UIMA-based language processing pipeline in order to allow for advanced processing capabilities.

We would like to encourage other researchers to participate in our efforts and invite them to explore our existing experimental setups as outlined in Section 5, run modified versions of our setups, and contribute own text similarity measures to the framework. For that, DKPro Similarity also comes with an example module for getting started, which guides first-time users through both the stand-alone and the UIMA-coupled modes.

Acknowledgements This work has been supported by the Volkswagen Foundation as part of the Lichtenberg Professorship Program under grant No. I/82806, and by the Klaus Tschira Foundation under project No. 00.133.2008. We thank Richard Eckart de Castilho and all other contributors.

[8] `code.google.com/p/airhead-research`

[9] `code.google.com/p/semanticvectors`

[10] `sourceforge.net/projects/wn-similarity`

[11] `sourceforge.net/projects/simmetrics`

[12] `sourceforge.net/projects/secondstring`

References

Eneko Agirre, Daniel Cer, Mona Diab, and Aitor Gonzalez-Agirre. 2012. SemEval-2012 Task 6: A Pilot on Semantic Textual Similarity. In *Proc. of the 6th Int'l Works. on Semantic Eval.*, pages 385–393.

Daniel Bär, Chris Biemann, Iryna Gurevych, and Torsten Zesch. 2012a. UKP: Computing Semantic Textual Similarity by Combining Multiple Content Similarity Measures. In *Proc. of the 6th Int'l Workshop on Semantic Evaluation*, pages 435–440.

Daniel Bär, Torsten Zesch, and Iryna Gurevych. 2012b. Text Reuse Detection Using a Composition of Text Similarity Measures. In *Proc. of the 24th Int'l Conf. on Computational Linguistics*, pages 167–184.

Sam Chapman, Barry Norton, and Fabio Ciravegna. 2005. Armadillo: Integrating Knowledge for the Semantic Web. In *Proceedings of the Dagstuhl Seminar in Machine Learning for the Semantic Web*.

Paul Clough, Robert Gaizauskas, Scott S.L. Piao, and Yorick Wilks. 2002. METER: MEasuring TExt Reuse. In *Proceedings of ACL*, pages 152–159.

William W. Cohen, Pradeep Ravikumar, and Stephen Fienberg. 2003. A Comparison of String Metrics for Matching Names and Records. In *Proc. of KDD Works. on Data Cleaning and Object Consolidation*.

Ido Dagan, Oren Glickman, and Bernardo Magnini. 2006. The PASCAL Recognising Textual Entailment Challenge. In *Machine Learning Challenges*, Lecture Notes in Computer Science, pages 177–190.

Liviu P. Dinu and Marius Popescu. 2009. Ordinal measures in authorship identification. In *Proceedings of the 3rd PAN Workshop. Uncovering Plagiarism, Authorship and Social Software Misuse*, pages 62–66.

David Ferrucci and Adam Lally. 2004. UIMA: An Architectural Approach to Unstructured Information Processing in the Corporate Research Environment. *Natural Language Engineering*, 10(3-4):327–348.

Evgeniy Gabrilovich and Shaul Markovitch. 2007. Computing Semantic Relatedness using Wikipedia-based Explicit Semantic Analysis. In *Proceedings of IJCAI*, pages 1606–1611, Hyderabad, India.

Konstantina Garoufi, Torsten Zesch, and Iryna Gurevych. 2008. Representational Interoperability of Linguistic and Collaborative Knowledge Bases. In *Proceedings of the KONVENS Workshop on Lexical-Semantic and Ontological Resources*.

Mark Hall, Eibe Frank, Geoffrey Holmes, Bernhard Pfahringer, Peter Reutemann, and Ian H. Witten. 2009. The WEKA Data Mining Software: An Update. *SIGKDD Explorations*, 11(1):10–18.

Vasileios Hatzivassiloglou, Judith L. Klavans, and Eleazar Eskin. 1999. Detecting text similarity over short passages: Exploring linguistic feature combinations via machine learning. In *Proceedings of EMNLP/VLC*, pages 203–212.

Jay J. Jiang and David W. Conrath. 1997. Semantic similarity based on corpus statistics and lexical taxonomy. In *Proceedings of ROCLING*, pages 19–33.

David Jurgens and Keith Stevens. 2010. The S-Space Package: An Open Source Package for Word Space Models. In *Proceedings of the ACL 2010 System Demonstrations*, pages 30–35, Uppsala, Sweden.

Donald E. Knuth. 1973. *The Art of Computer Programming: Volume 3, Sorting and Searching*. Addison-Wesley.

Thomas K. Landauer, Peter W. Foltz, and Darrell Laham. 1998. An Introduction to Latent Semantic Analysis. *Discourse Processes*, 25(2):259–284.

Vladimir I. Levenshtein. 1966. Binary codes capable of correcting deletions, insertions, and reversals. *Soviet Physics Doklady*, 10(8):707–710.

Philip M. McCarthy and Scott Jarvis. 2010. MTLD, vocd-D, and HD-D: A validation study of sophisticated approaches to lexical diversity assessment. *Behavior research methods*, 42(2):381–392.

Rada Mihalcea, Courtney Corley, and Carlo Strapparava. 2006. Corpus-based and Knowledge-based Measures of Text Semantic Similarity. In *Proceedings of AAAI-06*, pages 775–780, Boston, MA, USA.

Alvaro Monge and Charles Elkan. 1997. An efficient domain-independent algorithm for detecting approximately duplicate database records. In *Proceedings of the SIGMOD Workshop on Data Mining and Knowledge Discovery*, pages 23–29.

Ted Pedersen, Siddharth Patwardhan, and Jason Michelizzi. 2004. WordNet::Similarity - Measuring the Relatedness of Concepts. In *Proceedings of the HLT-NAACL: Demonstration Papers*, pages 38–41.

Lawrence Philips. 2000. The double metaphone search algorithm. *C/C++ Users Jour.*, 18(6):38–43.

Philip Resnik. 1995. Using Information Content to Evaluate Semantic Similarity in a Taxonomy. In *Proceedings of the IJCAI*, pages 448–453.

Efstathios Stamatatos. 2011. Plagiarism detection using stopword n-grams. *Journal of the American Society for Information Science and Technology*, 62(12):2512–2527.

Dominic Widdows and Trevor Cohen. 2010. The Semantic Vectors Package: New Algorithms and Public Tools for Distributional Semantics. In *Proceedings of IEEE-ICSC*, pages 9–15.

William E. Winkler. 1990. String Comparator Metrics and Enhanced Decision Rules in the Fellegi-Sunter Model of Record Linkage. In *Proceedings of the Survey Research Methods Section*, pages 354–359.

Michael J. Wise. 1996. YAP3: Improved detection of similarities in computer program and other texts. In *Proc. of the 27th SIGCSE Technical Symposium on Computer Science Education*, pages 130–134.

Fluid Construction Grammar for Historical and Evolutionary Linguistics

Pieter Wellens[1], **Remi van Trijp**[2], **Katrien Beuls**[1], **Luc Steels**[2,3]

[1]VUB AI Lab
Pleinlaan 2
1050 Brussels (Belgium)
pieter|katrien@ai.vub.ac.be

[2]Sony Computer Science Laboratory Paris
6 Rue Amyot
75005 Paris (France)
remi@csl.sony.fr

[3] ICREA Institute for Evolutionary Biology (UPF-CSIC)
PRBB, Dr Aiguidar 88
08003 Barcelona (Spain)
steels@ai.vub.ac.be

Abstract

Fluid Construction Grammar (FCG) is an open-source computational grammar formalism that is becoming increasingly popular for studying the history and evolution of language. This demonstration shows how FCG can be used to operationalise the cultural processes and cognitive mechanisms that underly language evolution and change.

1 Introduction

Historical linguistics has been radically transformed over the past two decades by the advent of corpus-based approaches. Ever increasing datasets, both in size and richness of annotation, are becoming available (Yuri et al., 2012; Davies, 2011), and linguists now have more powerful tools at their disposal for uncovering *which* changes have taken place. In this demonstration, we present Fluid Construction Grammar (Steels, 2011, FCG), an open-source grammar formalism that makes it possible to also address the question of *how* these changes happened by uncovering the cognitive mechanisms and cultural processes that drive language evolution.

FCG combines the expressive power of feature structures and unification with the adaptivity and robustnes of machine learners. In sum, FCG aims to be an open instrument for developing robust and open-ended models of language processing that can be used for both parsing and production. FCG can be downloaded at `http://www.fcg-net.org`.

2 Design Philosophy

Fluid Construction Grammar is rooted in a *cognitive-functional* approach to language, which is quite different from a *generative* grammar such as HPSG (Pollard and Sag, 1994). A generative grammar is a model of language competence that licenses well-formed structures and rejects ill-formed utterances. Such grammars often decide on the well- or ill-formedness of utterances by using a strong type system that defines a set of features and possible values for those features. The burden of efficient and robust language processing with a generative grammar largely rests on the shoulders of the language processor.

A cognitive-functional grammar, on the other hand, functions more like a transducer between meaning and form. In parsing, such a grammar tries to uncover as much meaning as possible from a given utterance rather than deciding on its grammaticality. In the other direction, the grammar tries to produce intelligible utterances, which are well-formed as a side-effect if the grammar adequately captures the conventions of a particular language. A cognitive-functional grammar can best be implemented without a strong type system because the set of possible features and values for them is assumed to be open-ended. Efficient and robust language processing also becomes a joint responsibility of the grammar and the linguistic processor.

3 Reversible Language Processing

As a construction grammar, FCG represents *all* linguistic knowledge as pairings of function and form (called constructions). This means that any linguistic item, be it a concrete lexical item (see Figure 1) or a schematic construction, shares the same fundamental representation in FCG.

Each construction consists of two poles (a semantic/functional one and a syntactic/form one), each represented as a feature structure. By using a separate semantic and syntactic pole, FCG allows the same construction to be efficiently parsed and produced by the same processing engine by simply changing the direction of application.

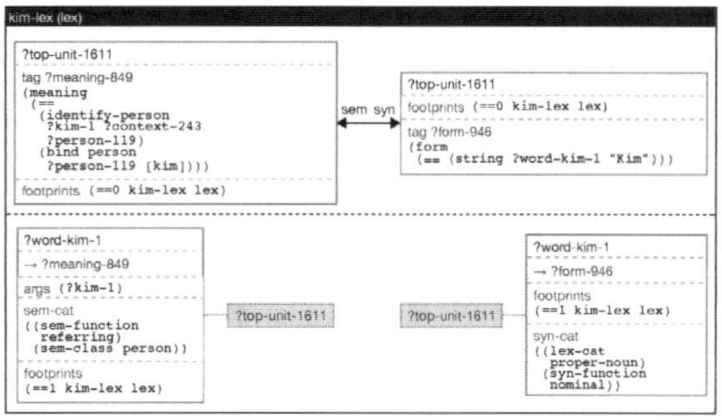

Figure 1: Lexical construction for the proper noun "Kim" as shown in the FCG web interface. All constructions are mappings between semantic (left) and syntactic feature structures (right).

FCG processing uses two different kinds of unification called *match* and *merge*. The match phase is a conditional phase which checks for applicability of the construction. The merge operation most closely resembles classical (yet untyped) unification. In production (i.e. going from meaning to form), the processor will consider a construction's semantic pole as a set of conditions that need to be satisfied, and the syntactic pole as additional information that can be contributed by the construction. In parsing (i.e. going from form to meaning), the roles of the poles are reversed.

Since FCG pays a lot of attention to the interaction between linguistic knowledge and processing, it makes it possible to investigate the consequences of particular aspects of grammar with regard to representation, production, parsing, learning and propagation (in a population of language users). For example, a small case system may be easier to represent and produce than a large system, but it might also lead to increased ambiguity in parsing and learning that the larger system would avoid. Fluid Construction Grammar can bring these differences to the surface for further computational analysis.

It is exactly this ability to monitor the impact of grammatical choices, that has sparked the interest of an increasingly wide audience of historical and evolutionary linguists. With FCG, different historical stages can be implemented (which addresses questions about representation and processing) but FCG also comes bundled with a reflective learning framework (Beuls et al., 2012) for learning the key constructions of each stage. That same architecture has proven to be adequately powerful to implement processes of grammaticalization so that actual linguistic change over time can be modeled (van Trijp, 2010; Beuls and Steels, 2013; Wellens and Loetzsch, 2012).

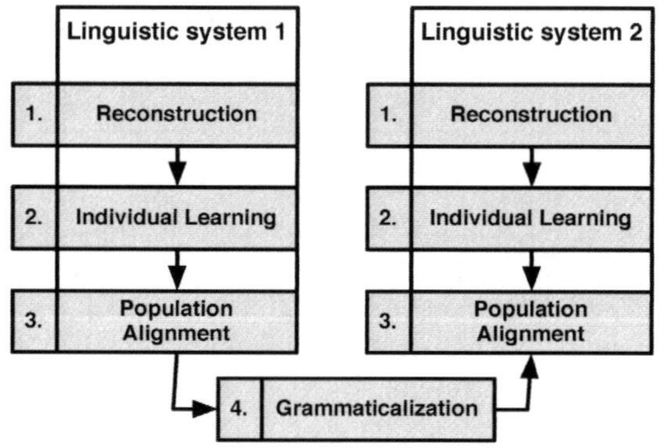

Figure 2: Schematic overview of the experimental methodology for historical and evolutionary linguists. The example here shows only two linguistic stages but there could be more.

4 How to set up an evolutionary linguistics experiment in FCG?

As the FCG processor can both produce and parse utterances it is possible to instantiate not one but a set or population of FCG processors (or FCG agents) that can communicatively interact with each other. Experiments in historical or evolutionary linguistics make use of this multi-agent approach where all agents engage in situated pairwise interactions (language games) (Steels, 2012b).

In this systems demo we will focus on a recent experiment in the emergence of grammatical agreement (Beuls and Steels, 2013). The language game consists of two agents in which one agent (the speaker) has to describe one or more (max three) objects in a scene to the other agent (the hearer). Each object can be described by one or more words. It follows that without any grammatical marking it would be difficult (often impossible) for the hearer to figure out which words describe the same object and thus to arrive at a successful interpretation. The hypothesis is that the introduction of agreement markers helps solve this ambiguity.

Next to setting up a language game script the methodology consists of operationalizing the *linguistic strategies* required for a population to bootstrap and maintain a particular *linguistic system* (in this case nominal agreement). Examples of lin-

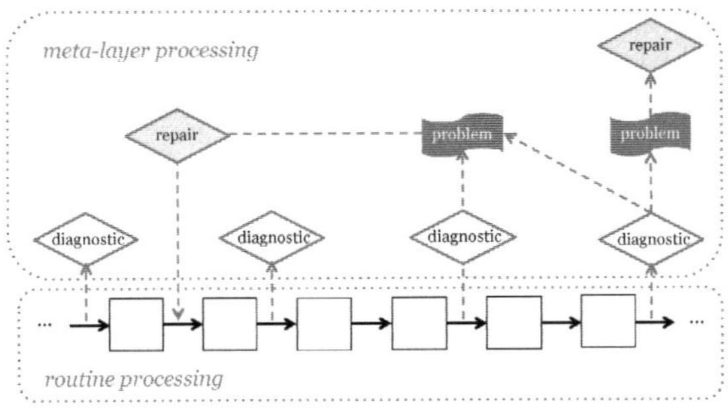

Figure 3: Reflective meta-layer architecture operating as part of an FCG agent/processor.

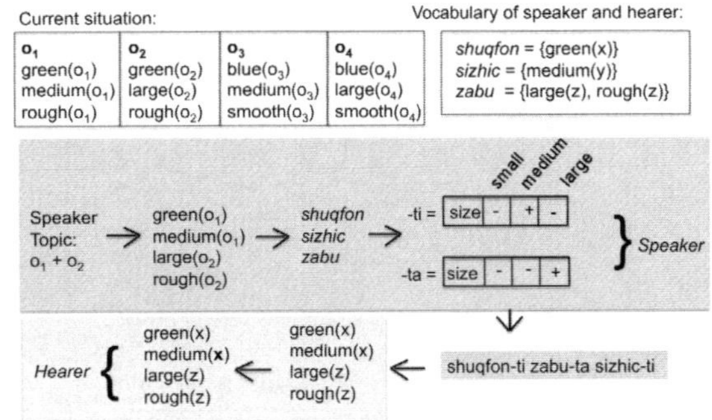

Figure 4: Meaningful marker strategy.

guistic systems already investigated include German case (van Trijp, 2012a; van Trijp, 2013), the grammatical expression of space (Spranger and Steels, 2012), the emergence of quantifiers (Pauw and Hilferty, 2012) and the expression of aspect in Russian (Gerasymova et al., 2012) [for an overview see (Steels, 2011; Steels, 2012a)].

An experiment generally investigates multiple linguistic systems of increasing complexity where each system can, but need not, map to a stage along an attested grammaticalization pathway. Most often a stage is introduced in order to gradually increase the complexity of the emergent dynamics. In this demo we posit four systems/strategies, (1) a baseline purely lexical strategy, (2) a strategy to bootstrap and align formal (meaningless) agreement markers, (3) a strategy to bootstrap and align meaningful agreement markers, and finally (4) a strategy that allows re-use of existing lexical constructions as markers (grammaticalization).

Implementing and linking together all the components involved in a single system is a highly non-trivial undertaking and our methodology prescribes the following four steps to undertake for each system (see also Figure 2).

Reconstruction: A full operationalization of all the constructions (lexical and grammatical) involved in the chosen linguistic phenomena. When multiple agents are initialized with these constructions they should be able to communicate successfully with each other. This stage serves primarily to test and verify intuitions about the different linguistic systems.

Individual Learning: Implementation of learning algorithms (or re-use of existing ones) so that one agent can learn the constructions based on the input of another agent. These learning operations are generally divided into *diagnostics* and *repair strategies* (see Figure 3). Diagnostics continually monitor FCG processing for errors or inefficiencies and generate problems if they are found. Repair strategies then act on these problems by altering the linguistic inventory (e.g. adding, removing or changing constructions).

Population Alignment: There exists a large gap between the cognitive machinary needed for learning an existing linguistic system (step 2) and bootstrapping, aligning and maintaining a complete linguistic system from scratch. In this step individual learning operators are extended with alignment strategies.

Grammaticalization: Moving from one linguistic system to another is the final step of the experiment. The challenge is to find and implement the mechanisms that drive grammaticalization (Heine and Kuteva, 2007) in line with observed grammaticalization pathways.

As an example we'll give a short sketch of one possible game as played in the meaningful marker strategy as schematically shown in Figure 4. The sketch shows a context of four objects (O_1 to O_4), each described by three features. The speaker chooses topic $O_1 + O_2$ which, given his vocabulary (shown top right), results in uttering "shuqfon sizhic zabu". Words "shuqfon" and "sizhic" both describe parts of O_1 and "zabu" of O_2. In order to explicitly communicate this linking the speaker attaches the markers "-ti" and "-ta" so that their meaning is compatible with the objects they are linking as shown in the Figure. This allows

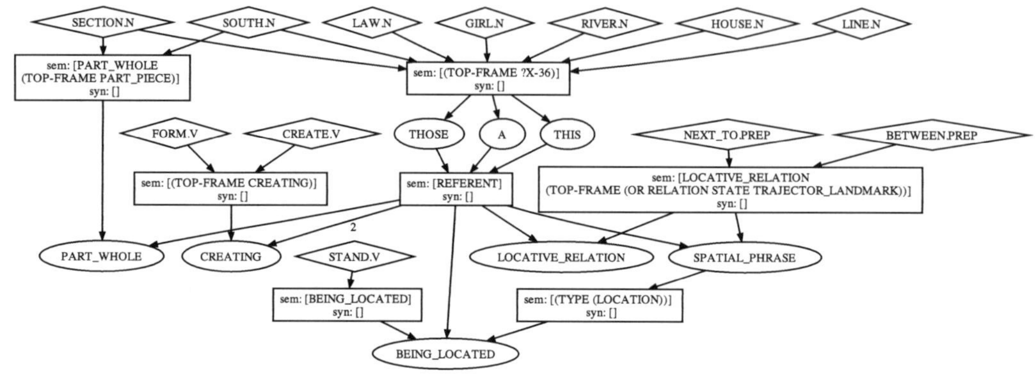

Figure 5: A network of constructions. Diamond shaped nodes represent lexical constructions, egg shaped nodes represent grammatical constructions and rectangular nodes represent semantic categories. Arrows can be read as "primes". For example the preposition between [BETWEEN.PREP] primes the category LOCATIVE RELATION which in turn primes both the [LOCATIVE RELATION] and [SPATIAL PHRASE] constructions. Both of these constructions also require a semantic category [REFERENT].

the hearer to arrive at a single non-ambiguous interpretation. For more details we refer the reader to (Beuls and Steels, 2013) and the web demo at http://ai.vub.ac.be/materials/plos-agreement/.

5 Features of FCG

A number of key features of FCG have already been introduced. Reversible bidirectional processing, a single data representation for all linguistic knowledge, a reflective meta-layer architecture for learning and a multi-agent component for managing multiple interacting FCG instances. Other features, some of which are unique to FCG, include, but are not limited to:

Web interface: FCG comes with a rich HTML/AJAX based web interface (Loetzsch, 2012) where it can show fine-grained information to the user in a user-friendly manner through the use of expandable elements. See Figure 6.

Customizable processing: Linguistic processing is implemented as a search process (Bleys et al., 2011). The user has easy access to the most important parameters influencing this process. Examples of these are the heuristics and the tests that determine whether a node represents an acceptable solution. FCG comes bundled with a library of heuristics and goal tests and with a bit of programming skills users can add new primitives easily.

Customizable construction inventory: By default, FCG stores all constructions in one large set. FCG however supplies a number of different taxonomies, both for conceptual and efficiency reasons. One popular option is to organize constructions in smaller subsets (Beuls, 2011) like lexical, morphological, functional, etc. Another option is to use networks (Wellens, 2011) that can learn co-occurrence relations between constructions and "prime" constructions when they are likely to apply (see Figure 5).

Interfaces to external repositories: FCG can connect to external repositories like Framenet (Baker et al., 1998) and Wordnet (Miller, 1995) to load thousands of lexical entries (Micelli et al., 2009; Wellens and Beule, 2010).

Robustness: FCG continues operation as far as it can get even if some constructions do not apply (Steels and van Trijp, 2011). Supplied with appropriate diagnostics and repair strategies FCG can even recover from errors (van Trijp, 2012b).

Open source: Best of all, FCG is freely downloadable and open source (http://www.fcg-net.org). It is written in Common Lisp (CLOS) and compatible with most popular lisp implementations (SBCL, CCL, Lispworks, ...).

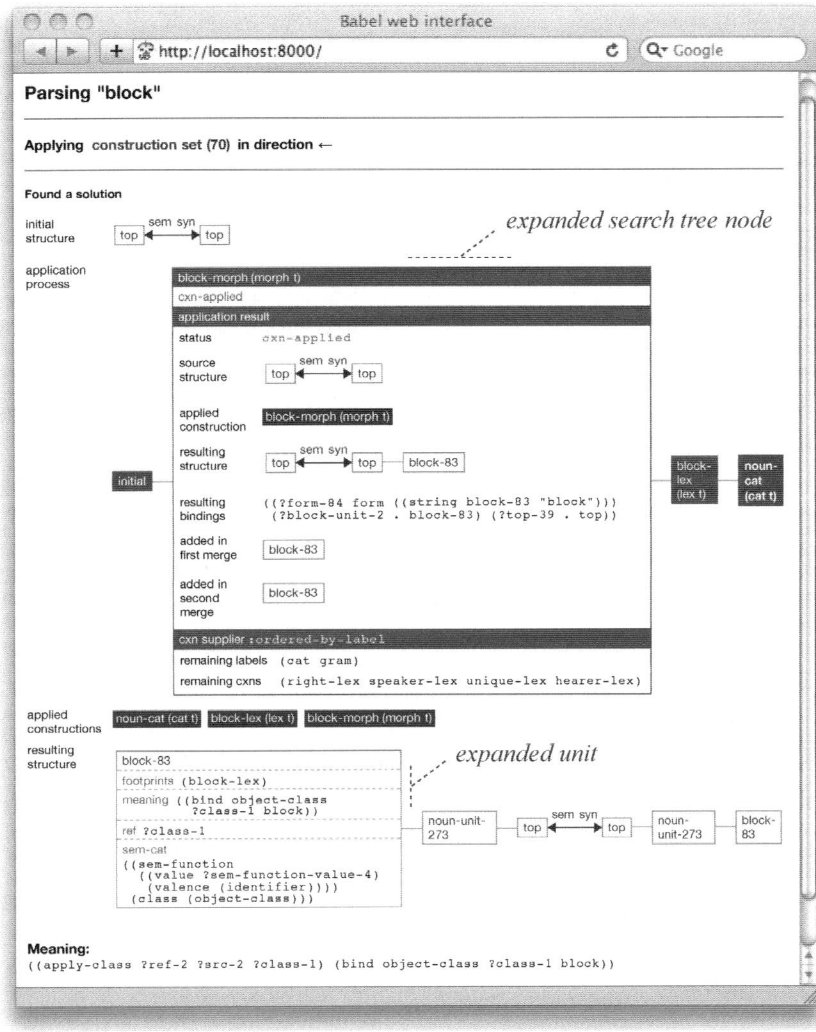

Figure 6: An example of parsing the noun "Block" as shown in the FCG web interface. Users can click on nearly every element to show an expanded version.

The reader is encouraged to take a look at http://www.fcg-net.org/projects/design-patterns-in-fluid-construction-grammar for a selection of demonstrations of Fluid Construction Grammar.

6 Conclusion

Fluid Construction Grammar is a mature technology that can be used by computational linguists to complement more traditional corpus-based approaches. FCG builds on many existing and proven technologies and adds new innovations to the mix resulting in a user friendly, yet powerful and extensible framework for in-depth investigations in natural language phenomena.

Acknowledgments

The FCG formalism is being developed at the Artificial Intelligence Laboratory of the Vrije Universiteit Brussel and the Sony Computer Science Laboratory in Paris. Pieter Wellens has been supported by the ESF EuroUnderstanding project DRUST funded by FWO and by the Vrije Universiteit Brussel. Katrien Beuls received funding from a strategic basic research grant from the agency for Innovation by Science and Technology (IWT). Remi van Trijp is funded by the Sony Computer Science Laboratory Paris. We would also like to thank Michael Spranger for his contributions to the FCG formalism.

References

Collin F. Baker, Charles J. Fillmore, and John B. Lowe. 1998. The Berkeley FrameNet Project. In *Proceedings of the 17th international conference on Computational linguistics*, Morristown, NJ, USA. Association for Computational Linguistics.

Katrien Beuls and Luc Steels. 2013. Agent-based models of strategies for the emergence and evolution of grammatical agreement. *PLoS ONE*, 8(3):e58960, 03.

Katrien Beuls, Remi van Trijp, and Pieter Wellens. 2012. Diagnostics and repairs in Fluid Construction Grammar. In Luc Steels and Manfred Hild, editors, *Language Grounding in Robots*. Springer Verlag, Berlin.

Katrien Beuls. 2011. Construction sets and unmarked forms: A case study for Hungarian verbal agreement. In Luc Steels, editor, *Design Patterns in Fluid Construction Grammar*, pages 237–264. John Benjamins, Amsterdam.

Joris Bleys, Kevin Stadler, and Joachim De Beule. 2011. Search in linguistic processing. In Luc Steels, editor, *Design Patterns in Fluid Construction Grammar*, pages 149–179. John Benjamins, Amsterdam.

Mark Davies. 2011. N-grams and word frequency data from the corpus of historical american english (coha).

Kateryna Gerasymova, Michael Spranger, and Katrien Beuls. 2012. A language strategy for aspect: Encoding aktionsarten through morphology. In Luc Steels, editor, *Experiments in Cultural Language Evolution*, pages 257 – 276. John Benjamins.

Bernd Heine and Tania Kuteva. 2007. *The Genesis of Grammar: A Reconstruction*. Oxford University Press, October.

Martin Loetzsch. 2012. Tools for grammar engineering. In Luc Steels, editor, *Computational Issues in Fluid Construction Grammar*. Springer Verlag, Berlin.

V. Micelli, R. van Trijp, and J. De Beule. 2009. Framing fluid construction grammar. In N.A. Taatgen and H. van Rijn, editors, *the 31th Annual Conference of the Cognitive Science Society*, pages 3023–3027. Cognitive Science Society.

George A. Miller. 1995. Wordnet: a lexical database for english. *Commun. ACM*, 38:39–41, November.

Simon Pauw and Joseph Hilferty. 2012. The emergence of quantifiers. In Luc Steels, editor, *Experiments in Cultural Language Evolution*, pages 277 – 304. John Benjamins.

Carl Pollard and Ivan A. Sag. 1994. *Head-Driven Phrase Structure Grammar*. University of Chicago Press, Chicago.

Michael Spranger and Luc Steels. 2012. Emergent functional grammar for space. In Luc Steels, editor, *Experiments in Cultural Language Evolution*, pages 207 – 232. John Benjamins, Amsterdam.

Luc Steels and Remi van Trijp. 2011. How to make construction grammars fluid and robust. In Luc Steels, editor, *Design Patterns in Fluid Construction Grammar*, pages 301–330. John Benjamins, Amsterdam.

Luc Steels, editor. 2011. *Design Patterns in Fluid Construction Grammar*. John Benjamins.

Luc Steels, editor. 2012a. *Computational Issues in Fluid Construction Grammar*, volume 7249 of *Lecture Notes in Computer Science*. Springer, Berlin.

Luc Steels, editor. 2012b. *Experiments in Cultural Language Evolution*. John Benjamins, Amsterdam.

Remi van Trijp. 2010. Grammaticalization and semantic maps: Evidence from artificial language evolution. *Linguistic Discovery*, 8:310–326.

Remi van Trijp. 2012a. Not as awful as it seems : Explaining german case through computational experiments in fluid construction grammar. In *Proceedings of the 13th Conference of the European Chapter of the Association for Computational Linguistics*, pages 829–839.

Remi van Trijp. 2012b. A reflective architecture for language processing and learning. In Luc Steels, editor, *Computational Issues in Fluid Construction Grammar*. Springer Verlag, Berlin.

Remi van Trijp. 2013. Linguistic assessment criteria for explaining language change: A case study on syncretism in German definite articles. *Language Dynamics and Change*, 3(1).

Pieter Wellens and Joachim De Beule. 2010. Priming through constructional dependencies: a case study in fluid construction grammar. In *The Evolution of Language (EVOLANG8)*, pages 344–351. World Scientific.

Pieter Wellens and Martin Loetzsch. 2012. Multi-dimensional meanings in lexicon formation. In Luc Steels, editor, *Experiments in Cultural Language Evolution*, pages 143–166. John Benjamins, Amsterdam.

Pieter Wellens. 2011. Organizing constructions in networks. In Luc Steels, editor, *Design Patterns in Fluid Construction Grammar*, pages 181–201. John Benjamins, Amsterdam.

Lin Yuri, Michel Jean-Baptiste, Lieberman Aiden Erez, Orwant Jon, Brockman Will, and Slav Petrov. 2012. Syntactic annotations for the google books ngram corpus. In *ACL (System Demonstrations)*. The Association for Computer Linguistics.

HYENA-live: Fine-Grained Online Entity Type Classification from Natural-language Text

Mohamed Amir Yosef[1] **Sandro Bauer**[2] **Johannes Hoffart**[1]
Marc Spaniol[1] **Gerhard Weikum**[1]
(1) Max-Planck-Institut für Informatik, Saarbrücken, Germany
(2) Computer Laboratory, University of Cambridge, UK
{mamir|jhoffart|mspaniol|weikum}@mpi-inf.mpg.de
sandro.bauer@cl.cam.ac.uk

Abstract

Recent research has shown progress in achieving high-quality, very fine-grained type classification in hierarchical taxonomies. Within such a multi-level type hierarchy with several hundreds of types at different levels, many entities naturally belong to multiple types. In order to achieve high-precision in type classification, current approaches are either limited to certain domains or require time consuming multi-stage computations. As a consequence, existing systems are incapable of performing ad-hoc type classification on arbitrary input texts. In this demo, we present a novel Web-based tool that is able to perform domain independent entity type classification under real time conditions. Thanks to its efficient implementation and compacted feature representation, the system is able to process text inputs on-the-fly while still achieving equally high precision as leading state-of-the-art implementations. Our system offers an online interface where natural-language text can be inserted, which returns semantic type labels for entity mentions. Further more, the user interface allows users to explore the assigned types by visualizing and navigating along the type-hierarchy.

1 Introduction

Motivation

Web contents such as news, blogs and other social media are full of named entities. Each entity belongs to one or more *semantic types* associated with it. For instance, an entity such as *Bob Dylan* should be assigned the types `Singer`, `Musician`, `Poet`, etc., and also the corresponding supertype(s) (hypernyms) in a type hierarchy, in this case `Person`. Such fine-grained typing of entities in texts can be a great asset for various NLP tasks including semantic role labeling, sense disambiguation and named entity disambiguation (NED). For instance, noun phrases such as "songwriter Dylan", "Google founder Page", or "rock legend Page" can be easily mapped to the entities Bob Dylan, Larry Page, and Jimmy Page if their respective types `Singer`, `BusinessPerson`, and `Guitarist` are available (cf. Figure 1 for an illustrative example).

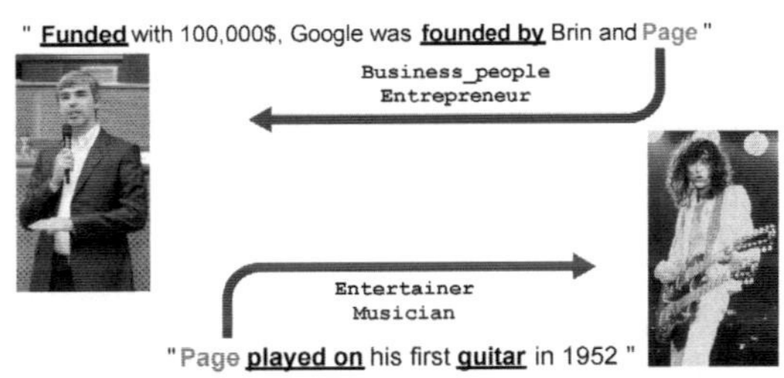

Figure 1: Fine-grained entity type classification

Problem Statement

Type classification is not only be based on hierarchical sub-type relationships (e.g. `Musician isA Person`), but also has to do on multi-labeling. Within a very fine-grained type hierarchy, many entities naturally belong to multiple types. For example, a guitarist is also a musician and a person, but may also be a singer, an actor, or even a politician. Consequently, entities should not only be assigned the most (fine-grained) label associated to them, but with all labels relevant to them. So we face a *hierarchical multi-label classification* problem (Tsoumakas et al., 2012).

Contribution

This paper introduces *HYENA-live*, which allows an on-the-fly computation of semantic types for entity mentions, based on a multi-level type hierarchy. Our approach uses a suite of features for a given entity mention, such as neighboring words and bigrams, part-of-speech tags, and also phrases from a large gazetteer derived from state-of-the-art knowledge bases. In order to perform "live" entity type classification based on ad-hoc text inputs, several performance optimizations have been undertaken to operate under real-time conditions.

2 Entity Type Classification Systems

State-of-the-art tools for named entity recognition such as the Stanford NER Tagger (Finkel et al., 2005) compute semantic tags only for a small set of coarse-grained types: `Person`, `Location`, and `Organization` (plus tags for non-entity phrases of type time, money, percent, and date). However, we are not aware of any online tool that performs *fine-grained typing* of entity mentions. The most common workaround to perform entity classification is a two-stage process: in first applying an online tool for Named-Entity Disambiguation (NED), such as DBpedia Spotlight (Mendes et al., 2011) or AIDA (Yosef et al., 2011; Hoffart et al., 2011), in order to map the mentions onto canonical entities and subsequently query the knowledge base for their types. In fact, (Ling and Weld, 2012) followed this approach when comparing their entity classification system results against those obtained by an adoption of the Illinois' Named-Entity Linking system (NEL) (Ratinov et al., 2011) and reached the conclusion that while NEL performed decently for prominent entities, it could not scale to cover long tail ones. Specifically, entity typing via NED has three major drawbacks:

1. NED is an inherently hard problem, especially with highly ambiguous mentions. As a consequence, accurate NED systems come at a high computation costs.
2. NED only works for those mentions that correspond to a canonical entity within a knowledge base. However, this fails for all out-of-knowledge-base entities like unregistered persons, start-up companies, etc.
3. NED heavily depends on the quality of the underlying knowledge base. Yet, only very few knowledge bases have comprehensive class labeling of entities. Even more, in the best case, coverage drops sharply for relatively uncommon entities.

We decided to adopt one of the existing approaches to make it suitable for online querying. We considered five systems. In the rest of this section we will briefly describe each of them.

(Fleischman and Hovy, 2002) is one of the earliest approaches to perform entity classification into subtypes of `PERSON`. They developed a decision-tree classifier based on contextual features that can be automatically extracted from the text. In order to account for scarcity of labeled training data, they tapped on WordNet synonyms to achieve higher coverage. While their approach is fundamentally suitable, their type system is very restricted. In order to account for more fine-grained classes, more features need to be added to their feature set.

(Ekbal et al., 2010) considered 141 subtypes of WordNet class `PERSON` and developed a maximum entropy classifier exploiting the words surrounding the mentions together with their POS tags and other contextual features. Their type hierarchy is fine-grained, but still limited to sub classes of `PERSON`. In addition, their experimental results have been flagged as non-reproducible in the ACL Anthology.

(Altaf ur Rahman and Ng, 2010) considered a two-level type hierarchy consisting of 29 top-level classes and a total of 92 sub-classes. These include many non-entity types such as date, time, percent, money, quantity, ordinal, cardinal, etc. They incorporated a hierarchical classifier using a rich feature set and made use of WordNet sense tagging. However, the latter requires human interception, which is not suitable for ad-hoc processing of out-of-domain texts.

(Ling and Weld, 2012) developed FIGER, which classifies entity mentions onto a two-level taxonomy based on the Freebase knowledge base (Bollacker et al., 2008). This results in a two-level hierarchy with top-level topics and 112 types. They trained a CRF for the joint task of recognizing entity mentions and inferring type tags. Although they handle multi-label assignment, their test data is sparse. Many classes are absent and plenty of instances come with only a single label (e.g. 216 of the 562 entities were of type `PERSON` without subtypes). Further, their results are instance based, which does not guarantee that the quality of their system will be reproducible for all the 112 types in their taxonomy.

(Yosef et al., 2012) is the most recent work in multi-label type classification. The HYENA system incorporates a large hierarchy of 505 classes organized under 5 top level classes, with 100 descendant classes under each of them. The hierarchy reaches a depth of up to 9 levels in some parts. The system is based on an SVM classifier using a comprehensive set of features and provides results for all classes of a large data set. In their experiments the superiority of the system in terms of precision and recall has been shown. However, the main drawback of HYENA comes from its large hierarchy and the extensive set of features extracted from the fairly large training corpus it requires. As a result, on-the-fly type classification with HYENA is impossible in its current implementation.

We decided to build on top of HYENA system by spotting the bottlenecks in the architecture and modifying it accordingly to be suitable for online querying. In Section 3 we explain in details HYENA's type taxonomy and their feature portfolio. Later on, we explain the engineering undertaken in order to develop the on-the-fly type classification system HYENA-live (cf. Section 4).

3 Type Hierarchy and Feature Set

3.1 Fine-grained Taxonomy

The type system is an automatically gathered fine-grained taxonomy of 505 classes. The classes are organized under 5 top level classes, with 100 descendant classes under each. The YAGO knowledge base (Hoffart et al., 2013) is selected to derive the taxonomy from because of its highly precise classification of entities into WordNet classes, which is a result of the accurate mapping YAGO has from Wikipedia Categories to WordNet synsets.

We start with five top classes namely `PERSON`, `LOCATION`, `ORGANIZATION`, `EVENT` and `ARTIFACT`. Under each top class, the most 100 prominent descendant classes are picked. Prominence is estimated by the number of YAGO entities tagged with this class. This results in a very-fine grained taxonomy of 505 types, represented as a directed acyclic graph with 9 levels in its deepest parts. While the classes are picked from the YAGO type system, the approach is generic and can be applied to derive type taxonomies from other knowledge bases such as Freebase or DBpedia (Auer et al., 2007) as in (Ling and Weld, 2012).

3.2 Feature Set

For the sake of generality and applicability to arbitrary text, we opted for features that can be automatically extracted from the input text without any human interaction, or manual annotation. The extracted features fall under five categories, which we briefly explain in the rest of this section.

Mention String
We derive four features from the entity mention string. The mention string itself, a noun phrase consisting of one or more consecutive words. The other three features are unigrams, bigrams, and trigrams that overlap with the mention string.

Sentence Surrounding Mention
We also exploit a bounded-size window around the mention to extract four features: all unigrams, bigrams, and trigrams. Two versions of those features are extracted, one to account for the occurrence of those tokens around the mention, and another to account for the position at which they occurred with respect to the mention (before or after). In addition, unigrams are also included with their absolute distance ignoring whether before of after the mention. Our demo is using a conservative threshold for the size of the window which is three tokens on each side of the mention.

Mention Paragraph
We also leverage the entire paragraph of the mention. This gives additional topical cues about the mention type (e.g., if the paragraph is about a music concert, this is a cue for mapping people names to musician types). We create three features here: unigrams, bigrams, and trigrams without including any distance information. In our demo, we extract those features from a bounded window of size 2000 characters before and after the mention.

Grammatical Features
We exploit the semantics of the text by extracting four features. First, we use part-of-speech tags of the tokens in a size-bounded window around the mention in distance and absolute distance versions. Second and third, we create a feature for the first occurrence of a "he" or "she" pronoun in the same sentence and in the subsequent sentence following the mention, along with the distance to the mention. Finally, we use the closest verb-preposition pair preceding the mention as another feature.

Gazetteer Features
We leverage YAGO2 knowledge base even further by building a type-specific gazetteer of words oc-

# of articles	50,000
# of instances (all types)	1,613,340
# of location instances	489,003 (30%)
# of person instances	426,467 (26.4%)
# of organization instances	219,716 (13.6%)
# of artifact instances	204,802 (12.7%)
# of event instances	176,549 (10.9%)
# instances in 1 top-level class	1,131,994 (70.2%)
# instances in 2 top-level classes	182,508 (11.3%)
# instances in more than 2 top-level classes	6,492 (0.4%)
# instances not in any class	292,346 (18.1%)

Table 1: Properties of the labeled data used for training HYENA-live

curring in the names of the entities of that type. YAGO2 knowledge base comes with an extensive dictionary of name-entity pairs extracted from Wikipedia redirects and link-anchor texts. We construct, for each type, a binary feature that indicates if the mention contains a word occurring in this type's gazetteer. Note that this is a fully automated feature construction, and it does by no means determine the mention type(s) already, as most words occur in the gazetteers of many different types. For example, "Alice" occurs in virtually every subclass of Person but also in city names like "Alice Springs" and other locations, as well as in songs, movies, and other products or organizations.

4 System Implementation

4.1 Overview

As described in Section 3, HYENA classifies mentions of named entities onto a hierarchy of 505 types using large set of features. A random subset of the English Wikipedia has been used for training HYENA. By exploiting Wikipedia anchor links, mentions of named entities are automatically disambiguated to their correct entities. Each Wikipedia named entity has a corresponding YAGO entity labeled with an accurate set of types, and hence we effortlessly obtain a huge training data set (cf. data properties in Table 1).

We build type-specific classifiers using the SVM software LIBLINEAR (cf. `http://liblinear.bwaldvogel.de/`). Each model comes with a comprehensive feature set. While larger models (with more features) improve the accuracy, they significantly affect the applicability of the system. A single model file occupies around 150MB disk space leading to a total of 84.7GB for all models. As a consequence, there is a substantial setup time to load all models in memory and a high-memory server (48 cores with 512GB of RAM) is required for computation. An analysis showed that each single feature contributes to the overall performance of HYENA, but only a tiny subset of all features is relevant for a single classifier. Therefore, most of the models are extremely sparse.

4.2 Sparse Models Representation

There are several workarounds applicable to batch mode operations, e.g. by performing classifications per level only. However, this is not an option for on-the-fly computations. For that reason we opted for a sparse-model representation.

LIBLINEAR model files are normalized textual files: a header (data about the model and the total number of features), followed by listing the weights assigned to each feature (line number indicates the feature ID). Each model file has been post-processed to produce 2 files:

- A compacted model file containing only features of non-zero weights. Its header reflects the reduced number of features.
- A meta-data file. It maps the new features IDs to the original feature IDs.

Due to the observed sparsity in the model files, particularly at deeper levels, there is a significant decrease in disk space consumption for the compacted model files and hence in the memory requirements.

4.3 Sparse Models Classification

By switching to the sparse model representation the architecture of the whole system is affected. In particular, modified versions of feature vectors need to be generated for each classifier; this is because

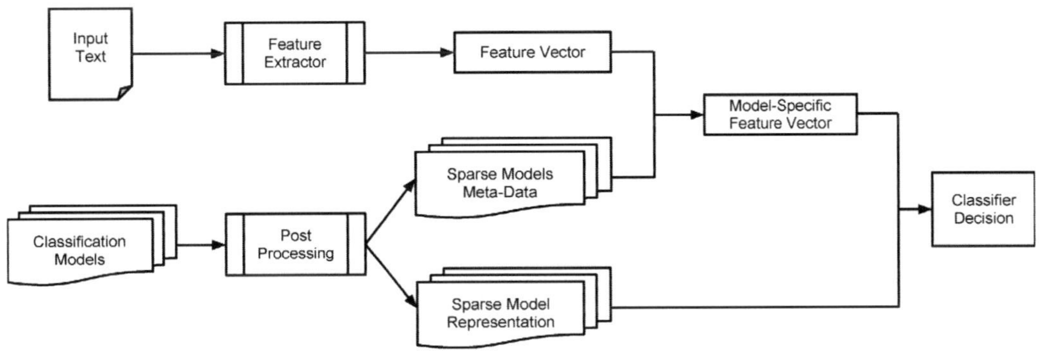

Figure 2: Modified system architecture designed for handling sparse models

a lot of features have been omitted from specific classifiers (those with zero weights). Consequently, the feature IDs need to be mapped to the new feature space of each classifier. The conceptual design of the new architecture is illustrated in Figure 4.2.

5 Demo Presentation

HYENA-live has been fully implemented as a Web application. Figure 5 shows the user interface of HYENA-live in a Web browser:

1) On top, there is a panel where a user can input any text, e.g. by copy-and-paste from news articles. We employ the Stanford NER Tagger to identify noun phrases as candidates of entity mentions. Alternatively, users can flag entity mentions by double brackets (e.g. "Harry is the opponent of [[you know who]]"). For the sake of simplicity, detected entity mentions by HYENA-live are highlighted in yellow. Each mention is clickable to study its type classification results.
2) The output of type classification is shown inside a tabbed widget. Each tab corresponds to a detected mention by the system and tabs are sorted by the order of occurrence in the input text. To open a tab, the tab header or the corresponding mention in the input area needs to be clicked.
3) The type classification of a mention is shown as a color-coded interactive tree. While the original type hierarchy is a directed acyclic graph, for the ease of navigation the classification output has been converted into a tree. In order to do so, nodes that belong to more than a parent have been duplicated. There are three different types of nodes:
   - Green Nodes: referring to a class that has been accepted by the classifier. These nodes can be further expanded in order to check which sub-classes have been accepted or rejected by HYENA-live.
   - Red Nodes: corresponding to a class that was rejected by the classifier, and hence HYENA-live did not traverse deeper to test its sub-classes.
   - White Nodes: matching classes that have not been tested. These nodes are either known upfront (e.g. `ENTITY`) or their super class was rejected by the system.

   It is worth noting that HYENA-live automatically adjusts the layouting so that as much as possible of the hierarchy is shown to the user. For the sake of explorability, this is being dynamically adjusted once the user decides to navigate along a certain (child-)node.

The system is available online at:
`d5gate.ag5.mpi-sb.mpg.de/webhyena/`.
The data transfer between the client and the server is done via JSON objects. Hence, we also provide HYENA-live as a JSON compliant entity classification Web-service. As a result, the back-end becomes easily interchangeable (e.g. by a different classification technique or a different type taxonomy) with minimum modifications required on the user interface side.

Acknowledgments

This work is supported by the 7th Framework IST programme of the European Union through the focused research project (STREP) on Longitudinal Analytics of Web Archive data (LAWA) under contract no. 258105.

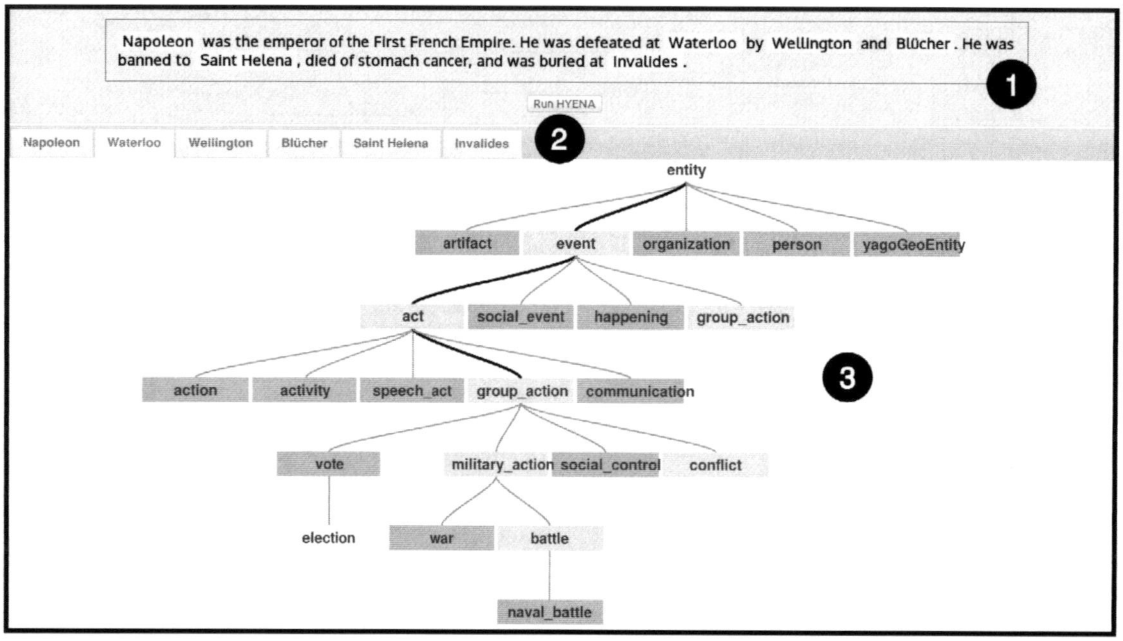

Figure 3: Interactively exploring the types of the "Battle of Waterloo" in the HYENA-live interface

References

Md. Altaf ur Rahman and Vincent Ng. 2010. Inducing fine-grained semantic classes via hierarchical and collective classification. In *COLING*, pages 931–939.

Sören Auer, Christian Bizer, Georgi Kobilarov, Jens Lehmann, and Zachary Ives. 2007. Dbpedia: A nucleus for a web of open data. In *ISWC*, pages 11–15. Springer.

Kurt D. Bollacker, Colin Evans, Praveen Paritosh, Tim Sturge, and Jamie Taylor. 2008. Freebase: a collaboratively created graph database for structuring human knowledge. In *SIGMOD*, pages 1247–1250.

Asif Ekbal, Eva Sourjikova, Anette Frank, and Simone P. Ponzetto. 2010. Assessing the challenge of fine-grained named entity recognition and classification. In *Named Entities Workshop*, pages 93–101.

Jenny Rose Finkel, Trond Grenager, and Christopher Manning. 2005. Incorporating non-local information into information extraction systems by gibbs sampling. In *ACL*, pages 363–370.

Michael Fleischman and Eduard Hovy. 2002. Fine grained classification of named entities. In *COLING*, pages 1–7.

Johannes Hoffart, Mohamed Amir Yosef, Ilaria Bordino, Hagen Fürstenau, Manfred Pinkal, Marc Spaniol, Bilyana Taneva, Stefan Thater, and Gerhard Weikum. 2011. Robust disambiguation of named entities in text. In *EMNLP*, pages 782–792.

Johannes Hoffart, Fabian M. Suchanek, Klaus Berberich, and Gerhard Weikum. 2013. YAGO2: A spatially and temporally enhanced knowledge base from wikipedia. *Artificial Intelligence*, 194(0):28 – 61.

Xiao Ling and Daniel S. Weld. 2012. Fine-grained entity recognition. In *AAAI*, pages 94–100.

Pablo N. Mendes, Max Jakob, Andrés García-Silva, and Christian Bizer. 2011. Dbpedia spotlight: shedding light on the web of documents. In *I-SEMANTICS*, pages 1–8.

Lev-Arie Ratinov, Dan Roth, Doug Downey, and Mike Anderson. 2011. Local and global algorithms for disambiguation to wikipedia. In *ACL*, pages 1375–1384.

Grigorios Tsoumakas, Min-Ling Zhang, and Zhi-Hua Zhou. 2012. Introduction to the special issue on learning from multi-label data. *Machine Learning*, 88(1-2):1–4.

Mohamed Amir Yosef, Johannes Hoffart, Ilaria Bordino, Marc Spaniol, and Gerhard Weikum. 2011. AIDA: An online tool for accurate disambiguation of named entities in text and tables. *PVLDB*, 4(12):1450–1453.

Mohamed Amir Yosef, Sandro Bauer, Johannes Hoffart, Marc Spaniol, and Gerhard Weikum. 2012. HYENA: Hierarchical Type Classification for Entity Names. In *COLING*, pages 1361–1370.

Linggle: a Web-scale Linguistic Search Engine for Words in Context

Joanne Boisson[+], Ting-Hui Kao[*], Jian-Cheng Wu[*], Tzu-His Yen[*], Jason S. Chang[*]
[+]Institute of Information Systems and Applications
[*]Department of Computer Science
National Tsing Hua University
HsinChu, Taiwan, R.O.C. 30013
{joanne.boisson, maxis1718, wujc86, joseph.yen, jason.jschang}
@gmail.com

Abstract

In this paper, we introduce a Web-scale linguistics search engine, *Linggle*, that retrieves lexical bundles in response to a given query. The query might contain keywords, wildcards, wild parts of speech (PoS), synonyms, and additional regular expression (RE) operators. In our approach, we incorporate inverted file indexing, PoS information from BNC, and semantic indexing based on Latent Dirichlet Allocation with Google Web 1T. The method involves parsing the query to transforming it into several keyword retrieval commands. Word chunks are retrieved with counts, further filtering the chunks with the query as a RE, and finally displaying the results according to the counts, similarities, and topics. Clusters of synonyms or conceptually related words are also provided. In addition, *Linggle* provides example sentences from *The New York Times* on demand. The current implementation of *Linggle* is the most functionally comprehensive, and is in principle language and dataset independent. We plan to extend *Linggle* to provide fast and convenient access to a wealth of linguistic information embodied in Web scale datasets including *Google Web 1T* and *Google Books Ngram* for many major languages in the world.

1 Introduction

As a non-native speaker writing in English, one encounters many problems. Doubts concerning the usage of a preposition, the mandatory presence of a determiner, the correctness of the association of a verb with an object, or the need for synonyms of a term in a given context are issues that arise frequently. Printed collocation dictionaries and reference tools based on compiled corpora offer limited coverage of word usage while knowledge of collocations is vital to acquire a good level of linguistic competency. We propose to address these limitations with a comprehensive system aimed at helping the learners "know a word by the company it keeps" (Firth, 1957). *Linggle* (**linggle.com**). The system based on Web-scaled datasets is designed to be a broad coverage language reference tool for English Second Language learners (ESL). It is conceived to search information related to word usage in context under various conditions.

First, we build an inverted file index for the *Google Web 1T* n-grams to support queries with RE-like patterns including PoS and synonym matches. For example, for the query "$V $D +important role", *Linggle* retrieves 4-grams that start with a verb and a determiner followed by a synonym of *important* and the keyword *role* (e.g., *play a significant role* 202,800). A natural language interface is also available for users who are less familiar with pattern-based searches. For example, the question *"How can I describe a beach?"* would retrieve two word chunks such as "*sandy beach* 413,300" and "*rocky beach* 16,800". The n-gram search implementation is achieved through filtering, re-indexing, populating an HBase database with the Web 1T n-grams and augmenting them with the most frequent PoS for words (without disambiguation) derived from the British National Corpus (BNC).

The n-grams returned for a query can then be linked to examples extracted from the New York Times Corpus (Sandhaus, 2008) in order to provide full sentential context for more effective learning.

In some situations, the user might need to search for words in a specific syntactic relation (e.g., *Verb-Object collocation*). The query *absorb $N* in n-grams display mode returns all the nouns that follow the verb ordered by decreasing n-gram counts. Some of these nouns might not be objects of the verb *absorb*. In contrast, the same query in cluster display mode will control that two words have been labeled *verb-object* by a parser. Moreover, n-grams grouped by object topic/domain give the learner an overview of the usage of the verb. For example the verb *absorb* takes clusters of objects related to the topics *liquid*, *energy*, *money*, *knowledge*, and *population*.

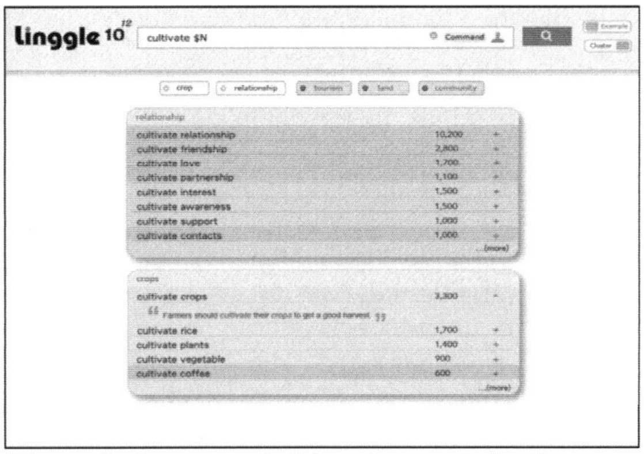

Figure 1. An example Linggle search for the query "absorb $N."

This tendency of predicates to prefer certain classes of arguments is defined by Wilks (1978) as selectional preferences and widely reported in the literature. Erk and Padó (2010) extend experiments on selectional preference induction to inverse selectional preference, considering the restriction imposed on predicates. Inverse sectional preference is also implemented in *linggle* (e.g. "$V apple").

Linggle presents clusters of synonymous collocates (adjectives, nouns and verbs) of a query keyword. We obtained the clusters by building on Lin and Pantel's (2002) large-scale repository of dependencies and word similarity scores. Using the method proposed by Ritter and Etzioni (2010) we induce selectional preference with a Latent Dirichlet Allocation (LDA) model to seed the clusters.

The rest of the paper is organized as follows. We review the related work in the next section. Then we present the syntax of the queries and the functionalities of the system (Section 3). We describe the details of implementation including the indexing of the n-grams and the clustering algorithm (Section 4) and draw perspective of development of Web scale search engines (Section 5).

2 Related work

Web-scale Linguistic Search Engine (LSE) has been an area of active research. Recently, the state-of-the-art in LSE research has been reviewed in Fletcher (2012). We present in this paper a linguistic search engine that provides a more comprehensive and powerful set of query features.

Kilgarriff et al. (2001) describe the implementation of the linguistic search engine Word Sketch (2001) that displays collocations and dependencies acquired from a large corpus such as the BNC. Word Sketch is not as flexible as typical search engines, only supporting a fixed set of *queries*.

Recently, researchers have been attempting to go one step further and work with Web scale datasets, but it is difficult for an academic institute to crawl a dataset that is on par with the datasets built by search engine companies. In 2006, Google released the *Web 1T* for several major languages of the world (trillion-word n-gram datasets for English, Japanese, Chinese, and ten European languages), to stimulate NLP research in many areas. In 2008, Chang described a prototype that enhances *Google Web 1T* bigrams with PoS tags and supports search in the dataset by wildcards (wild-PoS), to identify recurring collocations. Wu, Witten and Franken (2010) describe a more comprehensive system (FLAX) that combines filtered Google data with text examples from the BNC for several learning activities.

In a way similar to Chang (2008) and Wu, Witten and Franken (2010), Stein, Potthast, and Trenkmann (2010) describe the implementation and application of *NetSpeak*, a system that provides quick access to the Google Web 1T n-gram with RE-like queries (alternator "|", one arbitrary word "*", arbitrary number of words between two specified words "..."). In contrast to *Linggle*, *NetSpeak* does not support PoS wildcard or conceptual clustering.

An important function in both *Linggle* and *NetSpeak* is synonym query. *NetSpeak* uses WordNet (Fellbaum 2010) synsets to support synonym match. But WordNet synsets tend to contain very little synonyms, leading to poor coverage. Alternatively, one can use the distributional approach to similarity based on a very large corpus. Lin and Pantel (2002) report efforts to build a large repository of dependencies extracted from large corpora such as Wikipedia, and provide similarity between words (demo.patrickpantel.com). We use these results both for handling synonym queries and to organize the n-grams into semantic classes.

More recently, Ritter and Etzioni (2010) propose to apply an LDA model (Blei et al. 2003) to the problem of inducing selectional preference. The idea is to consider the verbs in a corpus as the documents of a traditional LDA model. The arguments of the verb that are encountered in the corpus are treated as the words composing a document in the traditional model. The model seems to successfully infer the semantic classes that correspond to the preferred arguments of a verb. The topics are semi-automatically labeled with WordNet classes to produce a repository of human interpretable class-based selectional preference. This choice might be due to the fact that if most LDA topic heads are usually reasonable upon human inspection, some topics are also incoherent (Newman 2010) and lower frequency words are not handled as successfully. We control the coherence of the topics and rearrange them into human interpretable clusters using a distributional similarity measure.

Microsoft Sempute Project (Sempute Team 2013) also explores core technologies and applications of semantic computing. As part of Sempute project, *NeedleSeek* is aimed at automatically extracting data to support general semantic Web searches. While *Linggle* focuses on n-gram information for language learning, *NeedleSeek* also uses LDA to support question answering (e.g., *What were the Capitals of ancient China?*) .

In contrast to the previous research in Web scale linguistic search engines, we present a system that supports queries with keywords, wildcard words, POS, synonyms, and additional regular expression (RE) operators and displays the results according the count, similarity, and topic with clusters of synonyms or conceptually related words. We exploit and combine the power of both LDA analysis and distributional similarity to provide meaningful semantic classes that are constrained with members of high similarity. Distributional similarity (Lin 1998) and LDA topics become two angles of attack to view language usage and corpus patterns.

3 Linggle Functionalities

The syntax of *Linggle* queries involves basic regular expression of keywords enriched with wildcard PoS and synonyms. *Linggle* queries can be either pattern-based commands or natural language questions. The natural language queries are currently handled by simple string matching based on a limited set of questions and command pairs provided by a native speaker informant.

3.1 Natural language queries

The handling of queries formulated in natural language has been implemented with handcrafted patterns refined from a corpus of questions found on various websites. Additionally, we asked both native and non-native speakers to use the system for text edition and to write down all the questions that arise during the exercise.

Linggle transforms a question into commands for further processing based on a set of canned texts (e.g., "How to describe a beach?" will be converted to "$A beach"). We are in the process of gathering more examples of language-related question and answer pairs from **Answers.com** to improve the precision, versatility, and coverage.

3.2 Syntax of queries

The syntax of the patterns for n-grams is shown in Table 1. The syntax supports two types of query functions: basic keyword search with regular expression capability and semantic search.

Basic search operators enable the users to query zero, one or more arbitrary words up to five words. For example, the query "*set off ... $N*" is intended to search for all nouns in the right context of *set off*, within a maximum distance of three words.

In addition, the "?" operator in front of a word represents a search for n-grams with or without the word. For example, a user wanting to determine whether to use the word *to* between *listen* and *music* can formulate the query "*listen ?to music*."

Yet another operation "|" is provided to search for information related to word choice. For example the query "build | construct ... dream" can be used to reveal that people *build* a dream much more often than they *construct* a dream.

A set of PoS symbols (shown in Table 2) is defined to support queries that need more precision than the symbol *. More work might be needed to resolve PoS ambiguity for n-grams. Currently, any word that has been labeled with the requested PoS in the BNC more than 5% of the time is displayed.

The "+" operator is provided to support semantic queries. Placed in front of a word, it is intended to search for synonyms in the context. For example the query "+sandy beach" would generate *rocky beach*, *stony beach*, *barren beach* in the top three results. The query "+abandoned beach" generates *deserted, destroyed and empty beach* at the top of the list. To support conceptual clustering of collocational n-grams, we need to identify synonyms related to different senses of a given word. Table 3 shows an example of the result obtained for the ambiguous word *bank* as a unigram query. We can see the two main senses of the word (*river bank* and *institution*) as clusters.

Operators	Description
*	Any Word
?	With/without the word
...	Zero or more words
|	Alternator
$	Part of speech
+	Synonyms

Table 1: Operators in the Linggle queries

Part of speech	Description
N	Noun
V	Verb
A	Adjective
R	Adverb
PP	Preposition
NP	Proper Noun
PR	Pronoun
D	Determiner

Table 2: Part-of-speech in the Linggle queries

A *cluster* button on the interface activates or cancels conceptual clustering. When *Linggle* is switched into a cluster display mode, adjective-nouns, verb-objects and subject-verb relations can be browsed based on the induced conceptual clusters (see Figure 1).

The New York Times Example Base

In order to display complete sentence examples for users, the New York Times Corpus sentences are indexed by word. When the user searches for words in a specific syntactic relation, morphological query expansion is performed and patterns are used to increase both the coverage and the precision of the provided examples. For example, the bi-gram *kill bacteria* will be associated with the example sentence "*The bacteria are killed by high temperatures*.".

3.3 Semantic Clusters

Two types of semantic clusters are provided in Linggle: selectional preference and clusters of synonyms. Selectional preference expresses for example that an *apple* is more likely to be *eaten* or *cooked* than to be *killed* or *hanged.* Different classes of arguments for a predicate (or of predicates for an argument) can be found automatically. The favorite class of objects for the verb *drink* is LIQUID with the noun *water* ranked at the top. Less frequent objects belonging to the same class include *liquor* in the tail of the list. We aim at grouping arguments and predicates into semantic clusters for better readability.

valley mountain river lake hill bay plain north ridge coast city district town area community municipality country village land region
route highway road railway bridge crossing canal railroad junction
stream creek tributary

organization business institution company industry organisation agency school department university government court board
channel network affiliate outlet
supplier manufacturer distributor vendor retailer investor broker provider lender owner creditor shareholder customer employer

Table 3: First two level-one clusters of synonyms for the word "*bank*"

We produce clusters with a two-layer structure. Level one represents loose topical relatedness roughly corresponding to broad domains, while level two is aimed at grouping together closely similar words. For example, among the objects of the verb *cultivate*, the nouns *tie* and *contact* belong to the same level-two cluster. *Attitude* and *spirit* belong to another level-two cluster but both pairs are in the same level-one cluster. The nouns *fruit* and *vegetable* are clustered together in another level-one cluster. This double-layer representation is a solution to express at once close synonymy and topic relatedness. The clusters of symonyms displayed in Table 3 follow the same representation.

4 Implementation of the system

In this section, we describe the implementation of *Linggle*, including how to index and store n-grams for a fast access (Section 4.1) and construction of the LDA models (Section 4.2). We will describe the clustering method in more details in section 5.

4.1 N-grams preprocessing

The n-grams are first filtered keeping only the words that are in WordNet and in the British National Corpus, and then indexed by word and position in the n-gram, in a way similar to the rotated n-gram approach proposed by Lin et. al. (2010). The files are then stored in an Apache

HBase NoSQL base. The major advantages of using a NoSQL database is the excellent performance in querying the ability of storing large amounts of data across several servers and the capability to scale up when we have additional entries in the dataset, or additional datasets to add to the system.

4.2 LDA models computations

Two types of LDA models are calculated for *Linggle*. The first type is a selectional preference model between heads and modifiers. Six models are calculated in total for the subject-verb, the verb-object and the adjective-noun relations done in a similar way to Ritter and Etzioni's (2010) model with binary relations instead of triples. The second is a word/synonyms model in which a word is considered as a document in LDA and its synonyms as the words of the document. This second model has the effect of splitting the synonyms of a word into different topics, as shown in Table 3.

Seeds	parameter: s_1
1. Consider the m first topics for a verb v according to the LDA per document-topic distribution (θ) 2. Consider $S = o_1,...,o_n$, a set of n objects of v. 3. Split S into m classes $C_1,..,C_m$ according to their LDA per topic-word probability: o_i is assigned to the topic in which it has the highest probability. 4. For each class C_i, move every object o_j that is not similar to any other o_k *of* C_i, *according to a* similarity threshold s_1 into a new created class.	
Level 2	parameter: s_2
While ($Argmax_{ci,cj}\ Sim(c_i, c_j) > s_2$): Merge $Argmax_{ci,cj}\ Sim(c_i, c_j)$ into one class.	
Level 1	parameter: s_3
While ($Argmax_{ci,cj}\ Sim(c_i, c_j) > s_3$): Group $Argmax_{ci,cj}\ Sim(c_i,c_j)$ under the same level 1 cluster.	

Table 4: Clustering Algorithm for the object of a given verb

The hyperparameters *alpha, eta,* that affect the sparsity of the document-topic (*theta*) and the topic-word (*lambda*) distributions are both set to 0.5 and the number of topics is set to 300. More research would be necessary to optimize the value for the parameters in the perspective of the clustering algorithm, as quickly discussed in the next section.

Sim (c_i, c_j):
1. Build the Cartesian product $C = c_i \times c_i$ 2. Get P the set of the similarity between all word pairs in C 3. Return Sim(c_i,c_j) the mean of the scores in P

Table 5: Similarity between two classes t_i and t_j

5 Clustering algorithm

The clustering algorithm combines topic modeling results and a semantic similarity measure. We use Pantel's dependencies repository to compute LDA models for subject-verbs, verbs-objects and adjective-nouns relations in both directions. Currently, we also use Pantel's similarity measure. It has a reasonable precision partly because it relies on parser information instead of bag of words windows. However the coverage of the available scores is lower than what would be needed for Linggle. We will address this issue in the near future by extending it with similarity scores computed from the n-grams.

We combine the two distributional semantics approaches in a simple manner inspired by clustering by committee algorithm (CBC). The similarity measure is used to refine the LDA topics and to generate finer grain clusters. Conversely, LDA topics can also be seen as the seeds of our clustering algorithm.

This algorithm intends to constrain the words that belong to a final cluster more strictly than LDA does in order to obtain clearly interpretable clusters. The exact same algorithm is applied to synonym models, for synonyms of nouns, adjectives and verbs (shown in Table 3).

Table 4 shows the algorithm for constructing double layer clusters for a set S of objects of a verb v. The objects are first roughly split into classes, attributing a single topic to every object o_i. The topic of a word o_i is determined according to its per topic-word probability. More experiments could be done using the product of the per document-topic and the per topic-word LDA probabilities instead, in order to take into account the specific verb when assigning a topic to the object. Such a way of assigning topics should also be more sensitive to the LDA hyperparameters.

At this stage, some classes are incoherent and that low frequency words that do not appear in the head of any topic are often misclassified. Words are rearranged between the classes and create new classes if necessary using the similarity measure. If any word of a class is not similar to any other word in this class (the threshold is set to $s_1 = 0.09$), a new class is created for it.

Any two classes are then merged if their similarity (computer accordingly to Table 5) is above $s_2=0.06$, forming the level 2 clusters. Classes are then grouped together if the similarity between them is above $s_3 = 0.02$ forming the level 1 clusters.

Finally, the classes that contain less than three words are not displayed in *Linggle* and the predicate-arguments counts in the *Web 1T* are retrieved using a few hand crafted RE and morphological expansion of the nouns and the verbs.

This algorithm appears to generate interpretable semantic classes and to be quite robust regarding the threshold parameters. More tests and rigorous evaluation are left to future work.

6 Conclusion

There are many different directions in which Linggle will be improved. The first one is to allow users to work with word forms and with multiword expressions. The second one concerns the extension of the coverage of the example base with several large corpora such as Wikipedia and the extension of the coverage of the similarity measure. The third direction concerns the development of automatic suggestions for text edition, such as suggesting a better adjective or a different preposition in the context of a sentence. Finally, Linggle is currently being extended to Chinese.

We presented a prototype that gives access to Web Scale collocations. Linggle displays both word usage and word similarity information. Depending on the type of the input query, the results are displayed under the form of lists or clusters of n-grams. The system is designed to become a multilingual platform for text edition and can also become a valuable resource for natural language processing research.

References

David Blei, A. Ng, and M. Jordan. 2003. Latent Dirichlet allocation. *Journal of Machine Learning Research*, 3:993–1022, January 2003.

Jason S. Chang, 2008. Linggle: a web-scale language reference search engine. *Unpublished manuscript*.

Katrin Erk and Sebastian Padó. 2010. A Flexible, Corpus-Driven Model of Regular and Inverse Selectional Preferences. *In Proceedings of ACL 2010*.

Christiane Fellbaum. 2010. WordNet. *MIT Press*, Cambridge, MA.

John Rupert Firth. 1957. The Semantics of Linguistics Science. *Papers in linguistics* 1934-1951. London: Oxford University Press.

William H Fletcher. 2012. Corpus analysis of the world wide web." In The Encyclopedia of Applied Linguistics.

Adam Kilgarriff , and David Tugwell. 2001. Word sketch: Extraction and display of significant collocations for lexicography. In *Proceedings of COLLOCTION: Computational Extraction, Analysis and Exploitation workshop, 39th ACL and 10th EACL*, pp. 32-38.

Dekang Lin. 1998. Automatic retrieval and clustering of similar words. In *Proceedings of the 17th international conference on Computational linguistics*, volume 2. Association for Computational Linguistics, pp. 768-774.

Dekang Lin, and Patrick Pantel. 2002. Concept Discovery from Text. In Proceedings of Conference on Computational Linguistics (COLING-02). pp. 577-583. Taipei, Taiwan.

Dekang Lin, Kenneth Ward Church, Heng Ji, Satoshi Sekine, David Yarowsky, Shane Bergsma, Kailash Patil, Emily Pitler, Rachel Lathbury, Vikram Rao, Kapil Dalwani, Sushant Narsale. 2010. New tools for web-scale n-grams. In Proceedings of LREC.

David Newman, Jey Han Lau, Karl Grieser and Timothy Baldwin (2010). Automatic Evaluation of Topic Coherence. In *Proceedings of Human Language Technologies, 11th NAACL HLT*, Los Angeles, USA, pp. 100—108.

Evan Sandhaus. 2008. "New york times corpus: Corpus overview." LDC catalogue LDC2008T19.

Sempute Team. 2013. What is NeedleSeek? http://needleseek.msra.cn/readme.htm

Benno Stein, Martin Potthast, and Martin Trenkmann. 2010. Retrieving customary Web language to assist writers. Advances in Information Retrieval. Springer Berlin Heidelberg, pp. 631-635.

Martin Potthast, Martin Trenkmann, and Benno Stein. Using Web N-Grams to Help Second-Language Speakers .2010. SIGIR 10 Web N-Gram Workshop, pages 49-49.

Alan Ritter, Mausam, and Oren Etzioni. 2010. A Latent Dirichlet Allocation method for Selectional Preferences. *In Proceedings of the 48th Annual Meeting of the Association for Computational Linguistics* (July 2010), pp. 424-434.

Yorick Wilks. 1978. Making preferences more active. *Artificial Intelligence* 11(3), pp. 197-223.

Shaoqun Wu, Ian H. Witten and Margaret Franken (2010). Utilizing lexical data from a web-derived corpus to expand productive collocation knowledge. ReCALL, 22(1), 83–102.

ParaQuery: Making Sense of Paraphrase Collections

Lili Kotlerman
Bar-Ilan University
Israel
lili.dav@gmail.com

Nitin Madnani and Aoife Cahill
Educational Testing Service
Princeton, NJ, USA
{nmadnani,acahill}@ets.org

Abstract

Pivoting on bilingual parallel corpora is a popular approach for paraphrase acquisition. Although such pivoted paraphrase collections have been successfully used to improve the performance of several different NLP applications, it is still difficult to get an intrinsic estimate of the quality and coverage of the paraphrases contained in these collections. We present *ParaQuery*, a tool that helps a user interactively explore and characterize a given pivoted paraphrase collection, analyze its utility for a particular domain, and compare it to other popular lexical similarity resources – all within a single interface.

1 Introduction

Paraphrases are widely used in many Natural Language Processing (NLP) tasks, such as information retrieval, question answering, recognizing textual entailment, text simplification etc. For example, a question answering system facing a question "*Who invented bifocals and lightning rods?*" could retrieve the correct answer from the text "*Benjamin Franklin invented strike termination devices and bifocal reading glasses*" given the information that "*bifocal reading glasses*" is a paraphrase of "*bifocals*" and "*strike termination devices*" is a paraphrase of "*lightning rods*".

There are numerous approaches for automatically extracting paraphrases from text (Madnani and Dorr, 2010). We focus on generating paraphrases by pivoting on bilingual parallel corpora as originally suggested by Bannard and Callison-Burch (2005). This technique operates by attempting to infer semantic equivalence between phrases in the same language by using a second language as a bridge. It builds on one of the initial steps used to train a phrase-based statistical machine translation system. Such systems rely on *phrase tables* – a tabulation of correspondences between phrases in the source language and phrases in the target language. These tables are usually extracted by inducing word alignments between sentence pairs in a parallel training corpus and then incrementally building longer phrasal correspondences from individual words and shorter phrases. Once such a tabulation of bilingual correspondences is available, correspondences between phrases in one language may be inferred simply by using the phrases in the other language as *pivots*, e.g., if both "*man*" and "*person*" correspond to "*personne*" in French, then they can be considered paraphrases. Each paraphrase pair (*rule*) in a pivoted paraphrase collection is defined by a *source* phrase e_1, the *target* phrase e_2 that has been inferred as its paraphrase, and a probability score $p(e_2|e_1)$ obtained from the probability values in the bilingual phrase table.[1]

Pivoted paraphrase collections have been successfully used in different NLP tasks including automated document summarization (Zhou et al., 2006), question answering (Riezler et al., 2007), and machine translation (Madnani, 2010). Yet, it is still difficult to get an estimate of the intrinsic quality and coverage of the paraphrases contained in these collections. To remedy this, we propose *ParaQuery* – a tool that can help explore and analyze pivoted paraphrase collections.

2 ParaQuery

In this section we first briefly describe how to set up *ParaQuery* (§2.1) and then demonstrate its use in detail for interactively exploring and characterizing a paraphrase collection, analyzing its utility for a particular domain, and comparing it with other word-similarity resources (§2.2). Detailed documentation will be included in the tool.

[1] There may be other values associated with each pair, but we ignore them for the purposes of this paper.

2.1 Setting up

ParaQuery operates on pivoted paraphrase collections and can accept collections generated using any set of tools that are preferred by the user, as long as the collection is stored in a pre-defined plain-text format containing the source and target phrases, the probability values, as well as information on pivots (optional but useful for pivot-driven analysis, as shown later). This format is commonly used in the machine translation and paraphrase generation community. In this paper, we adapt the Thrax and Joshua (Ganitkevitch et al., 2012) toolkits to generate a pivoted paraphrase collection using the English-French EuroParl parallel corpus, which we use as our example collection for demonstrating *ParaQuery*. Once a pivoted collection is generated, *ParaQuery* needs to convert it into an SQLite database against which queries can be run. This is done by issuing the *index* command at the *ParaQuery* command-line interface (described in §2.2.1).

2.2 Exploration and Analysis

In order to provide meaningful exploration and analysis, we studied various scenarios in which paraphrase collections are used, and found that the following issues typically interest the developers and users of such collections:

1. Semantic relations between the paraphrases in the collection (e.g. synonymy, hyponymy) and their frequency.
2. The frequency of inaccurate paraphrases, possible ways of de-noising the collection, and the meaningfulness of scores (better paraphrases should be scored higher).
3. The utility of the collection for a specific domain, i.e. whether domain terms of interest are present in the collection.
4. Comparison of different collections based on the above dimensions.

We note that paraphrase collections are used in many tasks with different acceptability thresholds for semantic relations, noisy paraphrases etc. We do not intend to provide an exhaustive judgment of paraphrase quality, but instead allow users to characterize a collection, enabling an analysis of the aforesaid issues and providing information for them to decide whether a given collection is suitable for their specific task and/or domain.

2.2.1 Command line interface

ParaQuery allows interactive exploration and analysis via a simple command line interface, by processing user issued *queries* such as:

***show* <query>:** display the rules which satisfy the conditions of the given *query*.

***show count* <query>:** display the number of such rules.

***explain* <query>:** display information about the pivots which yielded each of these rules.

***analyze* <query>:** display statistics about these rules and save a report to an output file.

The following information is stored in the SQLite database for each paraphrase rule:[2]

- The source and the target phrases, and the probability score of the rule.
- Are the source and the target identical?
- Do the source and the target have the same part of speech?[3]
- Length of the source and the target, and the difference in their lengths.
- Number of pivots and the list of pivots.
- Are both the source and the target found in WordNet (WN)? If yes, the WN relation between them (synonym, derivation, hypernym, hyponym, co-hyponym, antonym, meronym, holonym, pertainym) or the minimal distance, if they are not connected directly.

Therefore, all of the above can be used, alone or in combination, to constrain the queries and define the rule(s) of interest. Figure 1 presents simple queries processed by the *show* command: the first query displays top-scoring rules with "*man*" as their source phrase, while the second adds restriction on the rules' score. By default, the tool displays the 10 best-scoring rules per query, but this limit can be changed as shown. For each rule, the corresponding score and semantic relation/distance is displayed.

[2] Although some of this information is available in the paraphrase collection that was indexed, the remaining is automatically computed and injected into the database during the indexing process. Indexing the French-pivoted paraphrase collection (containing 3,633,015 paraphrase rules) used in this paper took about 6 hours.

[3] We use the simple parts of speech provided by WordNet (nouns, verbs, adjectives and adverbs).

The queries provide a flexible way to define and work with the rule set of interest, starting from filtering low-scoring rules till extracting specific semantic relations or constraining on the number of pivots. Figure 2 presents additional examples of queries. The tool also enables filtering out target terms with a recurrent lemma, as illustrated in the same figure. Note that *ParaQuery* also contains a batch mode (in addition to the interactive mode illustrated so far) to automatically extract the output for a set of queries contained in a batch script.

```
query> set limit 5
query> show source = "man"

  man => men      [0.02669] [synonym]
  man => people   [0.01404] [meronym]
  man => person   [0.01228] [hypernym]
  man => rights   [0.008373] [WN distance=6]
  man => citizen  [0.005146] [WN distance=3]

query> show source = "man" and prob < 0.001

  man => public       [0.0005019] [WN distance=3]
  man => anybody      [0.0004759] [not in WN]
  man => a person     [0.0004182] [not in WN]
  man => troops       [0.0002291] [WN distance=5]
  man => our citizens [0.0002023] [not in WN]
```

Figure 1: Examples of the *show* command and the probability constraint.

2.2.2 Analyzing pivot information

It is well known that pivoted paraphrase collections contain a lot of noisy rules. To understand the origins of such rules, an *explain* query can be used, which displays the pivots that yielded each paraphrase rule, and the probability share of each pivot in the final probability score. Figure 3 shows an example of this command.

We see that noisy rules can originate from stop-word pivots, e.g. "*l*'". It is common to filter rules containing stop-words, yet perhaps it is also important to exclude stop-word pivots, which was never considered in the past. We can use *ParaQuery* to further explore whether discarding stop-word pivots is a good idea. Figure 4 presents a more complex query showing paraphrase rules that were extracted via a single pivot "*l*'". We see that the top 5 such rules are indeed noisy, indicating that perhaps all of the 5,360 rules satisfying the query can be filtered out.

2.2.3 Analysis of rule sets

In order to provide an overall analysis of a rule set or a complete collection, *ParaQuery* includes the *analyze* command. Figure 5 shows the typical information provided by this command. In addition, a report is generated to a file, including the analysis information for the whole rule set and for its three parts: *top*, *middle* and *bottom*, as defined by the scores of the rules in the set. The output to the file is more detailed and expands on the information presented in Figure 5. For example, it also includes, for each part, rule samples and score distributions for each semantic relation and different WordNet distances.

The information contained in the report can be

```
query> show source = "man" and relation = "hypernym"

  man => person      [0.01228] [hypernym]
  man => individual  [0.003127] [hypernym]
  man => persons     [8.839e-05] [hypernym]
  man => individuals [6.799e-05] [hypernym]

query> set unique_tgt on
query> show source = "man" and relation = "hypernym"

  man => person     [0.01228] [hypernym]
  man => individual [0.003127] [hypernym]

query> show source = "man" and distance = 4

  man => member       [6.534e-05] [WN distance=4]
  man => businessmen  [6.249e-05] [WN distance=4]
  man => union        [5.766e-05] [WN distance=4]
  man => year         [1.685e-05] [WN distance=4]
  man => need         [3.17e-06] [WN distance=4]
```

Figure 2: Restricting the output of the *show* command using WordNet relations and distance, and the unique lemma constraint.

```
query> explain source = "man" and prob < 0.01

  man => rights     [0.008373] [WN distance=6]
    1.   homme : 0.005095152449060402
    2.   l' homme : 0.0032782141291460873

  man => citizen    [0.005146] [WN distance=3]
    1.   citoyen : 0.005146163785838685

  man => male       [0.004446] [synonym]
    1.   homme : 0.003821364336795302
    2.   hommes : 6.249019761606025E-4

  man => s          [0.003421] [WN distance=5]
    1.   l : 0.00341807739914768
    2.   ' : 3.328130356209791E-6

  man => politician [0.003397] [WN distance=3]
    1.   homme : 0.0033967682993736007

  man => individual [0.003127] [hypernym]
    1.   homme : 0.0021229801871085
    2.   personne : 9.042530177822003E-4
    3.   citoyen : 6.741699282758096E-5
    4.   humain : 3.232734671281396E-5
```

Figure 3: An example of the *explain* command.

```
query> set limit 5
query> show source = "*" and pivots = 1 and pivots include "l"

  evropa => s [0.2724] [not in WN]
     tym => s [0.2043] [not in WN]
      za => s [0.2043] [not in WN]
    gaat => s [0.1135] [not in WN]
     tak => s [0.1135] [not in WN]

query> show count source = "*" and pivots = 1 and pivots include "l"
5360
```

Figure 4: Exploring French stop-word pivots using the *pivots* condition of the *show* command.

```
query> analyze source = "man*" and prob > 0.1
Retrieving rules from the database ... found  155 paraphrase rules.
Analyzing...
10%... 20%... 30%... 40%... 50%... 60%... 70%... 80%... 90%...

Random rule sample:
--------------------
  mandate for negotiation => negotiating mandate  [0.351307189542]
  manifestly => obviously  [0.157373877673]
  manifestations => events  [0.116528555867]

Statistics for the 155 rule(s):
-------------------------------------
  Average number of pivots: 2.10322580645

  Results of WordNet analysis based on 20 rule(s) (12.9% of the 155 rule(s)):
      SYNONYM: 7 rule(s) (35.0%):
      DERIVATION: 2 rule(s) (10.0%):
      HYPERNYM: 2 rule(s) (10.0%):
      CO-HYPONYM: 1 rule(s) (5.0%):
      UNDEFINED RELATION: 6 rule(s) (30.0%):
      HYPONYM: 1 rule(s) (5.0%):
      PERTAINYM: 1 rule(s) (5.0%):

  Average WordNet distance for rules corresponding to UNDEFINED RELATION: 4.66666666667

  The number of unique source sides is: 134

  The average number of target sides per source is: 1.15671641791

   The average number of 'NOT IN WN' targets per source is: 1.00746268657
   The average number of 'SYNONYM' targets per source is: 0.0522388059701
   The average number of 'DERIVATION' targets per source is: 0.0149253731343
   The average number of 'HYPERNYM' targets per source is: 0.0149253731343
```

Figure 5: An example of the *analyze* command (full output not shown for space reasons).

TOP	BOTTOM
finest ⇒ better	approach ⇒ el
outdoors ⇒ external	effect ⇒ parliament
unsettled ⇒ unstable	comment ⇒ speak up
intelligentsia ⇒ intelligence	propose ⇒ allotted
caretaker ⇒ provisional	prevent ⇒ aimed
luckily ⇒ happily	energy ⇒ subject matter

Table 1: A random sample of *undefined relation* rules from our collection's top and bottom parts.

easily used for generating graphs and tables. For example, Figure 6 shows the distribution of semantic relations in the three parts of our example paraphrase collection. The figure characterizes the collection in terms of semantic relations it contains and illustrates the fact that the scores agree with their desired behavior: (1) the collection's top-scoring part contains significantly more synonyms than its middle and bottom parts, (2) similar trends hold for derivations and hypernyms, which are more suitable for paraphrasing than co-hyponyms and other relations not defined in WordNet (we refer to these relations as *undefined relations*), (3) such undefined relations have the highest frequency in the collection's bottom part, and are least frequent in its top part. Among other conclusions, the figure shows, that discarding the lower-scoring middle and bottom parts of the collection would allow retaining almost all the synonyms and derivations, while filtering out most of the co-hyponyms and a considerable number of undefined relations.

Yet from Figure 6 we see that undefined relations constitute the majority of the rules in the collection. To better understand this, random rule samples provided in the analysis output can be used, as shown in Table 1. From this table, we see that the top-part rules are indeed mostly valid for paraphrasing, unlike the noisy bottom-part rules. The score distributions reported as part of the analysis can be used to further explore the collection and set sound thresholds suitable for different tasks and needs.

2.2.4 Analysis of domain utility

One of the frequent questions of interest is whether a given collection is suitable for a specific domain. To answer this question, *ParaQuery* allows the user to run the analysis from §2.2.3 over rules whose source phrases belong to a specific domain, by means of the *analyze <query> using <file>* command. The *file* can hold either a list of domain terms or a representative domain text, from which frequent terms and term collocations will be automatically extracted, presented to the user, and utilized for analysis. The analysis includes the coverage of the domain terms in the paraphrase collection, and can also be restricted to top-K rules per source term, a common practice in many NLP applications. We do not show an example of this command due to space considerations.

2.2.5 Comparison with other collections

The output of the *analyze* command can also be used to compare different collections, either in general or for a given domain. Although *ParaQuery* is designed for pivoted paraphrase collections, it allows comparing them to non-pivoted paraphrase collections as well. Next we present an example of such a comparative study, performed using *ParaQuery* via several *analyze* commands.

Table 2 compares three different collections: the French pivoted paraphrase collection, a distributional similarity resource (Kotlerman et al., 2010) and a Wikipedia-based resource (Shnarch et al., 2009). The table shows the collection sizes, as well as the number of different (unique) source phrases in them and, correspondingly, the average number of target phrases per source. From the table we can see that the distributional similarity resource contains a lot of general language terms found in WordNet, while the Wikipedia resource includes only a small amount of such terms. A sample of rules from the Wikipedia collection explains this behavior, e.g. '*Yamaha SR500 ⇒ motorcycle*'. The table provides helpful information to decide which collection is (more) suitable for specific tasks, such as paraphrase recognition and generation, query expansion, automatic generation of training data for different supervised tasks, etc.

3 Conclusions and Future Work

We presented *ParaQuery*—a tool for interactive exploration and analysis of pivoted paraphrase collections—and showed that it can be used to estimate the intrinsic quality and coverage of the paraphrases contained in these collections, a task that is still somewhat difficult. *ParaQuery* can also be used to answer the questions that users of such collections are most interested in. We plan to release *ParaQuery* under an open-source license, including our code for generating paraphrase collections that can then be indexed and analyzed by

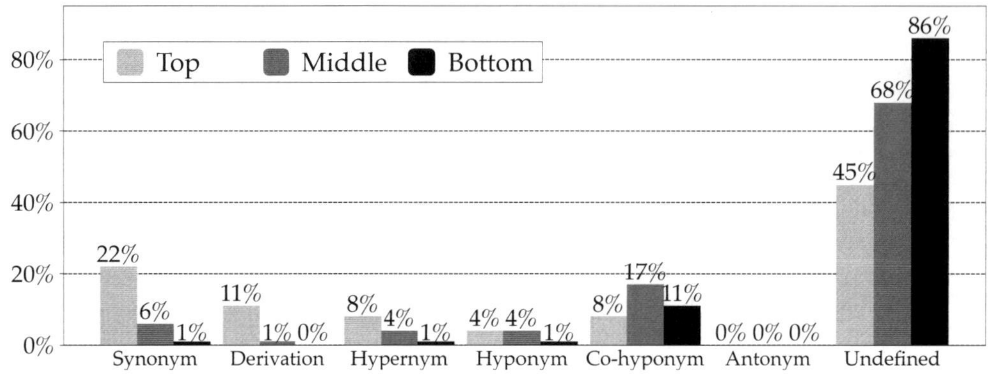

Figure 6: Distribution of semantic relations in the top, middle and bottom parts of the example collection. The parts are defined by binning the scores of the rules in the collection.

Collection	Size (rules)	In WordNet	Unique Src	Avg. Tgts per Src	d_{avg} for UR
Pivoted (FR)	3,633,015	757,994 (21%)	188,898	16.064	2.567
Dist.Sim.	7,298,321	3,252,967 (45%)	113,444	64.334	6.043
Wikipedia	7,880,962	295,161 (4%)	2,727,362	2.890	8.556

Table 2: Comparing the French-pivoted paraphrase collection to distributional-similarity based and Wikipedia-based similarity collections, in terms of total size, percentage of rules in WordNet, number of unique source phrases, average number of target phrases per source phrase, and the average WordNet distance between the two sides of the *undefined relation* (UR) rules.

ParaQuery. We also plan to include pre-generated paraphrase collections in the release so that users of *ParaQuery* can use it immediately.

In the future, we plan to use this tool for analyzing the nature of pivoted paraphrases. The quality and coverage of these paraphrases is known to depend on several factors, including (a) the genre of the bilingual corpus, (b) the word-alignment algorithm used during bilingual training, and (c) the pivot language itself. However, there have been no explicit studies designed to measure such variations. We believe that *ParaQuery* is perfectly suited to conducting such studies and moving the field of automated paraphrase generation forward.

Acknowledgments

This work was partially supported by the European Community's Seventh Framework Programme (FP7/2007-2013) under grant agreement no. 287923 (EXCITEMENT).

References

Colin Bannard and Chris Callison-Burch. 2005. Paraphrasing with Bilingual Parallel Corpora. In *Proceedings of ACL*, pages 597–604.

Juri Ganitkevitch, Yuan Cao, Jonathan Weese, Matt Post, and Chris Callison-Burch. 2012. Joshua 4.0: Packing, PRO, and Paraphrases. In *Proceedings of WMT*, pages 283–291.

Lili Kotlerman, Ido Dagan, Idan Szpektor, and Maayan Zhitomirsky-Geffet. 2010. Directional Distributional Similarity for Lexical Inference. *Natural Language Engineering*, 16(4):359–389.

Nitin Madnani and Bonnie J. Dorr. 2010. Generating Phrasal and Sentential Paraphrases: A Survey of Data-driven Methods. *Computational Linguistics*, 36(3):341–387.

Nitin Madnani. 2010. *The Circle of Meaning: From Translation to Paraphrasing and Back*. Ph.D. thesis, Department of Computer Science, University of Maryland College Park.

Stefan Riezler, Alexander Vasserman, Ioannis Tsochantaridis, Vibhu O. Mittal, and Yi Liu. 2007. Statistical Machine Translation for Query Expansion in Answer Retrieval. In *Proceedings of ACL*, pages 464–471.

Eyal Shnarch, Libby Barak, and Ido Dagan. 2009. Extracting lexical reference rules from Wikipedia. In *Proceedings of ACL-IJCNLP*, pages 450–458.

Liang Zhou, Chin-Yew Lin, Dragos Stefan Muntenau, and Eduard Hovy. 2006. ParaEval: Using Paraphrases to Evaluate Summaries Automatically. In *Proceedings of HLT-NAACL*, pages 447–454.

PATHS: A System for Accessing Cultural Heritage Collections

Eneko Agirre*, **Nikolaos Aletras**†, **Paul Clough**†, **Samuel Fernando**†,
Paula Goodale†, **Mark Hall**†, **Aitor Soroa*** and **Mark Stevenson**†

(*) IXA NLP Group, University of the Basque Country
Manuel Lardizabal, 1, 20.018 Donostia, Basque Country

(†) Department of Computer Science, Sheffield University
211 Portobello, Sheffield S1 4DP, United Kingdom

Abstract

This paper describes a system for navigating large collections of information about cultural heritage which is applied to Europeana, the European Library. Europeana contains over 20 million artefacts with meta-data in a wide range of European languages. The system currently provides access to Europeana content with meta-data in English and Spanish. The paper describes how Natural Language Processing is used to enrich and organise this meta-data to assist navigation through Europeana and shows how this information is used within the system.

1 Introduction

Significant amounts of information about cultural heritage has been digitised in recent years and is now easily available through online portals. However, this vast amount of material can also be overwhelming for many users since they are provided with little or no guidance on how to find and interpret this information. Potentially useful and relevant content is hidden from the users who are typically offered simple keyword-based searching functionality as the entry point into a cultural heritage collection. The situation is very different within traditional mechanisms for viewing cultural heritage (e.g. museums) where artefacts are organised thematically and users guided through the collection.

This paper describes a system that allows users to explore large cultural heritage collections. Navigation is based around the metaphor of pathways (or trails) through the collection, an approach that has been widely explored as an alternative to standard keyword-based search (Furuta et al., 1997; Reich et al., 1999; Shipman et al., 2000; White and Huang, 2010). Pathways are sets of artefacts organised around a theme which form access points to the collection.

Pathways are a useful way to access information about cultural heritage. Users accessing these collections are often unfamiliar with their content, making keyword-based search unsuitable since they are unable to formulate appropriate queries (Wilson et al., 2010). Non-keyword-based search interfaces have been shown to be suitable for exploratory search (Marchionini, 2006). Pathways support this exploration by echoing the organised galleries and guided tours found in museums.

2 Related Work

Heitzman et al. (1997) describe the ILEX system which acts as a guide through the jewellery collection of the National Museum of Scotland. The user explores the collection through a set of web pages which provide descriptions of each artefact that are personalised for each user. The system makes use of information about the artefacts the user has viewed to build up a model of their interests and uses this to customise the descriptions of each artefact and provide recommendations for further artefacts in which they may be interested.

Grieser et al. (2007) also explore providing recommendations based on the artefacts a user has viewed so far. They make use of a range of techniques including language modelling, geospatial modelling and analysis of previous visitors' behaviour to provide recommendations to visitors to the Melbourne Museum.

Grieser et al. (2011) explore methods for determining the similarity between museum artefacts, commenting that this is useful for navigation through these collections and important for personalisation (Bowen and Filippini-Fantoni, 2004; O'Donnell et al., 2001), recommendation (Bohnert et al., 2009; Trant, 2009) and automatic tour generation (Finkelstein et al., 2002; Roes et al., 2009). They also use exhibits from Melbourne

Museum and apply a range of approaches to determine the similarity between them, including comparing descriptions and measuring physical distance between them in the museum.

These approaches, like many of the systems that have been developed for online access to cultural heritage (e.g. (Hage et al., 2010)), are based around virtual access to a concrete physical space (i.e. a museum). They often provide tours which are constrained by the physical layout of the museum, such as virtual museum visits. However, these approaches are less suitable for unstructured collections such as databases of cultural heritage artefacts collected from multiple institutions or artefacts not connected with existing physical presentation (e.g. in a museum). The PATHS system is designed for these types of collections and makes use of natural language analysis to support navigation. In particular, similarity between artefacts is computed automatically (see Section 4.1), background information automatically added to artefact descriptions (see Section 4.2) and a hierarchy of artefacts generated (see Section 4.3).

3 Cultural Heritage Data

The PATHS system has been applied to data from Europeana[1]. This is a web-portal to collections of cultural heritage artefacts provided by a wide range of European institutions. Europeana currently provides access to over 20 million artefacts including paintings, films, books, archival records and museum objects. The artefacts are provided by around 1,500 institutions which range from major institutions, including the Rijksmuseum in Amsterdam, the British Library and the Louvre, to smaller organisations such as local museums. It therefore contains an aggregation of digital content from several sources and is not connected with any one physical museum.

The PATHS system makes use of three collections from Europeana. The first of these contains artefacts from content providers in the United Kingdom which has meta-data in English. The artefacts in the remaining two collections come from institutions in Spain and have meta-data in Spanish.

CultureGrid Culture Grid[2] is a digital content provider service from the Collection Trust[3]. It contains information about over one million artefacts from 40 different UK content providers such as national and regional museums and libraries.

Cervantes Biblioteca Virtual Miguel De Cervantes[4] contains digitalised Spanish text in various formats. In total, the online library contains about 75,000 works from a range of periods in Spanish history.

Hispana The Biblioteca Nacional de España[5] contains information about a diverse set of content including text and drawings. The material is collected from different providers in Spain including museums and libraries.

Europeana stores metadata for each artefact in an XML-based format which includes information such as its title, the digital format, the collection, the year of creation and also a short description of each artefact. However, this meta-data is created by the content providers and varies significantly across artefacts. Many of the artefacts have only limited information associated with them, for example a single word title. In addition, the content providers that contribute to Europeana use different hierarchical structures to organise their collections (e.g. Library of Congress Subject Headings[6] and the Art and Architecture Thesaurus[7]), or do not organise their content into any structure. Consequently the various hierarchies that are used in Europeana only cover some of the artefacts and are not compatible with each other.

3.1 Filtering Data

Analysis of the artefacts in these three collections revealed that many have short and uninformative titles or lack a description. This forms a challenge to language processing techniques since the artefact's meta-data does not contain enough information to model it accurately.

The collections were filtered by removing any artefacts that have no description and have either fewer than four words in their title or have a title that is repeated more than 100 times in the collection. Table 1 shows the number of artefacts in each of the Europeana collections before and

[1] http://www.europeana.eu
[2] http://www.culturegrid.org.uk
[3] http://www.collectionstrust.org.uk
[4] http://www.cervantesvirtual.com
[5] http://www.bne.es
[6] http://authorities.loc.gov/
[7] http://www.getty.edu/research/tools/vocabularies/aat/

after this filter has been applied. Applying the heuristic leads to the removal of around 31% of the artefacts, although the number varies significantly across the collections with 61% of the artefacts in CultureGrid being removed and only 1% of those in Hispana.

Collection	Lang.	Total	Filtered
CultureGrid	Eng.	1,207,781	466,958
Hispana	Sp.	1,235,133	1,219,731
Cervantes	Sp.	19,278	14,983
		2,462,192	1,701,672

Table 1: Number of artefacts in Europeana collections before and after filtering

4 Data Processing

A range of pre-preprocessing steps were carried out on these collections to provide additional information to support navigation in the PATHS system.

4.1 Artefact Similarity

We begin by computing the similarity between the various artefacts in the Europeana collections. This information is useful for navigation and recommendation but is not available in the Europeana collections since they are drawn from a diverse range of sources.

Similarity is computed using an approach described by Aletras et al. (2012). in which the topics generated from each artefact's metadata using a topic model are compared. Latent Dirichlet Allocation (LDA) (Blei et al., 2003) is a widely used type of topic model in which documents can be viewed as probability distributions over topics, θ. The similarity between a pair of documents can be estimated by comparing their topic distributions. This is achieved by viewing each distribution as a vector of probabilities and then computing the cosine of the angle between them:

$$sim(a,b) = \frac{\vec{\theta_a}.\vec{\theta_b}}{|\vec{\theta_a}| \times |\vec{\theta_b}|} \quad (1)$$

where $\vec{\theta_a}$ is the vector created from the probability distribution generated by LDA for document a.

This approach is evaluated using a set of 295 pairs of artefacts for which human judgements of similarity were obtained using crowdsourcing (Aletras et al., 2012). Pearson correlation between the similarity scores and human judgements was 0.53.

The similarity between all the artefacts in the collection is computed in a pairwise fashion. The 25 artefacts with the highest score are retained for each artefact.

4.2 Background Links

The metadata associated with Europeana artefacts is often very limited. Consequently links to relevant articles in Wikipedia were added to each the meta-data of each artefact using Wikipedia Miner (Milne and Witten, 2008) to provide background information. In addition to the link, Wikipedia Miner returns a confidence value between 0 and 1 for each link based on the context of the item.

The accuracy of the links added by Wikipedia Miner were evaluated using the meta-data associated with 21 randomly selected artefacts. Three annotators analysed the links added and found that a confidence value of 0.5 represented a good balance between accuracy and coverage. See Fernando and Stevenson (2012) for further details.

4.3 Hierarchies

The range of hierarchies used by the various collections that comprise the Europeana collection make navigation difficult (see Section 3). Consequently, the Wikipedia links added to the artefact meta-data were used to automatically generate hierarchies that the cover the entire collection. These hierarchies are used by the PATHS system to assist browsing and exploration.

Two approaches are used to generate hierarchies of Europeana artefacts (WikiFreq and WikiTax). These are combined to generate the WikiMerge hierarchy which is used in the PATHS system.

WikiFreq uses link frequencies across the entire collection to organise the artefacts. The first stage in the hierarchy generation process is to compute the frequency with which each linked Wikipedia article appears in the collection. The links in each artefact are these analysed to construct a hierarchy consisting of Wikipedia articles. The links in the meta-data associated with each artefact are ordered based on their frequency in the entire collection and that set of links then inserted into the hierarchy. For example, if the set of ordered links for an artefact is $a_1, a_2, a_3 \cdots a_n$ then the artefact is then inserted into the hierarchy under the branch $a_1 \rightarrow a_2 \rightarrow a_3 \cdots \rightarrow a_n$, with a_1 at the top level in the tree and the artefact appearing under the node a_n. If this branch does not already exist in the tree then it is created.

The hierarchy is pruned to removing nodes with fewer than 20 artefacts in them. In addition, if a node has more than 20 child nodes, only the 20 most frequent are used.

WikiTax uses the Wikipedia Taxonomy (Ponzetto and Strube, 2011), a taxonomy derived from Wikipedia categories. Europeana artefacts are inserted into this taxonomy using the links added by Wikipedia Miner with each artefact being added to the taxonomy for all categories listed in the links. This leads to a taxonomy in which artefacts can occur in multiple locations.

Each approach was used to generate hierarchies from the Europeana collections. The resulting hierarchies were evaluated via online surveys, see Fernando et al. (2012) for further details. It was found that WikiFreq performed well at placing items into the correct location in the taxonomy and grouping together similar items under the same node. However, the overall structure of WikiTax was judged to be more coherent and comprehensible.

WikiMerge combines combines WikiFreq and WikiTax. WikiFreq is used to link each artefact to Wikipedia articles $a_1 \ldots a_n$, but only the link to the most specific article, a_n, is retained. The a_n articles are linked to their parent WikiTax topics based on the Wikipedia categories the articles belong to. The resulting hierarchy is pruned removing all WikiTax topics that do not have a WikiFreq child or have only one child topic. Finally top-level topics in the combined hierarchy are then linked to their respective Wikipedia root node.

The resulting WikiMerge hierarchy has WikiFreq topics as its leaves and WikiTax topics as its interior and root nodes. Experiments showed that this approach was successful in combining the strengths of the two methods (Fernando et al., 2012).

5 The PATHS System

The PATHS system provides access to the Europeana collections described in Section 3 by making use of the additional information generated using the approaches described in Section 4. The interface of the PATHS system has three main areas:

Paths enables users to navigate via pathways (see Section 5.1).

Search supports discovery of both collection artefacts and pathways through keyword search (see Section 5.2).

Explore enables users to explore the collections using a variety of types of overview (see Section 5.3).

5.1 Paths Area

This area provides users with access to Europeana through pathways or trails. These are manually generated sets of artefacts organised into a tree structure which are designed to showcase the content available to the user in an organised way. These can be created by users and can be published for others to follow. An example pathway on the topic "railways" is shown in Figure 1. A short description of the pathway's content is shown towards the top of the figure and a graphical overview of its contents at the bottom.

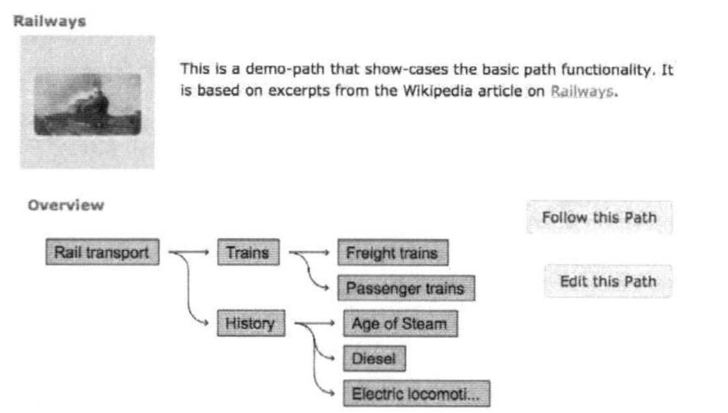

Figure 1: Example pathway on the topic "railways"

Figure 2 shows as example artefact as displayed in the system. The example artefact is a portrait of Catherine the Great. The left side of the figure shows information extracted directly from the Europeana meta-data for this artefact. The title and textual description are shown towards the top left together with a thumbnail image of the artefact. Other information from the meta-data is shown beneath the "About this item" heading. The right side of the figure shows additional information

Figure 2: Example artefact displayed in system interface. Related artefacts and background links are displayed on right hand side

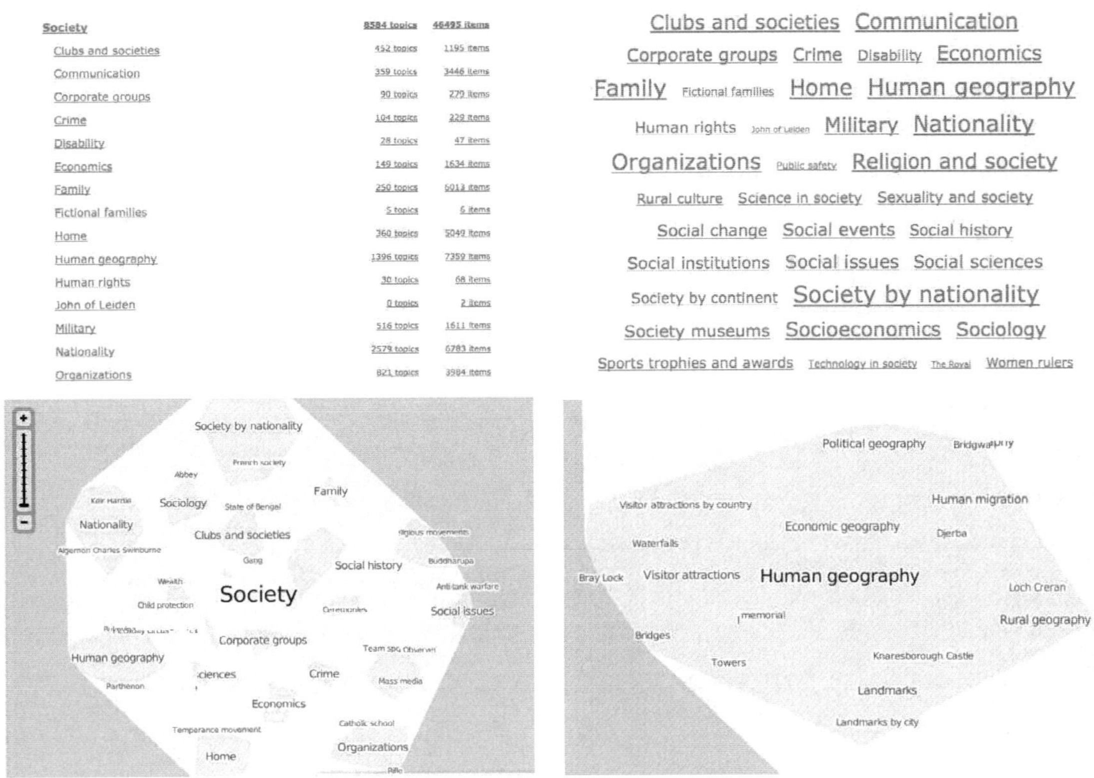

Figure 3: Example visualisations of hierarchy: thesaurus view (top left), tag cloud (top right), map views (bottom)

about the artefact generated using the approaches described in Sections 4.1 and 4.2. Related artefacts are shown to the user one at a time, clicking on the thumbnail image leads to the equivalent page for the related artefact. Below this are links to the Wikipedia articles that are identified in the text of the article's title and description.

5.2 Search Area

This area allows users to search for artefacts and pathways using standard keyword search implemented using Lucene (McCandless et al., 2010).

5.3 Explore Area

The system provides a variety of ways to view the hierarchies generated using the approach described in Section 4.3. Figure 3 shows how these are displayed for a section of the hierarchy with the label "Society". The simplest view (shown in the top left of Figure 3) is a thesaurus type view in which levels of the hierarchy are represented by indentation. The system also allows levels of the hierarchy to be viewed as a tag cloud (top right of Figure 3). The final representation of the hierarchy is as a map, shown in the bottom of Figure 3. In this visualisation categories in the hierarchy are represented as "islands" on the map. Zooming in on the map provides more detail about that area of the hierarchy.

6 Summary and Future Developments

This paper describes a system for navigating Europeana, an aggregation of collections of cultural heritage artefacts. NLP analysis is used to organise the collection and provide additional information. The results of this analysis are provided to the user through an online interface which provides access to English and Spanish content in Europeana.

Planned future development of this system includes providing recommendations and more personalised access. Similarity information (Section 4.1) can be used to provide information from which the recommendations can be made. Personalised access will make use of information about individual users (e.g. from their browsing behaviour or information they provide about their preferences) to generate individual views of Europeana.

Online Demo

The PATHS system is available at http://explorer.paths-project.eu/

Acknowledgments

The research leading to these results was carried out as part of the PATHS project (http://paths-project.eu) funded by the European Community's Seventh Framework Programme (FP7/2007-2013) under grant agreement no. 270082

References

N. Aletras, M. Stevenson, and P. Clough. 2012. Computing similarity between items in a digital library of cultural heritage. *Journal of Computing and Cultural Heritage*, 5(4):no. 16.

D. Blei, A. Ng, and M. Jordan. 2003. Latent dirichlet allocation. *Journal of Machine Learning Research*, 3:993–1022.

F. Bohnert, D. Schmidt, and I. Zuckerman. 2009. Spatial Process for Recommender Systems. In *Proc. of IJCAI 2009*, pages 2022–2027, Pasadena, CA.

J. Bowen and S. Filippini-Fantoni. 2004. Personalization and the Web from a Museum Perspective. In *Proc. of Museums and the Web 2004*, pages 63–78.

Samuel Fernando and Mark Stevenson. 2012. Adapting Wikification to Cultural Heritage. In *Proceedings of the 6th Workshop on Language Technology for Cultural Heritage, Social Sciences, and Humanities*, pages 101–106, Avignon, France.

Samuel Fernando, Mark Hall, Eneko Agirre, Aitor Soroa, Paul Clough, and Mark Stevenson. 2012. Comparing taxonomies for organising collections of documents. In *Proc. of COLING 2012*, pages 879–894, Mumbai, India.

L. Finkelstein, E. Gabrilovich, Y. Matias, E. Rivlin, Z. Solan, G. Wolfman, and E. Ruppin. 2002. Placing Search in Context: The Concept Revisited. *ACM Trans. on Information Systems*, 20(1):116–131.

R. Furuta, F.. Shipman, C. Marshall, D. Brenner, and H. Hsieh. 1997. Hypertext paths and the World-Wide Web: experiences with Walden's Paths. In *Proc. of the Eighth ACM conference on Hypertext*, pages 167–176, New York, NY.

K. Grieser, T. Baldwin, and S. Bird. 2007. Dynamic Path Prediction and Recommendation in a Museum Environment. In *Proc. of the Workshop on Language Technology for Cultural Heritage Data (LaTeCH 2007)*, pages 49–56, Prague, Czech Republic.

K. Grieser, T. Baldwin, F. Bohnert, and L. Sonenberg. 2011. Using Ontological and Document Similarity to Estimate Museum Exhibit Relatedness. *Journal of Computing and Cultural Heritage*, 3(3):1–20.

W.R. van Hage, N. Stash, Y. Wang, and L.M. Aroyo. 2010. Finding your way through the Rijksmuseum with an adaptive mobile museum guide. In *Proc. of ESWC 2010*, pages 46–59.

J. Heitzman, C. Mellish, and J. Oberlander. 1997. Dynamic Generation of Museum Web Pages: The Intelligent Labelling Explorer. *Archives and Museum Informatics*, 11(2):117–125.

G. Marchionini. 2006. Exploratory Search: from Finding to Understanding. *Comm. ACM*, 49(1):41–46.

M. McCandless, E. Hatcher, and O. Gospodnetic. 2010. *Lucene in Action*. Manning Publications.

D. Milne and I. Witten. 2008. Learning to Link with Wikipedia. In *Proc. of CIKM 2008*, Napa Valley, California.

M. O'Donnell, C. Mellish, J. Oberlander, and A. Knott. 2001. ILEX: An architecture for a dynamic hypertext generation system. *Natural Language Engineering*, 7:225–250.

S.P. Ponzetto and M. Strube. 2011. Taxonomy induction based on a collaboratively built knowledge repository. *Artificial Intelligence*, 175(9-10):1737–1756.

S. Reich, L. Carr, D. De Roure, and W. Hall. 1999. Where have you been from here? Trails in hypertext systems. *ACM Computing Surveys*, 31.

I. Roes, N. Stash, Y. Wang, and L. Aroyo. 2009. A personalized walk through the museum: the CHIP interactive tour guide. In *Proc. of the 27th International Conference on Human Factors in Computing Systems*, pages 3317–3322, Boston, MA.

F. Shipman, R. Furuta, D. Brenner, C. Chung, and H. Hsieh. 2000. Guided paths through web-based collections: Design, experiences, and adaptations. *Journal of the American Society for Information Science*, 51(3):260–272.

J. Trant. 2009. Tagging, folksonomies and art museums: Early experiments and ongoing research. *Journal of Digital Information*, 10(1).

R. White and J. Huang. 2010. Assessing the scenic route: measuring the value of search trails in web logs. In *Proc. of SIGIR 2010*, pages 587–594.

M. Wilson, Kulesm B., M. Schraefel, and B. Schneiderman. 2010. From keyword search to exploration: Designing future search interfaces for the web. *Foundations and Trends in Web Science*, 2(1):1–97.

Propminer: A Workflow for Interactive Information Extraction and Exploration using Dependency Trees

Alan Akbik, Oresti Konomi and Michail Melnikov
Technische Univeristät Berlin
Databases and Information Systems Group
Einsteinufer 17, 10587 Berlin, Germany
`firstname.lastname@tu-berlin.de`

Abstract

The use of deep syntactic information such as typed dependencies has been shown to be very effective in Information Extraction. Despite this potential, the process of manually creating rule-based information extractors that operate on dependency trees is not intuitive for persons without an extensive NLP background. In this system demonstration, we present a tool and a workflow designed to enable initiate users to interactively explore the effect and expressivity of creating Information Extraction rules over dependency trees. We introduce the proposed five step workflow for creating information extractors, the graph query based rule language, as well as the core features of the PROPMINER tool.

1 Introduction

Information Extraction (IE) is the task of generating structured information, often in the form of subject-predicate-object relation triples, from unstructured information such as natural language text. Although there are well-established methods for automatically training extractors from annotated data (Mintz et al., 2009), recent years have seen a renewed interest in manually created and maintained rule-based IE systems (Doan et al., 2009; Chiticariu et al., 2010). Advantages of such systems include a better transparency and explainability of extraction rules, and the resulting maintainability and customizability of rule sets.

Another trend in IE is to make increasing use of deep syntactic information in extractors (Bunescu and Mooney, 2005), as dependency parsers become faster and more robust on irregular text (Bohnet, 2010).

Bringing both trends together are recent works in the field of Open Information Extraction (OIE). The systems KRAKEN (Akbik and Löser, 2012) and CLAUSIE (Del Corro and Gemulla,) use a set of hand crafted rules on dependency trees to outperform previous classification based approaches. The latter system outperforms even OLLIE (Mausam et al., 2012), the machine learning based state-of-the art OIE system on dependency parses. Not only does CLAUSIE report significant precision gains over OLLIE, but also finds 2.5 to 3.5 times more relations.

These results indicate a strong potential for manually creating rule-based Information Extraction systems using dependency trees. The higher level syntactic representation, we argue, may even facilitate rule writing, as - unlike in shallow lexico-syntactic rules - much linguistic variation such as inserted clauses and expressions must not be specifically addressed. This enables the creation of more succinct IE rules, leading to better explainability and easier maintenance.

However, despite these advantages, experience has shown that deep syntactic information is difficult to read and understand for non NLP-experts.

In this system demonstration, we propose a workflow designed to tap into this potential, and present the PROPMINER tool that allows users to execute this workflow. It is specifically designed to help persons familiarize themselves with dependency trees and enable exploration and extraction of relations from parsed document collections. Core features of PROPMINER are:

Rule generation and modification. Initiate users are guided by a workflow in which they first enter and annotate an archetypical sentence with the desired relation. A rule generation process then pre-generates an overspecified rule that users modify along lines suggested by the tool. Our preliminary experiments show that this workflow of generating and modifying rules eases the learning curve for non NLP-experts to concepts such as part-of-speech tags and typed dependencies.

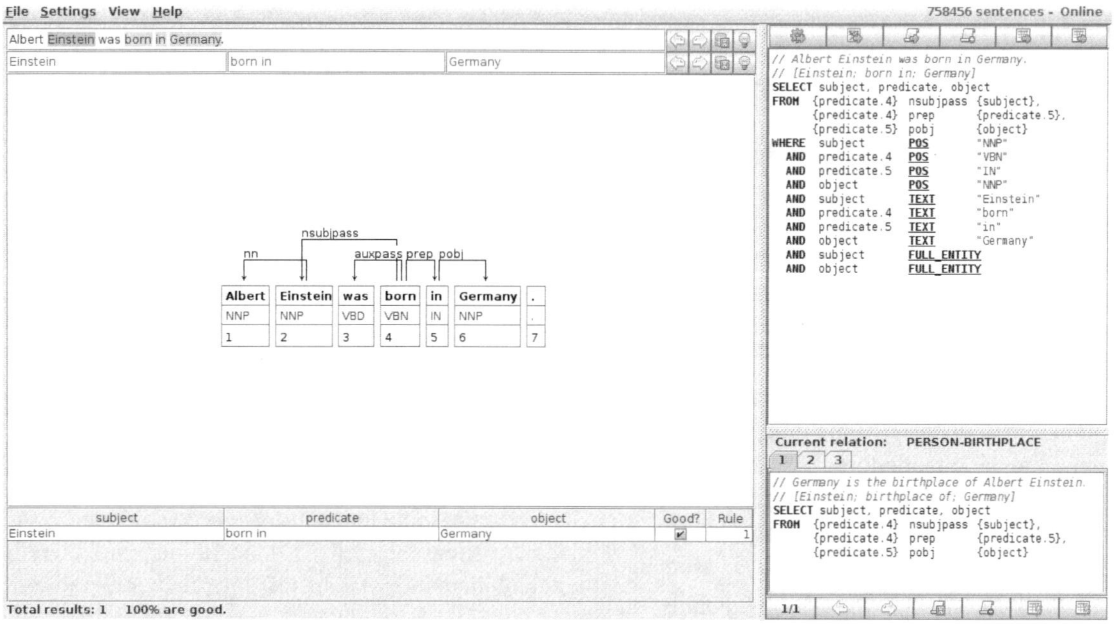

Figure 1: Sentence view of PROPMINER, where steps one and two of the workflow are executed. Users enter (or select) a sentence in the top input field and annotate subject, predicate and object for the desired relation. A rule is generated and displayed in the upper right panel. The lower right panel is the repository of already created rules. The parse of the input sentence is displayed in the center panel.

Interactivity and feedback. Each modification of a rule is immediately queried against a large collection of parsed sentences stored in a distributed graph database. The extraction results of the current state of the rule are presented at all times to the user, thereby explaining the rule by showing its effect.

Intuitive query language. Extraction rules are formulated as queries against a graph database. Our query language allows users to formulate subtree queries as *path expressions*, a concept borrowed from the SerQL query language (Broekstra and Kampman, 2003) because of its intuitive properties. We show a visualization of the parse tree of the current sentence next to the generated rule to ease users into understanding the query language (see Figure 1).

Guided workflow. All structured information generated by the user, such as extraction rules, sentence annotations and evaluation results, are stored to build up a repository of structured information. This information is used to suggest appropriate actions to the user.

A preliminary study shows that users without any NLP background are quickly able to use PROPMINER to create Information Extraction rules. We noted that users at first stay true to the workflow and limit manual effort to generalizing rules, but tend to more directly modify extraction rules as they grow more experienced. Furthermore, PROPMINER's interactive nature eases the process of understanding typed dependencies and enables the interactive exploration of parsed document collections.

2 Workflow and Query Language

PROPMINER implements a workflow that consists of five steps (*Annotate*, *Generate*, *Generalize*, *Evaluate* and *Store*). It is designed to allow users that are unfamiliar with syntactic annotation to create rule-based extractors. In the following subsections, we explain the five steps in detail. As a running example, we use the task of creating an extractor for the PERSONBIRTHPLACE relation.

2.1 Annotate

Users begin the process by constructing an *archetypical* sentence for the desired information type. This sentence constitutes an example that expresses the desired relation. For instance, a user interested in the PERSONBIRTHPLACE relation can choose a sentence such as *"Albert Einstein was born in Germany."*.

In this sentence, the user annotates the words

belonging to the relation triple, assigning the roles of *subject*, *predicate* and *object*. Subject and object are the entities in the example between which the relation holds. The predicate are the words in the sentence that express the relationship. Accordingly, the user marks "*Albert Einstein*" and "*Germany*" as subject and object, and "*born in*" as predicate in the example sentence.

Figure 1 shows the *sentence view* of PROPMINER, with the example sentence entered and annotated in the top input fields, and the parsed sentence shown in the center panel.

2.2 Generate

PROPMINER generates a rule from the annotated sentence by determining the minimal subtree in the sentence's dependency tree that connects all words labeled as subject, predicate and object. The rule consists of this minimal subtree, as well as constraints in the part-of-speech (POS) tags and lexical values of all involved words.

Rules are formulated as queries against a database in which parsed sentences are stored as graphs: Nodes represent words and edges represent typed dependencies. At each node, the POS tag and the lexical value of the word are stored as attributes.

A PROPMINER rule (or query) consists mainly of three parts: A SELECT clause, a FROM clause and a WHERE clause. The generated rule for the running example is displayed in Figure 1. Its individual parts are discussed in the following subsections.

2.2.1 SELECT and FROM

The SELECT clause determines the fields of tuple to be returned by the query. Typically, this consists of a subject-predicate-object triple, but queries with fewer or more fields are possible.

The FROM clause is a *path expression* that specifies the subgraph in the dependency tree the rule must match, and defines which nodes in the subgraph correspond to the fields in the SELECT clause. A path expression is a set of node-edge-node triples. Each of these triples defines one edge (typed dependency) that must hold between two nodes (words). The nodes are denoted in curly brackets, where the text inside curly brackets assigns a variable name to the node.

Consider the SELECT and FROM clauses for the rule generated for the running example, illustrated in the following:

```
SELECT subject, predicate, object
FROM
    {predicate.3}  nsubjpass  {subject},
    {predicate.3}  prep       {predicate.4},
    {predicate.4}  pobj       {object}
```

Here, the SELECT statement defines the desired result of this query, namely a tuple with a "subject", "object" and a "predicate" field: The path expression in this example is specified in the three lines in the FROM statement. It defines a subtree that consists of four nodes connected by three typed dependencies.

The nodes are assigned the variable names "subject", "object", "predicate.3" and "predicate.4". The node "subject" is defined to be a passive subject (typed dependency "*nsubjpass*") of the node "predicate.3". The node "predicate.3" is also connected via the dependency "*prep*" to the node "predicate.4", which in turn is connected to "object" with the dependency "*pobj*".

If this rule matches, the lexical values of the matching nodes are returned. Because the predicate in this example consists of two words ("born" and "in"), two nodes are assigned the "predicate" value, subtyped per convention with a dot and a number ("predicate.3" and "predicate.4").

2.2.2 WHERE

In the WHERE-clause, the attributes of words in the subtree can be further restricted. Auto-generated rules are maximally restricted. The rule for the running example is initially restricted as follows:

```
WHERE
AND subject      POS  "NNP"
AND predicate.3  POS  "VBN"
AND predicate.4  POS  "IN"
AND object       POS  "NNP"
AND subject      TEXT "Einstein"
AND predicate.3  TEXT "born"
AND predicate.4  TEXT "in"
AND object       TEXT "Germany"
AND subject      FULL_ENTITY
```

Word attributes are restricted by naming the variable followed either by "POS" or "TEXT" and the restricting value. Here, for instance, the POS tag of the "object" node is restricted to "NNP" (a proper noun), and its lexical value is restricted to "Germany".

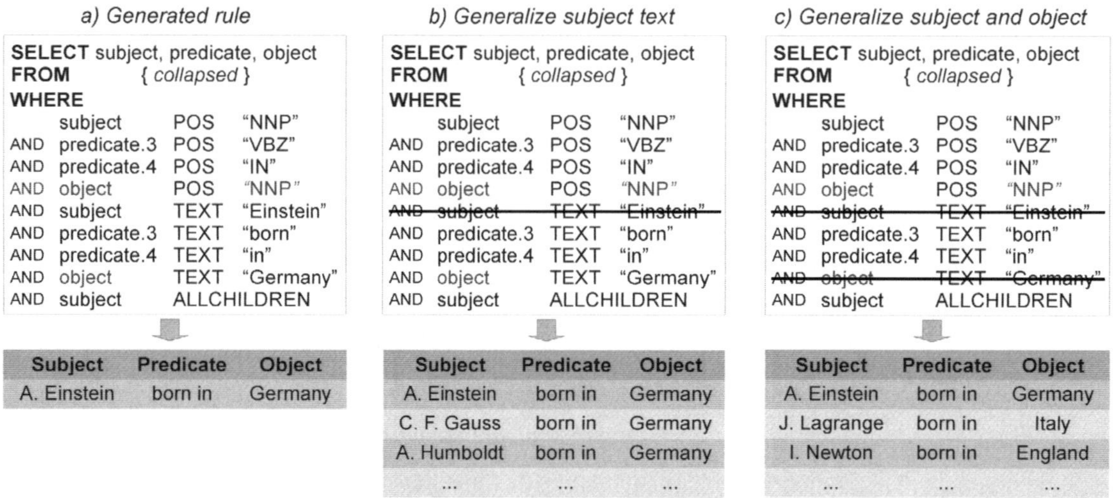

Figure 2: Conceptual example of rule modification through generalization. Below are example relation triples found for each rule. Rule a) is generated from the annotated sentence in the running example, and finds only one triple. Rule b) is the same rule without the restriction in the subject text. The rule now finds a number of relation triples in the document collection, representing different entities born in Germany. In Rule c) both subject and object text restrictions are removed. This yields a rule that finds different entities born in any entity.

Additionally, a number of subtree gathering mechanisms can be specified in the WHERE clause. For example, the keyword FULL_ENTITY causes the variable binding for the subject to expand to all children nodes expected to be part of a named entity.

2.3 Generalize

The rule generated in step two of the workflow is strongly overspecified to the annotated sentence; all features, including the shallow syntactic and lexical values of all words in the subtree, are constrained. The resulting rule only finds exact instances of the relations as seen in the archetypical sentence. Refer to Figure 2 a) for an example.

In step three of the workflow, the user generalizes the auto-generated rule with the help of suggestions. Common lines of generalizing rules focus on the WHERE clause; here, users can remove or modify constraints on the attributes of words. For example, by removing the restriction on the lexical value of the subject, the rule is generalized to finding *all entities* that were born in "*Germany*", instead of only entities with the lexical value "*Einstein*". This example is illustrated in Figure 2 b).

The rule can then be further generalized by removing the lexical constraint on the object, yielding the (desired) rule that finds all entities that were born in any location with an entity name. Figure 2 c) shows an example of this rule, as well as example results.

Further options of generalization include removing the lexical constraints in one or both of the predicate words, or modifying the POS tag constraints. At each modification, extraction results for the current state of the rule are displayed to assist the user. When the results match the desired relation, the user can proceed to the next step in the workflow.

2.4 Evaluate

Each rule created by the user is evaluated in the *corpus view* of PROPMINER, displayed in Figure 3. This view shows a sample of extraction results of the rule in a table. The user can scroll through the table and in each row see the extracted information as well as the sentence the information was extracted from. If the extracted information matches the statement in the sentence, the user can mark this fact as correct.

2.5 Store

If the user is satisfied with the extraction rule, he can assign it to a relation and store it in the rule repository. He can repeat the process with another sentence to find more patterns for the desired relation. As the workflow is repeated, the rule repository will build up, along with a repository of evalu-

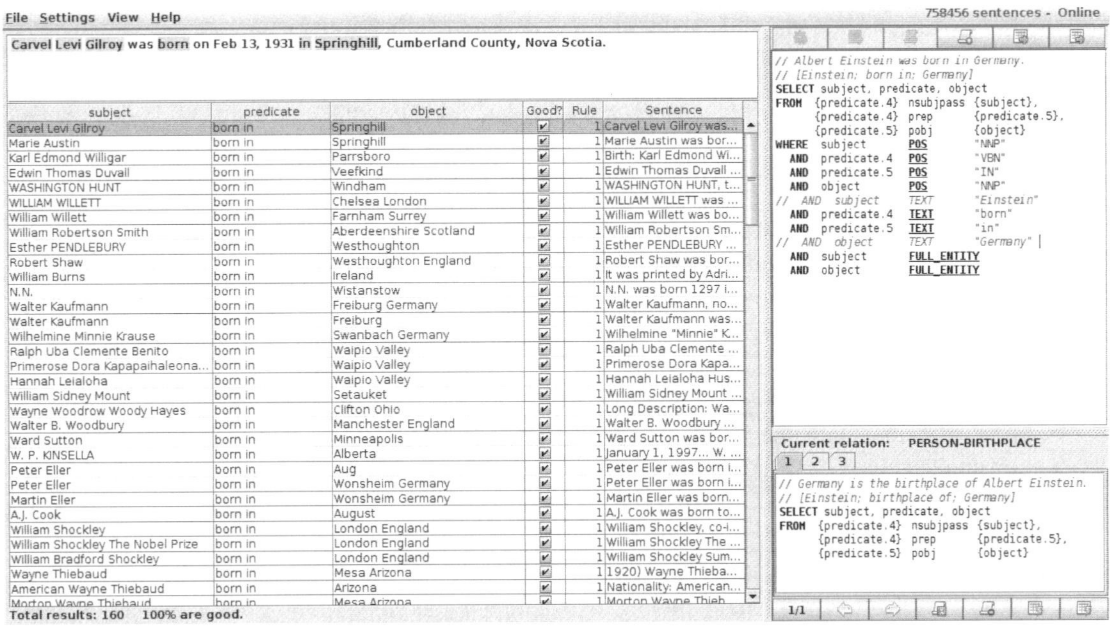

Figure 3: Corpus view of PROPMINER, where extraction rules are modified and evaluated. The center panel is a table that holds the extraction results for the current rule. Users can inspect each extracted triple by clicking on the row. This will display the sentence in which the triple was found.

ation results. This enables additional functionality in subsequent executions of the workflow:

Sentence suggestions. Evaluation results are used to assist the user in finding new sentences that might be relevant to the relation. For example, a user might mark a triple with the subject "C. F. Gauss" and object "Germany" as a correct instance of the PERSONBIRTHPLACE relation during evaluation. PROPMINER uses this information to retrieve all sentences that contain these two entities from its database. These sentences are treated as probable candidates for containing the PERSONBIRTHPLACE relation, because they contain two entities known to be in this relationship. Accordingly, they are suggested to the user upon request.

Conflict resolution. In order to prevent conflicts with existing rules, the entire rule set in the repository is applied to each sentence the workflow is started with. If any existing information extraction rule can be applied, the results of the extraction are presented to the user as annotations in the sentence. If this extraction result is already complete from the point of view of the user, he can proceed to a new sentence. If not, the user can proceed to generate a new rule, or modify existing ones.

3 Previous Work

Previous work on improving the rule creation process for IE systems has mainly focused on assisting users with machine learning techniques, such as pre-generation of regular expressions (Brauer et al., 2011) or pattern suggestions (Li et al., 2011). To improve usability, (Li et al., 2012) present a tool with a wizard-like environment to guide extractor development. While previous work focuses on shallow patterns, the focus of PROPMINER is to help create rules over dependency trees and aid in the exploration of parsed document collections.

4 Evaluation and Outlook

We conducted a preliminary study in which we asked 5 computer scientists unfamiliar with computational linguistics to use the tool to create extractors for the relations PERSONBIRTHPLACE, PERSONMARRIEDTOPERSON and PERSONWONPRIZE. The participants were given a two hour introduction explaining information extraction and subject-predicate-object triples. We introduced them to the five step workflow using the PERSONBIRTHPLACE example also used as running example in this paper, as well as other, more complex examples. The participants were given one hour for each relation and asked to create a rule set for each relation. After the conclusion we interviewed the participants and asked them to rate the usability both for information extraction, as well as for the exploration of dependency tree information.

In the latter category, participants generally gave positive feedback. Participants stated that the interactive nature of the tool helped understanding extraction rules and facilitated exploring information stated in the document collection. 4 out of 5 participants deviated from the suggested workflow and more directly edited rules as they became more comfortable with the tool. All participants consulted information on POS tags and typed dependencies during the process, in order to better understand the rules and query results. Participants suggested adding an explanation function for individual syntactic elements to the tool.

While all users were generally able to create rule sets for each of the relations, two main problems were cited for the creation of extraction rules. The first is a problem in conflict resolution; in some cases, users were not able to discern why a rule gave imperfect extraction results. We reviewed some rules and found that many of these cases stem from faulty dependency parses, which non NLP-experts cannot recognize. At present, we are searching for ways to address this problem.

A second problem were limitations of the rule language: Participants expressed the need for named entity types such as PERSON and LOCATION, which in the prototype were not included at the time of evaluation. However, because of the design of the query language and the underlying graph database, such additional operators can be incorporated easily.

Consequently, current work focuses on extending the range of user studies to gather more suggestions for the query language and the feature set, and integrating additional operators into the system.

5 Demonstration

In this demonstration we show how PROPMINER can be used for creating extractors or exploring the parsed document collection. The hands-on demonstration allows initiate users to execute the workflow presented in this paper, but also enables persons more familiar with syntactic annotation to more directly query the graph database using our query language and feature set.

Acknowledgements

We would like to thank the anonymous reviewers for their helpful comments. Alan Akbik received funding from the European Union's Seventh Framework Programme (FP7/2007-2013) under grant agreement no ICT-2009-4-1 270137 'Scalable Preservation Environments' (SCAPE).

References

Alan Akbik and Alexander Löser. 2012. Kraken: N-ary facts in open information extraction. In *AKBC-WEKEX*, pages 52–56. Association for Computational Linguistics.

Bernd Bohnet. 2010. Very high accuracy and fast dependency parsing is not a contradiction. In *COLING*, pages 89–97. Association for Computational Linguistics.

Falk Brauer, Robert Rieger, Adrian Mocan, and Wojciech M Barczynski. 2011. Enabling information extraction by inference of regular expressions from sample entities. In *CIKM*, pages 1285–1294. ACM.

Jeen Broekstra and Arjohn Kampman. 2003. Serql: a second generation rdf query language. In *Proc. SWAD-Europe Workshop on Semantic Web Storage and Retrieval*, pages 13–14.

Razvan C Bunescu and Raymond J Mooney. 2005. A shortest path dependency kernel for relation extraction. In *EMNLP*, pages 724–731. Association for Computational Linguistics.

Laura Chiticariu, Rajasekar Krishnamurthy, Yunyao Li, Sriram Raghavan, Frederick R Reiss, and Shivakumar Vaithyanathan. 2010. Systemt: an algebraic approach to declarative information extraction. In *ACL*, pages 128–137. Association for Computational Linguistics.

Luciano Del Corro and Rainer Gemulla. Clausie: Clause-based open information extraction. In *WWW (to appear in 2013)*.

AnHai Doan, Jeffrey F Naughton, Raghu Ramakrishnan, Akanksha Baid, Xiaoyong Chai, Fei Chen, Ting Chen, Eric Chu, Pedro DeRose, Byron Gao, et al. 2009. Information extraction challenges in managing unstructured data. *ACM SIGMOD Record*, 37(4):14–20.

Yunyao Li, Vivian Chu, Sebastian Blohm, Huaiyu Zhu, and Howard Ho. 2011. Facilitating pattern discovery for relation extraction with semantic-signature-based clustering. In *CIKM*, pages 1415–1424. ACM.

Yunyao Li, Laura Chiticariu, Huahai Yang, Frederick R Reiss, and Arnaldo Carreno-fuentes. 2012. Wizie: a best practices guided development environment for information extraction. In *Proceedings of the ACL 2012 System Demonstrations*, pages 109–114. Association for Computational Linguistics.

Mausam, Michael Schmitz, Stephen Soderland, Robert Bart, and Oren Etzioni. 2012. Open language learning for information extraction. In *EMNLP-CoNLL*, pages 523–534.

Mike Mintz, Steven Bills, Rion Snow, and Dan Jurafsky. 2009. Distant supervision for relation extraction without labeled data. In *ACL/IJCNLP. Volume 2-Volume 2*, pages 1003–1011. Association for Computational Linguistics.

SEMILAR: The Semantic Similarity Toolkit

Vasile Rus, Mihai Lintean, Rajendra Banjade, Nobal Niraula, and Dan Stefanescu
Department of Computer Science
The University of Memphis
Memphis, TN 38152
{vrus,rbanjade,mclinten,nbnraula,dstfnscu}@memphis.edu

Abstract

We present in this paper SEMILAR, the SEMantic simILARity toolkit. SEMILAR implements a number of algorithms for assessing the semantic similarity between two texts. It is available as a Java library and as a Java standalone ap-plication offering GUI-based access to the implemented semantic similarity methods. Furthermore, it offers facilities for manual se-mantic similarity annotation by experts through its component SEMILAT (a SEMantic simILarity Annotation Tool).

1 Introduction

We present in this paper the design and implementation of SEMILAR, the SEMantic simILARity toolkit. SEMILAR (www.semanticsimilarity.org) includes implementations of a number of algorithms proposed over the last decade or so to address various instances of the general problem of text-to-text semantic similarity. Semantic similarity is an approach to language understanding that is widely used in real applications. It is a practical alternative to the true understanding approach, which is intractable as it requires world knowledge, a yet to-be-solved problem in Artificial Intelligence.

Text A: *York had no problem with MTA's insisting the decision to shift funds had been within its legal rights.*
Text B: *York had no problem with MTA's saying the decision to shift funds was within its powers.*

Given such two texts, the paraphrase identification task is about automatically assessing whether Text A is a paraphrase of, i.e. has the same meaning as, Text B. The example above is a positive instance, meaning that Text A is a paraphrase of Text B and vice versa.

The importance of semantic similarity in Natural Language Processing (NLP) is highlighted by the diversity of datasets and shared task evaluation campaigns (STECs) that have been proposed over the last decade (Dolan, Quirk, and Brockett, 2004; McCarthy & McNamara, 2008; Agirre et al., 2012). These datasets include instances from various applications. Indeed, there is a need to identify and quantify semantic relations between texts in many applications. For instance, paraphrase identification, an instance of the semantic similarity problem, is an important step in a number of applications including Natural Language Generation, Question Answering, and dialogue-based Intelligent Tutoring Systems. In Natural Language Generation, paraphrases are a method to increase diversity of generated text (Iordanskaja et al. 1991). In Question Answering, multiple answers that are paraphrases of each other could be considered as evidence for the correctness of the answer (Ibrahim et al. 2003). In Intelligent Tutoring Sys-tems (Rus et al., 2009; Lintean et al., 2010; Lintean, 2011), paraphrase identification is useful to assess whether students' articulated answers to deep questions (e.g. conceptual physics questions) are similar-to/paraphrases-of ideal answers.

Generally, the problem of semantic similarity between two texts, denoted text A and text B, is defined as quantifying and identifying the presence of semantic relations between the two texts, e.g. to what extent text A has the same meaning as or is a paraphrase of text B (paraphrase relation; Dolan, Quirk, and Brockett, 2004). Other semantic relations that have been investigated systematically in the recent past are entailment, i.e. to what extent text A entails or logically infers text B (Dagan, Glickman, & Magnini, 2004), and elaboration, i.e. is text B is an elaboration of text A? (McCarthy & McNamara, 2008).

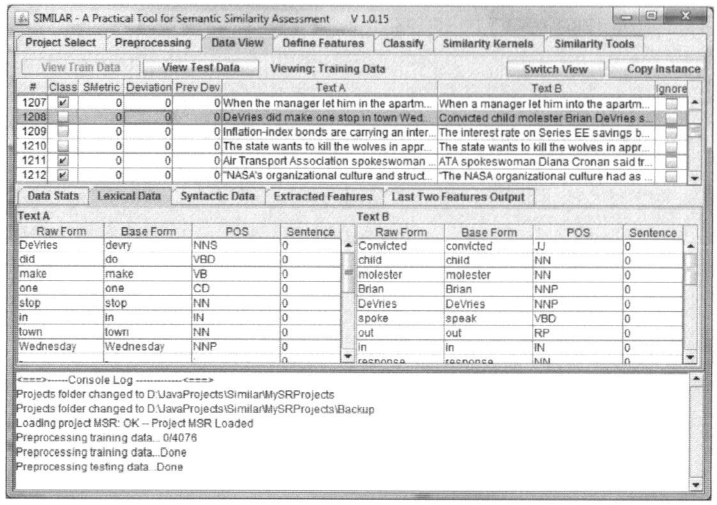

Figure 1. Snapshot of SEMILAR. The Data View tab is shown.

Semantic similarity can be broadly construed between texts of any size. Depending on the granularity of the texts, we can talk about the following fundamental text-to-text similarity problems: word-to-word similarity, phrase-to-phrase similarity, sentence-to-sentence similarity, paragraph-to-paragraph similarity, or document-to-document similarity. Mixed combinations are also possible such as assessing the similarity of a word to a sentence or a sentence to a paragraph. For instance, in summarization it might be useful to assess how well a sentence summarizes an entire paragraph.

2 Motivation

The problem of word-to-word similarity has been extensively studied over the past decades and a word-to-word similarity library (WordNet Similarity) has been developed by Pedersen and colleagues (Pedersen, Patwardhan, & Michelizzi, 2004).

Methods to assess the semantic similarity of larger texts, in particular sentences, have been proposed over the last decade (Corley and Mihalcea, 2005; Fernando & Stevenson, 2008; Rus, Lintean, Graesser, & McNamara 2009). Androutsopoulos & Malakasiotis (2010) compiled a survey of methods for paraphrasing and entailment semantic relation identification at sentence level. Despite all the proposed methods to assess semantic similarity between two texts, no semantic similarity library or toolkit, similar to the WordNet library for word-to-word similarity, exists for larger texts. Given the importance of semantic similarity, there is an acute need for such a library and toolkit. The developed SEMILAR library and toolkit presented here fulfill this need.

In particular, the development of the semantic similarity toolkit SEMILAR has been motivated by the need for an integrated environment that would provide:

- easy access to implementations of various semantic similarity approaches from the same user-friendly interface and/or library.
- easy access to semantic similarity methods that work at different levels of text granularity: word-to-word, sentence-to-sentence, paragraph-to-paragraph, document-to-document, or a combination (SEMILAR integrates word-to-word similarity measures).
- authoring methods for semantic similarity.
- a common environment for that allows systematic and fair comparison of semantic similarity methods.
- facilities to manually annotate texts with semantic similarity relations using a graphical user interface that make such annotations easier for experts (this component is called SEMILAT component - a SEMantic similarity Annotation Tool).

SEMILAR is thus a one-stop-shop for investigating, annotating, and authoring methods for the semantic similarity of texts of any level of granularity.

3 SEMILAR: The Semantic Similarity Toolkit

The authors of the SEMILAR toolkit (see Figure 1) have been involved in assessing the semantic similarity of texts for more than a decade. During this time, they have conducted a careful requirements analysis for an integrated software toolkit that would integrate various methods for semantic similarity assessment. The result of this effort is the prototype presented here. We briefly present the components of SEMILAR next and then describe in more detail the core component of SEMILAR, i.e. the set of semantic similarity methods that are currently available. It should be noted that we are continuously adding new semantic similarity methods and features to SEMILAR.

The SEMILAR toolkit includes the following components: project management; data view-browsing-visualization; preprocessing (e.g., collocation identification, part-of-speech tagging, phrase or dependency parsing, etc.), semantic similarity methods (word-level and sentence-level), classification components for qualitative decision making with respect to textual semantic relations (naïve Bayes, Decision Trees, Support Vector Machines, and Neural Network), kernel-based methods (sequence kernels, word sequence kernels, and tree kernels; as of this writing, we are still implementing several other tree kernel methods); debugging and testing facilities for model selection; and annotation components (allows domain expert to manually annotate texts with semantic relations using GUI-based facilities; Rus et al., 2012). For space reasons, we only detail next the main algorithms in the core component, i.e. the major text-to-text similarity algorithms currently available in SEMILAR.

4 The Semantic Similarity Methods Available in SEMILAR

The core component of SEMILAR is a set of text-to-text semantic similarity methods. We have implemented methods that handle both unidirectional similarity measures as well as bidirectional similarity measures. For instance, the semantic relation of entailment between two texts is unidirectional (a text T logically entails a hypothesis text H but H does not entail T) while the paraphrase relation is bidirectional (text A has same meaning as text B and vice versa).

Lexical Overlap. Given two texts, the simplest method to assess their semantic similarity is to compute lexical overlap, i.e. how many words they have in common. There are many lexical overlap variations. Indeed, a closer look at lexical overlap reveals a number of parameters that turns the simple lexical overlap problem into a large space of possibilities. The parameters include preprocessing options (collocation detection, punctuation, stopword removal, etc.), filtering options (all words, content words, etc.), weighting schemes (global vs. local weighting, binary weighting, etc.), and normalization factors (largest text, weighted average, etc.). A total of 3,456 variants of lexical overlap can be generated by different parameter settings in SEMILAR. Lintean (2011) has shown that performance on lexical overlap methods on the tasks of paraphrase identification and textual entailment tasks can vary significantly depending on the selected parameters. Some lexical overlap variations lead to performance results rivaling more sophisticated, state-of-the-art methods.

It should be noted that the overlap category of methods can be extended to include N-gram overlap methods (see the N-gram overlap methods proposed by the Machine Translation community such as BLEU and METEOR). SEMILAR offers bigram and unigram overlap methods including the BLEU and METEOR scores.

A natural approach to text-to-text similarity methods is to rely on word-to-word similarity measures. Many of the methods presented next compute the similarity of larger texts using individual word similarities.

Mihalcea, Corley, & Strappavara (2006; MCS) proposed a *greedy* method based on word-to-word similarity measures. For each word in text A (or B) the maximum similarity score to any word in the other text B (or A) is used. An idf-weighted average is then computed as shown in the equation below.

$$sim(T1,T2) = \frac{1}{2}\left(\frac{\sum_{w\in\{T_1\}} \max\{Sim(w,T_2) * idf(w)\}}{\sum_{w\in\{T_1\}} idf(w)} + \frac{\sum_{w\in\{T_2\}} \max\{Sim(w,T_1) * idf(w)\}}{\sum_{w\in\{T_2\}} idf(w)}\right)$$

The word-to-word similarity function *sim(w, T)* in the equation above can be instantiated to any word-to-word similarity measure (e.g. WordNet similarities or Latent Semantic Analysis). The vast majority of word-to-word similarity measures that rely on WordNet are concept-to-concept measures and to be able to use them one must map words in the input texts onto concepts in WordNet, i.e. word sense disambiguation (WSD) is needed. As of this writing, SEMILAR addresses the issue in two simple ways: (1) selecting the most frequent sense for each word, which is sense #1 in WordNet, and (2) using all the senses for each word and then take the maximum (or average) of the relatedness scores for each pair of word senses. We label the former method as ONE (sense one), whereas the latter is labeled as ALL-MAX or ALL-AVG (all senses maximum score or all senses average score, respectively). Furthermore, most WordNet-based measures only work within a part-of-speech category, e.g. only between nouns.

Other types of word-to-word measures, such as those based on Latent Semantic Analysis or Latent Dirichlet Allocation, do not have a word-sense disambiguation challenge.

Rus and Lintean (2012; Rus-Lintean-Optimal Matching or ROM) proposed an *optimal* solution for text-to-text similarity based on word-to-word similarity measures. The optimal lexical matching is based on the optimal assignment problem, a fundamental combinatorial optimization problem which consists of finding a maximum weight matching in a weighted bipartite graph.

Given a weighted complete bipartite graph $G = X \cup Y; X \times Y)$, where edge xy has weight $w(xy)$, the optimal assignment problem is to find a matching M from X to Y with maximum weight.

A typical application is about assigning a group of workers, e.g. words in text A in our case, to a set of jobs (words in text B in our case) based on the expertise level, measured by $w(xy)$, of each worker at each job. By adding dummy workers or jobs we may assume that X and Y have the same size, *n*, and can be viewed as $X = \{x_1, x_2, \dots, x_n\}$ and $Y = \{y_1, y_2, \dots, y_n\}$. In the semantic similarity case, the weight $w(xy)$ is the word-to-word similarity between a word x in text A and a word y in text B.

The assignment problem can also be stated as finding a permutation π of {1, 2, 3, … , n} for which $\sum_{i=1}^{n} w(x_i y_{\pi(i)})$ is maximum. Such an assignment is called optimum assignment. The Kuhn-Munkres algorithm (Kuhn, 1955) can find a solution to the optimum assignment problem in polynomial time.

Rus and colleagues (Rus et al., 2009; Rus & Graesser, 2006; Rus-Syntax-Negation or RSN) used a lexical overlap component combined with syntactic overlap and negation handling to compute an unidirectional subsumption score between two sentences, T (Text) and H (Hypothesis), in entailment recognition and student input assessment in Intelligent Tutoring Systems. Each text is regarded as a graph with words as nodes/vertices and syntactic dependencies as edges. The subsumption score reflects how much a text is subsumed or contained by another. The equation below provides the overall subsumption score, which can be averaged both ways to compute a similarity score, as opposed to just the subsumption score, between the two texts.

$$subsump(T, H) = (\alpha \times \frac{\sum_{V_h \in H_v} \max_{V_t \in T_v} match(V_h, V_t)}{|V_h|} + \beta \times \frac{\sum_{E_h \in H_e} \max_{E_t \in T_e} match(E_h, E_t)}{|E_h|}) \times \frac{(1 + (-1)^{\#neg\_rel})}{2}$$

The lexical component can be used by itself (given a weight of 1 with the syntactic component given a weight of 0) in which case the similarity between the two texts is just a compositional extension of word-to-word similarity measures. The *match* function in the equation can be any word-to-word similarity measure including simple word match, WordNet similarity measures, LSA, or LDA-based similarity measures.

Fernando and Stevenson (FST; 2008) proposed a method in which similarities among all pairs of words are taken into account for computing the similarity of two texts. Each text is represented as a binary vector (1 – the word occurs in the text; 0 – the word does not occur in the text). They use a similarity matrix operator W that contains word-to-word similarities between any two words.

$$sim(\vec{a}, \vec{b}) = \frac{\vec{a} W \vec{b}^T}{|\vec{a}||\vec{b}|}$$

Each element w_{ij} represents the word-level semantic similarity between word a_i in text A and word b_j in text B. Any word-to-word semantic similarity measure can be used.

Lintean and Rus (2010; weighted-LSA or wLSA) extensively studied methods for semantic similarity based on Latent Semantic Analysis (LSA; Landauer et al., 2006). LSA represents words as vectors in a 300-500 dimensional LSA space. An LSA vector for larger texts can be derived by vector algebra, e.g. by summing up the individual words' vectors. The similarity of two texts A and B can be computed using the cosine (normalized dot product) of their LSA vectors. Alternatively, the individual word vectors can be combined through weighted sums. Lintean and Rus (2010) experimented with a combination of 3 local weights and 3 global weights. All these versions of LSA-based text-to-text similarity measures are available in SEMILAR.

SEMILAR also includes a set of similarity measures based on the unsupervised method **Latent Dirichlet Allocation (LDA; Blei, Ng, & Jordnan, 2003; Rus, Banjade, & Niraula, 2013).** LDA is a probabilistic generative model in which documents are viewed as distributions over a set of topics (θ_d - text d's distribution over topics) and topics are distributions over words (φ_t – topic t's distribution over words). That is, each word in a document is generated from a distribution over words that is specific to each topic.

A first LDA-based semantic similarity measure among words would then be defined as a dot-product between the corresponding vectors representing the contributions of each word to a topic ($\varphi_t(w)$ – represents the probability of word w in topic t). It should be noted that the contributions of each word to the topics does not constitute a distribution, i.e. the sum of contributions is not 1. Assuming the number of topics T, then a simple word-to-word measure is defined by the formula below.

$$LDA-w2w(w,v)=\sum_{t=1}^{T}\varphi_t(w)\varphi_t(v)$$

More global text-to-text similarity measures could be defined in several ways as detailed next.

Because in LDA a document is a distribution over topics, the similarity of two texts needs to be computed in terms of similarity of distributions. The Kullback-Leibler (KL) divergence defines a distance, or how dissimilar, two distributions p and q are as in the formula below.

$$KL(p,q)=\sum_{i=1}^{T}p_i\log\frac{p_i}{q_i}$$

If we replace p with θ_d (text/document d's distribution over topics) and q with θ_c (text/document c's distribution over topics) we obtain the KL distance between two documents (documents d and c in our example). The KL distance has two major problems. In case q_i is zero KL is not defined. Then, KL is not symmetric. The Information Radius measure (IR) solves these problems by considering the average of p_i and q_i as below. Also, the IR can be transformed into a symmetric similarity measure as in the following (Dagan, Lee, & Pereira, 1997):

$$SIM(p,q)=10^{-\delta IR(c,d)}$$

The Hellinger and Manhattan distances between two distributions are two other options that avoid the shortcomings of the KL distance. Both are options are implemented in SEMILAR.

LDA similarity measures between two documents or texts c and d can also include similarity of topics. That is, the text-to-text similarity is obtained multiplying the similarities between the distribution over topics (θ_d and θ_c) and distribution over words (φ_{t1} and φ_{t2}). The similarity of topics can be computed using the same methods illustrated above as the topics are distributions over words (for all the details see Rus, Banjade, & Niraula, 2013).

The last semantic similarity method presented in this paper is based on **the Quadratic Assignment Problem (QAP).** The QAP method aims at finding an optimal assignment from words in text A to words in text B, based on individual word-to-word similarity measures, while simultaneously maximizing the match between the syntactic dependencies of the words.

The Koopmans-Beckmann (1957) formulation of the QAP problem best fits this purpose. The goal of the original QAP formulation, in the domain of economic activity, was to minimize the objective function QAP shown below where matrix F describes the flow between any two facilities, matrix D indicates the distances between locations, and matrix B provides the cost of locating facilities to specific locations. F, D, and B are symmetric and non-negative.

$$\min QAP(F,D,B)=\sum_{i=1}^{n}\sum_{j=1}^{n}f_{i,j}d_{\pi(i)\pi(j)}+\sum_{i=1}^{n}b_{i,\pi(i)}$$

The $f_{i,j}$ term denotes the flow between facilities i and j which are placed at locations $\pi(i)$ and $\pi(j)$, respectively. The distance between these locations is $d_{\pi(i)\pi(j)}$. In our case, F and D describe dependencies between words in one sentence while B captures the word-to-word similarity between words in opposite sentences. Also, we have weighted each term in the above formulation and instead of minimizing the sum we are maximizing it resulting in the formulation below.

$$\max QAP(F,D,B)=\alpha\sum_{i=1}^{n}\sum_{j=1}^{n}f_{i,j}d_{\pi(i)\pi(j)}+(1-\alpha)\sum_{i=1}^{n}b_{i,\pi(i)}$$

5 Discussion and Conclusions

The above methods were experimented with on various datasets for paraphrase, entailment, and elaboration. For paraphrase identification, the QAP method provides best accuracy results (=77.6%) on the test subset of the Microsoft Research Paraphrase corpus, one of the largest paraphrase datasets.

Due to space constraints, we have not described all the features available in SEMILAR. For a complete list of features, latest news, references, and updates of the SEMILAR toolkit along with downloadable resources including software and data files, the reader can visit this link: www.semanticsimilarity.org.

Acknowledgments

This research was supported in part by Institute for Education Sciences under award R305A100875. Any opinions, findings, and conclusions or recommendations expressed in this material are solely the authors' and do not necessarily reflect the views of the sponsoring agency.

References

Androutsopoulos, I. & Malakasiotis, P. 2010. A survey of paraphrasing and textual entailment methods. Journal of Artificial Intelligence Research, 38:135-187.

Agirre, E., Cer, D., Diab, M., & Gonzalez-Agirre, A. (2012). SemEval-2012 Task 6: A Pilot on Semantic Textual Similarity, First Joint Conference on Lexical and Computational Semantics (*SEM), Montreal, Canada, June 7-8, 2012.

Blei, D.M., Ng, A.Y., & Jordan, M.I. 2003. Latent dirichlet allocation, The Journal of Machine Learning Research 3, 993-1022.

Corley, C., & Mihalcea, R. (2005). Measuring the Semantic Similarity of Texts. In Proceedings of the ACL Workshop on Empirical Modeling of Semantic Equivalence and Entailment. Ann Arbor, MI.

Dagan, I., Glickman, O., & Magnini, B. (2004). The PASCAL Recognising textual entailment Challenge. In Quinorero-Candela, J.; Dagan, I.; Magnini, B.; d'Alche-Buc, F. (Eds.), *Machine Learning Challenges.* Lecture Notes in Computer Science, Vol. 3944, pp. 177-190, Springer, 2006.

Dolan, B., Quirk, C., & Brockett, C. (2004). Unsupervised construction of large paraphrase corpora: Exploiting massively parallel news sources. In *Proceedings of the 20th International Conference on Computational Linguistics (COLING-2004)*, Geneva, Switzerland.

Fernando, S. & Stevenson, M. (2008). A semantic similarity approach to paraphrase detection, *Computational Linguistics UK (CLUK 2008) 11th Annual Research Colloquium.*

Lintean, M., Moldovan, C., Rus, V., & McNamara D. (2010). The Role of Local and Global Weighting in Assessing the Semantic Similarity of Texts Using Latent Semantic Analysis. Proceedings of the 23rd International Florida Artificial Intelligence Research Society Conference. Daytona Beach, FL.

Lintean, M. (2011). Measuring Semantic Similarity: Representations and Methods, PhD Thesis, Department of Computer Science, The University of Memphis, 2011.

Ibrahim, A., Katz, B., & Lin, J. (2003). Extracting structural paraphrases from aligned monolingual corpora In Proceedings of the Second International Workshop on Paraphrasing, (ACL 2003).

Iordanskaja, L., Kittredge, R., & Polgere, A. (1991). Natural Language Generation in Artificial Intelligence and Computational Linguistics. *Lexical selection and paraphrase in a meaning-text generation model*, Kluwer Academic.

McCarthy, P.M. & McNamara, D.S. (2008). User-Language Paraphrase Corpus Challenge https://umdrive.memphis.edu/pmmccrth/public/ParaphraseCorpus/Paraphrase site.htm. Retrieved 2/20/2010 online, 2009.

Pedersen, T., Patwardhan, S., & Michelizzi, J. (2004). WordNet::Similarity - Measuring the Relatedness of Concepts, In the Proceedings of the Nineteenth National Conference on Artificial Intelligence (AAAI-04), pp. 1024-1025, July 25-29, 2004, San Jose, CA (Intelligent Systems Demonstration).

Rus, V., Lintean M., Graesser, A.C., & McNamara, D.S. (2009). Assessing Student Paraphrases Using Lexical Semantics and Word Weighting. In Proceedings of the 14th International Conference on Artificial Intelligence in Education, Brighton, UK.

Rus, V., Lintean, M., Moldovan, C., Baggett, W., Niraula, N., Morgan, B. (2012). The SIMILAR Corpus: A Resource to Foster the Qualitative Understanding of Semantic Similarity of Texts, In Semantic Relations II: Enhancing Resources and Applications, The 8th Language Resources and Evaluation Conference (LREC 2012), May 23-25, Instanbul, Turkey.

Rus, V., Banjade, R., & Niraula, N. (2013). Similarity Measures based on Latent Dirichlet Allocation, The 14th International Conference on Intelligent Text Procesing and Computational Linguistics, March 24-30, 2013, Samos, Greece.

Tag2Blog: Narrative Generation from Satellite Tag Data

Kapila Ponnamperuma **Advaith Siddharthan** **Cheng Zeng** **Chris Mellish**
Department of Computing Science
University of Aberdeen
{k.ponnamperuma, advaith, c.zeng, c.mellish}@abdn.ac.uk

René van der Wal
Aberdeen Centre for Environmental Sustainability (ACES)
University of Aberdeen
r.vanderwal@abdn.ac.uk

Abstract

The aim of the Tag2Blog system is to bring satellite tagged wild animals "to life" through narratives that place their movements in an ecological context. Our motivation is to use such automatically generated texts to enhance public engagement with a specific species reintroduction programme, although the protocols developed here can be applied to any animal or other movement study that involves signal data from tags. We are working with one of the largest nature conservation charities in Europe in this regard, focusing on a single species, the red kite. We describe a system that interprets a sequence of locational fixes obtained from a satellite tagged individual, and constructs a story around its use of the landscape.

1 Introduction

We present a system, Tag2Blog, that uses Natural Language Generation (NLG) in bringing up-to-date information about wild animals in their natural environment to nature enthusiasts. We focus on the reintroduction of the red kite to the UK. The red kite, a member of the raptor family, has been persecuted to near extinction in the UK. Since 1989, efforts have been underway to reintroduce the species across the UK with mixed success. Where less successful, illegal activities of humans are partly responsible (Smart et al., 2010).

We are working with the RSPB[1], one of the largest nature conservation charities in Europe, around a reintroduction site where the species struggles to get re-established. We propose to use NLG for public engagement around a small number of satellite tagged individuals. The nature conservation goal is to create a positive perception of the species through informative blogs based on the movements of individual birds. The NLG goal is the generation of these blogs; specifically, to put individual locations of a bird into an ecological context. This paper describes the design and implementation of the system. We are also carrying out concurrent ecological research on red kites that will further inform the NLG component.

2 Related work

There is increasing realisation of the potential of digital approaches, including the use of websites and social media, to increase public engagement with nature conservation issues. For instance, in the UK, the Open Air Laboratories (OPAL) network[2] is a large initiative led by Imperial College, which aims to create and inspire a new generation of nature-lovers by getting people to explore their local environment (Silvertown, 2009). Such initiatives are typically labour and time intensive, and require continual effort to maintain interest through the creation of new content. To date, initiatives such as OPAL have largely focused on biological recording as a public engagement tool, thereby using - for example - standard social networking sites to prompt the collection of species distributional data (Stafford et al., 2010), or web interfaces that use NLG to provide feedback to citizen scientists (Blake et al., 2012).

We propose something altogether different: the use of sensor data as a starting point for public engagement through the delivery of self-updating automatically generated blogs. This application provides fresh challenges for the field of NLG, where typically systems are designed to offer decision support in the workplace (Goldberg et al., 1994; Portet et al., 2009). Decision support requires accuracy and clarity first and foremost. We, on the other hand, aim to generate texts that are suffi-

[1]http://www.rspb.org.uk

[2]http://www.opalexplorenature.org

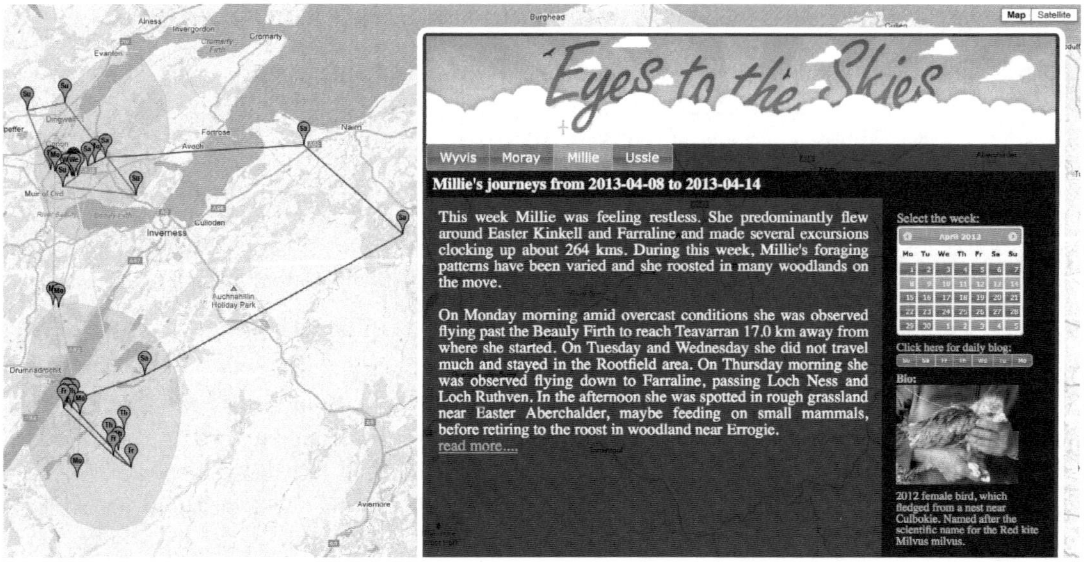

Figure 1: Screenshot of the Tag2Blog system.

ciently fluent and engaging for the general public to be attracted and informed by.

This does not mean that there is no precedent to our work. There are a handful of NLG systems that offer "info-tainment", such as Dial Your Disc (Van Deemter and Odijk, 1997) and Ilex (O'Donnell et al., 2001). Systems that generate sports commentary are particularly relevant, as they contextualise objects spatially and temporally and track the movement of objects as part of the game analysis (André et al., 2000). Rhodes et al. (2010) further explore dramatic narrative generation, to bring emotional content into the texts.

We subscribe to the same goals, adding to these the requirement that texts should be easy to read. For instance, ecological concepts (such as site fidelity) could be communicated by explicitly defining them. However, we would prefer these to be inferred from more engaging narratives, such as that in Fig. 1, which is a screenshot showing sample text generated by our system.

3 System architecture

The aim of the Tag2Blog system is to bring satellite tagged individuals of a species (e.g., the red kite) "to life" by constructing narratives describing their movements. In this regard, we need to interpret a sequence of locational fixes obtained from a tagged bird, and construct a story around its use of the landscape. To facilitate ecological interpretations, it is important to first supplement the locational data with other spatially relevant data; for example, landscape features and

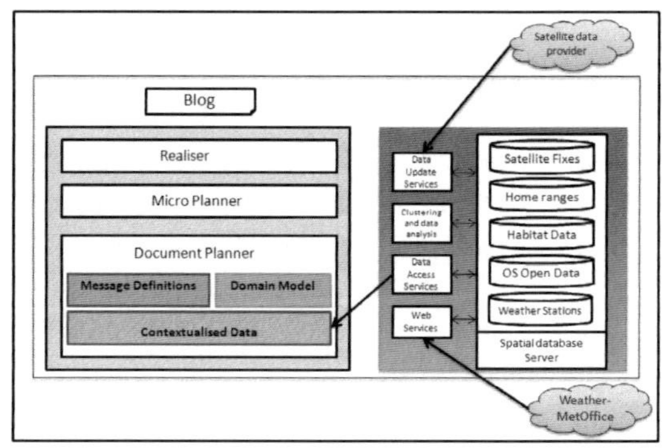

Figure 2: Architecture of the Tag2Blog system

weather. The Tag2Blog system therefore consists of two modules: Data Acquisition and Contextualisation (DAC), described in §3.1 and Natural Language Generation (NLG), described in §3.2.

3.1 Data acquisition and contextualisation

This module is composed of a spatial database and a set of services for updating and accessing data. We start with the information obtained from the satellite tags on the birds, which provide time-stamped locational information. This is augmented with data of associated habitat types, terrain features, place names and weather conditions. Our database thus stores rich information about the locations visited, acquired from a variety of sources summarised below:

Habitats: Land cover maps[3] are used to associate different habitat types (e.g., coniferous woodland, moorland, improved grassland, etc.) to

[3] http://www.ceh.ac.uk

locational fixes.

Terrain features: Ordnance Survey Vector Map data[4] are used to identify features (e.g., lochs, rivers, roads, etc.) in the vicinity of the fixes.

Names: Ordnance Survey Gazetteer data is used to obtain place and feature names.

Weather: The closest weather station to the fix is queried for historical weather data from the time of the fix, using an external web service.

The following services were implemented to update and enrich red kite location fixes:

Data update service: The satellite tags on the red kites have been programmed to transmit up to 5 GPS fixes per day, usually every two hours between 8am and 6pm[5]. The satellite data provider sends a daily email, using which we update the spatial database with red kite locations automatically. We also provide the conservation charity with a user interface, to allow them to censor ecologically sensitive locations (such as nesting sites), as and when required.

Data analysis service: Location data of each individual bird is periodically clustered (i.e., weekly) to identify their temporary *home ranges*. These clusters are spatially represented as ellipses and are stored in the database so that new fixes can be compared against known locational patterns.

Weather web service client: Weather data relevant to the time and location of each red kite locational fix is obtained on demand from a met office web service by providing the date, time, and the closest weather station.

Data access service: Each satellite fix is associated with a Java object (GeoLocation), which encapsulates the enriched data (habitats, place names, features, weather, etc.) for that location. Apart from individual locations, overall fight parameters such as distance from geographic features, displacement from or presence within known home ranges, are also computed and encapsulated into a Java object. These objects are generated on demand and passed onto the NLG module, described next.

3.2 Natural language generation module

The Tag2Blog system follows the NLG architecture proposed by Reiter and Dale (2000) and is composed of three components: a document planner (§3.2.2), a microplanner (§3.2.3) and a surface realiser (§3.2.4). The document planner utilises a domain model (§3.2.1) to populate and order message definitions, which are in turn passed on to the microplanner for creating sentence specifications. The surface realiser then generates text from these sentence.specifications.

3.2.1 Domain model and data analysis

The enriched data, as described above, be used as such to generate narratives of journeys. However in order to make these narratives insightful, an ecological interpretation is needed, and kite behaviours must also be included in the domain model. Siddharthan et al. (2012) has identified key behaviours that can be fruitfully communicated through such narratives. We broadly categorise these behaviours into:

- Site fidelity and exploratory behaviour
- Feeding and roosting behaviour
- Social behaviour (associations with other red kites)

A domain model was developed to infer likely kite behaviours from the enriched data. To build the domain model, we used explicit and implicit knowledge elicitation methods, such as data analysis and interviews, annotations of NLG produced blogs by ecologists, and analysis of hand-written blogs by ecologists from source data.

Site fidelity and exploratory behaviour: Historical location data is used to identify clusters (temporary home ranges) for each bird using the ADEHABITATHR[6] package (Calenge, 2006). In order to describe the overall movement pattern during the period, spatial data analysis is carried out and parameters, such as total distance travelled, displacement from clusters, percentage of fixes within each cluster, are calculated. These parameters are then used to identify the overall movement pattern. Fig. 3 shows three such patterns: Stationary, Short circular trip and Long distance movement.

Feeding and roosting behaviours: After conducting structured interviews with ecologists and analysing blogs written by ecologists, a set of rules were created to identify different feeding and roosting behaviours. Likely foraging patterns were defined on the basis of habitat type, season,

[4] http://www.ordnancesurvey.co.uk

[5] The satellite tags are solar powered, and only have power to provide a single fix per day in the winter months.

[6] http://cran.rstudio.com/web/packages/adehabitatHR

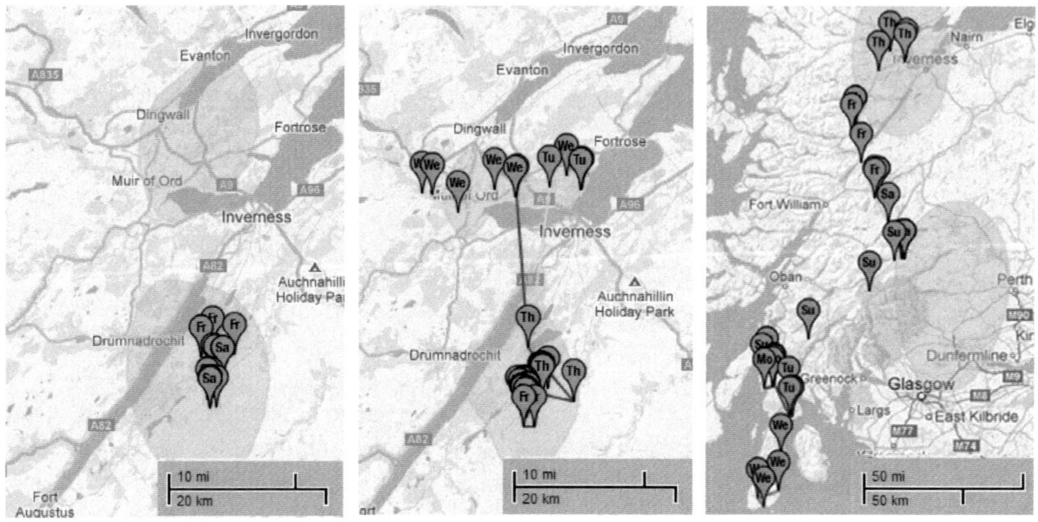

(a) (b) (c)

Figure 3: Movement patterns demonstrated in different weeks by different birds: (a) Stationary, staying within the temporary home range, (b) Short circular trip, moving out and returning to the temporary home range, and (c) Long distance movement, ending in a different location. The orange areas represent clusters of locations of the red kite from historical data that model temporary home ranges for the bird.

time of the day and weather conditions. The following extract from a blog written by an ecologist shows how experts can infer a behaviour from data. Note that it is acceptable in our application for such behaviours to be speculative, as long as they have a basis in kite ecology, and are plausible given the data.

> "Early that evening she was seen in farmland near Torness. Here, the rain must have brought up earthworms to the surface snacks well worth catching!"

From this text, we inferred the following rule:

> ***Rule: Feeding on Earthworms***
> IF it previously rained AND habitat is farm land, THEN it is likely that the red kite is feeding on earthworms.

We have expressed a range of such behaviours as JBoss[7] rules.

Social behaviours: Red kites being social birds, there are many social interactions that could be inferred from the type of data we brought together. Associations between red kites are typically inferred by analysing relative locations of different red kites. However, there is one specific behaviour, communal roosting, where a large group of red kites sleeps together in woodland during the winter months, for which we make use of our knowledge of known communal roost locations; i.e., local knowledge provided by ecologists.

[7]http://www.jboss.org/drools

3.2.2 Document planner

The document planner carries out content determination and document structuring.

Content determination: There are several types of message definitions, implemented as Java classes, that correspond to different narrative descriptions (flying, feeding, etc.). The message generator infers possible behaviours (feeding, roosting, exploring, etc.) using the domain model and then selects one or more based on content determination rules. For example, the message generator might infer possible behaviours such as feeding and exploring from the analyses described above in §3.2.1. However, the content determination rules would prioritise exploring behaviours over feeding (due to their rarity) and hence generate a EXPLORINGMESSAGE, which contains the information required to generate a description of the exploration journey. Similarly, corresponding messages would be generated for other flying, feeding, and social behaviours.

Document structuring: Our weekly blogs contain an introductory paragraph, which captures the overall movement pattern for the week, followed by a more detailed paragraph, which describes interesting behaviours during that week. Each paragraph is internally represented as a schema, which also orders the messages into a document plan.

3.2.3 Microplanner

The document plan generated at the previous stage is passed on to the microplanner for creating text specifications. This includes phrase specifications and their aggregation into sentences. Clauses are combined using discourse cues to express different discourse relations, such as concession, comparison and explanation.

3.2.4 Surface realiser

The role of the surface realiser is to convert the text specification received from the microplanner into text that the user can read and understand. This includes linguistic realisation (converting the sentence specifications into sentences) and structural realisation (structuring the sentences inside the document). Both the linguistic and structural realisations are performed by using functionalities provided by the SIMPLENLG realiser library (Gatt and Reiter, 2009).

4 Utility of blogs in this domain

Until recently, our partner charity was publishing hand-written blogs based on the journeys of these satellite tagged red kites. They have had to close down the site due to resource constraints: Such blogs are difficult, monotonous and time consuming to produce by hand. Tag2Blog will allow the charity to restart this form of public engagement.

We have earlier studied the use of ecological blogs based on satellite tag data (Siddharthan et al., 2012). Using hand-written blogs in a toy domain, we found that readers were willing to anthromorphise the bird, and generally formed a positive perception of it. Additionally, users were able to recall ecological insights communicated in the blog, demonstrating that such blogs are informative as well.

In this paper, we restrict ourselves to reporting a very preliminary evaluation of the quality of the computer generated blogs. We compared three blogs produced from the same data (the movements of one individual red kite during one week):

a) A computer generated blog of a journey, produced without using any domain knowledge as described in §3.2.1, and merely describing spatial movements of the red kite over time.

b) A computer generated blog of a journey with ecological insights, as described in §3.2.1. This is the production version used in Fig. 1.

c) Version (a), which has been post-edited by an ecologist to introduce ecological insights into the narrative. The ecologist was give access to a table containing habitat, terrain and weather information for each satellite fix.

Tab. 1 shows samples from the three versions. All three versions were shown to five human judges, without indication of provenance. They were asked to rate each blog on a scale of 1 (low) to 5 (high) for how readable, informative, engaging and ecologically sound they considered the texts. They were also asked to rate the relevance of each blog to different age groups (primary school children, secondary school children and adults).

We used as judges, a social scientist specialised in human–nature interactions, a public engagement officer at our University who interacts with local schools on a regular basis, a secondary school English teacher, and two school students, aged 14 and 16. Our goal was to obtain a diversity of opinion to inform system design.

Tab. 2 shows the ratings of our five evaluators for different aspects of each blog. The averages show that in most aspects, version (b) is rated higher than version (a) and, rather expectedly, the human edited/annotated version (c) is rated the highest. But, note that the two school students rated the automatically generated blogs highly, and that both felt that version (b) was the best suited for secondary schools. The public engagement officer rated (b) as less readable, and less relevant to schools. She specifically highlighted the use of terminology without introduction (e.g., "roost" and "foraging") as an issue.

Our focus will now be on improving the language, to address some of the readability and engagingness concerns.

5 Conclusions and Future Work

We have presented an NLG system that can generate ecologically informative and engaging narratives of animal (red kite) movements. Our initial evaluations have shown encouraging results and further evaluations are now planned. The system can be accessed through http://redkite.abdn.ac.uk/blog/.

Acknowledgements

This research is supported by an award made by the RCUK Digital Economy programme to the dot.rural Digital Economy Hub (ref. EP/G066051/1). We also thank our partner organisation, the RSPB (with special thanks to Stuart Benn), who manage the reintroduction project.

Text	First four sentences from each blog
(a)	This week, Millie did not travel far, but was actively exploring a small area. During this week, Millie has been observed on various habitats. However, except Thursday she chose to spend the night at the same woodland near Torness. No doubt Millie was not alone this week as kites Moray and Beauly were also observed often in the vicinity.
(b)	This week, Millie did not travel far, but was actively exploring a small area mainly within her home range. During this week, Millie's foraging patterns have been varied. However, except Thursday she chose to roost in the same woodland near Torness. No doubt Millie had a quite social week as kites Moray and Beauly were also observed often in the vicinity.
(c)	This week Millie did not travel far but was actively exploring a small area north-east of Loch Ness. Friday morning Millie left the woodland where she spend the night to fly to Loch Ruthven amid heavy rain. The poor visibility may have driven her to fly low when searching for food along the water sides. Early that evening she was seen in farmland near Torness.

Table 1: Excerpts of texts in each experimental condition

	Sociologist			Pub. Eng.			Teacher			16yo			14yo			Average		
Blog	a	b	c	a	b	c	a	b	c	a	b	c	a	b	c	a	b	c
Readability	3	3	5	4	3	5	3	2	4	3	4	4	3	4	4	3.2	3.2	4.4
Informativeness	3	4	5	5	5	5	2	1	2	3	4	5	3	3	4	3.2	3.4	4.4
Engagingness	2	4	5	3	3	4	2	1	3	3	4	5	2	4	4	2.4	3.2	4.2
Ecological soundness	4	3	3	4	4	4	5	5	5	3	4	4	3	4	3	3.8	4.0	3.8
Relevance to:																		
Primary Schools	3	4	5	3	2	4	4	4	4	4	4	3	3	2	3	3.4	3.2	3.8
Secondary Schools	3	4	5	4	3	4	2	2	2	4	5	3	3	4	3	3.2	3.6	3.4
Adults	3	4	5	4	4	4	3	1	3	3	4	5	3	4	4	3.2	3.4	4.2

Table 2: Evaluation of Blogs by Experts

References

E. André, K. Binsted, K. Tanaka-Ishii, S. Luke, G. Herzog, and T. Rist. 2000. Three robocup simulation league commentator systems. *AI Magazine*, 21(1):57.

S. Blake, A. Siddharthan, H. Nguyen, N. Sharma, A. Robinson, E. O Mahony, B. Darvill, C. Mellish, and R. van der Wal. 2012. Natural language generation for nature conservation: Automating feedback to help volunteers identify bumblebee species. In *Proceedings of the 24th International Conference on Computational Linguistics (COLING 2012)*, pages 311–324.

C. Calenge. 2006. The package adehabitat for the r software: tool for the analysis of space and habitat use by animals. *Ecological Modelling*, 197:1035.

A. Gatt and E. Reiter. 2009. SimpleNLG: A realisation engine for practical applications. In *Proceedings of the 112th European Workshop on Natural Language Generation (ENLG)*, pages 90–93.

E. Goldberg, N. Driedger, and R.I. Kittredge. 1994. Using natural-language processing to produce weather forecasts. *IEEE Expert*, 9(2):45–53.

M. O'Donnell, C. Mellish, J. Oberlander, and A. Knott. 2001. Ilex: an architecture for a dynamic hypertext generation system. *Natural Language Engineering*, 7(3):225–250.

F. Portet, E. Reiter, A. Gatt, J. Hunter, S. Sripada, Y. Freer, and C. Sykes. 2009. Automatic generation of textual summaries from neonatal intensive care data. *Artificial Intelligence*, 173(7-8):789–816.

E. Reiter and R. Dale. 2000. *Building Natural Language Generation Systems*. Cambridge University Press.

M. Rhodes, S. Coupland, and T. Cruickshank. 2010. Enhancing real-time sports commentary generation with dramatic narrative devices. In *Proceedings of the Third Joint Conference on Interactive Digital Storytelling, ICIDS 2010*, Lecture Notes in Computer Science, pages 111–116. Springer.

A. Siddharthan, M. Green, K. van Deemter, C. Mellish, and R. van der Wal. 2012. Blogging birds: Generating narratives about reintroduced species to promote public engagement. In *Proceedings of the Seventh International Natural Language Generation Conference (INLG)*, pages 120–124.

J. Silvertown. 2009. A new dawn for citizen science. *Trends in Ecology & Evolution*, 24(9):467–471.

J. Smart, A. Amar, I.M.W. Sim, B. Etheridge, D. Cameron, G. Christie, and J.D. Wilson. 2010. Illegal killing slows population recovery of a re-introduced raptor of high conservation concern–the red kite *milvus milvus*. *Biological Conservation*, 143(5):1278–1286.

R. Stafford, A.G. Hart, L. Collins, C.L. Kirkhope, R.L. Williams, S.G. Rees, J.R. Lloyd, and A.E. Goodenough. 2010. Eu-Social Science: The Role of Internet Social Networks in the Collection of Bee Biodiversity Data. *PloS one*, 5(12):e14381.

K. van Deemter and J. Odijk. 1997. Context modeling and the generation of spoken discourse. *Speech Communication*, 21(1-2):101–121.

TransDoop: A Map-Reduce based Crowdsourced Translation for Complex Domains

Anoop Kunchukuttan*, **Rajen Chatterjee***, **Shourya Roy**†, **Abhijit Mishra***, **Pushpak Bhattacharyya***

* Department of Computer Science and Engineering, IIT Bombay,
{anoopk,abhijitmishra,pb}@cse.iitb.ac.in, rajen.k.chatterjee@gmail.com

† Xerox India Research Centre,
Shourya.Roy@xerox.com

Abstract

Large amount of parallel corpora is required for building Statistical Machine Translation (SMT) systems. We describe the *TransDoop* system for gathering translations to create parallel corpora from online crowd workforce who have familiarity with multiple languages but are not expert translators. Our system uses a Map-Reduce-like approach to translation crowdsourcing where sentence translation is decomposed into the following smaller tasks: (a) translation of constituent phrases of the sentence; (b) validation of quality of the phrase translations; and (c) composition of complete sentence translations from phrase translations. *TransDoop* incorporates quality control mechanisms and easy-to-use worker user interfaces designed to address issues with translation crowdsourcing. We have evaluated the crowd's output using the METEOR metric. For a complex domain like judicial proceedings, the higher scores obtained by the map-reduce based approach compared to complete sentence translation establishes the efficacy of our work.

1 Introduction

Crowdsourcing is no longer a new term in the domain of Computational Linguistics and Machine Translation research (Callison-Burch and Dredze, 2010; Snow et al., 2008; Callison-Burch, 2009). Crowdsourcing - basically where task outsourcing is delegated to a largely unknown Internet audience - is emerging as a new paradigm of *human in the loop* approaches for developing sophisticated techniques for understanding and generating natural language content. *Amazon Mechanical Turk(AMT)* and *CrowdFlower* [1] are representative general purpose crowdsourcing platforms where as *Lingotek* and *Gengo*[2] are companies targeted at localization and translation of content typically leveraging freelancers.

Our interest is towards developing a crowdsourcing based system to enable general, non-expert crowd-workers generate natural language content equivalent in quality to that of expert linguists. Realization of the potential of attaining great scalability and cost-benefit of crowdsourcing for natural language tasks is limited by the ability of novice multi-lingual workers generate high quality translations. We have specific interest in Indian languages due to the large linguistic diversity as well as the scarcity of linguistic resources in these languages when compared to European languages. Crowdsourcing is a promising approach as many Indian languages are spoken by hundreds of Millions of people (approximately, Hindi-Urdu by 500M, Bangla by 200M, Punjabi by over 100M [3]) coupled with the fact that representation of Indian workers in online crowdsourcing platforms is very high (close to 40% in Amazon Mechanical Turk (AMT)).

However, this is a non-trivial task owing to lack of expertise of novice crowd workers in translation of content. It is well understood that familiarity with multiple languages might not be good enough for people to generate high quality translations. This is compounded by lack of sincerity and in certain cases, dishonest intention of earning rewards disproportionate to the effort and time spent for online tasks. Common techniques for quality control like *gold data based validation* and *worker reputation* are not effective for a subjective task

[1] http://www.mturk.com, http://www.crowdflower.com

[2] http://www.lingotek.com, http:///www.gengo.com

[3] http://en.wikipedia.org/wiki/List_of_languages_by_total_number_of_speakers

like translation which does not have any task specific measurements. Having expert linguists manually validate crowd generated content defies the purpose of deploying crowdsourcing on a large scale.

In this work, we propose a technique, based on the *Divide-and-Conquer* principle. The technique can be considered similar to a Map-Reduce task run on *crowd processors*, where the translation task is split into simpler tasks distributed to the crowd (the *map* stage) and the results are later combined in a *reduce* stage to generate complete translations. The attempt is to make translation tasks easy and intuitive for novice crowd-workers by providing translations aids to help them generate high quality of translations. Our contribution in this work is a end-to-end, crowdsourcing-platform-independent, translation crowdsourcing system that completely automates the translation crowdsourcing task by (i) managing the translation pipeline through software components and the crowd; (ii) performing quality control on workers' output; and (iii) interfacing with crowdsourcing service providers. The multi-stage, Map-reduce approach simplifies the translation task for crowd workers, while novel design of user interface makes the task convenient for the worker and discourages spamming. The system thus offers the potential to generate high quality parallel corpora on a large scale.

We discuss related work in Section 2 and the multi-staged approach which is central to our system in Section 3. Section 4 describes the system architecture and workflow, while Section 5 presents important aspects of the user interfaces in the system. We present our preliminary experiments and observations in Section 6. Section 7 concludes the paper, pointing to future directions.

2 Related Work

Lately, crowdsourcing has been explored as a source for generating data for NLP tasks (Snow et al., 2008; Callison-Burch and Dredze, 2010). Specifically, it has been explored as a channel for collecting different resources for SMT - evaluations of MT output (Callison-Burch, 2009), word alignments in parallel sentences (Gao et al., 2010) and post-edited versions of MT output (Aikawa et al., 2012). Ambati and Vogel (2010), Kunchukuttan et al. (2012) have shown the feasibility of crowdsourcing for collecting parallel corpora and pointed out that quality assurance is a major issue for successful translation crowdsourcing.

The most popular methods for quality control of crowdsourced tasks are based on sampling and redundancy. For translation crowdsourcing, Ambati et al. (2010) use inter-translator agreement for selection of a good translation from multiple, redundant worker translations. Zaidan and Callison-Burch (2011) score translations using a feature based model comprising sentence level, worker level and crowd ranking based features. However, automatic evaluation of translation quality is difficult, such automatic methods being either inaccurate or expensive. Post et al. (2012) have collected Indic language corpora data utilizing the crowd for collecting translations as well as validations. The quality of the validations is ensured using gold-standard sentence translations. Our approach to quality control is similar to Post et al. (2012), but we work at the level of phrases.

While most crowdsourcing activities for data gathering has been concerned with collecting simple annotations like relevance judgments, there has been work to explore the use of crowdsourcing for more complex tasks, of which translation is a good example. Little et al. (2010) propose that many complex tasks can be modeled either as iterative workflows (where workers iteratively build on each other's works) or as parallel workflows (where workers solve the tasks in parallel, with the best result voted upon later). Kittur et al. (2011) suggest a map-and-reduce approach to solve complex problems, where a problem is decomposed into smaller problems, which are solved in the *map* stage and the results are combined in the *reduce* stage. Our method can be seen as an instance of the map-reduce approach applied to translation crowdsourcing, with two map stages (phrase translation and translation validation) and one reduce stage (sentence combination).

3 Multi-Stage Crowdsourcing Pipeline

Our system is based on a multi-stage pipeline, whose central idea is to simplify the translation task into smaller tasks. The high level block diagram of the system is shown in Figure 1. Source language documents are sentencified using standard NLP tokenizers and sentence splitters. Extracted sentences are then split into phrases using a standard chunker and rule-based merging of small chunks. This step creates small phrases

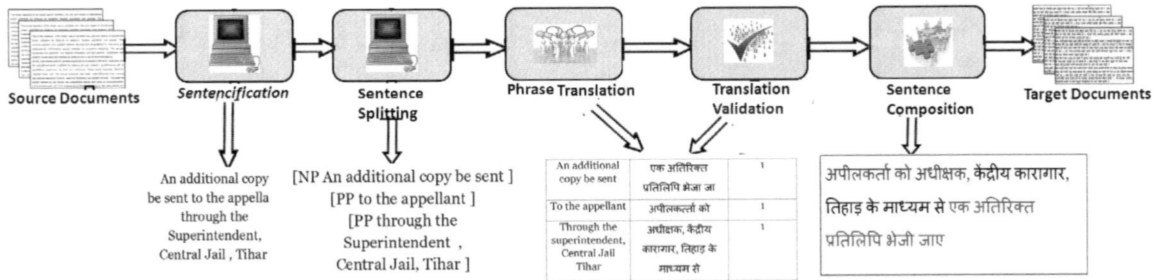

Figure 1: Multistage crowdsourced translation

from complex sentences which can be easily and independently translated. This leads to a crowdsourcing pipeline, with three stages of tasks for the crowd: Phrase Translation (PT), Phrase Translation Validation (PV), Sentence Composition (SC). A group of crowd workers translate source language phrases, the translations are validated by a different group of workers and finally a third group of workers put the phrase translation together to create target language sentences. The validation is done by workers by providing ratings on a k-point scale. This kind of divide and conquer approach helps to tackle the complexity of crowdsourcing translations since: (1) the tasks are simpler for workers; (2) uniformity of smaller tasks brings about efficiency as in any industrial assembly line; (3) pricing can be controlled for each stage depending on the complexity; and (4) quality control can be performed better for smaller tasks.

4 System Architecture

Figure 2 shows the architecture of *TransDoop*, which implements the 3-stage pipeline. The major design considerations were: (i) translation crowdsourcing pipeline should be independent of specific crowdsourcing platforms; (ii) support multiple crowdsourcing platforms; (iii) customize job parameters like pricing, quality control method and task design; and (iv) support multiple languages and domains.

The core component in the system is the **Crowdsourcing Engine**. The engine manages the execution of the crowdsourcing pipeline, lifecycle of jobs and quality control of submitted tasks. The Engine exposes its capabilities through the **Requester API**, which can be used by clients for setting up, customizing and monitoring translation crowdsourcing jobs and controlling their execution. These capabilities are made available to requesters via the **Requester Portal**. In order to make the crowdsourcing engine independent of any specific crowdsourcing platform, platform specific **Connectors** are developed. The Crowdsourcing system makes the tasks to be crowdsourced available through the **Connector API**. The connectors are responsible for polling the engine for tasks to be crowdsourced, pushing the tasks to crowdsourcing platforms, hosting worker interfaces for the tasks and pushing the results back to the engine after they have been completed by workers on the crowdsourcing platform. Currently the system supports the AMT crowdsourcing platform.

Figure 3 depicts the lifecycle of a translation crowdsourcing job. The requester initiates a translation job for a document (a set of sentences). The Crowdsourcing Engine schedules the job for execution. It first splits each sentence into phrases. For the job, PT tasks are created and made available through the Connector API. The connector for the specified platform periodically polls the Crowdsourcing Engine via the Connector API. Once the connector has new PT tasks for crowdsourcing, it interacts with the crowdsourcing platform to request crowdsourcing services. The connector monitors the progress of the tasks and on completion provides the results and execution status to the Crowdsourcing Engine. Once all the PT tasks for the job are completed, the crowdsourcing Engine initiates the PV task to obtain validations for the translations. The Quality Control system kicks in when all the PV tasks for the job have been completed.

The quality control (QC) relies on a combination of sampling and redundancy. Each PV task has a few gold-standard phrase translation pairs, which is used to ensure that the validators are honestly doing their tasks. The judgments from the

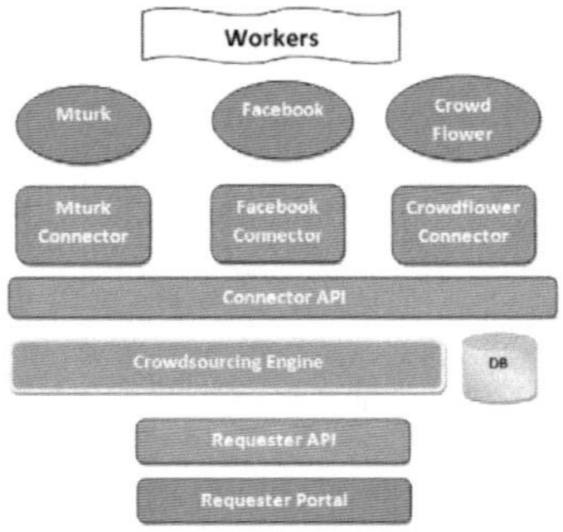

Figure 2: Architecture of *TransDoop*

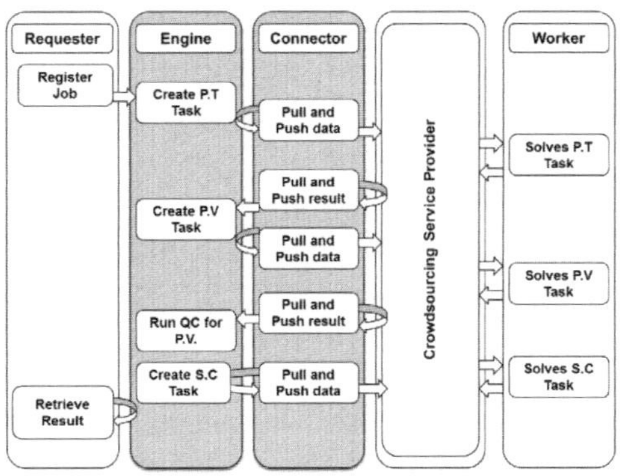

Figure 3: Lifecycle of a Translation Job

good validators are used to determine the quality of the phrase translation, based on majority voting, average rating, etc. using multiple judgments collected for each phrase translation. If any phrase validations or translations are incorrect, then the corresponding phrases/translations are again sent to the PT/PV stage as the case may be. This will continue until all phrase translations in the job are correctly translated or a pre-configured number of iterations are done.

Once phrase translations are obtained for all phrases in a sentence, the Crowdsourcing Engine creates SC tasks, where the workers are asked to compose a single correct, coherent translation from the phrase translation obtained in the previous stages.

5 User Interfaces

5.1 Worker User Interfaces

This section describes the worker user interfaces for each stage in the pipeline. These are managed by the **Connector** and have been designed to make the task convenient for the worker and prevent spam submissions. In the rest of the section, we describe the salient features of the PT and SC UI's. PV UI is similar to k-scale voting tasks commonly found in crowdsourcing platforms.

- **Translation UI:** Figure 4a shows the translation UI for the PT stage. The user interface *discourages spamming* by: (a) displaying source text as images; and (b) alerting workers if they don't provide a translation or spend very little time on a task. The UI also provides *transliteration support* for non-Latin scripts (especially helpful for Indic scripts). A *Vocabulary Support*, which shows translation suggestions for word sequences appearing in the source phrase, is also available. Suggested translations can be copied to the input area with ease and speed.

- **Sentence Translation Composition UI:** The sentence translation composition UI (shown in Figure 4b) facilitates composition of sentence translations from phrase translations. First, the worker can drag and rearrange the translated phrases into the right order, followed by reordering of individual words. This is important because many Indian languages have different constituent order (S-O-V) with respect to English (S-V-O). Finally, the synthesized language sentence can be post-edited to correct spelling, case marking, inflectional errors, etc. The system also captures the reordering performed by the worker, an important byproduct, which can be used for training reordering models for SMT.

5.2 Requester UI

The system provides a Requester Portal through which the requester can create, control and monitor jobs and retrieve results. The portal allows the requester to customize the job during creation by configuring various parameters: (a) domain and language pair (b) entire sentence vs multi-stage translation (c) price for task at each stage (d) task design (number of tasks in a task group, etc.) (e) translation redundancy (f) validation quality parameters. *Translation redundancy* refers to the number of translations requested for a source phrase. *Validation redundancy* refers to the number of validations collected for each phrase translation pair and the redundancy based acceptance criteria for phrase translations (majority, consensus, threshold, etc.)

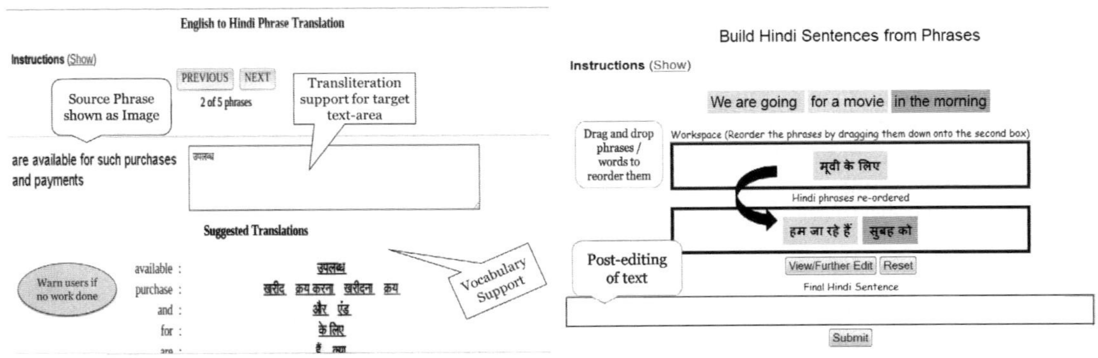

(a) Phrase Translation UI (b) Sentence Composition UI

Figure 4: Worker User Interfaces

6 Experiments and Observations

Using *TransDoop*, we conducted a set of small-scale, preliminary translation experiments. We obtained translations for English-Hindi and English-Marathi language pairs for the Judicial and Tourism domains. For each experiment, 15 sentences were given as input to the pipeline. For evaluation, we chose METEOR, a well-known translation evaluation metric (Banerjee and Lavie, 2005). We compared the results obtained from the crowdsourcing system with a expert human translation and the output of Google Translate. We also compared two expert translations using METEOR to establish a skyline for the translation accuracy. Table 1 summarizes the results of our experiments.

The translations with Quality Control and multistage pipeline are better than Google translations and translations obtained from the crowd without any quality control, as evaluated by METEOR. Multi-stage translation yields better than complete sentence translation. Moreover, the translation quality is comparable to that of expert human translation. This behavior is observed across the two language pairs and domains. This can be seen in some examples of crowdsourced translations obtained through the system which are shown in Table 2.

Incorrect splitting of sentences can cause difficulties in translation for the worker. For instance, discontinuous phrases will not be available to the worker as a single translation unit. In the English interrogative sentence, the noun phrase splits the verb phrase, therefore the auxiliary and main verb could be in different translation units. *e.g.*

*Why **did** you **buy** the book?*

In addition, the phrase structures of the source and target languages may not map, making translation difficult. For instance, the *vaala* modifier in Hindi translates to a clause in English. It does not contain any tense information, therefore the tense of the English clause cannot be determined by the worker. *e.g.*

***Lucknow vaalaa** ladkaa*

could translate to any one of:

*the boy **who lives/lived/is living in Lucknow***

We rely on the worker in sentence composition stage to correct mistakes due to these inadequacies and compose a good translation. In addition, the worker in the PT stage could be provided with the sentence context for translation. However, there is a tradeoff between the cognitive load of context processing versus uncertainty in translation. More elaborately, to what extent can the cognitive load be reduced before uncertainty of translation sets in? Similarly, how much of context can be shown before the cognitive load becomes pressing?

7 Conclusions

In this system demonstration, we present *TransDoop* as a translation crowdsourcing system which has the potential to harness the strength of the crowd to collect high quality human translations on a large scale. It simplifies the tedious translation tasks by decomposing them into several "easy-to-solve" subtasks while ensuring quality. Our evaluation on small scale data shows that the multistage approach performs better than complete sentence translation. We would like to extensively use this platform for large scale experiments on more language pairs and complex domains like Health, Parliamentary Proceedings, Technical and Scientific literature etc. to establish the utility of

Language Pair	Domain	Google Translate	No QC	Translation with QC *single stage*	*multi stage*	Reference Human
en-mr	Tourism	0.227*	0.30	0.368	0.372	0.48
en-hi	Tourism	0.292	0.363	0.387	0.422	0.51
en-hi	Judicial	0.252	0.30	0.388	0.436	0.49

Table 1: Experimental Results: Comparison of METEOR scores for different techniques, language pairs and domains
*Translated by an internal Moses-based SMT system

Accordingly the penalty imposed by AO is not justified and the same is cancelled.
इसके अनुसार ए औ द्वारा लगाये गये दंड उचित नहीं है और एक ही रद्द कर दिया है Accordingly A O by imposed penalty justified not is and one also cancel did
तदानुसार ए ओ द्वारा लगाया गया दंड जायज नहीं है और उसे रद्द कर दिया है Accordingly A O by imposed penalty justified not is and that cancel did

(a) English-Hindi Judicial Translation

A crowd of devotees engulf Haridwar during the time of daily prayer in the evening
शाम में दैनिक प्रार्थना के समय के दौरान भक्तों को अपनी चपेट में ले हरिद्वार की भीड evening in daily prayer of time during devotees its engulf in take Haridwar of crowd
श्रद्धालुओं की भीड शाम में दैनिक प्रार्थना के समय हरिद्वार को अपनी चपेट में लेती है devotees of crowd evening in daily prayer of time haridwar its engulf in take

(b) English-Hindi Tourism Translation

Table 2: Examples of translation from Google and three staged pipeline for source sentence (2nd, 3rd and 1st rows of each table respectively). Domains and languages are indicated above.

the method for collection of parallel corpora on a large scale.

References

Takako Aikawa, Kentaro Yamamoto, and Hitoshi Isahara. 2012. The impact of crowdsourcing post-editing with the collaborative translation framework. In *Advances in Natural Language Processing*. Springer Berlin Heidelberg.

Vamshi Ambati and Stephan Vogel. 2010. Can crowds build parallel corpora for machine translation systems? In *Proceedings of the NAACL HLT 2010 Workshop on Creating Speech and Language Data with Amazon's Mechanical Turk*.

Vamshi Ambati, Stephan Vogel, and Jaime Carbonell. 2010. Active learning and crowd-sourcing for machine translation. *Language Resources and Evaluation LREC*.

Satanjeev Banerjee and Alon Lavie. 2005. Meteor: An automatic metric for mt evaluation with improved correlation with human judgments. In *Proceedings of the ACL Workshop on Intrinsic and Extrinsic Evaluation Measures for Machine Translation and/or Summarization*.

Chris Callison-Burch and Mark Dredze. 2010. Creating speech and language data with amazon's mechanical turk. In *Proceedings of the NAACL HLT 2010 Workshop on Creating Speech and Language Data with Amazon's Mechanical Turk*.

Chris Callison-Burch. 2009. Fast, cheap, and creative: evaluating translation quality using amazon's mechanical turk. In *Proceedings of the 2009 Conference on Empirical Methods in Natural Language Processing*.

Qin Gao, Nguyen Bach, and Stephan Vogel. 2010. A semi-supervised word alignment algorithm with partial manual alignments. In *Proceedings of the Joint Fifth Workshop on Statistical Machine Translation and MetricsMATR*.

Aniket Kittur, Boris Smus, Susheel Khamkar, and Robert E Kraut. 2011. Crowdforge: Crowdsourcing complex work. In *Proceedings of the 24th annual ACM symposium on User interface software and technology*.

Anoop Kunchukuttan, Shourya Roy, Pratik Patel, Kushal Ladha, Somya Gupta, Mitesh Khapra, and Pushpak Bhattacharyya. 2012. Experiences in resource generation for machine translation through crowdsourcing. *Language Resources and Evaluation LREC*.

Greg Little, Lydia B Chilton, Max Goldman, and Robert C Miller. 2010. Exploring iterative and parallel human computation processes. In *Proceedings of the ACM SIGKDD workshop on human computation*.

Matt Post, Chris Callison-Burch, and Miles Osborne. 2012. Constructing parallel corpora for six indian languages via crowdsourcing. In *Proceedings of the Seventh Workshop on Statistical Machine Translation*.

Rion Snow, Brendan O'Connor, Daniel Jurafsky, and Andrew Y. Ng. 2008. Cheap and fast—but is it good?: evaluating non-expert annotations for natural language tasks. In *Proceedings of the Conference on Empirical Methods in Natural Language Processing*.

Omar Zaidan and Chris Callison-Burch. 2011. Crowdsourcing translation: Professional quality from non-professionals. In *Proceedings of the NAACL HLT 2010 Workshop on Creating Speech and Language Data with Amazon's Mechanical Turk*.

*t*SEARCH: Flexible and Fast Search over Automatic Translations for Improved Quality/Error Analysis

Meritxell Gonzàlez and **Laura Mascarell** and **Lluís Màrquez**
TALP Research Center
Universitat Politècnica de Catalunya
{mgonzalez,lmascarell,lluism}@lsi.upc.edu

Abstract

This work presents *t*SEARCH, a web-based application that provides mechanisms for doing complex searches over a collection of translation cases evaluated with a large set of diverse measures. *t*SEARCH uses the evaluation results obtained with the ASIYA toolkit for MT evaluation and it is connected to its on-line GUI, which makes possible a graphical visualization and interactive access to the evaluation results. The search engine offers a flexible query language allowing to find translation examples matching a combination of numerical and structural features associated to the calculation of the quality metrics. Its database design permits a fast response time for all queries supported on realistic-size test beds. In summary, *t*SEARCH, used with ASIYA, offers developers of MT systems and evaluation metrics a powerful tool for helping translation and error analysis.

1 Introduction

In Machine Translation (MT) system development, a qualitative analysis of the translations is a fundamental step in order to spot the limitations of a system, compare the linguistic abilities of different systems or tune the parameters during system refinement. This is especially true in statistical MT systems, where usually no special structured knowledge is used other than parallel data and language models, but also on systems that need to reason over linguistic structures. The need for analyzing and comparing automatic translations with respect to evaluation metrics is also paramount for developers of translation quality metrics, who need elements of analysis to better understand the behavior of their evaluation measures.

This paper presents *t*SEARCH, a web application that aims to alleviate the burden of manual analysis that developers have to conduct to assess the translation quality aspects involved in the above mentioned situations. As a toy example, consider for instance an evaluation setting with two systems, s_1 and s_2, and two evaluation metrics m_1 and m_2. Assume also that m_1 scores s_1 to be better than s_2 in a particular test set, while m_2 predicts just the contrary. In order to analyze this contradictory evaluation one might be interested in inspecting from the test set the particular translation examples that contribute to these results, i.e., text segments t for which the translation provided by s_1 is scored better by m_1 than the translation provided by s_2 *and* the opposite behavior regarding metric m_2. *t*SEARCH allows to retrieve (visualize and export) these sentences with a simple query in a fast time response. The search can be further constrained, by requiring certain margins on the differences, by including other systems or metrics, or by requiring some specific syntactic or semantic constructs to appear in the examples.

*t*SEARCH is build on top of ASIYA (Giménez and Màrquez, 2010), an open-source toolkit for MT evaluation; and it can be used along with the ASIYA ON-LINE INTERFACE (Gonzàlez et al., 2012), which provides an interactive environment to examine the sentences. ASIYA allows to analyze a wide range of linguistic aspects of candidate and reference translations using a large set of automatic and heterogeneous evaluation metrics. In particular, it offers a especially rich set of measures that use syntactic and semantic information. The intermediate structures generated by the parsers, and used to compute the scoring measures, could be priceless for MT developers, who can use them to compare the structures of several translations and see how they affect the performance of the metrics, providing more understanding in order to interpret the actual performance of the automatic translation systems.

*t*SEARCH consists of: 1) a database that stores

the resources generated by ASIYA, 2) a query language and a search engine able to look through the information gathered in the database, and 3) a graphical user interface that assists the user to write a query, returns the set of sentences that fulfill the conditions, and allows to export these results in XML format. The application is publicly accessible on-line[1], and a brief explanation of its most important features is given in the demonstrative video.

In the following, Section 2 gives an overview of the ASIYA toolkit and the information gathered from the evaluation output. Section 3 and Section 4 describe in depth the *t*SEARCH application and the on-line interface, respectively. Finally, Section 5 reviews similar applications in comparison to the functionalities addressed by *t*SEARCH.

2 MT Evaluation with the ASIYA Toolkit

Currently, ASIYA contains more than 800 variants of MT metrics to measure the similarity between two translations at several linguistic dimensions. Moreover, the scores can be calculated at three granularity levels: system (entire test-set), document and sentence (or segment).

As shown in Figure 1, ASIYA requires the user to provide a test suite. Then, the input files are processed in order to calculate the annotations, the parsing trees and the final metric scores. Several external components are used for both, metric computation and automatic linguistic analysis[2]. The use of these tools depends on the languages supported and the type of measures that one needs to obtain. Hence, for instance, lexical-based measures are computed using the last version of most popular metrics, such as BLEU, NIST, METEOR or ROUGE. The syntax-wise measures need the output of taggers, lemmatizers, parsers and other analyzers. In those cases, ASIYA uses the SVMTool (Giménez and Màrquez, 2004), BIOS (Surdeanu et al., 2005), the Charniak-Johnson and Berkeley constituent parsers (Charniak and Johnson, 2005; Petrov and Klein, 2007), and the MALT dependency parser (Nivre et al., 2007), among others.

In the *t*SEARCH platform, the system manages the communication with an instance of the ASIYA toolkit running on the server. For every test suite, the system maintains a synchronized representation of the input data, the evaluation results and the linguistic information generated. Then, the system updates a database where the test suites are stored for further analysis using the *t*SEARCH tool, as described next.

3 The *t*SEARCH Tool

*t*SEARCH offers a graphical search engine to analyze a given test suite. The system core retrieves all translation examples that satisfy certain properties related to either the evaluation scores or the linguistic structures. The query language designed is simple and flexible, and it allows to combine many properties to build sophisticated searches.

The *t*SEARCH architecture consists of the three components illustrated in Figure 2: the web-based interface, the storage system based on NoSQL technology and the *t*SEARCH core, composed of a query parser and a search engine.

The databases (Section 3.1) are fed through the *tSearch Data Loader* API used by ASIYA. At run-time, during the calculation of the measures, ASIYA *inserts* all the information being calculated (metrics and parses) and a number of precalculated variables (e.g., average, mean and percentiles). These operations are made in parallel, which makes the overhead of filling the database marginal.

The query parser (Section 3.2) receives the query from the on-line interface and converts it

[1] `http://asiya.lsi.upc.edu/demo`

[2] A complete list of external components can be found in the Technical Manual at the ASIYA web-site

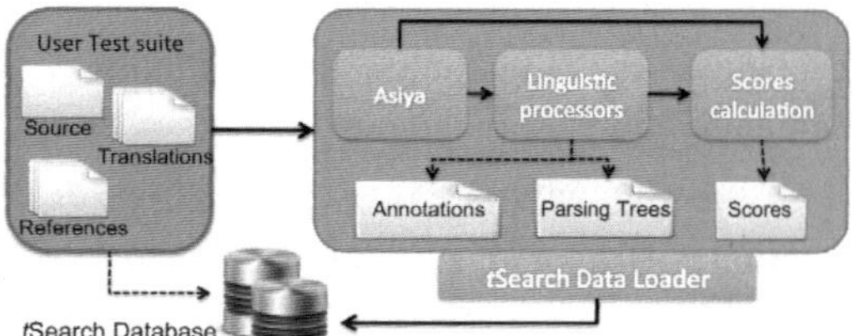

Figure 1: ASIYA processes and data files

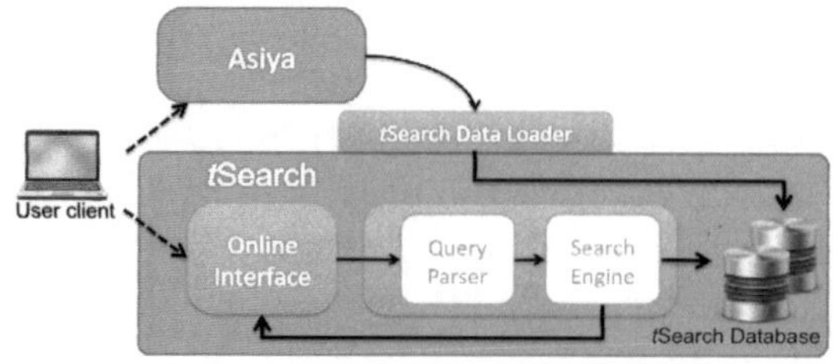

Figure 2: *t*SEARCH architecture

CF keys	CF values				
Testsuite_key + BLEU	0.2	...	0.6	1.0	
	s_1{seg3,seg5}, s_2{seg3,seg5}	...	s_1{seg8}	s_2{seg8}	
Testsuite_key + ULC	0.0	...	0.8	0.85	1.0
	s_1{seg2}	...	s_1{seg6}, s_2{seg7}	s_2{seg5}	s_2{seg8}

(a) Scores Column Family

CF keys	CF values							
Testsuite_key + BLEU	MIN	MAX	AVG	MEDIAN	PERC(1)	..	PERC(50)	PERC(100)
	0.0	1.0	0.34	0.27	0.0-0.1	...	0.34-0.36	0.99-1.0
Testsuite_key + ULC	MIN	MAX	AVG	MEDIAN	PERC(1)	...	PERC(50)	PERC(100)
	0.1	1.0	0.83	0.87	0.1-0.2	...	0.83-0.83	1.0-1.0

(b) Statistics Column Family

CF keys	CF values				
Testsuite_key + SP	DT	NN	VBZ	JJ	NNP
	s_1{seg1,seg2}, s_2{seg1,seg2}	s_2{seg1}	s_1{seg1,seg2}	s_2{seg1}	...
Testsuite_key + CP	ADJP	CONJP	ADVP	PP	WHPP
	s_1{seg3}	s_1{seg1}, s_2{seg2,seg5}	s_2{seg1}	s_1{seg1,seg2,seg3}	...

CF keys	CF values					
Testsuite_key + DP	N_nsubj_V	D_nsubj_V	C_cc_V	I_prep_N	M_aux_V	N_pobj_I
	s_1{seg1,seg2, seg3}	s_2{seg4}	s_1{seg1,seg2}	s_2{seg1}	s_2{seg3}	...
Testsuite_key + SR	A0	A1	AM-TMP	AM-LOC	AM-ADV	R-AM-LOC
	s_1{seg1}, s_2{seg2,seg5}	s_1{seg2}	s_1{seg1,seg2}, s_2{seg3,seg5}	s_2{seg1}	s_1{seg1,seg2}, s_2{seg1,seg2}	...

(c) Linguistic Elements Column Family

Figure 3: *t*SEARCH data model

into a binary tree structure where each leaf is a single part of an operation and each node combines the partial results of the children. The search engine obtains the final results by processing the tree bottom-up until the root is reached.

3.1 Data Representation, Storage and Access

The amount of data generated by ASIYA can be very large for test sets with thousands of sentences. In order to handle the high volume of information, we decided to use the Apache Cassandra database[3], a NoSQL (also known as *not only SQL*) solution that deals successfully with this problem.

It is important to remark that there is no similarity between NoSQL and the traditional relational database management system model (RDBMS). Actually, RDBMS uses SQL as its query language and requires a relational model, whereas NoSQL databases do not. Besides, the *t*SEARCH query language can be complex, with several conditions, which makes RDBMS perform poorly due the complexity of the tables. In contrast, NoSQL-databases use *big-tables* having many querying information precalculated as key values, which yields for direct access to the results.

The Cassandra data model is based on *column families* (CF). A CF consists of a set of rows that are uniquely identified by its key and have a set of columns as values. So far, the *t*SEARCH data model has the three CFs shown in Figure 3. The *scores* CF in Figure 3(a) stores information related to metrics and score values. Each row slot contains the list of segments that matches the column key.

[3]`http://cassandra.apache.org/`

The *statistics* CF in Figure 3(b) stores basic statistics, such as the minimum, maximum, average, median and percentiles values for every evaluation metric. The CF having the *linguistic elements* in Figure 3(c) stores the results of the parsers, such as part-of-speech, grammatical categories and dependency relationships.

One of the goals of NoSQL databases is to obtain the information required in the minimum access time. Therefore, the data is stored in the way required by the *t*SEARCH application. For instance, the query `BLEU > 0.4` looks for all segments in the test suite having a BLEU score greater than 0.4. Thus, in order to get the query result in constant time, we use the metric identifier as a part of the key for the *scores* CF, and the score 0.4 as the *column* key.

3.2 The Query Language and Parser

The Query Parser module is one of the key ingredients in the *t*SEARCH application because it determines the query grammar and the allowed operations, and it provides a parsing method to analyze any query and produce a machine-readable version of its semantics. It is also necessary in order to validate the query.

There are several types of queries, depending on the operations used: arithmetic comparisons, statistical functions (e.g., average, quartiles), range of values, linguistic elements and logical operators. Furthermore, the queries can be applied at segment-, document- and/or system-level, and it is even possible to create any group of systems or metrics. This is useful, for instance, in order to limit the search to certain type of systems (e.g., rule-based vs. statistical) and specific met-

Query Type	Query Structure	Example	Description
Arithmetic Comparison	METRIC op *real*	BLEU > 0.4	Operators: >, <, >=, <=, =
Statistical Functions	METRIC op SF	(1) BLEU > AVG (2) BLEU > TH(40)	Use precalculated statistical variables: average, median, min, max, percentiles [1..100], thresholds.
Range	METRIC IN [x,y] METRIC IN Q(n) METRIC IN PERC(m,m)	(1) BLEU IN [0.2,0.3) (2) BLEU IN Q(4) (3) BLEU IN [PERC(2,10),PERC(3,10)]	In a range of values that can be predefined by the user or statistical values precalculated by the system.
Linguistic Elements	LE[type(item+)+]	(1) LE[SP(NN), DP(conj), CP(PP)] (2) LE[SP(Fz, VC, Vai)] (3) LE[DP(VBG,dobj,NNS)] (4) LE[SR(want,A0,A1,AM-TMP)]	'type' is the type of linguistic processor: shallow (SP), constiency (CP), dependency (DP), semantic (SR). 'item' is a linguistic element that belongs to the type of processor: pos, categories, relationships, roles, as in example (1). It's possible to ask for N-grams, as shown in the example (2), a chain of pos and dep. relations (3), or a list of role arguments (4).
Logical Composition	Query1 AND|OR Query2	BLEU > 0.5 AND –PER < 0.7	Logical operators to concatenate several conditions

Query type	Example	Description
System-level queries	s_1[BLEU] > 0.4	Segments from system $s_1$translations that have a BLEU score avobe 0.4
Document level queries	(1) news[BLEU] > 0.3 (2) s_1[news[BLEU]] > 0.3	Segments from the *news* document (1) (and $s_1$translations (2)) having a BLEU score above 0.3
Groups of Systems and/or Metrics	▪s_{rb}={s_1, s_2} ▪LEX={BLEU, NIST} ▪SYN={CP-Op(*), SP-Oc(*)} (1) s_{rb}[LEX] > AVG (2) ((s_{rb}[LEX] > AVG) **OR** (s_3[LEX] < AVG)) **AND** ((s_{rb}[SYN] < AVG) **OR** (s_3[SYN] > AVG))	(1) Segments from s_{rb}={$s_1$and s_2) translations that have BLEU and NIST scores above the average (2) Segments from s_{rb} having good scores for lexical measures and bad scores for syntactic measures, and same segments for s_3 having bad and good scores for lexical and syntactic measures, respectively.

Figure 4: (top) Query operations and functions, (bottom) Queries for group of systems and metrics

rics (e.g., lexical vs. syntactic). All possible query types are described in the following subsections (3.2.1 to 3.2.3) and listed in Figure 4.

3.2.1 Segment-level and Metric-based Queries

The most basic queries are those related to segment level scores, i.e., *obtain all segments scored above/below a value for a concrete metric*. The common comparison operators are supported, such as for instance, `BLEU > 0.4` and `BLEU gt 0.4`, that are both correct and equivalent queries.

Basic statistics are also calculated at run-time, which allows to use statistic variables as values, e.g., obtain the segments scored in the fourth quartile of `BLEU`. The maximum, minimum, average, median and percentile values of each metric are precalculated and saved into the `MAX`, `MIN`, `AVG`, `MEDIAN` and `PERC` variables, respectively. The thresholds and quartiles (`TH`,`Q`) are calculated at run-time based on percentiles. `MIN` and `MAX` can also be used and allow to get all segments in the test set (i.e.,`BLEU ge MIN`).

The threshold function implies a percentage. The query `BLEU > TH(20)` gets all segments that have a BLEU score greater than the score value of the bottom 20% of the sentences.

It is also possible to specify an interval of values using the operator `IN[x,y]`. The use of parenthesis is allowed in order to exclude the boundaries. The arguments for this operator can be either numerical values or the predefined functions for quartiles and percentiles. Therefore, the following example `BLEU IN [TH(20), TH(30)]` returns all segments with a BLEU score in the range between the threshold of the 20% (included) and the 30% (excluded).

The quartile function `Q(X)` takes a value between 1 and 4 and returns all segments that have their score in that quartile. In contrast, the percentile function generalizes the previous: PERC(n,M), where $1 < M <= 100; 1 <= n <= M$, returns all the segments with a score in the nth part, when the range of scores is divided in M parts of equal size.

Finally, a query can be composed of more than one criterion. To do so, the logical operators `AND` and `OR` are used to specify intersection and union, respectively.

3.2.2 System- and Document-level Queries

The queries described next implement the search procedures for more sophisticated queries involving system and document level properties, and also the linguistic information used in the calculation of the evaluation measures. The purpose of this functionality is to answer questions related to groups of systems and/or metrics.

As explained in the introduction, one may want to find the segments with good scores for lexical metrics and, simultaneously, bad scores for syntactic-based ones, or viceversa. The following query illustrates how to do it: `((`s_{rb}`[LEX] > AVG) OR (`s_3`[LEX] < AVG)) AND ((`s_{rb}`[SYN] < AVG) OR (`s_3`[SYN] > AVG) )`, where $s_{rb} = \{s_1, s_2\}$ is the definition of a group of the rule-based systems s_1 and s_2, s_3 is another translation system, and `LEX=`{`BLEU,NIST`} and `SYN=`{`CP-Op(*),SP-Oc(*)`} are two groups of lexical- and syntactic-based measures, respectively. The output of this kind of queries can help developers to inspect the differences between the systems that meet these criteria.

Concerning queries at document level, its structure is the same but applied at document scope. They may help to find divergences when translating documents from different domains.

3.2.3 Linguistic Element-based Queries

The last functionality in *t*SEARCH allows searching the segments that contain specific linguistic elements (LE), estimated with any of the analyzers used to calculate the linguistic structures. Linguistic-wise queries will allow the user to find segments which match the criteria for any linguistic feature calculated by ASIYA: part-of-speech, lemmas, named entities, grammatical categories, dependency relations, semantic roles and discourse structures.

We have implemented queries that match n-grams of lemmas (`lemma`), parts-of-speech (`pos`) and items of shallow (`SP`) or constituent parsing (`CP`), dependency relations (`DP`) and semantic roles `SR`, such as `LE[lemma(be), pos(NN,adj), SP(NP,ADJP,VP), CP(VP,PP)]`. The `DP` function allows also specifying a compositional criterion (i.e., the categories of two words and their dependency relationship) and even a chain of relations, e.g., `LE[DP(N,nsubj,V,dep,V)]`. In turn, the `SR` function obtains the segments that match a verb and its list of arguments, e.g., `LE[SR(ask, A0, A1)]`.

The asterisk symbol can be used to substitute any LE-item, e.g., `LE[SP(NP,*,PP), DP(*,*,V)]`. When combined with semantic roles, one asterisk substitutes any verb that has all the arguments specified, e.g., `LE[SR(*, A0, A1)]`, whereas two asterisks in a row allow arguments to belong to different verbs in the same sentence. For instance, `LE[SR(**, A1, AM-TMP)]` matches the sentence *Those who prefer to save money, may try to wait a few more days*, where the verb *wait* has the argument `AM-TMP` and the verb *prefer* has the argument `A1`.

4 On-line Interface and Export of the Results

*t*SEARCH is fully accessible on-line through the ASIYA ON-LINE INTERFACE. The web application runs ASIYA remotely, calculates the scores and fills the *t*SEARCH database. It also offers the chance to upload the results of a test suite previously processed. This way it feeds the database directly, without the need to run ASIYA.

Anyhow, once the *t*SEARCH interface is already accessible, one can see a tools icon on the right of the search box. It shows the toolbar with all available metrics, functions and operations. The search box allows to query the database using the query language described in Section 3.2.

After typing a query, the user can navigate the results using three different views that organize them according to the user preferences: 1) *All segments* shows all segments and metrics mentioned in the query, the segments can be sorted by the score, in ascendent or descendent order, just tapping on the metric name; 2) *Grouped by system* groups the segments by system and, for

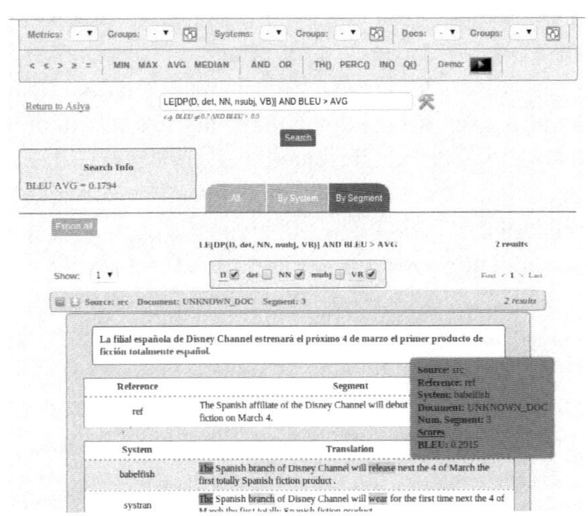

Figure 5: The *t*SEARCH Interface

each system, by document; 3) *Grouped by segment* displays the segment organization, which allows an easy comparison between several translations. Each group contains all the information related to a segment number, such as the source and the reference sentences along with the candidate translations that matched the query.

Additionally, moving the mouse over the segments displays a floating box as illustrated in Figure 5. It shows some relevant information, such as the source and references segments, the system that generated the translation, the document which the segment belongs to, and the scores.

Finally, all output data obtained during the search can be exported as an XML file. It is possible to export all segments, or the results structured *by system*, *by segment*, or more specific information from the views.

5 Related Work and Conclusions

The ultimate goal of *t*SEARCH is to provide the community with a user-friendly tool that facilitates the qualitative analysis of automatic translations. Currently, there are no freely available automatic tools for aiding MT evaluation tasks. For this reason, we believe that *t*SEARCH can be a useful tool for MT system and evaluation metric developers.

So far, related works in the field address (semi)-automatic error analysis from different perspectives. A framework for error analysis and classification was proposed in (Vilar et al., 2006), which has inspired more recent works in the area, such as (Fishel et al., 2011). They propose a method for automatic identification of various error types. The methodology proposed is language independent and tackles lexical information. Nonetheless, it can also take into account language-dependent information if linguistic analyzers are available. The user interface presented in (Berka et al., 2012) provides also automatic error detection and classification. It is the result of merging the Hjerson tool (Popović, 2011) and Addicter (Zeman et al., 2011). This web application shows alignments and different types of errors colored.

In contrast, the ASIYA interface and the *t*SEARCH tool together facilitate the qualitative analysis of the evaluation results yet providing a framework to obtain multiple evaluation metrics and linguistic analysis of the translations. They also provide the mechanisms to search and find relevant translation examples using a flexible query language, and to export the results.

Acknowledgments

This research has been partially funded by the Spanish Ministry of Education and Science (OpenMT-2, TIN2009-14675-C03), the European Community's Seventh Framework Programme under grant agreement number 247762 (FAUST, FP7-ICT-2009-4-247762) and the EAMT Sponsorhip of Activities: Small research and development project, 2012.

References

Jan Berka, Ondrej Bojar, Mark Fishel, Maja Popovic, and Daniel Zeman. 2012. Automatic MT error analysis: Hjerson helping Addicter. In *Proc. 8th LREC*.

Eugene Charniak and Mark Johnson. 2005. Coarse-to-Fine N-best Parsing and MaxEnt Discriminative Reranking. In *Proc. 43rd Meeting of the ACL*.

Mark Fishel, Ondřej Bojar, Daniel Zeman, and Jan Berka. 2011. Automatic Translation Error Analysis. In *Proc. 14th Text, Speech and Dialogue (TSD)*.

Jesús Giménez and Lluís Màrquez. 2004. SVMTool: A general POS tagger generator based on Support Vector Machines. In *Proc. 4th Intl. Conf. LREC*.

Jesús Giménez and Lluís Màrquez. 2010. Asiya: An Open Toolkit for Automatic Machine Translation (Meta-)Evaluation. *The Prague Bulletin of Mathematical Linguistics*, 94.

Meritxell Gonzàlez, Jesús Giménez, and Lluís Màrquez. 2012. A Graphical Interface for MT Evaluation and Error Analysis. In *Proc. 50th Meeting of the ACL. System Demonstration*.

Joakim Nivre, Johan Hall, Jens Nilsson, Atanas Chanev, Gülsen Eryigit, Sandra Kübler, Svetoslav Marinov, and Erwin Marsi. 2007. MaltParser: A language-independent system for data-driven dependency parsing. *Natural Language Engineering*, 13.

Slav Petrov and Dan Klein. 2007. Improved Inference for Unlexicalized Parsing. In *Proc. HLT*.

Maja Popović. 2011. Hjerson: An Open Source Tool for Automatic Error Classification of Machine Translation Output. *The Prague Bulletin of Mathematical Linguistics*, 96.

Mihai Surdeanu, Jordi Turmo, and Eli Comelles. 2005. Named Entity Recognition from Spontaneous Open-Domain Speech. In *Proc. 9th INTERSPEECH*.

David Vilar, Jia Xu, Luis Fernando D'Haro, and Hermann Ney. 2006. Error Analysis of Machine Translation Output. In *Proc. 5th LREC*.

Daniel Zeman, Mark Fishel, Jan Berka, and Ondrej Bojar. 2011. Addicter: What Is Wrong with My Translations? *The Prague Bulletin of Mathematical Linguistics*, 96.

VSEM: An open library for visual semantics representation

Elia Bruni
University of Trento
elia.bruni@unitn.it

Ulisse Bordignon
University of Trento
ulisse.bordignon@unitn.it

Adam Liska
University of Trento
adam.liska@unitn.it

Jasper Uijlings
University of Trento
jrr@disi.unitn.it

Irina Sergienya
University of Trento
irina.sergienya@unitn.it

Abstract

VSEM is an open library for visual semantics. Starting from a collection of tagged images, it is possible to automatically construct an image-based representation of concepts by using off-the-shelf VSEM functionalities. VSEM is entirely written in MATLAB and its object-oriented design allows a large flexibility and reusability. The software is accompanied by a website with supporting documentation and examples.

1 Introduction

In the last years we have witnessed great progress in the area of automated image analysis. Important advances, such as the introduction of local features for a robust description of the image content (see Mikolajczyk et al. (2005) for a systematic review) and the bag-of-visual-words method (**BoVW**)[1] for a standard representation across multiple images (Sivic and Zisserman, 2003), have contributed to make image analysis ubiquitous, with applications ranging from robotics to biology, from medicine to photography.

Two facts have played a key role in the rapid advance of these ideas. First, the introduction of very well defined challenges which have been attracting also a wide community of "outsiders" specialized in a variety of disciplines (e.g., machine learning, neural networks, graphical models and natural language processing). Second, the sharing of effective, well documented implementations of cutting edge image analysis algorithms, such as OpenCV[2] and VLFeat.[3]

A comparable story can be told about automatic text analysis. The last decades have seen a long series of successes in the processing of large text corpora in order to extract more or less structured semantic knowledge. In particular, under the assumption that meaning can be captured by patterns of co-occurrences of words, distributional semantic models such as Latent Semantic Analysis (Landauer and Dumais, 1997) or Topic Models (Blei et al., 2003) have been shown to be very effective both in general semantic tasks such as approximating human intuitions about meaning, as well as in more application-driven tasks such as information retrieval, word disambiguation and query expansion (Turney and Pantel, 2010). And also in the case of automated text analysis, a wide range of method implementations are at the disposal of the scientific community.[4]

Nowadays, given the parallel success of the two disciplines, there is growing interest in making the visual and textual channels interact for mutual benefit. If we look at the image analysis community, we discover a well established tradition of studies that exploit both channels of information. For example, there is a relatively extended amount of literature about enhancing the performance on visual tasks such as object recognition or image retrieval by replacing a purely image-based pipeline with hybrid methods augmented with textual information (Barnard et al., 2003; Farhadi et al., 2009; Berg et al., 2010; Kulkarni et al., 2011).

Unfortunately, the same cannot be said of the exploitation of image analysis from within the text community. Despite the huge potential that automatically induced visual features could represent as a new source of perceptually grounded

[1] Bag-of-visual-words model is a popular technique for image classification inspired by the traditional bag-of-words model in Information Retrieval. It represents an image with discrete image-describing features. **Visual words** are identified by clustering a large corpus of lower-level continuous features.

[2] http://opencv.org/

[3] http://www.vlfeat.org/

[4] See for example the annotated list of corpus-based computational linguistics resources at http://www-nlp.stanford.edu/links/statnlp.html.

semantic knowledge,[5] image-enhanced models of semantics developed so far (Feng and Lapata, 2010; Bruni et al., 2011; Leong and Mihalcea, 2011; Bergsma and Goebel, 2011; Bruni et al., 2012a; Bruni et al., 2012b) have only scratched this great potential and are still considered as proof-of-concept studies only.

One possible reason of this delay with respect to the image analysis community might be ascribed to the high entry barriers that NLP researchers adopting image analysis methods have to face. Although many of the image analysis toolkits are open source and well documented, they mainly address users within the same community and therefore their use is not as intuitive for others. The final goal of libraries such VLFeat and OpenCV is the representation and classification of images. Therefore, they naturally lack of a series of complementary functionalities that are necessary to bring the visual representation to the level of semantic concepts.[6]

To fill the gap we just described, we present hereby VSEM,[7] a novel toolkit which allows the extraction of image-based representations of concepts in an easy fashion. VSEM is equipped with state-of-the-art algorithms, from low-level feature detection and description up to the BoVW representation of images, together with a set of new routines necessary to move from an image-wise to a concept-wise representation of image content. In a nutshell, VSEM extracts visual information in a way that resembles how it is done for automatic text analysis. Thanks to BoVW, the image content is indeed discretized and visual units somehow comparable to words in text are produced (the visual words). In this way, from a corpus of images annotated with a set of concepts, it is possible to derive semantic vectors of co-occurrence counts of concepts and visual words akin to the representations of words in terms of textual collocates in standard distributional semantics. Importantly, the obtained visual semantic vectors can be easily combined with more traditional text-based vectors to arrive at a multimodal representation of meaning (see e.g. (Bruni et al., 2011)). It has been shown that the resulting multimodal models perform better than text-only models in semantic tasks such as approximating semantic similarity and relatedness ((Feng and Lapata, 2010; Bruni et al., 2012b)).

VSEM functionalities concerning image analysis is based on VLFeat (Vedaldi and Fulkerson, 2010). This guarantees that the image analysis underpinnings of the library are well maintained and state-of-the-art.

The rest of the paper is organized as follows. In Section 2 we introduce the procedure to obtain an image-based representation of a concept. Section 3 describes the VSEM architecture. Section 4 shows how to install and run VSEM through an example that uses the Pascal VOC data set. Section 5 concludes summarizing the material and discussing further directions.

2 Background

As shown by Feng and Lapata (2010), Bruni et al. (2011) and Leong and Mihalcea (2011), it is possible to construct an image-based representation of a set of target concepts by starting from a collection of images depicting those concepts, encoding the image contents into low-level features (e.g., SIFT) and scaling up to a higher level representation, based on the well-established BoVW method to represent images. In addition, as shown by Bruni et al. (2012b), better representations can be extracted if the object depicting the concept is first localized in the image.

More in detail, the pipeline encapsulating the whole process mentioned above takes as input a collection of images together with their associated tags and optionally object location annotations. Its output is a set of concept representation vectors for individual tags. The following steps are involved: (i) extraction of local image features, (ii) visual vocabulary construction, (iii) encoding the local features in a BoVW histogram, (iv) including spatial information with spatial binning, (v) aggregation of visual words on a per-concept basis in order to obtain the co-occurrence counts for each concept and (vi) transforming the counts into association scores and/or reducing the dimensionality of the data. A brief description of the individual

[5] In recent years, a conspicuous literature of studies has surfaced, wherein demonstration was made of how text based models are not sufficiently good at capturing the environment we acquire language from. This is due to the fact that they are lacking of perceptual information (Andrews et al., 2009; Baroni et al., 2010; Baroni and Lenci, 2008; Riordan and Jones, 2011).

[6] The authors of the aforementioned studies usually refer to words instead of concepts. We chose to call them concepts to account for the both theoretical and practical differences standing between a word and the perceptual information it brings along, which we define its concept.

[7] http://clic.cimec.unitn.it/vsem/

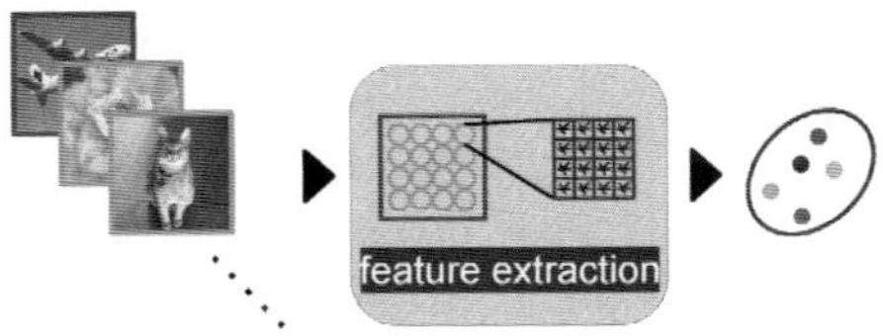

Figure 1: An example of a visual vocabulary creation pipeline. From a set of images, a larger set of features are extracted and clustered, forming the visual vocabulary.

steps follows.

Local features Local features are designed to find local image structures in a repeatable fashion and to represent them in robust ways that are invariant to typical image transformations, such as translation, rotation, scaling, and affine deformation. Local features constitute the basis of approaches developed to automatically recognize specific objects (Grauman and Leibe, 2011). The most popular local feature extraction method is the Scale Invariant Feature Transform (SIFT), introduced by Lowe (2004). VSEM uses the VLFeat implementation of SIFT.

Visual vocabulary To obtain a BoVW representation of the image content, a large set of local features extracted from a large corpus of images are clustered. In this way the local feature space is divided into informative regions (*visual words*) and the collection of the obtained visual words is called *visual vocabulary*. k-means is the most commonly used clustering algorithm (Grauman and Leibe, 2011). In the special case of Fisher encoding (see below), the clustering of the features is performed with a *Gaussian mixture model* (GMM), see Perronnin et al. (2010). Figure 1 exemplifies a visual vocabulary construction pipeline. VSEM contains both the k-means and the GMM implementations.

Encoding The encoding step maps the local features extracted from an image to the corresponding visual words of the previously created vocabulary. The most common encoding strategy is called *hard quantization*, which assigns each feature to the nearest visual word's centroid (in Euclidean distance). Recently, more effective encoding methods have been introduced, among which the Fisher encoding (Perronnin et al., 2010) has been shown to outperform all the others (Chatfield et al., 2011). VSEM uses both the hard quantization and the Fisher encoding.

Spatial binning A consolidated way of introducing spatial information in BoVW is the use of spatial histograms (Lazebnik et al., 2006). The main idea is to divide the image into several (spatial) regions, compute the encoding for each region and stack the resulting histograms. This technique is referred to as *spatial binning* and it is implemented in VSEM. Figure 2 exemplifies the BoVW pipeline for a single image, involving local features extraction, encoding and spatial binning.

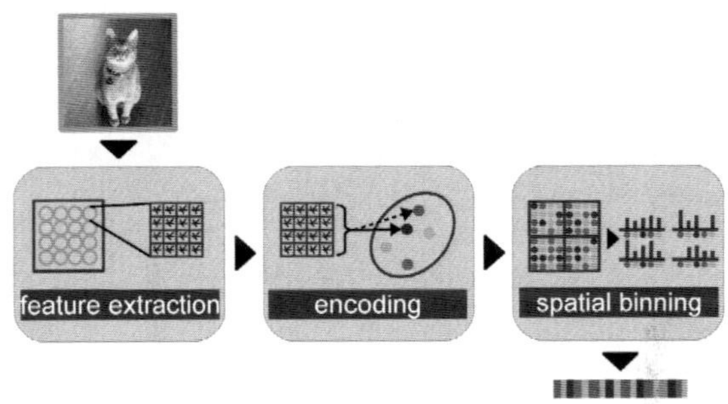

Figure 2: An example of a BoVW representation pipeline for an image. Figure inspired by Chatfield et al. (2011). Each feature extracted from the target image is assigned to the corresponding visual word(s). Then, spatial binning is performed.

Moreover, the input of spatial binning can be further refined by introducing localization. Three different types of localization are typically used: global, object, and surrounding. Global extracts visual information from the whole image and it is also the default option when the localization information is missing. Object extracts visual information from the object location only and the surrounding extracts visual information from outside the object location. Localization itself can either be done by humans (or ground truth annotation) but also by existing localization methods (Uijlings et al., 2013).

For localization, VSEM uses annotated object locations (in the format of bounding boxes) of the target object.

Aggregation Since each concept is represented by multiple images, an aggregation function for pooling the visual word occurrences across images has to be defined. As far as we know, the sum function has been the only function utilized so far. An example for the aggregation step is sketched in

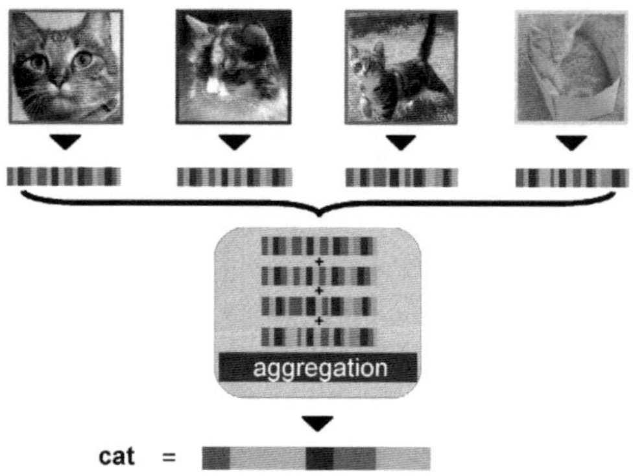

Figure 3: An example of a concept representation pipeline for **cat**. First, several images depicting a cat are represented as vectors of visual word counts and, second, the vectors are aggregated into one single concept vector.

figure 3. VSEM offers an implementation of the sum function.

Transformations Once the concept-representing visual vectors are built, two types of transformation can be performed over them to refine their raw visual word counts: *association scores* and *dimensionality reduction*. So far, the vectors that we have obtained represent co-occurrence counts of visual words with concepts. The goal of association scores is to distinguish interesting co-occurrences from those that are due to chance. In order to do this, VSEM implements two versions of mutual information (pointwise and local), see Evert (2005).

On the other hand, dimensionality reduction leads to matrices that are smaller and easier to work with. Moreover, some techniques are able to smooth the matrices and uncover latent dimensions. Common dimensionality reduction methods are singular value decomposition (Manning et al., 2008), non-negative matrix factorization (Lee and Seung, 2001) and neural networks (Hinton and Salakhutdinov, 2006). VSEM implements the singular value decomposition method.

3 Framework design

VSEM offers a friendly implementation of the pipeline described in Section 2. The framework is organized into five parts, which correspond to an equal number of MATLAB packages and it is written in object-oriented programming to encourage reusability. A description of the packages follows.

- `datasets` This package contains the code that manages the image data sets. We already provide a generic wrapper for several possible dataset formats (`VsemDataset`). Therefore, to use a new image data set two solutions are possible: either write a new class which extends `GenericDataset` or use directly `VsemDataset` after having rearranged the new data as described in **`help`** `VsemDataset`.

- `vision` This package contains the code for extracting the bag-of-visual-words representation of images. In the majority of cases, it can be used as a "black box" by the user. Nevertheless, if the user wants to add new functionalities such as new features or encodings, this is possible by simply extending the corresponding generic classes and the class `VsemHistogramExtractor`.

- `concepts` This is the package that deals with the construction of the image-based representation of concepts. `concepts` is the most important package of VSEM. It applies the image analysis methods to obtain the BoVW representation of the image data and then aggregates visual word counts concept-wise. The main class of this package is `ConceptSpace`, which takes care of storing concepts names and vectors and provides managing and transformation utilities as its methods.

- `benchmarks` VSEM offers a benchmarking suite to assess the quality of the visual concept representations. For example, it can be used to find the optimal parametrization of the visual pipeline.

- `helpers` This package contains supporting classes. There is a general `helpers` with functionalities shared across packages and several package specific `helpers`.

4 Getting started

Installation VSEM can be easily installed by running the file `vsemSetup.m`. Moreover, pascalDatasetSetup.m can be run to download and place the popular dataset, integrating it in the current pipeline.

Documentation All the MATLAB commands of VSEM are self documented (e.g. `help vsem`) and an HTML version of the MATLAB command documentation is available from the VSEM website.

The Pascal VOC demo The Pascal VOC demo provides a comprehensive example of the workings of VSEM. From the demo file `pascalVQDemo.m`multiple configurations are accessible. Additional settings are available and documented for each function, class or package in the toolbox (see Documentation).

Running the demo file executes the following lines of code and returns as output `conceptSpace`, which contains the visual concept representations for the Pascal data set.

```
% Create a matlab structure with the
% whole set of images in the Pascal
% dataset along with their annotation
dataset = datasets.VsemDataset(
    configuration.imagesPath,'
    annotationFolder',configuration.
    annotationPath);

% Initiate the class that handles
% the extraction of visual features.
featureExtractor = vision.features.
    PhowFeatureExtractor();

% Create the visual vocabulary
vocabulary = KmeansVocabulary.
    trainVocabulary(dataset,
    featureExtractor);

% Calculate semantic vectors
conceptSpace = conceptExtractor.
    extractConcepts(dataset,
    histogramExtractor);

% Compute pointwise mutual
% information
conceptSpace = conceptSpace.reweight();

% Conclude the demo, computing
% the similarity of correlation
% measures of the 190 possible
% pair of concepts from the Pascal
% dataset against a gold standard
[correlationScore, p-value] =
    similarityBenchmark.computeBenchmark
    (conceptSpace,similarityExtractor);
```

5 Conclusions

We have introduced VSEM, an open library for visual semantics. With VSEM it is possible to extract visual semantic information from tagged images and arrange such information into concept representations according to the tenets of distributional semantics, as applied to images instead of text. To analyze images, it uses state-of-the-art techniques such as the SIFT features and the bag-of-visual-words with spatial pyramid and Fisher encoding. In the future, we would like to add automatic localization strategies, new aggregation functions and a completely new package for fusing image- and text-based representations.

References

Mark Andrews, Gabriella Vigliocco, and David Vinson. 2009. Integrating experiential and distributional data to learn semantic representations. *Psychological Review*, 116(3):463–498.

Kobus Barnard, Pinar Duygulu, David Forsyth, Nando de Freitas, David Blei, and Michael Jordan. 2003. Matching words and pictures. *Journal of Machine Learning Research*, 3:1107–1135.

Marco Baroni and Alessandro Lenci. 2008. Concepts and properties in word spaces. *Italian Journal of Linguistics*, 20(1):55–88.

Marco Baroni, Eduard Barbu, Brian Murphy, and Massimo Poesio. 2010. Strudel: A distributional semantic model based on properties and types. *Cognitive Science*, 34(2):222–254.

Tamara Berg, Alexander Berg, and Jonathan Shih. 2010. Automatic attribute discovery and characterization from noisy Web data. In *ECCV*, pages 663–676, Crete, Greece.

Shane Bergsma and Randy Goebel. 2011. Using visual information to predict lexical preference. In *Proceedings of RANLP*, pages 399–405, Hissar, Bulgaria.

David M. Blei, Andrew Y. Ng, and Michael I. Jordan. 2003. Latent Dirichlet allocation. *Journal of Machine Learning Research*, 3:993–1022.

Elia Bruni, Giang Binh Tran, and Marco Baroni. 2011. Distributional semantics from text and images. In *Proceedings of the EMNLP GEMS Workshop*, pages 22–32, Edinburgh, UK.

Elia Bruni, Gemma Boleda, Marco Baroni, and Nam Khanh Tran. 2012a. Distributional semantics in Technicolor. In *Proceedings of ACL*, pages 136–145, Jeju Island, Korea.

Elia Bruni, Jasper Uijlings, Marco Baroni, and Nicu Sebe. 2012b. Distributional semantics with eyes: Using image analysis to improve computational representations of word meaning. In *Proceedings of ACM Multimedia*, pages 1219–1228, Nara, Japan.

Ken Chatfield, Victor Lempitsky, Andrea Vedaldi, and Andrew Zisserman. 2011. The devil is in the details: an evaluation of recent feature encoding methods. In *Proceedings of BMVC*, Dundee, UK.

Stefan Evert. 2005. *The Statistics of Word Cooccurrences*. Dissertation, Stuttgart University.

Ali Farhadi, Ian Endres, Derek Hoiem, and David Forsyth. 2009. Describing objects by their attributes. In *Proceedings of CVPR*, pages 1778–1785, Miami Beach, FL.

Yansong Feng and Mirella Lapata. 2010. Visual information in semantic representation. In *Proceedings of HLT-NAACL*, pages 91–99, Los Angeles, CA.

Kristen Grauman and Bastian Leibe. 2011. *Visual Object Recognition*. Morgan & Claypool, San Francisco.

Geoffrey Hinton and Ruslan Salakhutdinov. 2006. Reducing the dimensionality of data with neural networks. *Science*, 313(5786):504 – 507.

Girish Kulkarni, Visruth Premraj, Sagnik Dhar, Siming Li, Yejin Choi, Alexander C. Berg, and Tamara L. Berg. 2011. Baby talk: Understanding and generating simple image descriptions. In *Proceedings of CVPR*, Colorado Springs, MSA.

Thomas Landauer and Susan Dumais. 1997. A solution to Plato's problem: The latent semantic analysis theory of acquisition, induction, and representation of knowledge. *Psychological Review*, 104(2):211–240.

Svetlana Lazebnik, Cordelia Schmid, and Jean Ponce. 2006. Beyond bags of features: Spatial pyramid matching for recognizing natural scene categories. In *Proceedings of CVPR*, pages 2169–2178, Washington, DC.

Daniel D. Lee and H. Sebastian Seung. 2001. Algorithms for non-negative matrix factorization. In *In NIPS*, pages 556–562. MIT Press.

Chee Wee Leong and Rada Mihalcea. 2011. Going beyond text: A hybrid image-text approach for measuring word relatedness. In *Proceedings of IJCNLP*, pages 1403–1407.

David Lowe. 2004. Distinctive image features from scale-invariant keypoints. *International Journal of Computer Vision*, 60(2), November.

Chris Manning, Prabhakar Raghavan, and Hinrich Schütze. 2008. *Introduction to Information Retrieval*. Cambridge University Press, Cambridge, UK.

K. Mikolajczyk, T. Tuytelaars, C. Schmid, A. Zisserman, J. Matas, F. Schaffalitzky, T. Kadir, and L. V. Gool. 2005. A Comparison of Affine Region Detectors. *International Journal of Computer Vision*, 65(1).

Florent Perronnin, Jorge Sanchez, and Thomas Mensink. 2010. Improving the fisher kernel for large-scale image classification. In *Proceedings of ECCV*, pages 143–156, Berlin, Heidelberg.

Brian Riordan and Michael Jones. 2011. Redundancy in perceptual and linguistic experience: Comparing feature-based and distributional models of semantic representation. *Topics in Cognitive Science*, 3(2):1–43.

Josef Sivic and Andrew Zisserman. 2003. Video Google: A text retrieval approach to object matching in videos. In *Proceedings of ICCV*, pages 1470–1477, Nice, France.

Peter Turney and Patrick Pantel. 2010. From frequency to meaning: Vector space models of semantics. *Journal of Artificial Intelligence Research*, 37:141–188.

J.R.R. Uijlings, K.E.A. van de Sande, T. Gevers, and A.W.M. Smeulders. 2013. Selective search for object recognition. *IJCV*.

Andrea Vedaldi and Brian Fulkerson. 2010. Vlfeat – an open and portable library of computer vision algorithms. In *Proceedings of ACM Multimedia*, pages 1469–1472, Firenze, Italy.

Docent: A Document-Level Decoder for Phrase-Based Statistical Machine Translation

Christian Hardmeier   Sara Stymne   Jörg Tiedemann   Joakim Nivre
Uppsala University
Department of Linguistics and Philology
Box 635, 751 26 Uppsala, Sweden
firstname.lastname@lingfil.uu.se

Abstract

We describe Docent, an open-source decoder for statistical machine translation that breaks with the usual sentence-by-sentence paradigm and translates complete documents as units. By taking translation to the document level, our decoder can handle feature models with arbitrary discourse-wide dependencies and constitutes an essential infrastructure component in the quest for discourse-aware SMT models.

1 Motivation

Most of the research on statistical machine translation (SMT) that was conducted during the last 20 years treated every text as a "bag of sentences" and disregarded all relations between elements in different sentences. Systematic research into explicitly discourse-related problems has only begun very recently in the SMT community (Hardmeier, 2012) with work on topics such as pronominal anaphora (Le Nagard and Koehn, 2010; Hardmeier and Federico, 2010; Guillou, 2012), verb tense (Gong et al., 2012) and discourse connectives (Meyer et al., 2012).

One of the problems that hamper the development of cross-sentence models for SMT is the fact that the assumption of sentence independence is at the heart of the dynamic programming (DP) beam search algorithm most commonly used for decoding in phrase-based SMT systems (Koehn et al., 2003). For integrating cross-sentence features into the decoding process, researchers had to adopt strategies like two-pass decoding (Le Nagard and Koehn, 2010). We have previously proposed an algorithm for document-level phrase-based SMT decoding (Hardmeier et al., 2012). Our decoding algorithm is based on local search instead of dynamic programming and permits the integration of document-level models with unrestricted dependencies, so that a model score can be conditioned on arbitrary elements occurring anywhere in the input document or in the translation that is being generated. In this paper, we present an open-source implementation of this search algorithm. The decoder is written in C++ and follows an object-oriented design that makes it easy to extend it with new feature models, new search operations or different types of local search algorithms. The code is released under the GNU General Public License and published on Github[1] to make it easy for other researchers to use it in their own experiments.

2 Document-Level Decoding with Local Search

Our decoder is based on the phrase-based SMT model described by Koehn et al. (2003) and implemented, for example, in the popular Moses decoder (Koehn et al., 2007). Translation is performed by splitting the input sentence into a number of contiguous word sequences, called phrases, which are translated into the target language through a phrase dictionary lookup and optionally reordered. The choice between different translations of an ambiguous source phrase and the ordering of the target phrases are guided by a scoring function that combines a set of scores taken from the phrase table with scores from other models such as an n-gram language model. The actual translation process is realised as a search for the highest-scoring translation in the space of all the possible translations that could be generated given the models.

The decoding approach that is implemented in Docent was first proposed by Hardmeier et al. (2012) and is based on local search. This means that it has a state corresponding to a complete, if possibly bad, translation of a document at every

[1] `https://github.com/chardmeier/docent/wiki`

stage of the search progress. Search proceeds by making small changes to the current search state in order to transform it gradually into a better translation. This differs from the DP algorithm used in other decoders, which starts with an empty translation and expands it bit by bit. It is similar to previous work on phrase-based SMT decoding by Langlais et al. (2007), but enables the creation of document-level models, which was not addressed by earlier approaches.

Docent currently implements two search algorithms that are different generalisations of the hill climbing local search algorithm by Hardmeier et al. (2012). The original hill climbing algorithm starts with an initial state and generates possible successor states by randomly applying simple elementary operations to the state. After each operation, the new state is scored and accepted if its score is better than that of the previous state, else rejected. Search terminates when the decoder cannot find an acceptable successor state after a certain number of attempts, or when a maximum number of steps is reached.

Simulated annealing is a stochastic variant of hill climbing that always accepts moves towards better states, but can also accept moves towards lower-scoring states with a certain probability that depends on a temperature parameter in order to escape local maxima. *Local beam search* generalises hill climbing in a different way by keeping a beam of a fixed number of multiple states at any time and randomly picking a state from the beam to modify at each move. The original hill climbing procedure can be recovered as a special case of either one of these search algorithms, by calling simulated annealing with a fixed temperature of 0 or local beam search with a beam size of 1.

Initial states for the search process can be generated either by selecting a random segmentation with random translations from the phrase table in monotonic order, or by running DP beam search with sentence-local models as a first pass. For the second option, which generally yields better search results, Docent is linked with the Moses decoder and makes direct calls to the DP beam search algorithm implemented by Moses. In addition to these state initialisation procedures, Docent can save a search state to a disk file which can be loaded again in a subsequent decoding pass. This saves time especially when running repeated experiments from the same starting point obtained by DP search.

In order to explore the complete search space of phrase-based SMT, the search operations in a local search decoder must be able to change the phrase translations, the order of the output phrases and the segmentation of the source sentence into phrases. The three operations used by Hardmeier et al. (2012), *change-phrase-translation*, *resegment* and *swap-phrases*, jointly meet this requirement and are all implemented in Docent. Additionally, Docent features three extra operations, all of which affect the target word order: The *move-phrases* operation moves a phrase to another location in the sentence. Unlike *swap-phrases*, it does not require that another phrase be moved in the opposite direction at the same time. A pair of operations called *permute-phrases* and *linearise-phrases* can reorder a sequence of phrases into random order and back into the order corresponding to the source language.

Since the search algorithm in Docent is stochastic, repeated runs of the decoder will generally produce different output. However, the variance of the output is usually small, especially when initialising with a DP search pass, and it tends to be lower than the variance introduced by feature weight tuning (Hardmeier et al., 2012; Stymne et al., 2013a).

3 Available Feature Models

In its current version, Docent implements a selection of sentence-local feature models that makes it possible to build a baseline system with a configuration comparable to that of a typical Moses baseline system. The published source code also includes prototype implementations of a few document-level models. These models should be considered work in progress and serve as a demonstration of the cross-sentence modelling capabilities of the decoder. They have not yet reached a state of maturity that would make them suitable for production use.

The sentence-level models provided by Docent include the phrase table, n-gram language models implemented with the KenLM toolkit (Heafield, 2011), an unlexicalised distortion cost model with geometric decay (Koehn et al., 2003) and a word penalty cost. All of these features are designed to be compatible with the corresponding features in Moses. From among the typical set of baseline features in Moses, we have not implemented the lexicalised distortion model, but this model could easily be added if required. Docent uses the same binary file format for phrase tables as Moses, so the same training apparatus can be used.

DP-based SMT decoders have a parameter called distortion limit that limits the difference in word order between the input and the MT output. In DP search, this is formally considered to be a parameter of the search algorithm because it affects the algorithmic complexity of the search by controlling how many translation options must be considered at each hypothesis expansion. The stochastic search algorithm in Docent does not require this limitation, but it can still be useful because the standard models of SMT do not model long-distance reordering well. Docent therefore includes a separate indicator feature to indicate a violated distortion limit. In conjunction with a very large weight, this feature can effectively ensure that the distortion limit is enforced. In contrast with the distortion limit parameter of a DP decoder, the weight of our distortion limit feature can potentially be tuned to permit occasional distortion limit violations when they contribute to better translations.

The document-level models included in Docent include a *length parity model*, a *semantic language model* as well as a collection of document-level *readability models*. The length parity model is a proof-of-concept model that ensures that all sentences in a document have either consistently odd or consistently even length. It serves mostly as a template to demonstrate how a simple document-level model can be implemented in the decoder. The semantic language model was originally proposed by Hardmeier et al. (2012) to improve lexical cohesion in a document. It is a cross-sentence model over sequences of content words that are scored based on their similarity in a word vector space. The readability models serve to improve the readability of the translation by encouraging the selection of easier and more consistent target words. They are described and demonstrated in more detail in section 5.

Docent can read input files both in the NIST-XML format commonly used to encode documents in MT shared tasks such as NIST or WMT and in the more elaborate MMAX format (Müller and Strube, 2003). The MMAX format makes it possible to include a wide range of discourse-level corpus annotations such as coreference links. These annotations can then be accessed by the feature models. To allow for additional target-language information such as morphological features of target words, Docent can handle simple word-level annotations that are encoded in the phrase table in the same way as target language factors in Moses.

In order to optimise feature weights we have adapted the Moses tuning infrastructure to Docent. In this way we can take advantage of all its features, for instance using different optimisation algorithms such as MERT (Och, 2003) or PRO (Hopkins and May, 2011), and selective tuning of a subset of features. Since document features only give meaningful scores on the document level and not on the sentence level, we naturally perform optimisation on document level, which typically means that we need more data than for the optimisation of sentence-based decoding. The results we obtain are relatively stable and competitive with sentence-level optimisation of the same models (Stymne et al., 2013a).

4 Implementing Feature Models Efficiently

While translating a document, the local search decoder attempts to make a great number of moves. For each move, a score must be computed and tested against the acceptance criterion. An overwhelming majority of the proposed moves will be rejected. In order to achieve reasonably fast decoding times, efficient scoring is paramount. Recomputing the scores of the whole document at every step would be far too slow for the decoder to be useful. Fortunately, score computation can be sped up in two ways. Knowledge about how the state to be scored was generated from its predecessor helps to limit recomputations to a minimum, and by adopting a two-step scoring procedure that just computes the scores that can be calculated with little effort at first, we need to compute the complete score only if the new state has some chance of being accepted.

The scores of SMT feature models can usually be decomposed in some way over parts of the document. The traditional models borrowed from sentence-based decoding are necessarily decomposable at the sentence level, and in practice, all common models are designed to meet the constraints of DP beam search, which ensures that they can in fact be decomposed over even smaller sequences of just a few words. For genuine document-level features, this is not the case, but even these models can often be decomposed in some way, for instance over paragraphs, anaphoric links or lexical chains. To take advantage of this fact, feature models in Docent always have access to the previous state and its score and to a list of the state modifications that transform the previous state into the next. The scores of the new state are calculated by identifying the parts of a document that are affected by the modifications, subtracting the old scores of this part from the previous score and adding the new scores. This approach to scoring makes feature model implementation a bit more complicated than in DP search, but it gives the feature models full control over how they decompose a document while still permitting efficient decoding.

A feature model class in Docent implements three methods. The *initDocument* method is called once per document when decoding starts. It straightforwardly computes the model score for the entire document from scratch. When a state is modified, the decoder first invokes the *estimateScoreUpdate* method. Rather than calculating the new score exactly, this method is only required to return an upper bound that reflects the maximum score that could possibly be achieved by this state. The search algorithm then checks this upper bound against the acceptance criterion. Only if the upper bound meets the criterion does it call the *updateScore* method to calculate the exact score, which is then checked against the acceptance criterion again.

The motivation for this two-step procedure is that some models can compute an upper bound approximation much more efficiently than an exact score. For any model whose score is a log probability, a value of 0 is a loose upper bound that can be returned instantly, but in many cases, we can do much better. In the case of the n-gram language model, for instance, a more accurate upper bound can be computed cheaply by subtracting from the old score all log-probabilities of n-grams that are affected by the state modifications without adding the scores of the n-grams replacing them in the new state. This approximation can be calculated without doing any language model lookups at all. On the other hand, some models like the distortion cost or the word penalty are very cheap to compute, so that the *estimateScoreUpdate* method can simply return the precise score as a tight upper bound. If a state gets rejected because of a low score on one of the cheap models, this means we will never have to compute the more expensive feature scores at all.

5 Readability: A Case Study

As a case study we report initial results on how document-wide features can be used in Docent in order to improve the readability of texts by encouraging simple and consistent terminology (Stymne et al., 2013b). This work is a first step towards achieving joint SMT and text simplification, with the final goal of adapting MT to user groups such as people with reading disabilities.

Lexical consistency modelling for SMT has been attempted before. The suggested approaches have been limited by the use of sentence-level decoders, however, and had to resort to procedures like post processing (Carpuat, 2009), multiple decoding runs with frozen counts from previous runs (Ture et al., 2012), or cache-based models (Tiedemann, 2010). In Docent, however, we always have access to a full document translation, which makes it straightforward to include features directly into the decoder.

We implemented four features on the document level. The first two features are type token ratio (TTR) and a reformulation of it, OVIX, which is less sensitive to text length. These ratios have been related to the "idea density" of a text (Mühlenbock and Kokkinakis, 2009). We also wanted to encourage consistent translations of words, for which we used the Q-value (Deléger et al., 2006), which has been proposed to measure term quality. We applied it on word level (QW) and phrase level (QP). These features need access to the full target document, which we have in Docent. In addition, we included two sentence-level count features for long words that have been used to measure the readability of Swedish texts (Mühlenbock and Kokkinakis, 2009).

We tested our features on English–Swedish translation using the Europarl corpus. For training we used 1,488,322 sentences. As test data, we extracted 20 documents with a total of 690 sentences. We used the standard set of baseline features: 5-gram language model, translation model with 5 weights, a word penalty and a distortion penalty.

Baseline	Readability features	Comment
de ärade ledamöterna (the honourable Members)	ledamöterna (the members) / ni (you)	+ Removal of non-essential words
på ett sådant sätt att (in such a way that)	så att (so that)	+ Simplified expression
gemenskapslagstiftningen (the community legislation)	gemenskapens lagstiftning (the community's legislation)	+ Shorter words by changing long compound to genitive construction
Världshandelsorganisationen (World Trade Organisation)	WTO (WTO)	– Changing long compound to English-based abbreviation
handlingsplanen (the action plan)	planen (the plan)	– Removal of important word
ägnat särskild uppmärksamhet åt (paid particular attention to)	särskilt uppmärksam på (particular attentive on)	– Bad grammar because of changed part of speech and missing verb

Table 2: Example translation snippets with comments

Feature	BLEU	OVIX	LIX
Baseline	0.243	56.88	51.17
TTR	0.243	55.25	51.04
OVIX	0.243	54.65	51.00
QW	0.242	57.16	51.16
QP	0.243	57.07	51.06
All	0.235	47.80	49.29

Table 1: Results for adding single lexical consistency features to Docent

To evaluate our system we used the BLEU score (Papineni et al., 2002) together with a set of readability metrics, since readability is what we hoped to improve by adding consistency features. Here we used OVIX to confirm a direct impact on consistency, and LIX (Björnsson, 1968), which is a common readability measure for Swedish. Unfortunately we do not have access to simplified translated text, so we calculate the MT metrics against a standard reference, which means that simple texts will likely have worse scores than complicated texts closer to the reference translation.

We tuned the standard features using Moses and MERT, and then added each lexical consistency feature with a small weight, using a grid search approach to find values with a small impact. The results are shown in Table 1. As can be seen, for individual features the translation quality was maintained, with small improvements in LIX, and in OVIX for the TTR and OVIX features. For the combination we lost a little bit on translation quality, but there was a larger effect on the readability metrics. When we used larger weights, there was a bigger impact on the readability metrics, with a further decrease on MT quality.

We also investigated what types of changes the readability features could lead to. Table 2 shows a sample of translations where the baseline is compared to systems with readability features. There are both cases where the readability features help and cases where they are problematic. Overall, these examples show that our simple features can help achieve some interesting simplifications.

There is still much work to do on how to take best advantage of the possibilities in Docent in order to achieve readable texts. This attempt shows the feasibility of the approach. We plan to extend this work for instance by better feature optimisation, by integrating part-of-speech tags into our features in order to focus on terms rather than common words, and by using simplified texts for evaluation and tuning.

6 Conclusions

In this paper, we have presented Docent, an open-source document-level decoder for phrase-based SMT released under the GNU General Public License. Docent is the first decoder that permits the inclusion of feature models with unrestricted dependencies between arbitrary parts of the output, even crossing sentence boundaries. A number of research groups have recently started to investigate the interplay between SMT and discourse-level phenomena such as pronominal anaphora, verb tense selection and the generation of discourse connectives. We expect that the availability of a document-level decoder will make it substantially easier to leverage discourse information in SMT and make SMT models explore new ground beyond the next sentence boundary.

References

Carl-Hugo Björnsson. 1968. *Läsbarhet*. Liber, Stockholm.

Marine Carpuat. 2009. One translation per discourse. In *Proceedings of the Workshop on Semantic Evaluations: Recent Achievements and Future Directions (SEW-2009)*, pages 19–27, Boulder, Colorado.

Louise Deléger, Magnus Merkel, and Pierre Zweigenbaum. 2006. Enriching medical terminologies: an approach based on aligned corpora. In *International Congress of the European Federation for Medical Informatics*, pages 747–752, Maastricht, The Netherlands.

Zhengxian Gong, Min Zhang, Chew Lim Tan, and Guodong Zhou. 2012. N-gram-based tense models for statistical machine translation. In *Proceedings of the 2012 Joint Conference on Empirical Methods in Natural Language Processing and Computational Natural Language Learning*, pages 276–285, Jeju Island, Korea.

Liane Guillou. 2012. Improving pronoun translation for statistical machine translation. In *Proceedings of the Student Research Workshop at the 13th Conference of the European Chapter of the Association for Computational Linguistics*, pages 1–10, Avignon, France.

Christian Hardmeier and Marcello Federico. 2010. Modelling pronominal anaphora in statistical machine translation. In *Proceedings of the seventh International Workshop on Spoken Language Translation (IWSLT)*, pages 283–289, Paris, France.

Christian Hardmeier, Joakim Nivre, and Jörg Tiedemann. 2012. Document-wide decoding for phrase-based statistical machine translation. In *Proceedings of the 2012 Joint Conference on Empirical Methods in Natural Language Processing and Computational Natural Language Learning*, pages 1179–1190, Jeju Island, Korea.

Christian Hardmeier. 2012. Discourse in statistical machine translation: A survey and a case study. *Discours*, 11.

Kenneth Heafield. 2011. KenLM: faster and smaller language model queries. In *Proceedings of the Sixth Workshop on Statistical Machine Translation*, pages 187–197, Edinburgh, Scotland.

Mark Hopkins and Jonathan May. 2011. Tuning as ranking. In *Proceedings of the 2011 Conference on Empirical Methods in Natural Language Processing*, pages 1352–1362, Edinburgh, Scotland.

Philipp Koehn, Franz Josef Och, and Daniel Marcu. 2003. Statistical phrase-based translation. In *Proceedings of the 2003 conference of the North American chapter of the Association for Computational Linguistics on Human Language Technology*, pages 48–54, Edmonton.

Philipp Koehn, Hieu Hoang, Alexandra Birch, et al. 2007. Moses: open source toolkit for Statistical Machine Translation. In *Annual meeting of the Association for Computational Linguistics: Demonstration session*, pages 177–180, Prague, Czech Republic.

Philippe Langlais, Alexandre Patry, and Fabrizio Gotti. 2007. A greedy decoder for phrase-based statistical machine translation. In *TMI-2007: Proceedings of the 11th International Conference on Theoretical and Methodological Issues in Machine Translation*, pages 104–113, Skövde, Sweden.

Ronan Le Nagard and Philipp Koehn. 2010. Aiding pronoun translation with co-reference resolution. In *Proceedings of the Joint Fifth Workshop on Statistical Machine Translation and MetricsMATR*, pages 252–261, Uppsala, Sweden.

Thomas Meyer, Andrei Popescu-Belis, Najeh Hajlaoui, and Andrea Gesmundo. 2012. Machine translation of labeled discourse connectives. In *Proceedings of the Tenth Biennial Conference of the Association for Machine Translation in the Americas (AMTA)*, San Diego, California, USA.

Katarina Mühlenbock and Sofie Johansson Kokkinakis. 2009. LIX 68 revisited – an extended readability. In *Proceedings of the Corpus Linguistics Conference*, Liverpool, UK.

Christoph Müller and Michael Strube. 2003. Multi-level annotation in MMAX. In *Proceedings of the Fourth SIGdial Workshop on Discourse and Dialogue*, pages 198–207, Sapporo, Japan.

Franz Josef Och. 2003. Minimum error rate training in statistical machine translation. In *Proceedings of the 42nd Annual Meeting of the Association for Computational Linguistics*, pages 160–167, Sapporo, Japan.

Kishore Papineni, Salim Roukos, Todd Ward, and Wei-Jing Zhu. 2002. BLEU: A method for automatic evaluation of machine translation. In *Proceedings of the 40th Annual Meeting of the Association for Computational Linguistics*, pages 311–318, Philadelphia, Pennsylvania, USA.

Sara Stymne, Christian Hardmeier, Jörg Tiedemann, and Joakim Nivre. 2013a. Feature weight optimization for discourse-level SMT. In *Proceedings of the Workshop on Discourse in Machine Translation (DiscoMT)*, Sofia, Bulgaria.

Sara Stymne, Jörg Tiedemann, Christian Hardmeier, and Joakim Nivre. 2013b. Statistical machine translation with readability constraints. In *Proceedings of the 19th Nordic Conference of Computational Linguistics (NODALIDA 2013)*, pages 375–386, Oslo, Norway.

Jörg Tiedemann. 2010. Context adaptation in statistical machine translation using models with exponentially decaying cache. In *Proceedings of the ACL 2010 Workshop on Domain Adaptation for Natural Language Processing (DANLP)*, pages 8–15, Uppsala, Sweden.

Ferhan Ture, Douglas W. Oard, and Philip Resnik. 2012. Encouraging consistent translation choices. In *Proceedings of the 2012 Conference of the North American Chapter of the Association for Computational Linguistics: Human Language Technologies*, pages 417–426, Montréal, Canada.

Mr. MIRA: Open-Source Large-Margin Structured Learning on MapReduce

Vladimir Eidelman[1], **Ke Wu**[1], **Ferhan Ture**[1], **Philip Resnik**[2], **Jimmy Lin**[3]
[1] Dept. of Computer Science [2] Dept. of Linguistics [3] The iSchool
Institute for Advanced Computer Studies
University of Maryland
{eidelman,wuke,fture,resnik,jimmylin}@umd.edu

Abstract

We present an open-source framework for large-scale online structured learning. Developed with the flexibility to handle cost-augmented inference problems such as statistical machine translation (SMT), our large-margin learner can be used with any decoder. Integration with MapReduce using Hadoop streaming allows efficient scaling with increasing size of training data. Although designed with a focus on SMT, the decoder-agnostic design of our learner allows easy future extension to other structured learning problems such as sequence labeling and parsing.

1 Introduction

Structured learning problems such as sequence labeling or parsing, where the output has a rich internal structure, commonly arise in NLP. While batch learning algorithms adapted for structured learning such as CRFs (Lafferty et al., 2001) and structural SVMs (Joachims, 1998) have received much attention, online methods such as the structured perceptron (Collins, 2002) and a family of Passive-Aggressive algorithms (Crammer et al., 2006) have recently gained prominence across many tasks, including part-of-speech tagging (Shen, 2007), parsing (McDonald et al., 2005) and statistical machine translation (SMT) (Chiang, 2012), due to their ability to deal with large training sets and high-dimensional input representations.

Unlike batch learners, which must consider all examples when optimizing the objective, online learners operate in rounds, optimizing using one example or a handful of examples at a time. This online nature offers several attractive properties, facilitating scaling to large training sets while remaining simple and offering fast convergence.

Mr. MIRA, the open source system[1] described in this paper, implements an online large-margin structured learning algorithm based on MIRA (§2.1), for cost-augmented online large-scale training in high-dimensional feature spaces. Our contribution lies in providing the first published decoder-agnostic parallelization of MIRA with Hadoop for structured learning.

While the current demonstrated application focuses on large-scale discriminative training for machine translation, the learning algorithm is general with respect to the inference algorithm employed. We are able to decouple our learner entirely from the MT decoder, allowing users to specify their own inference procedure through a simple text communication protocol (§2.2). The learner only requires k-best output with feature vectors, as well as the specification of a cost function. Standard automatic evaluation metrics for MT, such as BLEU (Papineni et al., 2002) and TER (Snover et al., 2006), have already been implemented. Furthermore, our system can be extended to other structured learning problems with a minimal amount of effort, simply by implementing a task-specific cost function and specifying an appropriate decoder.

Through Hadoop streaming, our system can take advantage of commodity clusters to handle large-scale training (§3), while also being capable of running in environments ranging from a single machine to a PBS-managed batch cluster. Experimental results (§4) show that it scales linearly and makes fast parameter tuning on large tuning sets for SMT practical.

2 Learning and Inference

2.1 Online Large-Margin Learning

MIRA is a popular online large-margin structured learning method for NLP tasks (McDonald et al., 2005; Chiang et al., 2009; Chiang, 2012). The

[1] https://github.com/kho/mr-mira

main intuition is that we want our model to enforce a margin between the correct and incorrect outputs of a sentence that agrees with our cost function. This is done by making the smallest update we can to our parameters, $\mathbf{w}$, on every sentence, that will ensure that the difference in model scores $\delta \mathbf{f}_i(y') = \mathbf{w}^\top(\mathbf{f}(x_i, y^+) - \mathbf{f}(x_i, y'))$ between the correct output y^+ and incorrect output y' is at least as large as the cost, $\Delta_i(y')$, incurred by predicting the incorrect output:[2]

$$\mathbf{w}_{t+1} = \arg\min_{\mathbf{w}} \frac{1}{2}||\mathbf{w} - \mathbf{w}_t||^2 + C\xi_i$$
$$\text{s.t. } \forall y' \in \mathcal{Y}(x_i),\ \delta \mathbf{f}_i(y') \geq \Delta_i(y') - \xi_i$$

where $\mathcal{Y}(x_i)$ is the space of possible structured outputs we are able to produce from x_i, and C is a regularization parameter that controls the size of the update. In practice, we can define $\mathcal{Y}(x_i)$ to be the k-best output. With a passive-aggressive (PA) update, the $\forall y'$ constraint above can be approximated by selecting the single most violated constraint, which maximizes $y' \leftarrow \arg\max_{y \in \mathcal{Y}(x_i)} \mathbf{w}^\top \mathbf{f}(x_i, y) + \Delta_i(y)$. This optimization problem is attractive because it reduces to a simple analytical solution, essentially performing a subgradient descent step with the step size adjusted based on each example:

$$\alpha \leftarrow \min\left(C, \frac{\Delta_i(y') - \delta \mathbf{f}_i(y')}{||\mathbf{f}(x_i, y^+) - \mathbf{f}(x_i, y')||^2}\right)$$
$$\mathbf{w} \leftarrow \mathbf{w} + \eta\alpha\left(\mathbf{f}(x_i, y^+) - \mathbf{f}(x_i, y')\right)$$

The user-defined cost function is a task-specific external measure of quality that relays how bad selecting y' truly is on the task we care about. The cost can take any form as long as it decomposes across the local parts of the structure, just as the feature functions. For instance, it could be the Hamming loss for sequence labeling, F-score for parsing, or an approximate BLEU score for SMT.

Cost-augmented Inference For most structured prediction problems in machine learning, $y_i \in \mathcal{Y}(x_i)$, that is, the model is able to produce, and thus score, the correct output structure, meaning $y^+ = y_i$. However, for certain NLP problems this may not be the case. For instance in SMT, our model may not be able to produce or reach the correct reference translation, which prohibits our model from scoring it. This problem necessitates cost-augmented inference, where we select $y^+ \leftarrow \arg\max_{y \in \mathcal{Y}(x_i)} \mathbf{w}^\top \mathbf{f}(x_i, y) - \Delta_i(y)$ from the space of structures our model can produce, to stand in for the correct output in optimization. Our system was developed to handle both cases, with the decoder providing the k-best list to the learner, specifying whether to perform cost-augmented selection.

Sparse Features While utilizing sparse features is a primary motivation for performing large-scale discriminative training, which features to use and how to learn their weights can have a large impact on the potential benefit. To this end, we incorporate ℓ_1/ℓ_2 regularization for joint feature selection in order to improve efficiency and counter overfitting effects (Simianer et al., 2012). Furthermore, the PA update has a single learning rate η for all features, which specifies how much the feature weights can change at each update. However, since dense features (e.g., language model) are observed far more frequently than sparse features (e.g., rule id), we may instead want to use a per-feature learning rate that allows larger steps for features that do not have much support. Thus, we allow setting an adaptive per-feature learning rate (Green et al., 2013; Crammer et al., 2009; Duchi et al., 2011).

2.2 Learner/Decoder Communication

Training requires communication between the decoder and the learner. The decoder needs to receive weight updates and the input sentence from the learner; and the learner needs to receive k-best output with feature vectors from the decoder. This is essentially all the required communication between the learner and the decoder. Below, we describe a simple line-based text protocol.

Input sentence and weight updates Following common practice in machine translation, the learner encodes each input sentence as a single-line SGML entry named `seg` and sends it to the decoder. The first line of Figure 1 is an example sentence in this format. In addition to the required sentence ID (useful in parallel processing), an optional `delta` field is used to encode the weight updates, as a sparse vector indexed by feature names. First, for each name and update pair, a binary record consisting of a null-terminated string (name) and a double-precision floating point number in native byte order (update) is created. Then, all binary records are con-

[2]For a more formal description we refer the reader to (Crammer et al., 2006; Chiang, 2012).

```
<seg id="123" delta="TE0AexSuR+F6hD8="> das ist ein kleine haus </seg>
<seg id="124"> ein kleine haus </seg>\tein kleine ||| a small\thaus ||| house
```

Figure 1: Example decoder input in SGML

```
5
123 ||| 5 ||| this is a small house ||| TE0AAAAA... <base64> ||| 120.3
123 ||| 5 ||| this is the small house ||| <base64> ||| 118.4
123 ||| 5 ||| this was small house ||| <base64> ||| 110.5
<empty>
<empty>
```

Figure 2: Example k-best output

catenated and encoded in base64. In the example above, the value of `delta` is the base64 encoding of `0x4c 0x4d 0x00 0x7b 0x14 0xae 0x47 0xe1 0x7a 0x84 0x3f`. The first 3 bytes store the feature name (`LM`) and the next 8 bytes is its update (0.01), to be added to the decoder's current value of the corresponding feature weight.

The learner also allows the user to pass any additional information to the decoder, as long as it can be encoded as a single-line text string. Such information, if given, is appended after the `seg` entry, with a leading tab character as the delimiter. For example, the second line of Figure 1 passes two phrase translation rules to the decoder.

k-best output The decoder reads from standard input and outputs the k-best output for one input sentence before consuming the next line. For the k-best output, the decoder first outputs to standard output a line consisting of a single integer N. Next the decoder outputs N lines where each line can be either empty or an actual hypothesis. When the line is an actual hypothesis, it consists of the following parts:

```
SID ||| LEN ||| TOK ||| FEAT [ REST ]
```

`SID` is the sentence ID of the corresponding input; `LEN` is the length of source sentence;[3] `TOK` contains the tokens of the hypothesis sentence separated by spaces; `FEAT` is the feature vector, encoded in the same way as the weight updates, delimited by a whitespace. Everything after `FEAT` until the end of the line is discarded. See Figure 2 for an example of k-best output. Note the scores after the last `|||` are discarded by the learner.

Overall workflow The learner reads lines from standard input in the following tab-delimited format:

```
SRC<tab>REF<tab>REST
```

`SRC` is the actual input sentence as a `seg` entry; `REF` is the gold output for the input sentence, for example, reference translations in MT;[4] `REST` is the additional information that will be appended after the `seg` entry and passed to the decoder.

The learner creates a sub-process for the decoder and connects to the sub-process' standard input and output with pipes. Then it processes the input lines one by one. For each line, it first sends a composed input message to the decoder, combining the input sentence, weight updates, and user-supplied information. Next it collects the k-best output from the decoder, solves the QP problem to obtain weight updates and repeats.

The learner produces two types of output. First, the 1-best hypothesis for each input sentence, in the following format:

```
SID<tab>TOK
```

Second, when there are no more input lines, the learner outputs final weights and the number of lines processed, in the following format:

```
-1<tab>NUM ||| WEIGHTS
```

The 1-best hypotheses can be scored against references to obtain an estimate of cost. The final weights are stored in a way convenient for averaging in a parallel setting, as we shall discuss next.

3 Large-Scale Discriminative Training

3.1 MapReduce

With large amounts of data available today, distributed computations have become essential. MapReduce (Dean and Ghemawat, 2004) has emerged as a popular distributed processing framework for commodity clusters that has gained widespread adoption in both industry and academia, thanks to its simplicity and the availability of the Hadoop open-source implementation. MapReduce provides a higher level of

[3]This is used in computing the smoothed cost. Usually this is identical for all hypotheses if the input is a plain sentence. But in applications such as lattice-based translation, each hypothesis can be produced from different source sentences, resulting in different lengths.

[4]There can be multiple references, separated by `|||`.

abstraction for designing distributed algorithms compared to, say, MPI or pthreads, by hiding system-level details (e.g., deadlock, race conditions, machine failures) from the developer.

A single MapReduce program begins with a *map* phase, where mapper processes input key-value pairs to produce an arbitrary number of intermediate key-value pairs. The mappers execute in parallel, consuming data splits independently. Following the map phase, all key-value pairs emitted by the mappers are sorted by key and distributed to the reducers, such that all pairs sharing the same key are guaranteed to arrive at the same reducer. Finally, in the *reduce* phase, each reducer processes the intermediate key-value pairs it receives and emits final output key-value pairs.

3.2 System Architecture

Algorithm design We use Hadoop streaming to parallelize the training process. Hadoop streaming allows any arbitrary executable to serve as the mapper or reducer, as long as it handles key-value pairs properly.[5] One iteration of training is implemented as a single Hadoop streaming job. In the map step, our learner can be directly used as the mapper. Each mapper loads the same initial weights, processes a single split of data and produces key-value pairs: the one-best hypothesis of each sentence is output with the sentence ID as the key (non-negative); the final weights with respect to the split are output with a special negative key. In the reduce step, a single reducer collects all key-value pairs, grouped and sorted by keys. The one-best hypotheses are output to disk in the order they are received, so that the order matches the reference translation set. The reducer also computes the feature selection and weighted average of final weights received from all of the mappers. Assuming mapper i produces the final weights $\mathbf{w}_i$ after processing n_i sentences, the weighted averaged is defined as $\mathbf{w}^* = \frac{\sum_i \mathbf{w}_i \times n_i}{\sum_i n_i}$. Although averaging yields different result from running a single learner over the entire data, we have found the difference to be quite small in terms of convergence and quality of tuned weights in practice.

After the reducer finishes, the averaged weights are extracted and used as the initial weights for the next iteration; the emitted hypotheses are scored against the references, which allows us to track the learning curve and the progress of convergence.

Scalability In an application such as SMT, the decoder requires access to the translation grammar and language model to produce translation hypotheses. For small tuning sets, which have been typical in MT research, having these files transferred across the network to individual servers (which then load the data into memory) is not a problem. However, for even modest input on the order of tens of thousands of sentences, this creates a challenge. For example, distributing thousands of per-sentence grammar files to all the workers in a Hadoop cluster is time-consuming, especially when this needs to be performed prior to every iteration.

To benefit from MapReduce, it is essential to avoid dependencies on "side data" as much as possible, due to the challenges explained above with data transfer. To address this issue, we append the per-sentence translation grammar as user-supplied additional information to each input sentence. This results in a large input file (e.g., 75 gigabytes for 50,000 sentences), but this is not an issue since the data reside on the Hadoop distributed file system and MapReduce optimizes for data locality when scheduling mappers.

Unfortunately, it is much more difficult to obtain per-sentence language models that are small enough to handle in this same manner. Currently, the best solution we have found is to use Hadoop's distributed cache to ship the single large language model to each worker.

4 Evaluation

We evaluated online learning in Hadoop MapReduce by applying it to German-English machine translation, using our hierarchical phrase-based translation system with `cdec` as the decoder (Dyer et al., 2010). The parallel training data consist of the Europarl and News Commentary corpora from the WMT12 translation task,[6] containing 2.08M sentences. A 5-gram language model was trained on the English side of the bitext along with 750M words of news using SRILM with modified Kneser-Ney smoothing (Chen and Goodman, 1996).

We experimented with two feature sets: (1) a small set with standard MT features, including

[5] By default, each line is treated as a key-value pair encoded in text, where the key and the value are separated by a `<tab>`.

[6] http://www.statmt.org/wmt12/translation-task.html

Tuning set size		Time/iteration	# splits	# features	Tuning BLEU	Test	
(corpus)	(on disk, GB)	(in seconds)				BLEU	TER
dev	3.3	119	120	16	22.38	22.69	60.61
5k	7.8	289	120	16	32.60	22.14	59.60
10k	15.2	432	120	16	33.16	22.06	59.43
25k	37.2	942	300	16	32.48	22.21	59.54
50k	74.5	1802	600	16	32.21	22.21	59.39
dev	3.3	232	120	85k	23.08	23.00	60.19
5k	7.8	610	120	159k	33.70	22.26	59.26
10k	15.2	1136	120	200k	34.00	22.12	59.24
25k	37.2	2395	300	200k	32.96	22.35	59.29
50k	74.5	4465	600	200k	32.86	22.40	59.15

Table 1: Evaluation of our Hadoop implementation of MIRA, showing running time as well as BLEU and TER values for tuning and testing data.

	dev	test	5k	10k	25k	50k
Sentences	3003	3003	5000	10000	25000	50000
Tokens en	75k	74k	132k	255k	634k	1258k
Tokens de	74k	73k	133k	256k	639k	1272k

Table 2: Corpus statistics

phrase and lexical translation probabilities in both directions, word and arity penalties, and language model scores; and (2) a large set containing the top 200k sparse features that might be useful to train on large numbers of instances: rule id and shape, target bigrams, insertions and deletions, and structural distortion features.

All experiments were conducted on a Hadoop cluster (running Cloudera's distribution, CDH 4.2.1) with 16 nodes, each with two quad-core 2.2 GHz Intel Nehalem Processors, 24 GB RAM, and three 2 TB drives. In total, the cluster is configured for a capacity of 128 parallel workers, although we do not have direct control over the number of simultaneous mappers, which depends on the number of input splits. If the number of splits is smaller than 128, then the cluster is under-utilized. To note this, we report the number of splits for each setting in our experimental results (Table 1).

We ran MIRA on a number of tuning sets, described in Table 2, in order to test the effectiveness and scalability of our system. First, we used the standard development set from WMT12, consisting of 3,003 sentences from news domain. In order to show the scaling characteristics of our approach, we then used larger portions of the training bitext directly to tune parameters. In order to avoid overfitting, we used a jackknifing method to split the training data into $n = 10$ folds, and built a translation system on $n - 1$ folds, while adjusting the sampling rate to sample sentences from the other fold to obtain tuning sets ranging from 5,000 sentences to 50,000 sentences. Table 1 shows details of experimental results for each setting. The second column shows the space each tuning set takes up on disk when we include reference translations and grammar files along with the sentences. The reported tuning BLEU is from the iteration with best performance, and running times are reported from the top-scoring iteration as well.

Even though our focus in this evaluation is to show the scalability of our implementation to large input and feature sets, it is also worthwhile to mention the effectiveness aspect. As we increase the tuning set size by sampling sentences from the training data, we see very little improvement in BLEU and TER with the smaller feature set. This is not surprising, since sparse features are more likely to gain from additional tuning instances. Indeed, tuning scores for all sets improve substantially with sparse features, accompanied by small increases on test.

While tuning on dev data results in better BLEU on test data than when tuning on the larger sets, it is important to note that although we are able to tune more features on the larger bitext tuning sets, they are not composed of the same genre as the dev and test sets, resulting in a domain mismatch.

Therefore, we are actually comparing a smaller in-domain tuning set with a larger out-of-domain set. While this domain adaptation is problematic (Haddow and Koehn, 2012), the ability to discriminatively tune on larger sets remains highly desirable.

In terms of running time, we observe that the algorithm scales linearly with respect to input size, regardless of the feature set. With more features, running time increases due to a more complex translation model, as well as larger intermediate output (i.e., amount of information passed from mappers to reducers). The scaling characteristics point out the strength of our system: our scalable MIRA implementation allows one to tackle learning problems where there are many parameters, but also many training instances.

Comparing the wall clock time of parallelization with Hadoop to the standard mode of 10–20 learner parallelization (Haddow et al., 2011; Chiang et al., 2009), for the small 25k feature setting, after one iteration, which takes 4625 seconds using 15 learners on our PBS cluster, the tuning score is 19.5 BLEU, while in approximately the same time, we can perform five iterations with Hadoop and obtain 30.98 BLEU. While this is not a completely fair comparison, as the two clusters utilize different resources and the number of learners, it suggests the practical benefits that Hadoop can provide. Although increasing the number of learners on our PBS cluster to the number of mappers used in Hadoop would result in roughly equivalent performance, arbitrarily scaling out learners on the PBS cluster to handle larger training sets can be challenging since we'd have to manually coordinate the parallel processes in an ad-hoc manner. In contrast, Hadoop provides scalable parallelization in a manageable framework, providing data distribution, synchronization, fault tolerance, as well as other features, "for free".

5 Conclusion

In this paper, we presented an open-source framework that allows seamlessly scaling structured learning to large feature-rich problems with Hadoop, which lets us take advantage of large amounts of data as well as sparse features. The development of Mr. MIRA has been motivated primarily by application to SMT, but we are planning to extend our system to other structured prediction tasks in NLP such as parsing, as well as to facilitate its use in other domains.

Acknowledgments

This research was supported in part by the DARPA BOLT program, Contract No. HR0011-12-C-0015; NSF under awards IIS-0916043 and IIS-1144034. Vladimir Eidelman is supported by a NDSEG Fellowship. Any opinions, findings, conclusions, or recommendations expressed are those of the authors and do not necessarily reflect views of the sponsors.

References

S. Chen and J. Goodman. 1996. An empirical study of smoothing techniques for language modeling. In *ACL*.

D. Chiang, K. Knight, and W. Wang. 2009. 11,001 new features for statistical machine translation. In *NAACL-HLT*.

D. Chiang. 2012. Hope and fear for discriminative training of statistical translation models. *JMLR*, 13:1159–1187.

M. Collins. 2002. Ranking algorithms for named-entity extraction: boosting and the voted perceptron. In *ACL*.

K. Crammer, O. Dekel, J. Keshet, S. Shalev-Shwartz, and Y. Singer. 2006. Online passive-aggressive algorithms. *JMLR*, 7:551–585.

K. Crammer, A. Kulesza, and M. Dredze. 2009. Adaptive regularization of weight vectors. In *NIPS*.

J. Dean and S. Ghemawat. 2004. MapReduce: Simplified data processing on large clusters. In *OSDI*.

J. Duchi, E. Hazan, and Y. Singer. 2011. Adaptive subgradient methods for online learning and stochastic optimization. *JMLR*, 12:2121–2159.

C. Dyer, A. Lopez, J. Ganitkevitch, J. Weese, F. Ture, P. Blunsom, H. Setiawan, V. Eidelman, and P. Resnik. 2010. cdec: A decoder, alignment, and learning framework for finite-state and context-free translation models. In *ACL System Demonstrations*.

S. Green, S. Wang, D. Cer, and C. Manning. 2013. Fast and adaptive online training of feature-rich translation models. In *ACL*.

B. Haddow and P. Koehn. 2012. Analysing the effect of out-of-domain data on smt systems. In *WMT*.

B. Haddow, A. Arun, and P. Koehn. 2011. SampleRank training for phrase-based machine translation. In *WMT*.

T. Joachims. 1998. Text categorization with support vector machines: Learning with many relevant features. In *ECML*.

J. Lafferty, A. McCallum, and F. Pereira. 2001. Conditional random fields: Probabilistic models for segmenting and labeling sequence data. In *ICML*.

R. McDonald, K. Crammer, and F. Pereira. 2005. Online large-margin training of dependency parsers. In *ACL*.

K. Papineni, S. Roukos, T. Ward, and W.-J. Zhu. 2002. BLEU: a method for automatic evaluation of machine translation. In *ACL*.

L. Shen. 2007. Guided learning for bidirectional sequence classification. In *ACL*.

P. Simianer, S. Riezler, and C. Dyer. 2012. Joint feature selection in distributed stochastic learning for large-scale discriminative training in SMT. In *ACL*.

M. Snover, B. Dorr, R. Schwartz, L. Micciulla, and J. Makhoul. 2006. A study of translation edit rate with targeted human annotation. In *AMTA*.

Author Index